AF608001

IMAGINED TRUTHS

Realism in Modern Spanish Literature and Culture

EDITED BY MARY L. COFFEY AND
MARGOT VERSTEEG

Imagined Truths

Realism in Modern Spanish Literature and Culture

UNIVERSITY OF TORONTO PRESS
Toronto Buffalo London

Toronto Buffalo London
www.utorontopress.com

ISBN 978-1-4875-0517-2

Toronto Iberic

Library and Archives Canada Cataloguing in Publication

Title: Imagined truths : realism in modern Spanish literature and culture / edited by Mary L. Coffey and Margot Versteeg.
Other titles: Imagined truths (Toronto, Ont.)
Names: Coffey, Mary L., 1956– editor. | Versteeg, Margot, editor.
Series: Toronto Iberic ; 43.
Description: Series statement: Toronto Iberic ; 43 | Includes bibliographical references and index.
Identifiers: Canadiana 20190049324 | ISBN 9781487505172 (hardcover)
Subjects: LCSH: Spanish literature – 19th century – History and criticism. | LCSH: Realism in literature.
Classification: LCC PQ6073.R4 I43 2019 | DDC 860.9/005—dc23

This book has been published with the assistance of Pomona College and the University of Kansas.

University of Toronto Press acknowledges the financial assistance to its publishing program of the Canada Council for the Arts and the Ontario Arts Council, an agency of the Government of Ontario.

Canada Council for the Arts
Conseil des Arts du Canada

Funded by the Government of Canada
Financé par le gouvernement du Canada

Contents

Acknowledgments

We have many people to thank, beginning with our contributors, who took on our charge to re-examine Spanish realism with enthusiasm and scholarly brilliance. We are grateful for the support of the University of Toronto Press, especially Robert Davidson and Mark Thompson, who recognized the value of this project and encouraged us to move forward. The collection benefited enormously from the comments and suggestions of our anonymous readers, and we thank them for their willingness to read the original manuscript and our revisions with such care and insight. We thank Pam LeRow, who helped to prepare the manuscript for submission, and Judy Williams, whose meticulous copy editing was highly appreciated. We also wish to note the considerable financial support that we received from Pomona College and the University of Kansas's College of Liberal Arts and Sciences Research Excellence Fund. Scholars in the humanities depend more than ever on the support of institutions of higher education, and we are fortunate indeed that our respective institutions continue to value the study of literatures and cultures and helped us bring the project to fruition. Above all we wish to acknowledge and thank Harriet Turner, without whom this collection would not exist. Her unmatched love of the aesthetic complexities of literary realism, particularly in nineteenth-century Spanish literature, has been an inspiration to her colleagues and her students. Our goal has been to follow in Harriet's footsteps in making the complexity and richness of realist texts written in Spanish accessible and comprehensible to new generations of readers. Accordingly, this volume is dedicated to her.

IMAGINED TRUTHS

Realism in Modern Spanish Literature and Culture

Introduction

MARY L. COFFEY AND MARGOT VERSTEEG

To tell the truth, realism has never gone out of fashion. The realist mode in popular cultural production, literary or visual, has always spoken, and will continue to speak, to readers and viewers in a way unlike any other communicative mode. In its literary form, realism has demonstrated an unusually flexible linguistic capacity to represent the world as we think we see it and understand it. Realism's intrinsic adaptability is what allows it to continue to attract the attention of writers, readers, and scholars and to remain vibrant, ultimately transcending its historical boundaries. But any study of literary realism must, by necessity, attempt to address both the complex nature of the term "realism" itself, as one which contains within it the broad conceptual questions of what it means for language to be perceived as representing the "real," and the historical factors which led to its dominance as an artistic movement in the nineteenth century in Europe.

The concept of realism, in both a formal and historical sense, is notoriously hard to define. Realism is traditionally understood in an aesthetic and conceptual sense as a mimetic mode of representation that approximates our experience of the world we inhabit, thus endowing it with an exceptional flexibility, given the physical, emotional, and psychological ways in which human beings understand their environment. Attempts to define realism as a literary movement are equally amorphous, and they invariably seem to focus on what distinguishes it from other forms of representation. From a historical perspective, realism is often described as a literary movement bookended by romanticism in the early decades of the nineteenth-century and modernism by century's end. Fredric Jameson, in one of his most recent books, *The Antinomies of Realism* (2013), acknowledges the difficulty of assigning parameters to literary realism, both in historical and formal terms, indicating that "it is as though the object of our meditation began to wobble, and the attention to it to slip insensibly away from it in two opposite directions, so that at length we find we are thinking, not about realism, but about its emergence; not about the thing itself, but about its dissolution" (1). By situating realism between the poles of romanticism and modernism, Jameson not only invokes the issue of periodization and the traditional historical contextualization of European literary realism within the nineteenth century but also places the literary movement of realism within contemporary debates on the very nature of modernity. In presenting this collection of essays, we, too, must address both the formal and historical nature of realism, but our choice has been to do so within the specific framework of works written and/or published in Spain, predominantly within the nineteenth century. There are compelling reasons to look at the example of Spain, though it is useful to begin with a brief review of theoretical and critical approaches to realism as a literary movement and discursive mode capable of transcending national boundaries.

By its very nature, realism will always be both an aesthetic and historical concept. Any study of this literary form will find an antinomical tension situated between the philosophical concept of defining and describing in language the nature of perceived reality and the historical framing of that attempt within a particular space and time. Erich Auerbach's foundational study of literary realism, *Mimesis: The Representation of Reality in Western Literature*, is a case in point. The book begins with the famous chapter "Odysseus' Scar," which compares *The Odyssey*'s "fully externalized description" and "few elements of historical development" to the Old Testament's "suggestive influence of the unexpressed" and its "development of the concept of the historically becoming" (23). Auerbach's binary constitutes a useful description of two styles of realist expression even as it provides a structural framework of binaries for subsequent critical approaches. Pam Morris points out that one of the *Oxford English Dictionary*'s definitions for realism is "any view or system contrasted with idealism," thus underscoring not only the tendency to define realism by what it is not but also the fact that "the term realism almost always involves both claims about the nature of reality and an evaluative attitude toward it" (2).[1] For contemporary theorists, realism serves as a vital touchstone for articulating a wide range of intellectual and ideological perspectives, for example Michael Riffaterre's exploration of the paradox of truth in fiction (*Fictional Truth*, 1990), Roland Barthes's poststructuralist perspective on the socially constructed nature of language (*S/Z*, 1992), or

Mikhail Bakhtin's exploration of the intrinsically "polyphonic" and dialogic qualities of the novel (*The Dialogic Imagination*, 1981). Alongside the studies of the formal and linguistic aspects of realism, there are the scholarly approaches to the historicity of the realist novel, and the advent of realism as a literary movement traditionally situated within the context of Europe in the eighteenth and nineteenth centuries. Influential studies written from this perspective include Ian Watt's *The Rise of the Novel* (1957) and Lilian Furst's *All Is True: The Claims and Strategies of Realist Fiction* (1995), while Georg Lukács's historical-materialist explanation of the rise of the novel – in *The Theory of the Novel* (1920), and his subsequent study, *The Historical Novel* (1932) – has provided another fruitful approach. The focus of nearly all of these critical analyses of realism as a literary form has been on fiction produced in the nineteenth century. This should come as no surprise, given the rise of the popular realist novel and the historical novel during that period.

Yet it is somewhat surprising that studies of nineteenth-century European literature in general and of European literary realism in particular tend to address almost exclusively the works of French and English authors, and only in some cases include references to Russian writers such as Dostoevsky and Tolstoy and occasionally a nod to German authors such as Theodor Fontane.[2] Even recent critical studies of the genesis of the realist novel, in their attempts to question long-held critical opinions, continue to focus on the literary histories of northern Europe.[3] Nonetheless, with the historical re-examination of Spain's particular situation within the advent of modernity in Europe, scholars are beginning to look more closely at the ways in which that country's participation in various literary movements reflects its unique position within a larger system of global relationships. It is our intention, with this collection of essays, to begin the process of mapping out the unique nature of Spanish realism within the framework of modern Spanish literature and culture.

Contextualizing Spanish Realism and Naturalism within European Literary History

Jameson's framing of realism – as a literary mode that grew out of a reaction to the excesses of romanticism and in turn spurred a modernist and avant-garde rejection of its own bourgeois morality – reflects a long-standing critical assessment in European literary history. According to this assessment, the excess of feeling and the exoticism of place and time that often defined European romanticism, particularly in France and England, gave way to a focus on the representation of everyday life, itself a reflection of critical aspects associated with modernity: the growing dominance of a nascent middle class, the advent of political liberalism, and the development of economic capitalism.

While scholars have identified the nineteenth century as "the great age of realism," the countries considered primary producers of realist fiction have traditionally been France and England (Morris 47). General histories of European literature and even specific studies of European realism rarely contain references to such important Spanish realist novelists as Benito Pérez Galdós, Leopoldo Alas (Clarín), Emilia Pardo Pazán, José María de Pereda, Juan Valera, Pedro Antonio de Alarcón, Armando Palacio Valdés, and Vicente Blasco Ibáñez.[4] One reason for this tendency is the oft-repeated argument that the realist novel first flourished in England and France and only came later, in less compelling and mostly imitative fashion, to other countries in Europe.[5] Another reason is that Spain was widely considered a nation slow to adopt economic, political, or artistic innovation in comparison to the nations of northern Europe.[6] Yet as Carlos Alonso has correctly clarified, there are two definitions to be considered: "modernity as a concept or aesthetic idea as manifested in several discursive modalities, and modernity as a socio-economic reality, as a phase of Western historical development" (29). In the case of Spain, these two views were often conflated. Elisa Martí-López, grounding her argument on Franco Moretti's examination of the literary landscape in Europe, has commented on the reasons for this tendency:

> The weakness of [Spain's] industrialization process, the violence of the civil wars, the unfinished character of its political revolution (the constant *alzamientos*), the well-rooted centrifugal forces of regionalism (the *juntas* undermining the authority of the state) and the loss of the empire (when the most prosperous European nations were busy building them) did not find a vehicle of expression in the "solid and well-regulated world" that characterizes the "Realistic temper" of both the British novel of social manners and, after the revolution of 1848, the new generation of French novelists. (136)

The very notion of realist narrative as a way of representing the lives of a growing middle class was seen, at its heart, as an original concept.

French realist writers and critics (Flaubert, Sainte-Beuve, the Goncourt brothers, Balzac, and Huysmans) defined the realist movement as a new tendency in tune with modern times. This was also the case for Zola's late nineteenth-century naturalist strain of French realist narrative. For these authors, the movement's modernity justifies some of its most noticeable characteristics (i.e., the impartial narrator, the representation of emergent social classes, the scientific method). Accordingly, the proclaimed modernity of both realist and naturalist aesthetics in the nineteenth century seemed at odds with Spain's status among European nations. According to politicians and historians, Spain was a nation in decline, suffering from more than a century of economic mismanagement and stagnation.[7] Until recently, this disdainful way of contextualizing Spain's engagement with modernity has had a profound impact on European historiography – political, economic, cultural, and literary – and has created a framework by which nearly all Spanish literary production from the late eighteenth until the mid-twentieth centuries, not just realism, was defined as largely imitative of the cultural production of northern European countries. Recent historical scholarship, however, has begun to dismantle the long-standing perceptions of Spain's "backwardness" and question the nature of a historical narrative that places Spain at the periphery of a modern Europe.[8] If, as one scholar has opined, modernity is Europe's "leading definition," then any attempt to deconstruct modernity involves an examination of European imperialism (Pieterse 114). As a result, within recent literary studies we are seeing a process of rethinking the nature of Spain's imperial history and the impact of that history on the very processes that allowed Europe to transition into the modern age.[9]

For that reason, the marginalization of Spain has had real consequences. Michael Iarocci has correctly noted that "this symbolic amputation of Spain from 'modernity,' 'Europe,' and the 'West' was arguably among the most profound historical determinants in defining modern Spanish culture" (8). Most important, perhaps, in Iarocci's re-examination of Spanish romanticism, is his recognition of the fact that the eighteenth- and nineteenth-century northern European discourse regarding Spain's global stature "elided modern Europe's roots in the Iberoamerican Atlantic by marking the Spanish empire as modernity's exterior" (15). If the Spanish empire could be labelled as barbarous, then northern European imperialism could be considered "civilized, liberating, tolerant, fair-minded, peaceful, and rational" (15). While Iarocci's observations focus on the cultural production of Spanish romanticism, similar comments have been made with respect to literary modernism and the avant-garde.

For example, in their introduction to a 2007 special issue of the *Journal of Iberian and Latin American Studies* devoted to Spanish modernism, Elena Delgado, Jordana Mendelson, and Oscar Vázquez echo Iarocci's language to describe what they see as the systematic exclusion of Spain and Spanish letters from many studies on modernism. They note, for example, that "scholars have failed to examine Spain both because it is and is not Europe, both because of its incorporation into Western European institutions and simultaneously because of its isolation and its exceptionality from them" (108). Moreover, they observe, "in describing the forms of modernity that do not conform to the Northern European paradigm, scholars have used terms like 'alternative', 'marginal', and 'peripheral', some within the context of Europe, others within the framework of globalization and colonialism" (108). Spain, in other words, is always different from other European nations, politically, economically, and culturally.

If we accept these new calls to understand modernity less as a concept of absence and presence and more appropriately as a network of shifting relations on a global scale, then it makes sense to look at the ways scholars in the past have tried to explain the absence of Spanish realism from literary histories of European realism. Indeed, scholars of Spanish literature in the twentieth century certainly recognized that Spain's contributions to literary realism were often overlooked on the map of European realism, but the explanations they provided for such lacunae were ultimately unconvincing, and in hindsight quite revealing. James Mandrell, in a 1988 article entitled "Realism in Spain: Galdós, Pardo Bazán, Clarín and the European Context," offered the following explanation:

> The reasons for the relative neglect of Spanish literature and its tradition of realist fiction are several, and prominent among them are that of language, what in the past was a general lack of familiarity with Spanish along with the until recently concomitant dearth of good translations, and that of the psychological and cultural barrier that is formed by the Pyrenees, for those both inside and outside Spain. (84)[10]

Mandrell correctly notes that a lack of understanding of Spanish realism "tends to distort the nature of our understanding of literary trends and traditions in Europe" (85). This is certainly true if we fail to see the relationship Spanish writers had with their English and French counterparts. Yet more to the point, Mandrell's reference to the cultural barrier of the Pyrenees constitutes an acceptance of the idea that Spain was not truly a part of Europe. This is an example of the "imperial difference" that Walter Mignolo identifies, and Iarocci cites, as a fundamental component of the definition of European modernity, with Spain representing an uncivilized past and the expansion of English and French colonialism as positively different (Mignolo 165).

In the early nineteenth century, France became the country that provided a model of innovation and progressivism for its southern neighbour, particularly with respect to cultural production. Indeed, the connections between Spanish and French literary traditions have perhaps attracted the most attention, given the nations' shared border and the popularity of works translated from French into Spanish from the very beginning of the nineteenth century (Martí-López 34). More recently, Jesús Torrecilla has taken up the issue of France's literary dominance and Spain's absence from most general studies on realism. Taking direct aim at long-held attitudes of French superiority, he attributes the scant attention paid to Spanish letters to the country's marginal position in Europe in the last two centuries (98). But he also counters the traditional view that Spain simply imitated the works of other national literatures by demonstrating that Spanish realism exhibits "a unique idiosyncrasy" that must be taken into account if we want to understand the protean nature of this movement that encompasses works and authors of extraordinary importance (98). Both liberal and conservative Spanish authors, he argues, had a conflicted relationship with the realist movement that they perceived not only as new but also as a humiliating imposition of French cultural hegemony. With respect to Zola's naturalism, Spanish authors like Galdós, Clarín, and Pardo Bazán were clear in stressing that foreign literary trends could not simply be imitated by Spanish authors but instead needed to be transformed in keeping with the cultural limits of Spanish society and the reading public. Notably, Spanish writers often found solutions in turning to their own national traditions, in aspects of Spanish Golden Age literature and in *costumbrista* narrative sketches of local customs. Reluctant to imitate the French trends that they simultaneously admired and rejected, they chose to appropriate the realist movement even as they redefined it as authentically Spanish (Torrecilla 100, 103). Accordingly, if we reconsider the relationship of Spain to the rest of Europe in the nineteenth century, we see a series of writers who, in the midst of a complex global reconfiguration of power and a persistently negative representation of Spain's engagement with European modernity, nonetheless attempted to establish themselves as writers within a unique national literary tradition.

Curiously, while not all foreign influences were considered negative, the way in which Spanish authors understood and incorporated these in a literary product defined as uniquely Spanish allows us to reconceptualize several literary connections. The English model is a case in point, and Linda Willem's essay in this volume explores these connections with respect to Galdós and Charles Dickens. In an 1868 article on Dickens, Galdós presents the English writer as a model because he had achieved in England what Galdós intended to accomplish in Spain: to write a modern realist novel free from the influence of French literature (452–3). The fact that Spanish Golden Age literature was a source of inspiration for some of Dickens's works made the author even more attractive to Galdós. In his 1870 manifesto, "Observaciones sobre la novela contemporánea en España" [Observations on the Contemporary Novel in Spain], Galdós clearly showed that he was aware of the new realist trends originating from outside of Spain, but he considers their adoption by contemporary authors to be problematic:

> El gran defecto de la mayor parte de nuestros novelistas, es el haber utilizado elementos extraños, convencionales, impuestos por la moda, prescindiendo por completo de los que la sociedad nacional y coetánea les ofrece con extraordinaria abundancia. (105)
>
> [The greatest weakness of most of our novelists is having used conventional foreign elements imposed by fashion, precluding those that contemporary national society offers them with extraordinary abundance.]

Galdós does not recommend that Spanish writers follow in the footsteps of his admired Balzac and Flaubert, but, associating anything French with "literatura de folletín" [serial literature] (not surprising considering the gulf of translations that flooded the Spanish publishing market), he proposes instead the imitation of Dickens's novels and, above all, of the Spanish realist tradition of the Golden Age. In short, and in the words of Jesús Torrecilla, Galdós proposes "to use Spanish realism to achieve a double objective: to create a genuinely Spanish and at the same time modern literature free from foreign influences and rooted in the most authentic national tradition" (101).[11]

In his 1900 "Prólogo" [Prologue] to Leopoldo Alas's novel *La Regenta*, Galdós does admit that the naturalist trend in realist narrative arrived from France, but he is quick to point out that Spanish writers were already familiar with naturalism as far back as the sixteenth century, when they employed it with great mastery: "todo lo esencial del Naturalismo lo teníamos en casa desde tiempos remotos" [everything that is essential about Naturalism we already had at home since ancient times] (198). What's more, it was precisely from these Golden Age authors that English and French writers learnt their craft: "En resumidas cuentas: Francia, con su poder incontrastable, nos imponía una reforma de nuestra propia obra" [In short, France, with its incontrovertible power, imposed on us a reformulation of our own work] (199). Consequently, when in the second half of the nineteenth century France imposed all over Europe a new version of the realist movement, Spanish novelists adopted this trend, but not without restoring the humour of the Cervantine tradition that the French had taken away. Galdós's ideas were shared by many of his contemporaries, not only by the more conservative Pereda and Alarcón but also by novelists like Clarín and Pardo Bazán, who were both favourably disposed to the new trends but demanded nevertheless a new reading of them.

In her foreword to *Un viaje de novios* [A Honeymoon] (1881), for example, Pardo Bazán recognizes the importance of French naturalism and praises its efforts to produce a faithful reproduction of reality. She repudiates, however, the crude topics, the absolute lack of humour, the overly detailed descriptions, and the degrading animalization of human beings that she finds in much of French naturalist fiction. The author opposes this defective kind of realism with what she called *our* Spanish realism: that of *La Celestina* and *Don Quijote*, the picaresque novel, and the works by Diego de Velázquez, Francisco de Goya, and Ramón de la Cruz. Later in *La cuestion palpitante* [The Burning Question] (1883) she expresses a positive opinion of Zola's *Le Roman expérimental* [The Experimental Novel], but because of her fervent Catholicism and her doctrinaire faith in the possibility of individual free will, she can't accept the pseudo-scientific nature of Zola's naturalistic techniques or any type of biological or social determinism. This famously caused the French writer to raise his eyebrows: how could this woman pretend to be a staunch, militant Catholic and, at the same time, a naturalist (qtd in Davis 284)?

The dynamics unleashed by this reinterpretation of French realism through the lens of Spanish literary tradition is one of the most important factors that shaped Spanish realism, and it can be observed in some of the greatest works of the movement. Cervantes's seminal text provides the history of Spanish realist fiction with a unique point of departure, one that is inextricably bound up in the questions surrounding the nature of what constitutes reality. *Don Quijote* is widely considered by critics to be the first modern novel, because of its approach to representing the realities of everyday life, human psychology, and literary self-reflexivity, while both capturing and transcending the historical and cultural framework of Miguel de Cervantes's time. Harry Levin, a literary scholar whose 1963 study of French realism, *The Gates of Horn*, still stands as a masterful work of literary criticism, wrote that in *Don Quijote* Cervantes found "the formula for realism" (42). "By attacking literary illusions," Levin opined, "[Cervantes] could capture the illusion of reality" (43). That unique ability to create the sense of an "imagined truth" has not been lost on critics and authors from the time of Cervantes to the present, hence the title of our volume. In his introduction to Edith Grossman's 2003 translation of *Don Quijote*, Harold Bloom wrote that Cervantes's novel "contains within itself all the novels that have followed in its sublime wake" (xxii). Many critics have noted the influence of Spanish Golden Age literature, especially of *Don Quijote* and of the picaresque novel, on Spanish realist authors such as Galdós, Clarín, and Pardo Bazán.[12] The works of Cervantes and other Golden Age masters provided the nineteenth-century Spanish realist authors with an exceptionally fertile ground for representing and questioning the nature of lived reality and for exploiting the metafictional phenomenon of self-reflexivity, giving Spanish realism what is probably its most distinctive feature.

Harriet Turner, following Harry Levin, notes that, etymologically, realism is thing-ism, and that the nineteenth-century realists place great emphasis on mimesis, on depicting the things in this world as they "really" are ("The Realist Novel" 81). But, as Turner observes, these authors also expanded and critiqued this notion of mimesis: "they fused, in a single text, social critique, a theory of representation, and a reproduction, faithfully mirrored, of the mores, costumes, objects, actions, beliefs, and rites of their times" (100).

In Stendhal's famous definition (1830) of the novel as a mirror being walked along a road, the mirror reflects that which is visible, constant, and verifiable. But since the novelist carries his mirror along the road, that image is moving and thus subjective, variable, and uncertain. It forms part of the process of change itself. The artistic and intellectual fascination with the unstable nature of the mimetic mirror exhibits what Lilian Furst has identified as the tension between the claims of referentiality, on the one hand, and those of textuality on the other. This tension becomes "the distinctive hallmark of the realist novel" (Furst 12; Turner, "The Realist Novel" 85). Sensitive to the quixotic phenomenon of "enchantment," that is of transforming one person or thing into another, authors such as Galdós and Clarín exploit the possibilities of mimesis to question whether or not imitation leads to knowledge. Recognition of the shadowy forces and fusions that move just below the apparent surfaces of texts caused a readjustment in their thinking about the nature and boundaries of texts and things. Nineteenth-century Spanish writers came to display this readjustment through a kind of self-reflexive perspectivism: the depiction, within a story or picture or novel or newspaper article, of the act of writing, painting, or creating that particular work. This instance of self-reflexivity resembles similar moments in the *Quijote* or *Las meninas* (1656), in which the painter Diego de Velázquez reflects the creative process of painting, as the *Quijote* does of writing, thus questioning the idea of origins and of identity. In nineteenth-century Spain, such instances almost become an artistic norm (Turner, "The Realist Novel" 94).

But questions of representation aside, there is no doubt that realism developed in Spain at a time of cultural and economic change. The country's engagement with the socio-economic impact of European modernity, quite visible in the exodus of Spaniards from the countryside to the cities and the development of new urban cultures, unquestionably affected writers' perspectives of reality. Jo Labanyi argues that the shift from a mimesis of things to a mimesis of perception is "linked inextricably to the rise of mercantilism," to paper money and credit. If what is real is merely a representation, a piece of fiction in a manner similar to the relationship of paper money to coins and bars of gold, without any stable referent, then reality and representation can be collapsed into one single entity and realism becomes nothing but "the representation of a reality constituted by exchange relations" ("Realism, Modernity" 390). The Spanish realist novel claimed to document a reality that it was effectively constructing, while at the same time exposing the process of representation itself. While some critics have seen this as a precocious anticipation of twentieth-century modernism – an ironic conclusion given the established narrative of Spain's supposed backwardness – Labanyi argues that, in their perception that reality is constituted by representation, the Spanish realist novels are closer to the postmodern loss of the real and its replacement by simulacra than to the modernist stress on the gap between the two ("Realism, Modernity" 385, 401). In this sense, Spanish realism might be seen as a particular manifestation of the literary genre that, far from imitative of French or English models, actually anticipated future developments in literature.

Yet however "modern" scholars might interpret nineteenth-century realism, Spanish realism always maintained identifiable connections to Spain's unique past. Certainly the insistence on the influence of early modern Spanish literature is one of the ways that Spanish realism differed from its European counterparts. Yet it is worth noting that other literary forms influenced the way in which writers adapted realism to the specific circumstances of Spanish culture. In particular, the literary form of *costumbrismo,* with its focus on producing short narratives describing social customs, participated in this process. Accordingly this volume dedicates considerable space to understanding *costumbrismo* and its connections to modern Spanish literature. The *costumbrista* texts of the 1830s and 1840s allowed Spanish writers the opportunity to both comment on the economic developments associated with modernity and mourn, in many ways, the perceived loss of earlier forms of social engagement. There is no doubt that the surprising vibrancy and endurance of Spanish *costumbrismo* was part of the cultural response to the rise of capitalism. But in complex ways *costumbrismo* affirmed the pace of change in Spanish society even as it nostalgically acknowledged the nation's past and what was lost with the advent of modernity.

Contemporary studies use the term "panoramic literature" to define the nineteenth-century European short narrative works that described the particulars of various national cultures, yet in Spain the term *costumbrismo* remains the preferred term.[13] The distinction in the term alone is indicative of the developmental history of this narrative subgenre. Like nineteenth-century literary realism, *costumbrista* depictions of Spanish culture – in quaint narratives scenes (*cuadros*), newspaper columns (*artículos*), and collections of types (*tipos*) – owe their roots to French and English models.[14] But *costumbrismo* quickly gained traction within the Spanish-speaking world in ways that it did not in the rest of Europe. It rapidly developed into a vibrant and durable representational form that lasted throughout the nineteenth and early twentieth centuries, long after the genre quickly faded from sight in England and France. Similar to the argument made by Spanish realist authors – that realism itself was already a fundamental component of Spain's literary traditions – some scholars have argued that *costumbrismo* has roots in sixteenth- and seventeenth-century Spanish literature.[15] Perhaps most important for our purposes here is that nineteenth-century *costumbrismo* is now considered a uniquely Spanish literary form. As Jo

Labanyi has noted, the earliest *costumbrista* collections of social types constituted "an attempt to construct a national identity out of those features that most clearly distinguished Spaniards from Europeans," adding that "the function of such works was to turn the people into 'Spaniards'; that is, members of a single national community" (*Gender and Modernization* 17)

That said, the relationship between Spanish *costumbrista* writing and Spanish realism is a rather complex one. Though many *costumbrista* texts in the early part of the nineteenth century evidence aesthetic qualities more properly attributable to romanticism, by the mid-nineteenth century, the representational quality of the genre became a fertile ground for realist authors. As the essays in this collection by Enrique Rubio Cremades and Rebecca Haidt make clear, the relationship of *costumbrismo* to Spanish realism is unique in that the descriptive qualities of *costumbrismo* eventually lose their preoccupation with the universal or essential qualities of "lo español" [Spanishness] in order to represent something more specific and individual; portraits of daily life that more appropriately can be considered realist.[16] Moreover, it is important to recognize that part of the incorporation of *costumbrista* writing into the traditions of Spanish realism involves a shift in ideology, from a conservative to a more liberal perspective, as manifested in different attitudes towards the changing fortunes of Spanish society.[17] Ignacio Boix's collection, *Los españoles pintados por sí mismos* [The Spaniards Portrayed by Themselves], for example, explicitly tries to capture social types that were being lost due to the advent of modernity. As Boix indicates in the prologue to his volume, he has included a large number of social types in the collection in order to "no dejar en el tintero uno solo de pocos tipos que conservamos" [not leave in the inkwell even one of the few original types that we still have] (vii). The collection, therefore, looks to the past rather than the future. This remains true for much of *costumbrismo* up to and including the Isabeline period of the 1860s. *Costumbrista* writers often manifested a decidedly conservative perspective, presenting portraits of Spanish society in which individuals who respect the virtues of throne and altar are rewarded and those who fail to honour those virtues suffer.[18] Yet as the essay by Rebecca Haidt in this collection demonstrates, in the later decades of the nineteenth century, *costumbrismo* became a useful narrative tool for realist writers as they attempted to reflect the effects of modernity on Spanish society.

It is also important to note that the path by which European panoramic literature connected with Spanish literary traditions, past and present, to produce its Spanish counterpart clearly involves issues of empire. From the perspective of contemporary postcolonial theories of literature, it makes sense that nineteenth-century Spanish *costumbrismo* developed precisely when and how it did as a part of Spanish national literary history. On the one hand, the rise of *costumbrismo* in the 1830s in Spain begins precisely at the moment when Fernando VII's death and the end of his monarchy's close control of journalism afforded the popular press in Spain the space to develop. Indeed, some scholars have insisted that it is a literary movement particular to the eighteenth and nineteenth centuries, an outgrowth of the newly established field of journalism (Herrero, Montesinos). On the other hand, the establishment of *costumbrismo* as a narrative subgenre within Spanish popular literature also occurred at a moment when Spain was coming to terms with the loss of the bulk of its imperial territories in the Americas.

Accordingly, it should come as no surprise that conservative Spanish *costumbrista* writers would prefer to look backward to a Spain that existed in the past, before the nation's dramatic change of position on the global stage. Yet not all *costumbrismo* constituted solely a nostalgic examination of the past. As Joyce Tolliver's essay in this collection demonstrates, the *costumbrista* insistence on the details of everyday life in late nineteenth- and early twentieth-century short realist writings by Emilia Pardo Bazán encouraged readers to address Spanish identity within a postcolonial framework. In this sense *costumbrismo* points to the ongoing work of Spanish authors and readers to understand the nature of Spanish identity, work that sometimes takes the form of denial and rejection of the changing nature of daily life and other times becomes a vehicle for accepting and evaluating the consequences of those changes.

Unquestionably one of the issues that *costumbrista* literature had to address, directly and indirectly, was the changed environment for the Spanish metropolis, once the centre of a global hegemonic empire but reduced by the start of the nineteenth century to being considered a peripheral extension of a new, northern European imperialism. Given *costumbrismo*'s preoccupation with Spanish identity and its influence on the development of Spanish narrative traditions, it is not surprising that Spanish realist texts demonstrate a similar engagement with Spain's changing fortunes on the global stage. We have already indicated that one of the unique aspects of Spanish realism is precisely the fact that the genre is developing in Spain in a distinctly postcolonial environment while in other European nations, most notably England and France, it is tied inexorably to periods of imperial expansion. One could argue that it is exactly the imperial framework that makes Spanish realism distinct not only from realist traditions in other European national literatures but also from those developed in Latin America. As Alejandro Mejías-López has noted, "Spanish American literary history has been written by and large with its back to Spain, read instead in relation to other European and North American centers" (206). This has led, ironically, to a situation in which, rather than being assessed within its own imperial framework, Spanish literature was evaluated in terms "of exclusion and inclusion, of being European or not European enough" (Mejías-López 208).

In the early twentieth century, realist fiction gave way across Europe to modernist literature, the avant-garde in poetry and theatre, and a wide range of literary "isms." Many authors at the turn of the century, like Unamuno, Valle-Inclán, and Azorín – whose ascendence in the Spanish literary canon became forever associated with the Spanish American War of 1898 and Spain's loss of its last major colonial territories – turned to more experimental forms of fiction and openly rejected realist aesthetics. But as we have seen, Spanish *modernismo* was still considered as somehow different and apart from innovative literary movements sweeping across the rest of Europe. José Ortega y Gasset became a prominent voice in recognizing the move away from realist aesthetics and towards experimentation.[19] In his 1925 work *La deshumanización del arte* [The Dehumanization of Art], Ortega depicted how the "human" gradually disappeared from the arts. In the same year, Guillermo de Torre presented the different forms of the post-realist literary avant-garde in his pioneering *Literaturas europeas de vanguardia* [European Literatures of the Avant-Garde]. At the same time, general accounts both in Spain and abroad kept emphasizing the essentially realist nature of Spanish literature, at times also considering this an inherent weakness. Two years after the assessments of Ortega and Torre, Dámaso Alonso, during the Generation of 1927's Góngora celebrations, gave a lecture at Seville's Ateneo in which he criticized the myth of Spanish literature as predominantly realist. Alonso praised the artistic merits of Spain's Golden Age poets and dramatists, but dismissed what he considered an outdated characterization of Spanish literature as realist and lacking "universal" appeal. Alonso's remarks did not fail to leave a mark. For a few years around 1930 it seemed odd for any serious author to take an explicitly realist stance (Gagen 245–6).

Despite the flourishing of avant-garde literature in Spain, the rejection of realist aesthetics did not last. It is of course not surprising that, in Spain's grim *posguerra* [postwar era], Spanish writers, above all of fiction and drama, returned to a more realist mode, whether represented by the *tremendista* fiction of the 1940s or the apparently naturalistic tone of Buero Vallejo's *Historia de una escalera* [History of a Stairway] of 1949 (Gagen 247). Starting in the early 1950s, social realism emerged as a provocative form of narrative and existed in Spain for over a decade. Above all, the social realist writers aspired to depict life and human experience within the harsh realities of postwar Spain. Juan Marsé wrote in 1962 that "il est bien connu que le premier devoir de tout romancier consiste à décrire la réalité sans la falsifier. Même si ce n'était qu'à cela, je servirais à quelque chose dans mon temps" [it is well known that the most important obligation of a novelist is to describe reality without falsifying. Even if it were only for that, I would have been useful in my time] (qtd in Herzberger 156). Harry Levin once called the literary realist "a professional iconoclast, bent on shattering the false images of his day" (248). David Herzberger argues that such thinking is particularly relevant to the social realists in postwar Spain. While Franco's historiographers pretended to dispose of the problematic (and sought, in Paul Ricoeur's words, to forget the unforgettable) by forging a discourse that omitted discord, the social realists, in contrast, transformed the experiential into a discourse that is a multiplicity of alternative worlds, calling forth what the same Ricoeur in another context has termed "the sphere of the horrible" that circumscribed all of the historical present. Social realism is thus placed in service of the unforgettable (i.e., counter-myths of poverty, isolation, alienation, and the like), which the Franco state plainly had set out both to forget and to annul (Herzberger 158, 162)

Social realism ebbed away in the early 1960s. But the force of realism remains, even in the twenty-first century. In his 2018 book *Memory Battles of the Spanish Civil War*, Sebastiaan Faber underscores the urgency with which contemporary Spanish authors are addressing the issue of truthful representation in the recent burst of narrative fiction dealing with the Spanish Civil War and its collective memory. What are the ethical and civic responsibilities of the author when it comes to the representation of memory? How do we represent the past faithfully and without distorting it? How does an author avoid creating an all too comfortable cultural and historical distance between past and present that allows readers to passively consume the atrocities of the Civil War and its aftermath?

Many writers today grapple with these issues. A case in point is Javier Cercas, who in his 2009 *Anatomía de un instante* [*The Anatomy of a Moment*] self-reflectively describes his failing efforts to produce an adequate account of the February 1981 coup attempt in Madrid, known as the *Tejerazo,* six years after Franco's death: "Comprendí que los hechos del 23 de febrero poseían por sí mismos toda la fuerza dramática y el potencial simbólico que exigimos de la literatura y ... por una vez la realidad importaba más que la ficción" (*Anatomía* 24) [I understood that the events of 23 February on their own possessed all the dramatic force and symbolic power that we demand of literature ... for once reality mattered more to me than fiction] (*Anatomy* 13). Ignoring the question whether Cercas actually keeps his promises, here is, once again, an author who finds himself confronted with the problem of how to achieve a realist narrative through language. One wonders, with Derek Gagen, what advice Galdós would have had for Cercas (249–50).

Imagined Truths as a Contemporary Reassessment of Spanish Realism

The essays in *Imagined Truths* take both formalist and historical approaches to realism into account, even as they examine the way in which current reassessments of European modernity are impacting our understanding of the relationships between national literary traditions. This collection brings together the work of the foremost specialists in the field of contemporary Spanish letters. It is not only the first volume to focus exclusively on the phenomenon of realism within the context of modern Spanish literature in more than a quarter-century (since Yvan Lissorgues's 1988 publication) but also the first to be written in English since Jeremy Medina's 1979 study. Our understanding of Spanish realism has grown and developed in the decades since the studies by Lissorgues and Medina. The essays in this collection represent new and innovative approaches to literary and cultural criticism. They thoughtfully address the ways in which Spanish realist fiction in the nineteenth century dealt with the conceptual and visible markers of modernity. They acknowledge the critical importance of women writers and our dramatically different contemporary approaches to questions of gender. They address the impact of economics on our perceptions of reality and our constructions of everyday life. They argue for the importance of emotions in the social construction of individual identity. They also acknowledge the post-imperial turn in literary studies. As such, this is a long overdue collection. *Imagined Truths* also appears at a significant moment of renewed interest in realism as a literary, historical, and cultural phenomenon.[20]

The collection is designed to continue the ongoing and vibrant intellectual discussion of the nature of mimetic representation by addressing a broad range of authors, works, and topics. *Imagined Truths* contains essays that explore the continued relevance of Cervantes's *Don Quijote* as well as the heretofore poorly understood role of nineteenth-century *costumbrismo* within the traditions of Spanish narrative. Other sections address how Spanish realism portrays the advent of modernity and the ways in which language can represent the complexity of modern thoughts and emotions. We have included essays in this collection that address how Spanish realism moved beyond narrative to inhabit the spaces of both theatre and film. Other essays explore the relationship between realism as a literary mode and philosophical approaches to understanding the workings of both the mind and body. Together the essays constitute a series of meditations on new ways of comprehending and processing narratives as representative of a certain kind of reality. By participating in a critical scholarly dialogue that expands our understanding of the unique place of realism in Spain's cultural history, *Imagined Truths* offers insights for specialists in a wide range of disciplines – literature, cultural studies, gender studies, history, philosophy – and, equally important, for readers just becoming acquainted with realist narrative as a central component of Spanish literary history.

The collection is structured into four sections. The first section, with a reference to the metaphor of root and branch, examines important points of departure and early developments relative to realist narrative in Spain. This section begins by acknowledging the continuing importance of Cervantes for discussions of Spanish realism while also identifying the role played by Spanish *costumbrismo*, a narrative subgenre focusing on the presentation of uniquely Spanish social customs. Rather than revisit the ways in which nineteenth-century realist narratives incorporate aspects of Cervantes's self-reflexivity into their modes of representation, already so well studied by authors throughout the twentieth century, Catherine Jaffe's essay, "Arabella's Veil: Translating Realism in *Don Quijote con faldas* (1808)," examines a gendered version of the quixotic through an analysis of the 1808 publication *Don Quijote con faldas, o los perjuicios morales de las disparatadas novelas* [Don Quixote in Skirts, or the Moral Harm of Ridiculous Novels], translated into Spanish from Charlotte Lennox's 1752 English novel, *The Female Quixote*. Jaffe's essay provides an insightful example of cultural transference, from Spanish to English and back again, thus undercutting the very cultural imperialism that northern European literature often unrightfully claimed. Moreover, this essay examines the gendered progressivism of Lennox's text and its role in inserting a feminist model of reading and thinking that would eventually lead to such texts as Galdós's *La desheredada* and Clarín's *La Regenta*.

The other essays in part 1, by Enrique Rubio Cremades and Rebecca Haidt, turn the reader's attention to the critical importance of *costumbrismo* in the development of Spanish realism. *Costumbrismo*, long considered peripheral to the development of realism and certainly a lesser form of literary mimesis, is now proving to be a rich source of information for helping us recontextualize the relationships between various literary traditions, both European and transatlantic in nature. Rubio Cremades is a leading specialist on *costumbrista* literature whose work has not heretofore been available to English readers. True to the long-standing tradition of literary scholarship in Spain, his essay "Between *Costumbrista* Sketch and Short Story: Armando Palacio Valdés's *Aguas fuertes*" presents not only a useful overview of *costumbrismo* as a literary genre but also a detailed close reading of how the work of a less often studied author of nineteenth-century realism is able to link together the literary models of such *costumbrista* luminaries as Mariano José de Larra and Ramón Mesonero Romanos with the deep insights that are more typical of realist authors like Galdós. Rubio Cremades's attention to textual detail clearly highlights how texts were able to hover between the poles of *costumbrismo* and realism. By examining the history of public spaces in the nation's capital, Rubio Cremades also points a spotlight on the important ways in which Spanish society was changing and adapting to the new realities associated with the advent of modernity. His essay provides an essential scaffold for the last article in this section, particularly in its contextual framing of a uniquely Spanish genre that offers new perspectives for understanding Spain in the nineteenth century. Haidt's essay, "Money, Capital, Monstrosity: Metaphorical Matrices of Realism in Antonio Flores's *Ayer, hoy y mañana*," is an exceptional example of cutting-edge scholarship that is able to identify the way in which previously overlooked *costumbrista* texts made visible the complex yet often unexamined nature of economic change and its impact on the day-to-day lives of Spain's metropolitan citizens. Her essay foregrounds the radical modernity that Flores's work represents, in its sensitive understanding of the effects of capitalism on nineteenth-century Spanish society. Haidt reveals that *Ayer, hoy y mañana* functions as a text with an uncanny ability to understand and metaphorically represent the alienating effects of political economy.

The next section of *Imagined Truths* looks at how the fictional works of perhaps the best-known nineteenth-century Spanish realists – Benito Pérez Galdós, Leopoldo Alas (Clarín), and Emilia Pardo Bazán – address questions of modernity while testing realism's limits as a literary mode. Peter A. Bly, Maryellen Bieder, Linda M. Willem, and Susan M. McKenna examine the ways in which literary texts present figures and spaces strongly associated with modern life in the last decades of the nineteenth century. Bly, in "The Physician in the Narratives of Galdós and Clarín," recounts the history of the development of modern medicine in late nineteenth-century Spain and then delves into works by both authors (Galdós's *Gloria* and Clarín's *La Regenta*) as examples that demonstrate how realist narratives portrayed the role of the doctor. While Galdós situates the physician as a character who plays an important role in shaping the choices of his patients, Clarín represents the doctor as evidence of a more elemental struggle between past and present. For Galdós, modern science is employed in the service of representing human nature, the development and the testing of faith, within the physical realm of the body. For Clarín, Bly argues, the conflict between faith and science is laid bare as a struggle for dominion and power, as a binary that represents the opposition between past and present, a "backward" Spain and a modern European nation. Bieder's contribution, "Travelling by Streetcar through Madrid with Galdós and Pardo Bazán," focuses on the streetcar as a manifestation of urban modernity and compares the way in which Galdós and Pardo Bazán employ that physical manifestation in their respective portraits of life in the Spanish capital. Following the spatial turn in literary studies, Bieder shows how the authors position realist narrative within the context of sentimental, pseudo-romantic, moralistic, and other discourses.

Willem's contribution, "Urban Hyperrealism: Galdós's Dickensian Descriptions of Madrid," echoes Bieder's examination of the representation of space, but turns to Galdós's employment of techniques that originated with Charles Dickens. While Roland Barthes, in his 1968 essay "The Reality Effect," famously argued that no analysis of a text can be considered complete if it does not take into account the seemingly insignificant details that, while contributing little or nothing to the narrative, make the story feel real, Willem's essay demonstrates that neither Dickens's London nor Galdós's Madrid is made real to readers through meticulously accurate descriptions. Instead, their narratives build on the ability of readers to supplement the imagined fictional universe based on their familiarity with the external world.

McKenna's essay, "Observed versus Imaginative Communities: Creative Realism in Galdós's *Misericordia*," argues that *Misericordia* [Mercy] represents a text in which Galdós exploits and explores the limitations of traditional realist discourse. By producing a fusion of reality and fiction, Galdós moves to the extreme limits of realism to promote concepts of national regeneration through a self-reflexive examination of turn-of-the-century Spain. McKenna argues that the novel's presentation of both the hybrid character of Almudena Mordejai, a reflection of Muslim, Christian, and Jewish cultures, and the figure of Benina, at once caretaker and servant, becomes a symbol of Galdós's hope that Spanish society can transcend the severe restrictions of Spain's bourgeois morality. Combined, the essays by Bly, Bieder, Willem, and McKenna help underscore how Spanish authors actually wrestled with realist processes of representation when describing a rapidly changing world. They remind us of how Spanish realist fiction engaged with the visible experience of modernity for both authors and readers in the nineteenth century.

Part 3 of the volume contains essays that build on the essays in the first two sections to provide dramatically new and provocative readings of the works by Galdós, Clarín, and Pardo Bazán. Joyce Tolliver analyses several short writings by Emilia Pardo Bazán that, although of realist nature, employ the techniques of *costumbrismo*, and in particular techniques of layered description, as a way of providing a commentary on Spain's post-1898 and postcolonial social milieu. Her essay, "Colonialism, Collages, and Thick Description: Pardo Bazán and the Rhetoric of Detail," shows how Pardo Bazán makes reference to articles of everyday life in metropolitan Spain that contain within them resonances of Spanish imperialism – i.e., the *mantón de Manila* and hot chocolate – thus addressing discourses of empire within the discourses of metropolitan female domesticity. The result is an essay that connects literary analysis with anthropology as a way of understanding Pardo Bazán's attitudes towards the end of empire and the consequences for Spanish national identity. The essays by Randolph D. Pope and Roberta Johnson approach Spanish realism from equally contemporary but also decidedly philosophical perspectives. In "Embodied Minds: Critical Erotic Decisions in *La Regenta*," Pope reaches across a wide spectrum of twentieth- and twenty-first-century philosophers to explore the extent to which Clarín's realist novel, and its description of characters' embodied thought processes in decision making, can be understood from the perspective of various philosophical approaches to the connections between mind and body and the processes of cognition. It is exactly

Clarín's recognition of the embodiment of thought, Pope argues, that continues to make *La Regenta* a narrative that readers experience as real. In a similar vein, Johnson looks at the philosophical writings of twentieth-century philosopher María Zambrano, a figure who was almost erased from Spanish history during the last half of the twentieth century and whose importance as a philosopher and feminist is only now becoming clear to new generations of scholars. Johnson's essay, "María Zambrano on Women, Realism, and Freedom," examines Zambrano's fascination with Benito Pérez Galdós's narratives, particularly at a time in which her mentor, José Ortega y Gasset, and early twentieth-century thinkers and writers like Miguel de Unamuno and Pío Baroja rejected the Canarian author outright and eschewed the literary value of realism in favour of the avant-garde. Zambrano's re-examination of Ortega y Gasset's prominence as a philosopher within the framework of Eurocentric philosophical thought and her refusal to denigrate Spanish realism represent an early recognition of realism's ability to question heretofore established notions of Spain's engagement with modernity as well as northern European claims to cultural centrality. Zambrano's independence in this sense, argues Johnson, is rooted in her appreciation for Galdós's creation of female characters and her recognition that Galdós's realism provided an avenue for human liberty and independence. The unique nature of Zambrano's contributions to feminist philosophy and literary criticism lies, as Johnson notes, in the fact that she saw the importance of Spanish realism as a tool for understanding both personal and national realities.

The final section of the volume attempts to push the envelope of our examination of Spanish realism even further, by extending the analysis to various genres with their own particular relationship to mimetic representation: epistolary, theatrical, and cinematographic. The first essay in this section, by Cristina Patiño Eirín, offers a distinctly different and provocative understanding of the limits of imagination by examining the one-sided epistolary evidence of the 1889 love affair between Galdós and Pardo Bazán, a subject that has prompted a number of studies.[21] The essay, "Writing (Un)clear Code: The Letters and Fiction of Emilia Pardo Bazán and Benito Pérez Galdós," offers up provocative possibilities of what Galdós's missing letters might have been. Patiño Eirín looks at a detailed series of references to the letters and fictions written by both authors as well as at previously unpublished letters sent to Pardo Bazán by her confessor, who privately chastised her for her public and private behaviour. Patiño Eirín does not collapse biography and fiction but explicitly recognizes the impact of life on fiction, and she challenges notions of how we might interpret the realist fiction of both authors as reflections of lived reality and experienced emotions. In this sense, Patiño Eirín's essay participates in the current scholarship on the significance of emotions in Spanish culture.[22]

David T. Gies and Stephanie Sieburth examine how realist narratives connect with other genres in ways that challenge the very framework of realism. Both essays address forms of Spanish cultural production in the twentieth century, and underscore the ways in which realism continued to be a powerful force in Spanish letters well beyond the nineteenth century. In "'Volvía Galdós triunfante': *Fortunata y Jacinta* on Stage (1930)," Gies explores the complex process of trying to adapt Galdós's monumental realist novel for the stage, noting the spatial and temporal limitations that any theatrical production would necessarily place on the author's sweeping narrative. Gies includes heretofore overlooked journalistic reviews and descriptions of this theatrical venture, spearheaded by Spain's leading actress of the day, Margarita Xirgu, that provide contemporary scholars with useful information in analysing the various ways in which literary realism is translated to the theatre. Sieburth's essay, "When Reality Is Too Harsh to Bear: Role-Play in Juan Marsé's 'Historia de detectives,'" involves a similar connection to artistic genres beyond narrative. Though Marsé's short story is, at heart, a work of narrative fiction, the originality of Sieburth's approach lies primarily in that she shows how the story also depends on the generic expectations of film in providing a vision of reality that allows the fictional characters to manage the unbearable privations of post–Civil War Spain through role-play. Sieburth cleverly links Marsé's short story to the traditions of Spanish realism as found in both Cervantes's *Quijote* and Clarín's *La Regenta*. She points to the psychological impulse that encouraged the character of Don Quixote to read chivalric novels as one that similarly drives Marsé's characters to imagine themselves to be detectives on the trail of solving a mystery, underscoring the fact that Cervantes's approach to realist fiction remains alive and well in contemporary Spanish realism. At the same time, Marsé's use of the metaphors of dissolution for post–Civil War Spain echo those employed half a century earlier by Clarín to signal the moral corruption of the town of Vetusta. Sieburth's essay constitutes a fitting conclusion to *Imagined Truths* in that it not only demonstrates the enduring legacy of Spanish realism well into contemporary Spanish literature but also illustrates yet once more that Spanish realism is never too far from its Cervantine origins.

Conclusion

To bring this Introduction to a close, we wish to acknowledge that *Imagined Truths* is inspired by the work of Harriet Turner, who has devoted her entire career to the exploration of how texts create the illusion of reality through the purposeful layering of linguistic references. To describe the complex ways in which nineteenth-century Spanish authors approached realist narrative, Turner has drawn critical attention to a moment near the end of Benito Pérez Galdós's novel *Fortunata y Jacinta*, when a secondary character, Segismundo Ballester, is given the role of presenting a metaphor for the author's own theory of realism: "que la fruta cruda bien madura es cosa muy buena, y que también lo son las compotas, si el repostero sabe lo que trae entre manos" [ripe fruit is a good thing, but so is cooked fruit, if the pastry chef knows what he has in his hands] (2:535). The metaphor of the artist shaping reality into something richer is essential to our understanding of the interface between reality and fiction, truth and imagination. This interface, Turner has shown us, becomes an exploration of cognition itself, and of the power of language to create a sense of the reality of things: "In ... realist novels ... texts have the power to become 'objects,' 'objects' have the power to turn into 'people,' and people keep pausing as they engage in writing their lives, while we, as readers, engage in breath-taking moments that permit our minds to imagine a fictional thing as real" ("Why the Face of the Voice" 227–8). In other words, while texts may have no material reality, Turner will argue that the mind's engagement with the descriptive and metaphoric components of realist narrative triggers a moment of cognition that is then experienced with the senses, making an author's work capable of shaping a reader's mind. Turner's fascination with the nature of realism has led her to explore its manifestations in the work of many authors from different national traditions, but nowhere was the pull as strong as with Spanish literature of the nineteenth century. In her essay "Afterlives – Experiences of Space and Time in the Spanish Realist Novel," Turner brings together the many paths of her scholarship with respect to literary realism, turning to the two authors who have most thoroughly engaged her imagination: Benito Pérez Galdós and Leopoldo Alas. She argues that the best of realist fiction, in framing its images in space and time, encourages readers to reflect on themselves, in addition to the characters portrayed, thus creating an "afterlife" which imbues the literary text with a constantly renewed sense of relevance and vibrancy (297/1161). *Imagined Truths* is intended to be a testament to the afterlives of Spanish realism, a form of literary representation that continues to engage our imaginations, to cause us to formulate images of places and times that, despite often being beyond our own space and time, continue to speak to us as readers about the possibilities of what it means to be a human being.

NOTES

1 As Jameson notes, realism is invariably used as one pole of opposition in a series of literary binaries: "realism vs. romance, realism vs. epic, realism vs. melodrama, realism vs. idealism, realism vs. naturalism ... and of course, most frequently rehearsed of all, realism vs. modernism" (2).

2 A typical example is Peter Brooks's *Realist Vision*, a classic example of contemporary critical approaches to nineteenth-century European realism. Brooks limits his analysis to France and England, and he begins his analysis with Balzac, then moves through a series of authors such as Dickens, Flaubert, Eliot, Zola, and Henry James, and concludes with the connections between modernism and realism in such authors as James Joyce, Marcel Proust, and Virginia Woolf.

3 Margaret Cohen and Carolyn Dever's collection of essays focuses almost exclusively on the interrelationship between French and English narratives in the formation of the novel, eliding the importance of Spain's literary traditions in this regard. Jenny Mander's collection, while certainly acknowledging the importance of Spanish literary history, provides only brief glimpses into the importance of realism in Spanish letters. Notably, Pedro Javier Pardo argues that formal studies of the novel, starting with Ian Watt's *The Rise of the Novel* and including the recent collections by Cohen, Dever, and Mander, are inevitably incomplete and insular examinations of the genre, given their failure to recognize the contributions of uniquely Spanish modes of fictional representation to the history of the realist novel.

4 The work of Edward Said is a case in point. Though not solely focused on the realist novel, *Culture and Imperialism* presents concepts that prove particularly useful for recent scholarship on nineteenth-century and early twentieth-century Spanish realism, but the study itself is limited to French and English literary history. Jameson's recent *Antinomies* is a notable exception, given that it provides an unusually wide-ranging analysis of authors, including the usual suspects, such as Zola, Balzac, Dickens, Tolstoy, Scott, and Eliot, and other authors less often included in studies of realism,

such as Goethe, Mann, Twain, Faulkner, Crane, and Dos Passos. Most notable for scholars of Spanish literature is the fact that Jameson includes an entire chapter devoted to Benito Pérez Galdós, and in that sense his study represents a modest first step in recuperating Spanish contributions to the corpus of nineteenth- and twentieth-century realist literature.

5 The demand for translations of French and English novels in Spain, in particular the novels of Dickens and Sir Walter Scott, helps support that perspective. As Jeremy Medina has noted, "most of the great English and French novelists had died by the time Galdós and other Spanish realists produced their best works: Balzac in 1850, Thackeray in 1863, Dickens in 1870 and Flaubert in 1880" (51).

6 Walter Mignolo has argued that Hegel's seminal identification of a distinction between early modern and modern Europe in *The Phenomenology of the Spirit* (1807) underscores the idea of northern Europe as the centre of the modern world and creates a framework by which other European nations such as Spain and Portugal, not mentioned in his analysis, become marginalized and peripheral to the project of modernity (165).

7 Immanuel Wallerstein points to Spain's decline as an economic issue, and notes that in the seventeenth and eighteenth centuries, despite its imperial status, the country became "at best a rather passive conveyor belt between the core countries and Spain's colonies" (2:185). The focus on Spain's economic structures as a marker of "backwardness" continues even today; see, for example, Regina Grafe, who, to her credit, does not confuse the complex structures of market integration and state formation with cultural manifestations of modernity, which were, as the essays by Peter Bly, Maryellen Bieder, and Linda Willem in this volume will show, quite thoroughly in evidence in Spanish society of the nineteenth century.

8 See, for example, Christopher Schmidt-Nowara's interview with the Spanish historian Josep Fradera. Jesús Pérez Magallón has also convincingly shown that Spanish intellectuals and writers participated fully in the conceptual and philosophical debates that characterized the advent of modernity in Europe. Moreover, it is worth noting Carlos Alonso's belief that "the aesthetic manifestation of modernity can indeed thrive in the absence of the material conditions of the modern" (31).

9 See, for example, Blanco; Surwillo; and Tsuchiya and Acree.

10 Mandrell's reference to Spain's border with France evokes the racial theories of William Z. Ripley, who claimed, in his 1899 book *The Races of Europe* that "beyond the Pyrenees begins Africa" (272). Such theories, it should be noted, fit into a narrative of Spanish decline popularized by the American historian William Hickling Prescott (see Kagan).

11 Torrecilla makes clear that these compensatory strategies do not belong exclusively to nineteenth-century Spain. On the contrary, they represent a general tendency common to all literatures and epochs (102).

12 The connections between nineteenth-century Spanish realism and the narrative art of Cervantes have been well documented. See, for example, Gilman; Gullón; Urey; Benítez; Gold; Jagoe; Willem; Kronik; Delgado; Labanyi, "Modernity as Representation"; and Valis.

13 The term "panoramic literature" has its origins in Benjamin's *Das Paris des Second Empire bei Baudelaire* [The Paris of the Second Empire in Baudelaire] (1938). For a discussion of this particular literary subgenre within the framework of English, French, and German literature, see Lauster. Despite its thorough examination of panoramic literature in various national traditions, Lauster's study does not include a discussion of Spanish texts, which serves to echo the scholarly approaches to European realism that have tended to overlook Spanish contributions. Yet the lack of inclusion can also be read as evidence that perhaps the Spanish manifestations of these literary genres are uniquely distinct from their European counterparts.

14 The 1843–4 collection *Los españoles pintados por sí mismos* was a seminal text in the history of Spanish *costumbrista* writing. The collection took its name from *Les Français peint par eux-mêmes*, a multi-volume collection of social types published between 1839 and 1842 in France, itself a nationalized adaptation of an English-language collection, *Heads of the People*, published in serial form in London in 1838 and reprinted in France in 1839 under the title *Les anglais peints par eux-mêmes*. For a thorough history of this collection, see Ucelay Da Cal. In addition, *cuadros de costumbres*, short narrative descriptions designed to be portraits of quintessential social scenes, were already appearing regularly in the Spanish press, most notably in the *Seminario pintoresco*, which began publication in Madrid in 1836.

15 Scholars have noted the generic evidence of *costumbrismo* in Cervantes's *novela ejemplar*, *Rinconete y Cortadillo*, as well as specific eighteenth-century texts. See Correa Calderón and Montgomery.

16 See Rubio Cremades, "Costumbrismo."

17 See Kirkpatrick.

18 One particularly representative example of such conservative neo-Catholic ideology can be found in the short story by Cecilia Böhl de Faber (Fernán Caballero), "La corruptora y la buena maestra," originally published in 1868 and reprinted in 1961 as part of the collection *Biblioteca de Autores Españoles*, 411–31.

19 Notably, Ortega y Gasset's high profile as a philosopher and cultural theorist in Spain in the twentieth century is also being re-evaluated as more

evidence of the powerful influence of northern European philosophical thought in contextualizing Spain as a "backward" nation. See, for example, Villacañas Berlanga. Accordingly, Roberta Johnson's contribution to this volume, which notes the marginalized role of María Zambrano, one of Ortega y Gasset's students, within the history of philosophy in Spain, and her celebration of Galdósian realism in the face of the popularity of the avant-garde, becomes even more important for a reassessment of Spanish literary history in general and Spanish realism in particular.

20 In addition to Jameson's aforementioned study, others include Walder's anthology; Morris's *Realism*, part of the New Critical Idiom series; and Brooks.

21 Two noteworthy studies of Pardo Bazán's letters to Pérez Galdís are Bravo-Villasante; and González Arias.

22 See the collection edited by Delgado, Fernández, and Labanyi.

WORKS CITED

Alonso, Carlos. *The Burden of Modernity: The Rhetoric of Cultural Discourse in Spanish America*. New York: Oxford UP, 1998. Print.

Auerbach, Erich. *Mimesis: The Representation of Reality in Western Literature*. Trans. Willard Trask. Princeton: Princeton UP, 1953. Print.

Bahktin, Mikhail. *The Dialogic Imagination: Four Essays*. Ed. Michael Holquist. Trans. Caryl Emerson. Austin: U of Texas P, 1981. Print.

Barthes, Roland. "The Reality Effect." In *The Rustle of Language*, trans. R. Howard. Berkeley: U of California P, 1989. 141–8. Print.

– *S/Z*. Trans. Richard Miller. London: Blackwell, 1992. Print.

Benítez, Rubén. *Cervantes en Galdós*. Murcia: Universidad de Murcia, 1990. Print.

Blanco, Alda. *Cultura y conciencia imperial en la España del siglo XIX*. Valencia: Publicaciones Universitat de Valéncia, 2012. Print.

Bloom, Harold. Introduction. In Miguel de Cervantes, *Don Quixote*, trans. Edith Grossman. New York: HarperCollins, 2003. Print.

Böhl de Faber, Cecilia (Fernán Caballero). "La corruptora y la buena maestra." In *Biblioteca de Autores Españoles. Obras de Fernán Caballero*, vol. 4, ed. José María Castro Calvo. Madrid: Colección Rivadeneira, Real Academia Española, 1961. 411–31. Print.

Boix, Ignacio, ed. *Los españoles pintados por sí mismos*. Madrid, 1843. Print.

Bravo-Villasante, Carmen. *Vida y obra de Emilia Pardo Bazán. Correspondencia amorosa con Pérez Galdós*, Madrid: Magisterio Español, 1973. Print.

Brooks, Peter. *Realist Vision*. New Haven: Yale UP, 2005. Print.

Cercas, Javier. *Anatomía de un instante*. Barcelona: Mondadori, 2009. Print.

– *The Anatomy of a Moment: Thirty-five Minutes in History and Imagination.* Trans. Anne McLean. New York: Bloomsbury, 2011. Print.

Cohen, Margaret, and Carolyn Dever, eds. *The Literary Channel: The Inter-National Invention of the Novel.* Princeton: Princeton UP, 2002. Print.

Correa Calderón, Evaristo. *Costumbristas españoles.* Vol. 1. Madrid: Aguilar, 1964. Print.

Davis, Gifford. "Catholicism and Naturalism: Pardo Bazán's Reply to Zola." *MLN* 90.2 (1975): 282–7. Print. http://doi.org/10.2307/2906864.

Delgado, Luisa Elena. *La imagen elusiva: Lenguaje y representación en la narrativa de Galdós.* Amsterdam: Rodopi, 2000. Print.

Delgado, Luisa Elena, Pura Fernández, and Jo Labanyi, eds. *Engaging the Emotions in Spanish Culture and History.* Nashville: Vanderbilt UP, 2016. Print.

Delgado, Luisa Elena, Jordana Mendelson, and Oscar Vázquez. "Introduction: Recalcitrant Modernities – Spain, Cultural Difference and the Location of Modernism." *Journal of Iberian and Latin American Studies* 13.2–3 (2007): 105–19. Print. https://doi.org/10.1080/14701840701776173.

DuPont, Denise. *Realism as Resistance: Romanticism and Authorship in Galdós, Clarín and Baroja.* Lewisburg, PA: Bucknell UP, 2006. Print.

Faber, Sebastiaan. *Memory Battles of the Spanish Civil War: History, Fiction, Photography.* Nashville: Vanderbilt UP, 2018.

Les Français peints par eux-mêmes. Paris, 1838–42. Print.

Furst, Lilian. *All Is True: The Claims and Strategies of Realist Fiction.* Durham, NC: Duke UP, 1995. Print.

Gagen, Derek. "Scylla or Charybdis? Spain's 'Special' Realism." *Romance Studies* 30:3–4 (2012): 244–50. Print. https://doi.org/10.1179/0263990412Z.00000000024.

Gilman, Stephen. *Galdós and the Art of the European Novel: 1867–1887.* Princeton: Princeton UP, 1981. Print.

Ginger, Andrew. "Spanish Modernity Revisited: Revisions of the Nineteenth Century." *Journal of Iberian and Latin American Studies* 13.2–3 (2007): 121–32. Print. https://doi.org/10.1080/14701840701776181.

Gold, Hazel. *The Reframing of Realism.* Durham, NC: Duke UP, 1993. Print.

González Arias, Francisca. "Diario de un viaje: las cartas de Emilia Pardo Bazán a Benito Pérez Galdós." *In Textos y contextos de Galdós: Actas del Simposio Centenario de "Fortunata y Jacinta"*, coord. Harriet S. Turner and John W. Kronik. Madrid: Castalia, 1994. 169–78.

Grafe, Regina. *Distant Tyranny: Markets, Power, and Backwardness in Spain, 1650–1800.* Princeton: Princeton UP, 2012. Print.

Gullón, Ricardo. "Estructura y diseño en *Fortunata y Jacinta.*" In Benito Pérez Galdós, *Fortunata y Jacinta.* Madrid: Taurus, 1986. 175–235. Print.

Herrero, Javier. "El naranjo romántico: esencia del costumbrismo." *Hispanic Review* 46 (1978): 343–54. Print. http://doi.org/10.2307/472418.

Herzberger, David K. "Social Realism and the Contingencies of History in the Contemporary Spanish Novel." *Hispanic Review* 59.2 (1991): 153–73. Print. http://doi.org/10.2307/473720.

Iarocci, Michael. *Properties of Modernity: Romantic Spain, Modern Europe, and the Legacies of Empire*. Nashville: Vanderbilt UP, 2006. Print.

Jagoe, Catherine. "Disinheriting the Feminine: Galdós and the Rise of the Realist Novel in Spain." *Revista de Estudios Hispánicos* 27.2 (1993): 226–48. Print.

Jameson, Fredric. *The Antinomies of Realism*. London: Verso, 2013. Print.

Kagan, Richard. "Prescott's Paradigm: American Historical Scholarship and the Decline of Spain." *American Historical Review* 101.2 (April 1996): 423–46. Print. https://doi.org/10.1086/ahr/101.2.423.

Kirkpatrick, Susan. "The Ideology of Costumbrismo." *Ideologies and Literature* 2.7 (1978): 28–44. Print.

Kronik, John. "La resonancia del realismo: Galdós y Clarín entre fines de siglo." *Revista de Filología Hispánica* 15.1 (1999): 93–104. Print.

Labanyi, Jo. *Gender and Modernization in the Spanish Realist Novel*. Oxford: Oxford UP, 2000. Print.

– "Modernity as Representation: The Self-Reflexivity of the Spanish Realist Novel." *Romance Studies* 30.3–4 (2012): 238–43. Print. https://doi.org/10.1179/0263990412Z.00000000023.

– "Realism, Modernity and the Critique of Representation." *Letras Peninsulares* 13.1 (2000): 385–404. Print.

Lauster, Martina. *Sketches of the Nineteenth Century: European Journalism and Its Physiologies 1830–1850*. London: Palgrave Macmillan, 2007. Print.

Levin, Harry. *The Gates of Horn: A Study of Five French Realists*. Oxford: Oxford UP, 1963.

Lissorgues, Yvan, coord. *Realismo y naturalismo en España en la segunda mitad del siglo XIX*. Barcelona: Anthropos, 1988. Print.

Lukács, Georg. *The Historical Novel*. Trans. Hannah and Stanley Mitchell. Lincoln: U of Nebraska P, 1983. [1932] Print.

– *The Theory of the Novel*. Trans. Anna Bostock. London: MIT P, 1971 [1920]. Print.

Mander, Jenny, ed. *Remapping the Rise of the European Novel*. Oxford: Voltaire Foundation, 2007. Print.

Mandrell, James. "Realism in Spain: Galdós, Pardo Bazán, Clarín and the European Context." *Neohelicon* 15.2 (1988): 83–112. Print. http://doi.org/10.1007/BF02129078.

Martí-López, Elisa. *Borrowed Words: Translation, Imitation, and the Making of the Nineteenth-Century Novel in Spain*. Lewisburg: Bucknell UP, 2002. Print.

Medina, Jeremy T. *Spanish Realism: The Theory and Practice of a Concept in the Nineteenth Century*. Potomac, MD: Studia humanitatis/José Porrúa Turanzas, S.A., 1979. Print.

Mejías-López, Alejandro. "Hispanic Studies and the Legacies of Empire." In *Empire's End. Transnational Connections in the Hispanic World*, ed. Akiko Tsuchiya and William G. Acree, Jr. Nashville: Vanderbilt UP, 2016. 204–21. Print.

Mignolo, Walter. "Rethinking the Colonial Model." In *Rethinking Literary History: A Dialogue on Theory*, ed. Linda Hutcheon and Mario Valdés. Oxford: Oxford UP, 2002. 155–93. Print.

Montesinos, José F. *Costumbrismo y novela*. Madrid: Castalia, 1983. Print.

Montgomery, Clifford Marvin. *Early Costumbrista Writers in Spain, 1750–1830*. Philadelphia: U of Pennsylvania, 1931. Print.

Moretti, Franco. "Modern European Literature: A Geographical Sketch." *New Left Review* 206 (1994): 86–109. Print.

Morris, Pam. *Realism*. New Critical Idiom Series. London: Routledge, 2003. Print.

Pardo, Pedro Javier. "Spanish Speculations on the Rise of the Novel: The Romantic, the Picaresque and the Quixotic." *Comparative Critical Studies* 12.1 (2015): 49–69. Print. http://doi.org/10.3366/ccs.2015.0154.

Pardo Bazán, Emilia. "Prólogo." In *Un viaje de novios*, ed. Marisa Sotelo Vázquez. Madrid: Alianza, 2003. Print.

Pérez Galdós, Benito. "Carlos Dickens." In *Los Artículos de Galdós en "La Nación"*, ed. William H. Shoemaker. Madrid: Insula, 1972. 450–4. Print.

– "Observaciones sobre la novela contemporánea en España." In *Benito Pérez Galdós: Ensayos de crítica literaria*, ed. Laureano Bonet. Barcelona: Península, 1972. 105–20. Print.

– "Prólogo."In Leopoldo Alas, *La Regenta*. Reprinted in *Ensayos de Crítica Literaria*, ed. Laureano Bonet. Barcelona: Ediciones Península, 1990. 195–205. Print.

– "La sociedad presente como materia novelable." In *Benito Pérez Galdós: Ensayos de crítica literaria*, ed. Laureano Bonet. Barcelona: Península, 1972. 167–72. Print.

Pérez Magallón, Jesús. *Construyendo la modernidad: la cultura española en el tiempo de los novatores (1675–1725)*. Madrid: CSIC, 2002. Print.

Pieterse, Jan. "Unpacking the West: How European Is Europe?" In *Racism, Modernity, Identity on the Western Front*, ed. Ali Rattani and Sallie Westwood. Cambridge: Polity P, 1994. 129–50. Print.

Riffaterre, Michael. *Fictional Truth*. Baltimore: Johns Hopkins UP, 1990. Print.
Ripley, William Z. *The Races of Europe: A Sociological Study*. London: Kegan Paul, Trench, Trübner and Co., 1899. Print.
Rubio Cremades, Enrique. "Costumbrismo. Definición, cronología y su relación con la novela." *Siglo diecinueve* 1.1 (1995): 7–25. Print.
Said, Edward. *Culture and Imperialism*. New York: Knopf, 1994 [1993]. Print.
Schmidt-Nowara, Christopher. "After 'Spain': A Dialogue with Josep M. Fradera on Spanish Colonial Historiography." In *After the Imperial Turn: Thinking with and through the Nation*, ed. Antoinette Burton. Durham, NC: Duke UP, 2003. 157–69. Print.
Sieburth, Stephanie. *Inventing High and Low: Literature, Mass Culture, and Uneven Modernity in Spain*. Durham, NC: Duke UP, 1994. Print.
Surwillo, Lisa. *Monsters by Trade*. Stanford: Stanford UP, 2014. Print.
Torrecilla, Jesús. "Power and Resistance: The Reality of Spanish Realism." *Symposium: A Quarterly Journal in Modern Literatures* 67.2 (2013): 98–110. Print. https://doi.org/10.1080/00397709.2013.790282.
Tsuchiya, Akiko, and William G. Acree, Jr, eds. *Empire's End*. Nashville: Vanderbilt UP, 2016. Print.
Turner, Harriet. "Afterlives – Experiences of Space and Time in the Spanish Realist Novel." *Anales de la literatura española contemporánea* 41.4 (2016): 283/1147–300/1164. Print.
– "The Realist Novel." In *The Cambridge Companion to the Realist Novel from 1600 to the Present*, ed. Harriet Turner and Adelaida López de Martínez. Cambridge: Cambridge UP, 2003. 81–101. Print.
– "'Silent Writing' and the Power of Form in *Anna Karenina* and *Fortunata y Jacinta*." In *Prosa y poesía: homenaje a Gonzalo Sobejano*, coord. Christopher Maurer, Jean-François Botrel, Yvan Lissorgues, and Leonardo Romero Tobar. Madrid: Gredos, 2001. 407–18. Print.
– "Why the Face of the Voice Is in the Hand: On the Poetics of Realist Fiction." In *Studies in Honor of Vernon Chamberlin*, ed. Mark Harpring. Newark, DE: Juan de la Cuesta, 2013.
Ucelay Da Cal, Margarita. *Los españoles pintados por sí mismos (1843–44). Estudio de un género costumbrista*. México: El colegio de México, 1951. Print.
Ugarte, Michael. "The Spanish Empire on the Wane: Africa, Galdós, and the Moroccan Wars." In *Empire's End*, ed. Akiko Tsuchiya and William G. Acree, Jr. Nashville: Vanderbilt UP, 2016. 177–90. Print.
Urey, Diane. *The Novel Histories of Galdós*. Princeton: Princeton UP, 1989. Print.
Valis, Noël. "On the Matter of Inner Realism: Clarín's *La Regenta* and Galdós' *Fortunata y Jacinta*." In *A History of the Spanish Novel*, ed. J.A. Garrido Ardila. Oxford: Oxford UP, 2015. 255–74. Print.

Villacañas Berlanga, José Luis. "Ortega y el monopolio de la modernidad." *Journal of Iberian and Latin American Studies* 13.2–3, special issue, ed. L. Elena Delgado, Jordana Mendelson, and Oscar Vázquez (2007): 169–84. Print.

Walder, Dennis, ed. *The Realist Novel: An Introduction*. London: Routledge, 1995.

Wallerstein, Immanuel. *The Modern World-System II: Mercantilism and the Consolidation of the European World-Economy, 1600–1750*. New York: Academic P, 1980. Print.

Watt, Ian. *The Rise of the Novel: Studies in Defoe, Richardson and Fielding*. Berkeley: U of California P, 1957.

Willem, Linda. *Galdós's Segunda Manera: Rhetorical Strategies and Affective Response*. Chapel Hill: U of North Carolina P, 1998. Print.

PART ONE

Nineteenth-Century Spanish Realism: Root and Branch

1 Arabella's Veil: Translating Realism in *Don Quijote con faldas* (1808)

CATHERINE JAFFE

In ... realist novels ... texts have the power to become "objects," "objects" have the power to turn into "people," and people keep pausing as they engage in writing their lives, while we, as readers, engage in breath-taking moments that permit our minds to imagine a fictional thing as real.

Harriet Turner, "Why the Face of the Voice" 227–8

Whether invoked as a formal model, as an intertextual trope, or as a character type, Cervantes's *Don Quijote* is a touchstone for the study of realism in Spanish literature. Harriet Turner and Adelaida López de Martínez assert the centrality of the *quixotic* to the Spanish novel:

> Regardless of the age, past or present, in the development of the Spanish novel we discern a fundamental element: the *quixotic* or what Nabokov has called "play in collusion with reality." ... Even when it appears that play is all, that there is no meaning, no message to take away from the novel, the imprint of the text, of the spectacle of verbal thinking, feeling, and imagining, creates meaning as it discloses collusion with a particular cultural moment. The depiction of things or ideas or actions or simply of dialogue, of the acts of reading, remembering, and writing, evolves as various novelistic forms of enchantment in a disenchanted world. ("On the Novel" 1–2)

Scenes of novel reading and novel readers mirror this formal tension between enchantment and disenchantment that lies at the heart of the realist novel. The motif of fictional female novel readers began to connect women and quixotism early in Spain's nineteenth century. *Don Quijote* is perhaps the foremost example among realist novels of how a text becomes an object and a character, because it thematizes this process of reading as enchantment, which in turn draws its reader into its play of mirrors.

Texts travel through cultures by means of translations and imitations, adapting old genres to new behaviours and abandoning others that no longer fit, explains Eve Bannet. She describes a satiric vision of transnational models of conduct in eighteenth-century quixotic works. In the intense transnational circulation of people, ideas, and texts in the eighteenth century, she argues, quixotic works questioned the validity of transnational imitation, "the continued applicability of anachronistic transnational imitations in conduct and writing to different ranks, localities, and genders" (553).[1] At the close of the eighteenth century, Spaniards debated their sense of national identity and often rejected foreign, especially French, political and cultural models. In this context of ambivalence towards foreign models, the Spanish translation of one of the most significant eighteenth-century British quixotic fictions – Charlotte Lennox's 1752 *The Female Quixote or the Adventures of Arabella* – was published in Madrid in 1808, without acknowledging the author's name or gender: *Don Quijote con faldas; ó Perjuicios morales de las disparatadas novelas; escrito en inglés, sin nombre de autor; y en castellano, por Don Bernardo María de Calzada, Teniente Coronel de los Reales Exércitos é individuo de varios cuerpos literarios*.[2] Calzada used a 1773 French translation by Isaac-Mathieu Crommelin (reprinted in 1801) as an unacknowledged mediating text for his *Don Quijote con faldas*.[3] This chapter argues that Calzada's translation pioneered female quixotism in nineteenth-century Spain as a multivalent topos that subtly connected the feminine to the new genre of the novel and to unrealistic and nostalgic idealism. However, by also introducing a female protagonist who wins sympathy for her intelligence, kindness, virtue, and above all, eloquence, the novel subverts its stated didactic purpose to control and repress unruly women readers, offering instead an ambivalent message to its public about women's abilities and behaviour. Realism emerges as both a metaliterary theme and a technique in Lennox's novel and in its successive French and Spanish translations.

Menudencias [Trifles]

Don Quijote con faldas engages with the realist tradition in the nineteenth-century Spanish novel by offering a metaliterary critique of the grounds of empiricism, of how one can interpret what one sees and what one reads as real, and by its focus on concrete objects and persons, an aspect of the quixotic: "In the *Quijote* a mimetic focus on *menudencias* – the trifling things of life – acts as a kind of inset mirror that reflects those trifles within a nexus of relations that confers upon the ordinary an extraordinary range of meaning" (López de Martínez and Turner 3). Both French and Spanish prologues to the translations of *Don Quijote con faldas*, for example, allege that English novels are often too detailed: "chargés de détails minutieux" (1:i); "sobradamente cargados de menudencias" (1:ii). The translators seem to anticipate that their audiences may not understand or appreciate this aspect of realism, and they try to excuse it as a "foreign" aspect of the texts that they find exaggerated.

Even though the translations of Lennox's novel have reduced some of the details of the original, the "menudencias" to which Calzada refers still work to convey meaning both vertically as metaphor and horizontally across time as metonymy. Harriet Turner has eloquently explained the function of metaphor and metonymy in realist fiction:

> The images, denoting the "verticality" associated with metaphor, suggest that what is real or true lies at the center of things, and that it is possible, by effort, intuition or grace, to feel, know and express the fullness of this truth. Conversely, the metonymic or "horizontal" dimension of recorded experience specifies that the truth of something – the quintessential nature of traits or perceptions, actions or events – lies hidden, mixed into experience, subject to duration and qualified by links to other contexts. While a center exists ... what is real, true or authentic perforce emerges as bitty and piecemeal, contingent and *not* absolute nor ever whole. ("Metaphor and Metonymy" 887)

An article of clothing, Arabella's veil, is an example of how "menudencias" are transformed in the process of translation from Lennox's English novel through the French and Spanish versions, acquiring new meanings and functions while losing others through a process of appropriation and cultural transfer.

Arabella's Veil

Lennox describes how Arabella, neither knowing nor caring about contemporary fashion, decides to wear a veil when she first visits the Pump Room in Bath with her cousins: "instead of a Capuchin [a hood] she wore something like a Veil, of black Gauze, which covered almost all her Face, and Part of her Waist, and gave her a very singular Appearance"

(*The Female Quixote* 262). The French and Spanish translations, however, imply that wearing a veil was not necessarily unusual, and simply say that Arabella chooses "prendre son voile" (2:86); "se [puso] el velo" (2:191). Arabella's strange appearance, however, excites the curiosity of the crowd in the Pump Room, and they imagine romantic or exotic stories that reveal nationalistic prejudices to explain her strange appearance: "Some of the wiser Sort took her for a Foreigner; others, of still more Sagacity, supposed her a *Scots* lady, covered with her Plaid; and a third Sort, infinitely wiser than either, concluded she was a *Spanish* nun, that had escaped from a Convent, and had not yet quitted her Veil" (263). The French and Spanish translations omit most of the irony of Lennox's gradation of the wit of the spectators and re-nationalize the references to Arabella's strange appearance: "Un cercle la prenait pour une Portugaise; un autre se persuaduit qu'elle était Flamande; d'autres infiniment plus fins, la soupçonnaient d'être une religieuse espagnole échappée de son couvent" (2:87); "Unos la tuvieron por portuguesa; otra por natural de Flandes; y algunos, que presumian de mas astutos, sospecharon que era alguna monja escapada de su convento" (2:192). Lennox writes that Arabella was "ignorant of the Diversity of Opinions" caused by her strange, veiled, appearance, while the French and Spanish versions omit the interesting phrase that alludes to a public sphere – the diversity of opinion that Jürgen Habermas had described developing in British coffee houses during the eighteenth century – and reduce the crowd's reading of Arabella to a more uniform reaction: "Arabella ne se doutant pas de la sensation qu'elle faisait" (2:87); "Arabella ... no creia haber hecho sensacion alguna" (2:192).

Arabella's veil, which she wears in imitation of her heroines and to screen herself from public view, gives rise in this scene to additional, imaginative narratives by which the crowd tries to explain her strange appearance. When the spectators in the Pump Room learn that Arabella is the daughter of a Marquis, they indulgently accept her oddity by recalling three other examples of aristocratic women's "Whims": wearing a hooped skirt to Court; sitting astride a horse; and inventing a strange title for herself (264). Yet in contrast with their usual strategy of omitting details from the English original, the French and Spanish translations of this scene in the Pump Room instead elaborate on the spectators' imagined stories of analogies to Arabella's behaviour by adding another half-dozen anecdotes of aristocratic pretensions and vanity: presumptuous *petimetras* who imagine that old leather aprons are their families' escutcheons, exhibiting "mal-adroitement le ton impudent de la noblesse moderne" (2:88); "fingieron, con impropiedad, el porte descarado de la nobleza moderna" (2:194); a vain Countess someone knew; proud and ridiculous Marqueses and Marquesas they have seen who exhibit "la manie de se marquiser" (2:89); "la manía de enmarquesar" (2:194). Where Lennox presented the crowd's interpretations of eccentric aristocratic behaviour that could be excused as harmlessly whimsical, the French and Spanish translators suggest an interpretation of Arabella's unusual behaviour as vain social pretension, a portrait at odds with the young woman's overall virtuous character portrayed in the text. The two translators' imaginatively embroidered adaptations of the scene reveal more, perhaps, about the relation between fiction and class tensions of their own times, during the transition from the Old Regime to the liberal state during the late eighteenth and early nineteenth centuries, than a deep understanding of Arabella's character as Lennox had portrayed her in the mid-eighteenth century.

Arabella's veil later on plays a crucial role in provoking the crisis that leads to the conclusion of the novel. Arabella's cousin and suitor, Mr Glanville, suspicious of his rival Sir George's subterfuges to win her favour, thinks he sees Arabella from his window "cover'd with her veil as usual" going out to meet someone in the garden. Glanville hurries out and attacks and seriously wounds Sir George, "while the Lady, who had lost her Veil in her running, and to the great Astonishment of Mr. *Glanville,* prov'd to be his Sister, came up to them, with Tears and Exclamations, blaming herself for all that had happen'd" (357). His sister Charlotte's loss of the veil, her recognition of her guilt, and her repentance come all at the same moment in the English version, while the French and Spanish versions do not mention her repentance, only Glanville's. We learn later that one of Arabella's servants "propos'd [Charlotte's] putting on one of her Lady's Veils" in order to meet Sir George (365). The translations both recount Charlotte's jealousy of Arabella and the purposes of subterfuge to which the veil is put for the clandestine rendezvous with Sir George: "Cette fille lui conseilla, sans hésiter, de prendre un des voiles de sa maitresse" (2:197); "La moza la aconsejó, sin vacilar, que se pusiese uno de los velos de su ama" (3:138). Arabella's strange dress and behaviour, her idealistic, quixotic, self-fashioning, cause confusion but also win her admiration. But when others, her jealous cousin, for example, attempt to imitate her by "putting on" her characteristic veil, the consequences are nearly disastrous.

Thus we see that the details, the "menudencias" of Arabella's dress and especially the motif of her veil, convey metaphorically and metonymically, through time, in the text, the quixotic themes of imitation, self-fashioning, and the veiling and unveiling of character, and help Arabella to both fashion her appearance and discover the truth about her heart: "the romance plot she consistently adopts allows her to veil her own desires from herself while taking the liberty of imagining the male libidos around her" (Doody xxix). Like Don Quixote, Arabella imitates her heroines and manages to be odd, but somehow also heroic and authentic, while her "Whimsical" behaviour inspires imitations, continuations, and elaborations that can provoke and unveil less admirable aspects of the characters who interact with her.

Translation, Translators, and Gender

Since the republication of Lennox's novel in a modern edition in 1970, feminist critics have hailed it for its representation of feminine power and women's agency, for its foregrounding of the relation between gender and romance, for its probing of the gendered opposition between the novel and history (Doody, Spacks, Langbauer, Gallagher), and as a self-reflective text for women writers (Borham Puyal). Other critics have analysed its relationship to discourses on nationalism and gender, on quixotism, sentimentalism, and political economy, and on the epistemology of the novel (Motooka, Wood, Gordon, Mack, Bender). Many of these recent approaches focus on the final chapters of Lennox's novel, when the romance-deluded Arabella debates with a cleric the truth status of her favourite seventeenth-century French romances. At stake is the empirical grounding of history and fiction, and the ability of individual perception to prove whether reality is relative or absolute. Although the female Quixote Arabella maintains that her romances represent a better, more heroic, standard of behaviour, she finally yields to the cleric's assertion that such romances immorally sanction violence and suffering for the heroine's admirers, and therefore cannot be believed as "truth" or followed as a model for behaviour. Paul Gordon calls Lennox's novel an "orthodox" quixotic tale that rejects the Quixote's romantic or self-serving interpretation of the real as a delusion and affirms a normative reality grounded in perception and commonly shared social practices (184–5). Both the feminist vindications of the transcendence of Lennox's heroine and the materialist approaches that focus on nationalism and epistemology help us to understand the significance of Calzada's 1808 translation for the development of realism in nineteenth-century Spain. It inserted female quixotism – a cultural import from Britain via a mediating French translation – into a Spanish national discourse of aesthetic transformation from neoclassical didacticism to pre-romanticism, and of political transformation from absolutism to the beginnings of representative democracy.

The 1808 translation of Lennox's *The Female Quixote* as *Don Quijote con faldas* introduced into Spain a text not only quixotic but also doubly "other," both feminine and foreign, at a historical moment – the beginning of the Guerra de la Independencia [Peninsular War] – when national identity and foreign influence were being contested. Two years after its publication, the formation of the "national subject" would begin to be debated in the constitutional congresses in Cádiz. The public role some women had claimed in the late eighteenth century in, for example, the *Junta de Damas* and as active patriots during the Guerra de la Independencia would be repressed, and women as political subjects would be given secondary status to men (Bolufer 341–401; Smith 111–77; Romeo Mateo 61–72).

Nevertheless, despite its otherness – British and feminine – the translated novel *Don Quijote con faldas* sympathetically invokes for its Spanish public Spain's most significant contribution to European culture, "nuestro don Quijote" (1:vi) as the translator's introduction claims. Calzada's translation of *The Female Quixote* is thus an example of what Peter Burke has called the "circularity" of the cultural hybrid: "adaptations of foreign items of culture that are so thorough that the result can sometimes be 're-exported' successfully to the place from which the item originated" (96). Rather than relegating translation to a lesser status than that accorded an original work in the history of the Spanish novel, it is illuminating to inquire what cultural work the translation is executing. Stephanie Stockhorst describes translation as "cultural transfer" that takes into account "the complexity, processuality, and reciprocity of intercultural exchange relations" (20). In translation studies, it matters who translated what, for whom, and Peter Burke reminds us that "[t]ranslators are often displaced people" (100). Calzada's translation also appeared at a moment of change in translation theory that mirrored shifting political philosophies. Mary Helen McMurran discusses the circulation of novels through translation and claims that, during the eighteenth century, pre-modern translation theory grounded in "authority, temporality, and imitation" gradually gave way by the early nineteenth century to "a new bifurcated matrix of translation: the national and the foreign" (15). Calzada's 1808 translation reflects this early nineteenth-century translation strategy to nationalize the text by merely gesturing towards the authority of the original novel when describing "las novelas inglesas," effacing the author's name and the French mediating translation, to present the text as uniquely appropriate for his Spanish public. This female, British Don Quixote imported to Spain by Calzada had peculiar resonances for its Spanish audience and effected significant cultural work or transfer. It recalled a Spanish classic text that had been admired and imitated by the English and was a source of proud nostalgia for the apogee of Spanish cultural influence in Europe; it suggested a close or familial relation between British and Spanish contemporary readers, as opposed to the French, who remain unmentioned; and it specifically linked the prestigious English novel tradition to the Spanish literary tradition by mentioning "Fyeldings" and "Richardsons" in the prologue (1:ii). As a novel about a woman novel reader, it cemented the connection between the new class of women readers and novels.[4]

Lennox's French translator Crommelin subtitled his work "traduction libre de l'anglois." Crommelin seeks to foreground the comedy of the protagonist's romantic delusions rather than reproduce the metaliterary aspect of Lennox's parody of French romances. Through omission of dialogue and concision of description, Crommelin renders the characters of Lennox's novel more as comedic "types" than as psychologically convincing individuals, thus subtly minimizing the subversive effect of the protagonist's discourse (Tran-Gervat 288–9).[5] Calzada follows Crommelin's translation quite closely. The ironies of this translation situation multiply: Calzada translated a French translation of a British novel published half a century earlier, which was about a girl who reads bad translations of antique French novels; Lennox's novel is a feminized imitation of a character from Cervantes's novel, itself supposedly a translation from Arabic into Spanish. Calzada therefore simultaneously enacts and thematizes the "opposition between productive and reproductive work [that] organizes the way a culture values work," according to Lori Chamberlain, distinguishing writing as "masculine" and translating as "feminine" (254–5). In the gendered polemic over translation, the commonplace "les belles infidèles" suggests that, like women, "translations should be either beautiful or faithful" (Chamberlain 254–5). Both the novel *Don Quijote* and its imitation *The Female Quixote* take as their theme the tension inherent in translation between the relative value of original and copy and the distinction between "good" and "bad" translations; the French and Spanish translations of Lennox's novel enact this thematized, mirrored opposition.

During his visit to a print shop in Barcelona, Don Quixote famously refers to the ambivalence that attends on translation: "es como quien mira los tapices flamencos por el revés; que aunque se veen las figuras, son llenas de hilos que las escurecen ... Y no por esto quiero inferir que no sea loable este ejercicio del traducir" (2:62) ["[it] is like looking at Flemish tapestries from the wrong side, for although the figures are visible, they are covered by threads that obscure them ... And I do not wish to infer from this that the practice of translating is not deserving of praise" (873–4)]. Lennox makes poor translations a theme of her quixotic imitation. Her protagonist Arabella reads the books left by her deceased mother in her father's library: a "great Store of Romances, and, what was still more unfortunate, not in the original *French,* but very bad Translations" (7); "une quantité de vieux romans français, et plus malheureusement encore, tous mal traduits" (1:6); "un gran número de novelas modernas y antiguas, y, por mayor desgracia todavia, malditamente traducidas todas" (1:6). The English and French versions claim that the novels are French, but Calzada omits the French origin of the novels as part of his general strategy to repress French influence in his translation, and perhaps to avoid problems with his censors.

As if to align himself more closely with the famous Spanish original, and not with the British female novelist or with the French translator, Calzada appropriates the French translation's prologue with only minor changes, adding a new final paragraph:

> Como á nuestra heroina se la trastornó su buen juicio con la lectura de los mencionados libros heroicos, (cuyas ideas gigantescas é impracticables se propuso adoptar, á imitacion de nuestro Don Quijote famosísimo, no parece que la sienta mal llamarla *Don Quijote con Faldas,* título con que se anuncia al público esta obra. (1:vi)[6]

Both French and Spanish versions of the prologue show an awareness of national rivalry and admit the pre-eminence of English novels simply because they are English: "Las Novelas Inglesas tienen aceptacion tan constante, que basta serlo para grangearse reputacion" (1:ii), as they both claim in the prologues. Both translators stress that the English novels' style is less "delicate" than their own ("que nous" [1:i] in the French; "que otros" [1:ii] in the Spanish).

The French and Spanish prologues explain that the protagonist is a young girl, isolated from society, who reads "las obras, ridiculamente heroicas, de Magdalena Scudery" (1:iii). Calzada supplies Scudéry's first name, which is not in the French version, showing that he knows who she is. Calzada's text claims that Arabella read both "novelas modernas y antiguas" (1:6) and not solely the seventeenth-century French romances satirized by Lennox, most of which had not been translated into Spanish (Jaffe, "From the *Female Quixote*" 122).

Both French and Spanish prologues emphasize that the protagonist is impressionable: "un jeune coeur susceptible des premières impressions" (1:ii); "Se vén los efectos que semejante lectura puede producir en una muchacha de alma honrada y sencilla, que recibe aquellas primeras impresiones" (1:iv). The focus on the female reader as impressionable, receiving the text's message as pliantly as paper receives ink during printing, is a common metaphor of the time for the anxiety regarding the extension of literacy to many new classes of readers and how to regulate their reading and the new ideas they might derive from it (Jaffe, "Lectora"). Arabella is a synecdoche for all newly literate women readers as well as for other newly literate social classes; the lesson in realism she is taught in the novel, her process of disenchantment, serves to repress variant and subversive readings of texts and possibly of political, cultural, and social realities. Such a lesson would also be taught to other quixotic female protagonists, such as Isidora Rufete and Ana Ozores, later in the century.

Discourses of Realism and the Novel

In the novel's conclusion, Arabella jumps into the Thames to escape imagined ravishers. As she recovers from a serious illness caused by this accident, she discusses with a respected cleric whether her favourite romance novels are true histories or fictions. She demands that the cleric prove to her that her favourite novels are untrue, absurd, and dangerous. This final scene is disappointing for critics like Patricia Meyer Spacks, who defend romance as a feminine genre: "Romances tell the truth of female desire" (533).[7] Likewise, Margaret Anne Doody, who argues that Lennox wanted to use the novel form to tell a woman's story (xxvii), finds that "[t]he conversion scene represents a brainwashing session as a sexual taming" (xxxi). This identification of gender with genre is apparent when the cleric tells Arabella that her "Books soften the heart to love, and harden it to murder" (380), while the Spanish version explicitly genders the novel and says that the works "afeminan y endurecen a un mismo tiempo el corazón" (3:173).

The translations of this metaliterary conversion scene show a marked terminological difference from the original. When Arabella argues the case for the verisimilitude of her romances, the translations omit many references to the terms "fiction" and "narrative." Arabella demands to know why the cleric censures her fictions as absurd: "why, supposing them Fictions, and intended to be received as Fictions, you censure them as absurd?" (378); "prouvez-moi que ces histoires sont absurdes" (2:216); "probadme que las tales historias son absurdas" (3:167). Both Crommelin and Calzada omit Lennox's discourse regarding the status of fiction, its reception by the reader as a generic convention, and its relationship to reality, to "History and Nature." And in an imaginative addition to the text, when describing the peculiar truth value of fiction, the translators opt to illustrate the point through an analogy to the theatre rather than using the technical term "narrative":

> —The only Excellence of Falshood, answered he, is its Resemblance to Truth; as therefore any Narrative is more liable to be confuted by its Inconsistency with known Facts, it is at a greater distance from the Perfection of Fiction; for there can be no Difficulty in framing a Tale, if we are left at Liberty to invert all History and Nature for our own Conveniency. When a Crime is to be concealed, it is easy to cover it with an imaginary Word." (378)

> —La qualité la plus dangereuse du mensonge, répliqua le ministre, est de ressembler à la vérité; et l'on ne peut le réfuter que par le manque de rapports qu'il a avec les faits connus. Rien n'est plus aisé que de fabriquer une histoire, et de la rendre intéressante, si l'on permet à l'imagination de se servir des moyens employés dans les opéras, comme de faire croitre une forêt pour cacher un criminel ... (2:216–17)

> —La qualidad mas peligrosa de la mentira, replicó el sabio Cura, es la de parecerse á la verdad; y unicamente se la puede refutar por la falta de relacion que tiene con los hechos conocidos. No hay cosa mas facil que fabricar una historia, y hacerla gustosísima, si se permite á la imaginacion servirse de los medios empleados en los teatros para la representacion de las piezas, como figurar un bosque espeso para esconder á un delinqüente ... (3:167–8)

To make the cleric's point about the power of the fiction and the imagination, the translators use an analogy to a popular genre, the theatre, where a real/false "forest" of scenery can be manufactured to hide a criminal (on stage). They significantly omit the cleric's reference to the subversive potential of "Liberty to invert all History and Nature for our own Conveniency" and the wielding of the "imaginary Word" that bring to the foreground the potential power of language to shape reality. The translators invoke more concrete examples that were likely to be in their audience's field of reference to describe fiction's power, especially to conceal, "esconder," which reminds us again of Arabella's obscuring veil that incited such elaborate narrative speculation and deception.

Women Readers, Orators, and Writers

Despite these significant differences in discourse about narrative, the three versions end the same way, with Arabella's "cure" and marriage. The novel's suppression of the female Quixote's challenge to the socially accepted norm of marriage to her thoroughly acceptable cousin, the exclusion of the "other" in discourse, is a conclusion that has disappointed many readers (Spacks, Langbauer, Doody). Joseph Bartolomeo notes that, like Samuel Richardson, Lennox explored what was possible for women (164), and finds Lennox's ending positive because she "manages to examine the dangers women face, the options they have and the threats to patriarchal order they can represent" through her use of the comic mode (173). For April Alliston, quixotism is not about verisimilitude, but "about juxtaposing prescriptive and descriptive verisimilitudes of character" (264). In the character of Arabella, the feminine seems to be opposed to realism.

On the other hand, even though Calzada fails to acknowledge that the English novel's author was a woman, he publishes a translated novel whose very plot turns on a strong woman reader who argues logically with a cleric about her interpretation of texts and reality, according to the laws of disputation. At various times in the novel, the other characters express their admiration of Arabella's eloquence and reason that outshine her odd delusions. Her uncle, Sir Charles, "listen'd to her with many Signs of Admiration" and tells her, "you speak like an Orator" (269); "vous raisonnez comme un docteur" (2:95); "racionçinas como un doctor" (2:205). Again, Sir Charles "express'd much Admiration of her Wit, telling her, if she had been a Man, she would have made a great Figure in Parliament, and that her Speeches might have come to be printed in time" (311); "Sir Charles, enthousiasmé, lui dit: 'Quel dommage, ma nièce, que vous ne soyez pas homme! vous auriez sûrement figuré dans le parlement, peut-être même auriez-vous eu la gloire de voir vos discours imprimés'" (2:142); "El Barón, arrebatado de entusiasmo, dixo: '¡Qué lástima, sobrina mia, que no hayas sido hombre! Seguramente hubieras representado papel en el parlamento, y aun, acaso, tenido la gloria de ver impresos tus discursos'" (3:52). Sir Charles claims that "when she was out of those Whims, [Arabella] was a very sensible young Lady, and sometimes talk'd as learnedly as a Divine" (314), a statement changed to "como un ministro" (3:53) in the translations, doubtless in a nod to the censors. Even in Arabella's defeat through her acceptance of marriage, the example Calzada presents of Arabella raises the status of women, who were assuming more importance in the Spanish literary marketplace as readers and writers, and alludes to their ability to reason, debate, and write, only a few years before the beginning of the Cortes de Cádiz.[8]

Conclusion

Calzada's translation, even with its somewhat caricatured and truncated style, introduces into early nineteenth-century Spain a female Quixote connected to a discourse questioning the social and political status quo. As Joaquín Varela has recently argued, in the 1700s the interpretation in Spain shifted from seeing Britain as a constitutional monarchy to seeing it as a parliamentary monarchy, and this model was compared in debates to the French constitutional model. Calzada's text, a cultural hybrid, stands as a forerunner to female quixotic novels later in the century that would refer to debates regarding political legitimacy and the political subject (Benito Pérez Galdós's *La desheredada* or Leopoldo Alas's *La Regenta*, for example).[9] Lennox's model of female quixotism, via Calzada's translation, can be studied alongside later iterations of quixotism in the Spanish realist novel. *Don Quijote con faldas* is an example of the work of translation as cultural transfer at the end of the Enlightenment when intense debates about national identities accompanied the expansion of the reading public and the widening transnational circulation of texts and people, of knowledge and ideas. Eve Bannet finds that eighteenth-century writers used the quixotic trope "to address the crises of individuation and of 'national character' that transnational imitation was now perceived to create" (554). *Don Quijote con faldas* reintroduces the autochthonous quixotic trope, gendered and altered by its journeys through different cultures and imbued with Enlightenment ideologies and new narrative realism, back into Spain, at a moment when the nation's political and social structures were on the brink of profound change, as Spaniards looked nostalgically back to their past and forward to an uncertain future.

NOTES

1 Enlightenment imitations and continuations of the *Quijote* in Spain satirized the bad education of youth, scholasticism, and aristocratic presumptions, while early nineteenth-century Spanish quixotic imitations denounced liberal or Napoleonic ambitions (Álvarez de Miranda, "Sobre el 'Quijotismo'" 31–4). On eighteenth-century Quixotes and quixotism in Spain, see also Álvarez Barrientos, Aguilar Piñal, Barrero Pérez, Giménez, Lewis, and Lopez. Amelia Dale claims that in eighteenth-century England, "Quixotism was domesticated and naturalized as an English quality," while Aaron Hanlon argues that Don Quixote became "globalized" in the eighteenth century, untied from his relation to Cervantes and to Spain. For a study of parodies of *Don Quijote* in eighteenth-century English novels, see also Ardila (149–86). Paulson describes the aesthetic significance of *Don Quijote* in the same period.

2 Unless otherwise indicated, all quotations from the novels are taken from the original texts. Accents, punctuation, and spelling remain as in the original texts, and italics from the original have been retained. All quotations from Lennox's text are from the Dalziel edition. All quotations from the French translation are from Crommelin's 1801 edition, listed by volume and page, and quotations from Calzada's 1808 translation are listed by volume and page. For an analysis of Calzada's translation as a gendered text, see Lorenzo-Modia, and Jaffe, "From *The Female Quixote*" and "El Quijotismo femenino." A new Spanish translation by Manuel Broncano of Lennox's novel, *La mujer Quijote*, was published in 2004, edited by Cristina Garrigós.

3 María Jesús Lorenzo-Modia suggests that this omission was a translation strategy meant to foreground Calzada's work as an "author-translator" rather than a "mediator-translator" (108).

4 Calzada's translations contributed to the widening variety of novels available to readers at the end of the eighteenth century in Spain, which both met a demand in the market and helped to shape readers' expectations for the literary form (Haidt 33–4). On Calzada's translations, see Freire López. On translation in Spain, see García Garrosa and Lafarga.

5 Maurice Bardon finds that *Le don Quichotte femelle* "se rebela contra lo novelesco" and that it is "en perfecta sintonía con el *Quijote* español" (775).

6 The rest of the prologue is:

> La obra que doy á luz es de un género estraño, y me atrevo á esperar que agradará, quando no sea mas que por su singularidad misma. La encuentro, no obstante, el defecto principal de que critíca algunas

novelas, cuya lectura ya no es peligrosa, como la de varias que corren en nuestros dias. Pero, como quiera que sea, se trata de una señorita inglesa, nacida en un parage retirado, distante de toda suerte de sociedad, sin madre, sin guia, y sin tener, para minorar su tédio, mas libros que las obras, ridiculamente heroicas, de Magdalena Scudery. Se vén los efectos que semejante lectura puede producir en una muchacha de alma honrada y sencilla, que recibe aquellas primeras impresiones.

Arabela hermosa, joven modesta, viva y conseqüente, aun en su heroismo extravagante, merece promover la compasion, y no el desprecio. Su confidenta es una moza simple, que rie, llora, y solo se presenta en la Escena para entregar una carta, abrir una puerta, alargar una silla, hacer alguna comision ridícula, ó estropear algunas frases de su ama. (1:ii–iii)

7 Many critics have discussed this conversion scene, finding it unsatisfying and perhaps influenced by Samuel Johnson. See Doody, xxix–xxxii. Close describes the romantic interpretation of *Don Quijote*.

8 For studies of different aspects of the phenomenon of women readers and writers, and women's reading in the eighteenth century, see Urzainqui Miqueleiz, "Nuevas propuestas" and "La mujer como receptora literaria," and Jaffe, "Lectora y Lectura femenina en la modernidad."

9 López-Cordón analyses the shift from the concept of monarchy to nation. For a study of a female Quixote in nineteenth-century Spanish theatre, see Jaffe, "Female Quixotism and National Identity."

WORKS CITED

Aguilar Piñal, Francisco. "Anverso y reverso del 'quijotismo' en el siglo XVIII español." *Anales de literatura española* 1 (1982): 207–16. Print. https://doi.org/10.14198/aleua.1982.1.07.

Alliston, April. "Female Quixotism and the Novel: Character and Plausibility, Honesty and Fidelity." *Eighteenth-Century* 52.3–4 (2011): 249–69. Print. http://doi.org/10.1353/ecy.2011.0021.

Álvarez Barrientos, Joaquín. *La novela del siglo XVIII*. Madrid: Júcar, 1991. Print.

Álvarez de Miranda, Pedro. *Palabras e ideas. El léxico de la Ilustración temprana en España (1680-1760)*. Madrid: Real Academia Española, 1992. Print.

– "Sobre el 'Quijotismo' dieciochesco y las imitaciones reaccionarias del Quijote en el primer siglo XIX." *Dieciocho* 27.1 (2004): 31–45. Print.

Ardila, J.A.G. *Cervantes en Inglaterra: El Quijote y la novela inglesa del siglo XVIII.* 2nd ed. Alcalá de Henares: Centro de Estudios Cervantinos, 2014. Print.

Bannet, Eve Tavor. "Quixotes, Imitations, and Transatlantic Genres." *Eighteenth-Century Studies* 40.4 (2007): 553–69. Print. http://doi.org/10.1353/ecs.2007.0035.

Bardon, Maurice. *El "Quijote" en Francia en los siglos XVII y XVIII.* Ed. Françoise Étienvre. Trans. Jaime Lorenzo Miralles. Alicante: Universidad de Alicante, 2010. Print.

Barrero Pérez, Óscar. "Los imitadores y continuadores del 'Quijote' en la novela española del siglo XVIII." *Anales Cervantinos* 24 (1986): 103–21. Print.

Bartolomeo, Joseph. "Female Quixotism v. 'Feminine' Tragedy: Lennox's Comic Revision of *Clarissa.*" In *New Essays on Samuel Richardson*, ed. Albert J. Rivero. New York: St Martin's, 1996. 163–75. Print.

Bender, John. "Novel Knowledge: Judgement, Experience, Experiment." In *This Is Enlightenment*, ed. Clifford Siskin and William Warner. Chicago: U of Chicago P, 2010. 284–300. Print.

Bolufer Peruga, Mónica. *Mujeres e Ilustración: La construcción de la feminidad en la España del siglo XVIII.* Valencia: Institució Alfons el Magnanim, 1998. Print.

Borham Puyal, Miriam. *Quijotes con enaguas: Encrucijada de géneros en el siglo XVIII británico.* Valencia: JPM Ediciones, 2015. Print.

Burke, Peter. *Cultural Hybridity.* Cambridge: Polity, 2009. Print.

Cervantes, Miguel de. *Don Quixote.* Trans. Edith Grossman. New York: HarperCollins, 2003. Print.

Chamberlain, Lori. "Gender and the Metaphorics of Translation." In *The Translation Studies Reader*, ed. Lawrence Venuti. 3rd ed. New York: Routledge, 2012. 254–68. Print.

Close, Anthony J. *The Romantic Approach to "Don Quixote": A Critical History of the Romantic Tradition in Quixote Criticism.* New York: Cambridge UP, 1978. Print.

"Crommelin, Isaac-Mathieu." In *Biographie Universelle Ancienne et Moderne*, ed. Michaud. Paris: Chez Madame C. Desplaces, 1854. 9:519. Print.

Dale, Amelia. "'National Character' and Quixotic Masculinity in Eighteenth-Century England." *SECC* 46 (2017): 5–19. Print. doi:10.1353/sec.2017.0003.

Doody, Margaret Anne. Introduction. In Charlotte Lennox, *The Female Quixote or the Adventures of Arabella*, ed. Margaret Dalziel, Margaret Anne Doody, and Duncan Isles. Oxford: Oxford UP, 1989. xi–xxxii. Print.

Freire López, Ana María. "Un traductor del reinado de Carlos III: Bernardo María de Calzada." *Investigación franco-española* 2 (1989): 71–80. Print.

Gallagher, Catherine. *Nobody's Story: The Vanishing Acts of Women Writers in the Marketplace 1670–1820.* Los Angeles: U of California P, 1994. Print.

García Garrosa, María Jesús, and Francisco Lafarga. *El discurso sobre la traducción en la España del siglo XVIII. Estudio y antología*. Kassel: Reichenberger, 2004. Print.

Garrigós, Cristina. Introduction. In Charlotte Lennox, *La mujer Quijote*. Madrid: Cátedra, 2004. 9–71. Print.

Giménez, Enrique, ed. *El Quijote en el siglo de las luces*. Alicante: Universidad de Alicante, 2006. Print.

Gordon, Scott Paul. *The Practice of Quixotism: Postmodern Theory and Eighteenth-Century Women's Writing*. New York: Palgrave Macmillan, 2006. Print.

Habermas, Jürgen. *The Structural Transformation of the Public Sphere: An Inquiry into a Category of Bourgeois Society*. Trans. Thomas Burger and Frederick Lawrence. Cambridge, MA: MIT P, 1991. Print.

Haidt, Rebecca. "The Enlightenment and Fictional Form." In *The Cambridge Companion to the Spanish Novel: From 1600 to the Present*, ed. Harriet Turner and Adelaida López de Martínez. New York: Cambridge UP, 2003. 31–46. Print.

Hanlon, Aaron. "Quixotism as Global Heuristic." *SECC* 46 (2017): 49–62. Print. doi:10.1353/sec.2017.0006.

Jaffe, Catherine M. "Female Quixotism and National Identity in *Contigo pan y cebolla* (1833)." In *Variantes de la modernidad: Estudios en honor de Ricardo Gullón*, ed. Carlos Javier García and Cristina Martínez-Carazo. Newark, DE: Juan de la Cuesta, 2011. 169–85. Print.

– "From the *Female Quixote* to *Don Quijote con faldas*: Translation and Transculturation." *Dieciocho* 28.2 (2005): 120–6. Print.

– "Lectora y lectura femenina en la modernidad: el *Semanario de Salamanca* (1793–1798)." *Ayer: Revista de Historia Contemporánea* 72.2 (2010): 69–91. Print.

– "El Quijotismo femenino: Mujer y lectura al fin de la Ilustración." In *Avanzando hacia la igualdad*, ed. Antonia Mª Medina Guerra. Málaga: Diputación de Málaga y la Asociación de Estudios Históricos Sobre la Mujer, 2007. 73–87. Print.

Langbauer, Laurie. *Women and Romance: The Consolations of Gender in the English Novel*. Ithaca: Cornell UP, 1990. Print.

Lennox, Charlotte. *Arabella ou le Don Quichote Femelle*. Trans. Isaac Mathieu Crommelin. 2 vols. Paris: Bertaudet, 1801. Print.

– *Don Quichotte femelle: traduction libre de l'anglois*. Trans. Isaac Mathieu Crommelin. 2 vols. Lyon: Les libraires associés, 1773. Print.

– *Don Quijote con faldas o perjuicios morales de las disparatadas novelas*. Trans. Bernardo María de Calzada. 3 vols. Madrid: Fuentenebro, 1808. Print.

– *The Female Quixote or the Adventures of Arabella*. Ed. Margaret Dalziel, Margaret Anne Doody, and Duncan Isles. Oxford: Oxford UP, 1989. Print.

– *La mujer Quijote*. Trans. Manuel Broncano. Ed. Cristina Garrigós. Madrid: Cátedra, 2004. Print.

Lewis, Elizabeth Franklin. "Maps, Travelers, and the 'Real' *Don Quixote de la Mancha*." *SECC* 46 (2017): 35–48. Print. doi:10.1353/sec.2017.0005.

Lopez, François. "Los *Quijotes* de la Ilustración." *Dieciocho* 22.2 (1992): 247–64. Print.

López de Martínez, Adelaida, and Harriet Turner. "On the Novel: Mirror and Text." In *The Cambridge Companion to the Spanish Novel: From 1600 to the Present*, ed. Turner and López de Martínez. New York: Cambridge UP, 2003. 1–11. Print.

López-Cordón, María Victoria. "De monarquía a nación." *Norba. Revista de Historia* 19 (2006): 151–73. Print.

Lorenzo-Modia, María Jesús. "Charlotte Lennox's *The Female Quixote* into Spanish: A Gender-Biased Translation." *Yearbook of English Studies* 36.1 (2006): 103–14. Print.

Mack, Ruth. "Quixotic Ethnography: Charlotte Lennox and the Dilemma of Cultural Observation." *Novel: A Forum on Fiction* 38.2/3 (2005): 193–213. Print. http://doi.org/10.1215/ddnov.038020193.

McMurran, Mary Helen. *The Spread of Novels: Translation and Prose Fiction in the Eighteenth Century*. Princeton: Princeton UP, 2010. Print.

Motooka, Wendy. *The Age of Reasons: Quixotism, Sentimentalism and Political Economy in Eighteenth-Century Britain*. New York: Routledge, 1998. Print.

Paulson, Ronald. *Don Quixote in England: The Aesthetics of Laughter*. Baltimore: Johns Hopkins UP, 1998. Print.

Romeo Mateo, María Cruz. "Destinos de mujer: esfera pública y políticos liberales." In *Historia de las mujeres en España y América Latina*, vol. 3, ed. Isabel Morant, Guadalupe Gómez-Ferrer, Gabriel Cano, Dora Barrancos, and Asunción Lavrin. Madrid: Cátedra, 2006. 61–83. Print.

Smith, Theresa Ann. *The Emerging Female Citizen: Gender and Enlightenment in Spain*. Los Angeles: U of California P, 2006. Print.

Spacks, Patricia Meyer. "The Subtle Sophistry of Desire: Dr. Johnson and *The Female Quixote*." *Modern Philology* 85.4 (May 1988): 532–42. Print. http://doi.org/10.1086/391661.

Stockhorst, Stefanie. "Introduction: Cultural Transfer through Translation: A Current Perspective in Enlightenment Studies." In *Cultural Transfer through Translation: The Circulation of Enlightened Thought in Europe by Means of Translation*, ed. Stefanie Stockhorst. New York: Rodopi, 2010. 7–26. Print.

Tran-Gervat, Yen-Mai. "La Première Traduction de *The Female Quixote* de Ch. Lennox: Le Choix de la Comédie." In *La traduction Romanesque au XVIIIe Siècle*, ed. Annie Cointre, Alain Lautel, and Annie Rivara. Arras: Artois Presses Université, 2003. 285–93. Print.

Turner, Harriet. "Metaphor and Metonomy in Galdós and Tolstoy." *Hispania* 75.4 (1992): 884–96. Print. http://doi.org/10.2307/343857.

– "'Why the Face of the Voice Is in the Hand': On the Poetics of Realist Fiction." In *Studies in Honor of Vernon Chamberlin*, ed. Mark A. Harpring. Newark, DE: Juan de la Cuesta. 215–30. Print.

Turner, Harriet, and Adelaida López de Martínez, eds. *The Cambridge Companion to the Spanish Novel: From 1600 to the Present*. New York: Cambridge UP, 2003. Print.

Urzainqui Miqueleiz, Inmaculada. "La mujer como receptora literaria en el siglo XVIII." In *Ecos silenciados: la mujer en la literatura española, siglos XII al XVIII*, ed. Susana Gil-Albarellos Pérez-Pedrero and Mercedes Rodríguez Pequeño. León: Junta de Castilla y León, 2006. 289–314. Print.

– "Nuevas propuestas a un público femenino." In *Historia de la edición y la lectura en España, 1472–1914*, ed. Nieves Baranda, Víctor Infantes de Miguel, François Lopez, and Jean François Botrel. Madrid: Fundación Germán Sánchez Ruipérez, 2003. 481–91. Print.

Varela Suanzes-Carpegna, Joaquín. "The Image of the British System of Government in Spain (1759–1814)." In *The Spanish Enlightenment Revisited*, ed. Jesús Astigarraga. Oxford: Voltaire Foundation, 2015. 193–211. Print.

Wood, Sarah F. *Quixotic Fictions of the USA 1792–1815*. Oxford: Oxford UP, 2005. Print.

2 Between *Costumbrista* Sketch and Short Story: Armando Palacio Valdés's *Aguas fuertes*

ENRIQUE RUBIO CREMADES
TRANSLATION BY MARGOT VERSTEEG

In both literature and in painting, the term *aguafuerte* (etching) refers to an art of reproduction. The text or the image arrives in the hands of the reader or before the eyes of the viewer, just as the artist or writer wanted to express or draw it, without preliminary considerations or sketches; it is the most natural expression of the mind of the artist, in this case of the writer Armando Palacio Valdés. His collection *Aguas fuertes* is a distinctive and subtle literary work whose narratives physically and visually capture a series of sensations, and the short narratives that make up the volume range from the abstract-descriptive *costumbrista* sketch to the anecdote that has been fitted with a storyline that lends the piece an animated, lively tone, with characters and movement. *Aguas fuertes* contains not only writings rooted in the impeccable *costumbrista* tradition of Mesonero Romanos and Larra, but also a number of short stories that lend the volume its miscellaneous character.

The first edition of *Aguas fuertes* (1884)[1] coincides with the publication of other volumes similar in focus and content written by, among others, Father Luis Coloma, Ángela Grassi, and Manuel Ossorio y Bernard.[2] Earlier in the decade, Spanish publishers had issued several collections that alternated short stories, novellas, and *costumbrista* sketches in their various forms, such as José Ortega y Munilla's *Pruebas de imprenta, cuentos y artículos* [Print Drafts, Stories and Articles] (1883) and Pereda's *Esbozos y rasguños* (1881) [Sketches and Notes], a volume that combines multifaceted contents in a hybrid form halfway between short story and *costumbrista* sketch, and that is linked together by the characters and a thin narrative thread.[3]

The members of Palacio Valdés's generation often published their *cuadros de costumbres* and short stories in newspapers and magazines and collected them later in volumes or anthologies.[4] I am convinced that the first anthology or collective volume had its origin in journalism. The nineteenth century witnessed the development of a public sphere in Spain as a result of the proliferation of the periodical press that had started a century earlier. Journals, newspapers, and magazines became the primary medium of public exchange for a growing bourgeoisie. This development saw the emergence of the professional writer, changed the notion of what a text was, and shaped new forms of readerly reception (Iarocci 385–6). *Costumbrismo* has a distinctive realist dimension, as the fundamentally new form of literary mimesis in the *cuadros de costumbres* reveals an increasing focus on the representation of contemporary social life. Like the realist novel, these articles became a venue in which the new middle classes contemplated and analysed their social world. They helped to make sense of an increasingly heterogeneous society (Iarocci 388).[5]

The *costumbrista* articles in the journals and magazines were only short-lived, but, once they were published in book form, these journalistic texts prevailed and could be read at any moment. This is illustrated by the first edition of *Figaro*'s articles published by the printer Repullés (1835). With the birth of the modern press – *Cartas Españolas, Revista Española, El Artista, Semanario Pintoresco Español* – the editors, in connivance with the authors, would reprint articles that had been published scattered in journals and magazines in order to cash in on the author's fame and thus obtain ample benefits. This practice of publishing was common in the nineteenth century and also occurred with pieces written by Palacio Valdés.

The first edition of *Aguas fuertes*, for instance, contains a total of seventeen miscellaneous texts by Palacio Valdés. *El Retiro de Madrid* is a long *costumbrista* sketch that consists of four subdivisions: *Mañanas de junio y julio* [June and July Mornings], *El estanque grande* [The Great Pond], *La casa de fieras* [The Wild Animal House], and *El paseo de los coches* [Carriage Way]. In the second edition (1907), three new texts have been added; well-written pieces of undeniable literary quality that enrich the collection: *El crimen de la calle de la Perseguida* [The Crime on Perseguida Street], *El potro del señor cura* [The Curate's Colt], and *Polifemo* [Polyphemus]. The reader is not given any explanation about the criteria that guide the inclusion of the additional texts, and in the second and final edition of *Aguas fuertes* the subtitle *novelas y cuadros* [novels and scenes] has been omitted. This is also the case in the 1921 and 1947 editions of the *Obras completas* [Complete Works] by Palacio Valdés.

Specific stories and *cuadros de costumbres* have been pulled out of the final corpus of *Aguas fuertes* to be published either in collective volumes, in anthologies of work by the author himself, or in isolated form. *El pájaro en la nieve* [The Bird in the Snow], for instance, was published in 1918 in *Los Contemporáneos* [The Contemporaries], and in 1925 this text appeared in a collection of short stories illustrated by the well-known illustrator Enrique Martínez Echevarría, "Echea." The same happened with *Los Puritanos* [The Puritans], a story that had always been included in *Aguas fuertes* and that would later be published together with other stories in, for example, W.T. Faulkner's 1904 collection *Los puritanos y otros cuentos*, and in the 1929 edition *Los Puritanos*. Although this last volume is named after a single story, *Los Puritanos*, it also contains stories that figure in *Aguas fuertes* – *El pájaro en la nieve*, *El drama de las bambalinas* [Stage Curtain Drama], *Los amores de Clotilde* [Clotilde's Romance], and *Polifemo* [Polyphemus], or in other publications, such as *Solo* [Alone], *Ramonín*, *Seducción* [Seduction], and *Vida de canónigo* [The Life of a Canon]. What we have described here was common practice during Palacio's time (Lorenzo Álvarez 215–36), and the author was no exception in allowing publications of his *cuadros* or stories in a variety of venues.

The publication of *Aguas fuertes* also coincided with another literary practice typical of the second half of the nineteenth and the beginning of the twentieth century: the publication of *artículos de costumbres* in *costumbrista* collections. With the disappearance of the masters of *costumbrismo* – Larra and Mesonero Romanos – the interest in the genre did not diminish but rather revived in the second half of the nineteenth century, as demonstrated by the writings of Valera, Alarcón, Galdós, Pardo Bazán, Pereda, and others. This success of the *costumbrista* article led to the publication of *costumbrista* collections, such as *Las españolas pintadas por los españoles* [Spanish Women, Portrayed by Spanish Men] (1871–2), *Las mujeres españolas, portuguesas y americanas* [Spanish, Portuguese, and American Women] (1872, 1873, 1876), *Los españoles de ogaño* [The Spaniards of Today] (1872), *Madrid por dentro y por fuera* [Madrid Inside and Out] (1873), *Los hombres españoles, americanos y lusitanos pintados por sí mismos* [Spanish, American, and Lusitanian Men, Portrayed by Themselves] (1882), and *Las mujeres españolas, americanas y lusitanas pintadas por sí mismas* [Spanish, American, and Lusitanian Women, Portrayed by Themselves] (1882). The *crème de la crème* of Spanish intellectuals, writers, and journalists collaborated in these collections. Even at the dawn of the twentieth century, these volumes occupied a privileged place, such as *El Álbum de Galicia* [The Book of Galicia] or those whose titles evoked the very first volume in its genre, *Los españoles pintados por sí mismos* [The Spanish Portrayed by Themselves]. In this sense, Palacio Valdés's pieces *El Paseo de Recoletos* and *La Castellana*, to name only two, appear as classic texts alongside other *costumbrista* scenes written by Rafael Ramiro y Doreste, Enrique Sepúlveda, Eusebio Blasco, Luis Taboada, Ramón Gómez de la Serna, and many others. To this list of writers we could obviously add the above-mentioned authors of the great realist and naturalist novels.

The publication of *Aguas fuertes* was well received, as the volume garnered the approval of the caustic, famous, and feared Clarín, who from the pages of *El Globo* (1 February 1885) began his critical discussion of the work with a series of eloquent literary and pictorial references: "En *Aguas fuertes* hay miniaturas que, a encontrarlas en un abanico *El Primo Pons* [Cousin Pons], las hubiera comprado por obra de Watteau a peso de oro" [In *Aguas fuertes* there are miniatures that, upon finding them painted on a fan, Cousin Pons would have purchased for their weight in gold, thinking them the work of Watteau] (Alas 802). Clarín did not choose this literary comparison frivolously. *El Primo Pons* is a translation of a novel by Balzac, *Le cousin Pons* (1847), that together with *La prima Bette* forms the diptych *Los parientes pobres – Les parents pauvres* [Poor Relations] – included in Balzac's *Comedia humana*. What's important for Clarín is Pons's incredible journey. We are dealing with a simple and good-hearted character, who has a great fondness for art and who, with the modest income from his harmony lessons and after cutting down on all his expenses, accumulates a highly select and extremely beautiful collection of paintings and curiosities while remaining unaware of the works' commercial value. To compare *Aguas fuertes* to the paintings of Jean Antoine Watteau, whose works are on display in Europe's foremost national museums, means to highly value the volume's excellence. To situate *Aguas fuertes* among the works of the universal masters – Balzac and Watteau – is the highest praise that Clarín could give to Palacio's book. Accordingly, it should come as no surprise that he defines the work in laudatory terms:

> Y tal como es difícil salir de la bodega-catedral González-Wias sin un poco de alegría en el cuerpo, cuando se termina la lectura de *Aguas fuertes* se está un poco ebrio de luz, calor, armonía, sentimiento, y también de esa malicia bonachona, que en el fondo no es más que un perdón de

todas las flaquezas, aderezadas con la gracia de la experiencia horaciana. (Alas 893–4)

[And just as it is difficult to leave the González-Wias winery-cathedral without a bit of joy in the body, when one finishes the reading of *Aguas fuertes* one is a little drunk with light, heat, harmony, feeling, and also with that good-natured malice, which is in essence no more than a forgiveness of all weaknesses, seasoned with the grace of the Horacian experience.]

According to Clarín, Palacio Valdés's volume is perfect. There is not a word too many; everything is delight and joy, and no individual narrative component is preferred or critiqued. The amalgam of *cuadros de costumbres*, disparate in content and scope, of short stories and novels, forms an exceptional whole. To please the reader accustomed to his sharp criticism, Clarín only points out minor oversights in language that nonetheless do not diminish the quality of *Aguas fuertes*.

Palacio Valdés begins *Aguas fuertes* with a *costumbrista* scene in the style of *El Curioso Parlante* [The Curious Speaker]. Mesonero Romanos often described Madrid's Retiro Park, both in his *Manual de Madrid* and in his *Nuevo Manual de Madrid*. His characters stroll through the Buen Retiro, although not in any specific or concrete way. Later followers of Larra and Mesonero, on the contrary, would describe and analyse the social behaviour of characters very different in appearance and social origin that so frequently visited this urban context. Only a few years before Palacio Valdés published *Agua fuertes*, Pedro de Répide commented on the political life in Madrid at that time in his *Madrid a vista de pájaro* [A Bird's-Eye View of Madrid] (1874) when he described passers-by in Madrid's Retiro discussing the manipulative moves of Rosas Samaniego and the followers of King Alfonso. Another example is found in *Las fieras del Retiro* [The Beasts of the Retiro], by Vital Aza, who levels a scathing critique of politicians and their venality by comparing them to the caged monkeys in the Buen Retiro (287–300).[6] Palacio Valdés, however, adopts in his article the detailed *costumbrismo* style of Adolfo Mentaberry, author of the article *Los jardines del Retiro* (255–64), published together with the article by Aza in the *costumbrista* collection *Madrid por dentro y por fuera*.

Palacio Valdés pays particular attention to an urban landscape populated by characters who make brief appearances and, for whatever reason, run into the author during his daily stroll, including, for example, the seamstresses and other persons whose occupations require them to start early, at daybreak, when Don Armando used to take his walk. In this first *cuadro de costumbres*, we clearly notice some of the characteristics of the genre, not only in the literary devices used by the author but also in the words with which Palacio Valdés, following the masters of *costumbrismo*, expresses his intentions: "Antes de ponerme a escribir a cerca de ellas [La casa de fieras del Retiro], quizá debiera examinar algunos documentos referentes a su erección y desenvolvimiento, a fin de que las futuras generaciones, cuando lean el presente estudio, sepan a quien deben las fieras el piadoso hospital que hoy disfrutan" [Before I write about them [the animal cages in the Retiro Park], perhaps I should examine some documents about their construction and history, so that future generations, when they read this study, know to whom the beasts owe the compassionate hospital they now enjoy] (*Aguas fuertes* 20).

Several generations later, Palacio Valdés's perspective provides today's reader with a keen understanding of the lively environment that was Madrid's Retiro, where a variety of social types mingled with tradesmen and artisans. The author takes the reader on a journey through Madrid's urban environment; he presents us with the city's customs, courtship traditions, and forms of entertainment, and shows us a thousand ways to idly pass time, the driving force of the characters' actions, from sunset to sundown. For Palacio Valdés, the "madrileños, mejor que ningún otro pueblo antiguo o moderno, han llevado el refinamiento a este goce exquisito; en las iglesias, en los teatros, en los paseos, en los salones. Se apuran todos los medios de contemplarse con más comodidad" [Madrileños, better than any other ancient or modern people, have brought refinement to this exquisite enjoyment; in the churches, in the theatres, in the boulevards, in the salons. They take advantage of every means to indulge themselves with greater comfort] (*Aguas fuertes* 33–4). Palacio's intentions are in a way similar to those of Galdós, when the latter writes his *costumbrista* article *Aquel* [That One] (266–74), in which the narrator, from the beginning to the end of the text, follows a character during his walk, his journey through the city, his stops and observations, as if he were following a mysterious being. In the end Galdós will reveal the profession of this mysterious individual: he is an idler, an inactive person. Even before Baudelaire and Walter Benjamin, the *costumbristas* used the term *flanear*, from the French *flâner*, since they were masters in the art of strolling, wandering and doing nothing. Palacio Valdés puts this *galicismo* into practice, knowing that his *flanear* will provide him with sufficient noteworthy material to publish in a newspaper.

El Retiro de Madrid is an exemplary *cuadro de costumbres*, since the writer accounts for his observations in a way that is fluid and careful, without ignoring the urban context or the people who pass by. It's an animated sketch that describes at the same time as it analyses or satirizes. The observation is detailed, the tone very personal. We clearly sense that Palacio Valdés is present in this piece. We notice his characteristic tics in the way he observes his surroundings, and his tolerance, sense of humour, and temperament keep charming us. During his urban journey he refers to classical antiquity to describe the peacefulness and beauty of the Retiro, its pond, its romantic gardens, its hidden corners, while at the same time denouncing the misconceived modernity of Madrid's city council for its inability to solve specific problems with the *Casa de fieras* or the so-called *Paseo de los coches*. In a humorous tone, he approaches the deplorable situation of the Retiro's wild animals, which are hungry and basically abandoned to their fate or to the generosity and thoughtfulness of the onlookers. The origins of the passers-by, army recruits and seamstresses, betray their working-class culture and their natural vivacity, and Palacio Valdés portrays them with subtle charm. He paints a lively and diverse world in which the protagonists spontaneously begin to converse, using a language riddled with vulgarisms, syntactic distortions, borrowings, and idiomatic variations that make the described situations feel real. In this sense, Palacio Valdés is very close to an author such as Mesonero Romanos, or Antonio Flores, *costumbrista* writers who equipped their characters with all the features of the language that corresponded with their social status, just as Galdós situated his fictional world in specific social contexts of the city of Madrid.

In *Aguas fuertes* we clearly perceive the *costumbrista* writer's attitude when it comes to analysing the past in relation to the present. Palacio Valdés shows a certain tolerance, benevolence, and sympathy for the configuration of the Retiro in a time before its alteration, its remodelling. The author contemplates the innovations from a negative perspective. Something similar occurs with his vision or analysis of this same society characterized by *cursilería*, the notorious "quiero y no puedo" [I want and I can't] that Galdós will describe in his fictional world, equipping it with a life of its own. Noël Valis, in *The Culture of Cursilería: Bad Taste, Kitsch and Class in Modern Spain*, defines *cursilería* as a phenomenon inhabiting the conflictive face of modernity in Spain and one that has its roots in a sense of cultural inadequacy felt by Spain's lower middle classes. Palacio Valdés writes on the topic that "hay hombre que se queda calvo, y defrauda al Estado, y arruina a varias familias, solamente para que dos caballos le lleven a todas partes a contemplar a otros hombres que también se han quedado calvos y han defraudado al Estado y a los particulares con el mismo objeto" [There are men who have gone broke, have defrauded the state, ruined various families, only so that two horses might carry them everywhere so that they can contemplate other men who have also gone broke, defrauded the state and other individuals, all with the same goal] (*Aguas fuertes* 33).

Palacio Valdés also uses fantastic elements in his sketches, such as animals that dialogue with each other and denounce their owners or those who live nearby. These animals are not conceived as subjects of the story or symbols of the virtues or vices of human beings, but rather as beings that are qualified to judge their owners and reproach them their lack of understanding or common sense. These sketches portray a diverse world populated by colts that pass themselves off as legitimate descendants of the most renowned London stables, while in reality they originate in Spanish soil. Middle-class bipeds contemplate without blinking the magnificent entourage of the aristocratic quadrupeds. The result is a courtly life with an intimate connection to the urban world, analysed from different viewpoints, as if Palacio Valdés wanted to offer it to his readers from multiple perspectives, besides his own.

In the same vein of the sketch *El Retiro de Madrid* is *El Paseo de Recoletos,* in those days the promenade of the middle classes. It was a place frequented by the *cursi,* another exponent of the widespread phenomenon of *cursilería* (see above). A character from the illustrious nineteenth-century literary tradition, the *cursi* is generally considered false because of her eagerness to boast about an elegance or refinement that she does not have: "cursililla de media tostada" [slow-witted snobs] (*Aguas fuertes* 170), Palacio Valdés called them, recalling famous examples of *cuadros de costumbres* that describe the adventures and misfortunes of this character.[7] The Paseo de Recoletos, which in the beginning of the nineteenth century was called the Paseo Nuevo de las Delicias de la Princesa, was also known as the Fuente de la Castellana and Paseo de Isabel II. Palacio Valdés describes this promenade as the preferred leisure zone of Madrid's inhabitants, an urban framing that is characteristic and typical of his time. While he walks along Madrid's principal arteries that converge into the Castellana, the author, in typical *costumbrista* style, digresses from his topic into what can be seen as a tribute to his admired Galdós. The style and literary devices of Palacio's urban trajectory differ in nothing from those of the masters of *costumbrismo,* and the same is true for the sketches *La Academia de Jurisprudencia, La Biblioteca Nacional,* and *La Abeja (periódico científico y literario).*

La Academia de Jurisprudencia is one of several articles that deal with political or scientific debates and that are meant to condemn the elections and the tricks that aspiring lawyers use to obtain a position as full members of the Madrid's Royal Academy of Jurisprudence. In these heated discussions, the enthusiasm for the debate is more important than the truth of the matter that is being discussed. The article brings into question the inscrutable behaviour of the legal authorities, since not even they respect the opinions and reflections that lead to the explanation of certain facts. The text resuming the debate is sufficiently eloquent: "Indescriptible confusión. Dos espectadores apostrofan duramente al orador. Algunos académicos tratan de imponerles silencio. El presidente rompe la campanilla" [Indescribable confusion. Two spectators shout down the speaker. Some academicians try to silence them. The president vigorously rings the bell] (*Aguas fuertes* 78). In this scathing sketch, Palacio Valdés highlights the ambition of those who desire at all costs to occupy privileged positions in the Academy by revealing the poverty and misery that surround the academic life of its representatives:

> ¡Qué de intrigas espantables y tenebrosas! ¡Qué de crueles asechanzas! ¡Cuántas palabras pérfidas! ¡Cuántas sonrisas traidoras! El espíritu se estremece y los cabellos se erizan al acercase a este hervidero de las pasiones humanas. Ni tampoco faltan los arranques brutales de la fuerza, o sea las coacciones escandalosas, como se dice en términos técnicos. (*Aguas fuertes* 81)
>
> [What frightening and sinister intrigues! What cruel snares! So many perfidious words! So many traitorous smiles! One's spirit shudders and hair stands on end upon approaching this boiling pot of human passions. Neither are there lacking brutal outbursts of force, that is to say, scandalous coercions, as they say in technical terms.][8]

The sketch is aggressive, and similar to those of Larra. The teasing, humorous tone, in the vein of Mesonero Romanos, disappears, revealing a caustic Palacio Valdés who is upset and disappointed with those who should, in fact, model exemplary behaviour.

Similar to this article is another titled *La Biblioteca Nacional* [The National Library] in which Palacio Valdés, rather than offering a detailed description of this building, as was usual in the descriptive articles of Mesonero Romanos (for instance, *El Patio de correos, La Casa de Cervantes, El Camposanto, La Filarmonía,* and *La Casa de baños*), instead sticks his nose into the lives of those who work there. He passes judgment on the management of the National Library that does nothing to prevent the employees from being rude in their dealings with the visiting readers and researchers. Indeed, Palacio Valdés spares nobody. The only ones who escape his criticism are the long-suffering and humble researchers who in their distress have no other option than to put up with a pile of obstacles to obtain the desired book that, in most cases, will fail to reach its destination because of the ineffectiveness of the librarians or the Library's absurd hours of operations. Both in *La Academia de Jurisprudencia* and in the present piece, Palacio Valdés is an eyewitness and observer of what he describes and denounces in his sketches. One can see reflections of Larra's critical perspective in the author's mind when he judges Spain's bureaucracy, the country's official institutions, in short, the state. Everything is chaos: the public servants are poorly educated, the custodians are inept, the organization of the borrowing system is chaotic, and the establishment is filthy. Instead of being a centre of research and culture, the National Library is an inhospitable place, cold and dirty, and closed with unusual frequency. To write and to do research in Spain, as *Fígaro* would say, is impossible because of the deplorable condition of the National Library, and the incompetence of its employees, from its highest official to its lowest clerk.

Given the history of nineteenth-century *costumbrismo*, the article entitled *La Abeja* [The Bee] could be considered an atypical piece. It is true that there are articles that deal with and analyse a certain periodical, but this piece is unusual. *La Abeja* is the story of a newspaper, from its conception, its first publication and journalistic history to its final issue and disappearance. At certain moments, the piece echoes the introductory phrases in Larra's *El Pobrecito Hablador – Dos palabras* (17 August 1832) – or *Ya soy redactor*, published in the *Revista Española* on 19 March 1833. Prior to this piece by Palacio Valdés, there were other articles published in the second half of the nineteenth century that analysed a media outlet – a newspaper and its editors – such as the sketches included in *Los españoles de ogaño* and written by José Garay de Sarti, *El periodista de oficio* [Journalist by Trade] (1:352–64); Florencio Moreno Rodino, *El crítico* [The Critic] (2:183–8); and Andrés Ruigómez e Ibarbia, *El periodista peatón* [The Pedestrian Journalist] (1872, 2:377–86). There were also pieces that contained references to the creation of a newspaper, the establishment of its editorial corps, and the distribution of its issues. In the collection *Madrid por dentro y por fuera*, for instance, Eduardo de Lustonó published *La redacción de un periódico demoledor* [The Incendiary Newsroom] (1:89–96), Manuel Matoses's *El periódico callejero* [The Street Newspaper] (1:447–56), and Galdós's *El artículo de fondo* [The Background Article]. It is unusual, however, to see authors limiting themselves to a specific publication, as is the case of Palacio Valdés. In *Aguas fuertes* there are constant references to the Spanish press, as the author continually mentions publications of unquestionable prestige and quality such as the *Ilustración Española y Americana, La Correspondencia de España, El Imparcial,* and *El Globo*, among others.

La Abeja. Periódico científico y literario [The Bee. A Scientific and Literary Journal] is a document that contains newsworthy material of indisputable value for those who want to learn about this newspaper, which aimed to become the official publication of Madrid's Ateneo, along the same lines as other journals that included cultural activities and historical and literary publications. The sketch is a faithful representation of the author's years as a student at the Universidad de Madrid. At twenty-one he had finished his university career and a year earlier he had become a member of Madrid's Ateneo. According to Ángel Cruz Rueda, during the first months of his stay in Madrid, Clarín, Tuero, and Palacio Valdés himself

> publicaron unos cuantos números de la revista hebdomadaria *Rabagás*, el título del drama de Victoriano Sardou, entonces tan en boga, y en el que unos vieron personificados Ollivier o Gambetta ... El dinero preciso lo facilitó un tío de don Armando; y el cuadro de *La Abeja (periódico científico y literario)* está inspirado, con delicado humorismo, en los comienzos y epílogo de aquella publicación juvenil. (Cruz Rueda 77–8)

> [published several editions of the weekly paper *Rabagás*, the title of Victoriano Sardou's drama, then much in fashion, and in which some saw Ollivier or Gambetta personified ... The necessary funds were provided by an uncle of Don Armando; and the framework of *The Bee (A Scientific and Literary Journal)* is inspired, with delicate humour, by the beginnings and epilogue of that youthful publication.]

In the history of Spanish journalism, the title *La Abeja* has always referred to a literary publication, even if the journal did not usually belong to cultural communities related to Liceos or Ateneos. The word *abeja* denoted not only a literary but also a satirical bend. This is the case with *La Abeja Española* (1812) and *La Abeja Madrileña* (1814), whose editor-in-chief was Bartolomé José Gallardo; *La Abeja* (1834–6), led by Joaquín Francisco Pacheco, *La Abeja Literaria* (1845–6), *La Abeja Literaria, Científica e Industrial* (1864–5), and *La Abeja* (1864–5), among other publications of the same name that had similar intentions to the one mentioned in Palacio Valdés's article. These journals had two things in common: first was their lack of financial resources, a circumstance that prevented them from surviving for very long, and second was the fact that the editors were usually a group of friends united by their love of literature. Accordingly, Palacio Valdés's documentation of *La Abeja* is a detailed account of the creation and disappearance of a newspaper.

The collection *Aguas fuertes* also contains a series of *cuadros de costumbres* that mainly focus on the death penalty, the description of a public execution and its circumstances. From different perspectives, Palacio Valdés provides a detailed description of a public execution, a spectacle that Madrid's population witnessed with particular enthusiasm. In *El hombre de los patíbulos* [The Man of the Gallows], a diverse crowd gathers at dawn in the centre of Madrid. At seven in the morning a stream of people fill the Puerta del Sol and the Calle de la Montera. Above the noisy multitude we hear the shouts of the *criers* as they announce the *Salve Regina* that the prisoners will sing in the chapel for those who will be put to death. Palacio Valdés provides other details that turn this often-censored Madrid custom into a Dantesque spectacle. From the very beginning of the article, the author perfectly captures the incessant stream of people:

> Una fila de carruajes marchaba lentamente hacia la Red de San Luis. Los cocheros, arrebujados en sus capotes raídos, se balanceaban perezosamente sobre los pescantes. Otra fila de ómnibus, con las portezuelas abiertas, convidaba a los curiosos a subir. Los cocheros nos animaban con voces descompensadas. Uno de ellos gritaba al pie de su carruaje:
> -¡Eh, eh! ¡al patíbulo! ¡dos reales al patíbulo! (*Aguas fuertes* 88)

> [A line of carriages marched slowly toward the Red de San Luis. The coachmen, huddled in their threadbare cloaks, swayed lazily in their seats. Another row of coaches, with doors open, invited the curious to climb aboard. The coachmen encouraged us with unrestrained voices. One of them was shouting at the foot of his carriage: Eh, eh! To the gallows! Two *reales* to the gallows!]

Earlier works by Larra and Alarcón expressed similar feelings opposed to the death penalty.[9] Yet, unlike these great writers, Palacio Valdés enlivens his piece with the appearance and disappearance of characters, and with dialogues that give us the impression of a lively scene, with an anecdotal structure. In this way, the narrator and the new characters that appear in the sketch, such as a passionate spectator who has witnessed all the executions that have been carried out since his childhood, provide a series of considerations for the reader who peers into the action of the sketch as if he were another spectator of this macabre scene.

Palacio Valdés addresses the topic of public executions in other narratives in *Aguas fuertes* as well. In the sketch *El sueño de un reo de muerte* [The Dream of a Condemned Man], for instance, the author presents the same emotions and convictions opposed to capital punishment found in *El hombre de los patíbulos*, but the literary devices he employs are now completely different. Although his intention has not changed – to denounce the sad sight of these public executions that are made into a spectacle in which the person who is put to death is the tragedy's main character – in this latter article, the protagonist-narrator falls asleep and dreams that he has received the death sentence. All his suffering boils down to being made into the principal character of the show; far more than the garotte, he fears being observed by a crowd that is eager to see the accused in a bloody and humiliating situation. Contrary to what happens in *El hombre de los patíbulos*, in this sketch Madrid's inhabitants do not attend the execution. The streets are deserted and the prisoner will be transferred without spectators. The only witnesses of the execution are the representatives of the law and the executioner. The silent streets contrast with the brutality and contempt that the crowd shows for the condemned in the previously mentioned article. We could say that the silence that surrounds the execution is the true protagonist. This silence and the total absence of witnesses make the accused happy, since he is not afraid of the execution but of the horrible spectacle and the idea that he will be observed by a multitude of voyeurs. Just before the condemned receives punishment, he wakes up. It all has been a bad dream.[10]

The newsworthy material that Palacio Valdés offers both in *El sueño de un reo de muerte* and in *El hombre de los patíbulos* is impressive. Instead of presenting a detailed examination of what he has observed, Palacio provides his material with a little storyline so that at certain moments the sketch resembles a short story. The perspective of the *costumbrista* writer, the accumulation of all kinds of details, objects, and characters that surround the description, form one side of the coin. In *El hombre de los patíbulos*, Palacio Valdés describes the crowd gathered in the streets of Madrid, the balconies and shopping stalls, the shouts of the street vendors. The description of the prisoner's itinerary, from El Saladero (the city jail) to the Campo de Guardias where he will be executed, is lively, dynamic, and colourful. Conversely – on the other side of the coin – we have the dialogue between the narrator and a character whose past is heartbreaking because his father was put to death when he was still a child. Since that moment in his childhood, this character has never missed an execution, and he will tell his interlocutor several stories about persons who have been put to death, all equally scabrous. Palacio Valdés inserts in this tenuous frame a series of short narratives that resemble those sometimes embedded in novels. We learn about the history of a woman who is put to death or of people who more or less courageously face their upcoming execution. The life of the protagonist himself, a specialist in executions, is the kernel of a short story.

Given its title, *La confesión de un crimen* [A Criminal Confession] resembles the previously mentioned pieces. By situating the action of the piece in the Prado, Palacio Valdés uses a literary device that was typical of *costumbristas* such as Larra or Mesoneros; he listens to a series of conversations by anonymous characters who reveal their personal issues without realizing that they are being overheard. Just as Larra did in *El café* [The Café] or Mesonero Romanos in *Las sillas del Prado* [The Chairs in the Prado], Palacio Valdés uses this technique to inform his readers about a sad event: the death of the fiancé of one of the female characters. By subtly expressing the amorous feelings of a group of girls who get together in the Prado to tell each other about their respective heartbreaks, Palacio Valdés enters this adolescent world with a very precise perception of the human mind. The death of the young man will not divide but unite those who have loved him most.

Aguas fuertes offers the reader a rich variety of scenes that reveal the behaviours and what Raymond Williams would call structures of feeling of Spanish society in Palacio Valdés's time, from things utterly insignificant to the new forms of expression and social satire. The article *Lloviendo* [Raining], for instance, describes people walking through Madrid's streets on a rainy day. While the protagonist of the sketch seeks shelter in an entryway to protect himself from the rain, he describes a social mosaic whose protagonists are the passers-by. The most successful moment of the sketch is when the rain appears to have stopped. As the character prepares to move on, a mysterious hand that checks if the rain has stopped unexpectedly touches him. It is a beautiful hand that announces the presence of an equally beautiful woman, and the narrator, instead of avoiding it, kisses the hand delicately. There is a subtle, almost imperceptible eroticism in the descriptions of the women that appear before the scrutinizing gaze of Palacio Valdés.

In many pieces in *Agua fuertes* we note the presence of the masters of *costumbrismo*, and also the writers of the generation that preceded Palacio, such as Alarcón. The sketch *El profesor León* [Professor León], for instance, recalls Alarcón's *Un maestro de antaño* [A Teacher of Yesteryear]. Something similar occurs with the articles in which Palacio Valdés denounces certain behaviours and social attitudes that are deeply rooted in the literary world. In *Los mosquitos literarios* [The Literary Flies], the author dissects his material in the same vein as Larra in *Los calaveras* [The Skulls] or Alarcón in *La fea* [The Ugly One], even if the content of these articles is highly different, since what Palacio Valdés is really interested in is the dissection of the diverse world of poets that abound in the society of his time, from the *mosquitos sentimentales* [sentimental flies] or *filósofos trascendentes* [transcendent philosophers] to the *mosquitos legendarios* [legendary flies] or *mosquitos clásicos* [classic flies].

To conclude, *Aguas fuertes* is an excellent work of literature, presenting a textual social mosaic that has been inspired by a new vision, but with respect for the literary tradition of the previous *costumbrista* writers. The literary pieces in *Aguas fuertes* skilfully reveal the customs, social habits, and behaviours of a society that experienced substantial changes. Produced in the later part of the nineteenth century, these short sketches demonstrate how *costumbrismo* gradually lost its romantic fixation on the universal or essential qualities of "lo español" [Spanishness] and evolved into a series of more realist portraits of daily life. It is precisely this representational quality of *costumbrismo* that will become a useful narrative model for realist writers in their efforts to reflect the effects of modernity on Spanish society.

NOTES

1 This first edition of *Aguas fuertes* (1884) is slightly different from the second (1907).

2 See, for instance, Luis Coloma, *Lecturas recreativas* (1884–7); Ángela Grassi, *Palmas y laureles* (1884); Casta Esteban, *Mi primer ensayo* (1884); José María Matheu, *La casa y la calle* (1884); Manuel Ossorio y Bernard, *Cuentos novelescos* (1884); and Juan Tomás Salvany, *De tarde en tarde* (1891.

3 Other publications in the same vein are *Páginas en prosa* (1882) by Ángel Rodríguez Chaves; *El Salterio. Cuentos y apuntes* (1881) by José Ortega y Munilla; *La capa del estudiante. Cuentos y artículos* (1880) by Eduardo de Lustonó; *Cuadros y cuentos de aldea* (1877) by Julián Peño Carrero; *Flores*

de invierno, cuentos, leyendas y costumbres populares (1882) by Federico Castro; *Cuadros contemporáneos* (1871) by José de Castro y Serrano; *Cuadros al fresco, cuentos de todos colores* (1880) by Carlos Navarro y Rodrigo; and *El libro azul. Novelitas y bocetos de costumbres* (1879) by Eduardo Bustillo. The list is long and abundant, and with only minor variations in line with the volume by Palacio Valdés.

4 It is evident that *costumbrismo* can be analysed from a double perspective: as a reflection of social customs in literature or in its connection with the rise of the periodical press at the end of the eighteenth century and the first third of the nineteenth century. Montgomery is the first to explore the connection between journalism and *costumbrismo*, and he identifies the first *cuadros de costumbres* in *El Duende especulativo* and in newspapers such as *El Pensador, El Censor, El Diario de Madrid, El Regañon General, El Duende Satírico del Día*, and *El Correo Literario Mercantil*, as well as other periodical publications. Le Gentil has noted the literary connections between *costumbrismo* and journalism, with regard to the first articles by Estébanez Calderón and Mesonero Romanos and with certain publications that anticipate the famous magazine *Cartas Españolas*. The work of critics such as Blanco García, Cejador, Lomba, Tarr, Correa, and Montesinos has provided additional corroboration and nuance with respect to a direct relationship between romantic *costumbrismo* and the periodical press of that time.

5 The connection between *costumbrismo* and the realist novel has been analysed with special attention by critics in the second half of the twentieth century. According to José F. Montesinos, *costumbrismo* not only does not determine the advent of the Spanish realist novel but considerably delays its appearance. *Costumbrismo*, in his opinion, was lethal for the Spanish novel, imposing a dismal discrimination in the dispute of the Spanish and the non-Spanish. In recent decades, Montesinos's theory has been analysed by critics from a different perspective, as in the case, for example, of Baquero Goyanes, Herrero, Sebold, Fontanella, Rubio Cremades, Palomo, Escobar, Ayala, Alborg, Sotelo, and Penas. These studies highlight the indisputable literary quality of *costumbrismo* and its incorporation into the great Spanish novel of the second half of the nineteenth century. They provide a mosaic of opinions that also link with the reflections of writers belonging to Spanish realism-naturalism, such as Fernán Caballero, Alarcón, Pereda, Galdós, Pardo Bazán, Palacio Valdés, and Blasco Ibáñez. Thus, the great novelist Galdós, in his collection *Los apostólicos* [The Apostolics], will affirm that Mesonero Romanos was destined to resuscitate in the nineteenth century the almost forgotten portrait of Spanish social reality, beginning in 1832 with "su labor fecunda, que había de ser principio

y fundamento de una larga escuela de prosistas. Él trajo el cuadro de costumbres, la sátira amena, la rica pintura de la vida, elementos de que toma su substancia y hechura la novela" [his fruitful work, which was to be the beginning and the foundation of an extensive school of prose writers. He brought the picture of customs, the pleasant satire, and the rich painting of life, elements from which the novel takes its substance and form] (2:197). In addition, Fernán Caballero's *La Gaviota*, considered by critics to be the first sample of the realist fictional genre in Spain, would corroborate precisely the influence of *costumbrismo* in the realist novel, since its prologue indicates the influence of the *costumbrista* collection *Los españoles pintados por sí mismos* [The Spaniards painted by themselves] in its tale.

6 We quote here from the 2008 edition of *Madrid por dentro y por fuera* prepared by María de los Ángeles Ayala. See, for instance, the following text: "Lo mismo que sucede en la jaula de los monos, ocurre en la política de nuestro país. Todos corren, se arañan y se persiguen por llegar a conseguir sus deseos. Con la facilidad que uno de aquellos monos saltaba desde el suelo al trapecio y desde éste al punto más elevado posible, con la misma facilidad, digo, salta un político en España desde periodista a gobernador, y de gobernador a ministro. Lo mismo trepan esos hombres por las gradas del presupuesto que los monos por la alambrera de su jaula. El alegre *tití* que satisfecho desenvuelve el cartuchito de almendras que una mano caritativa le arroja, representa al que lanzado en el palenque político se encuentra de pronto con una credencial de cuarenta mil reales de sueldo" [The same thing that happens in the monkey cages occurs in the politics of our country. All run, scratch, and chase each other to get their way. With the same ease that one of those monkeys jumped from the ground to the trapeze and from there to the highest possible position, I would say a politician in Spain jumps from journalist to governor, and from governor to minister. These men climb up the rungs of the budget in the same way the monkeys climb the netting of their cage. The happy capuchin who, satisfied, unrolls the package of almonds that a charitable hand throws at him exemplifies him who, thrown into the political stockade, finds himself suddenly with a position bringing in forty thousand *reales* in salary] (325).

7 Vulgarity [*lo cursi*], the quality of tackiness, is closely related to a type of person who considers herself or himself fine and elegant without being so, or who, with an appearance of elegance or wealth that is ridiculous or in bad taste, is happily accepted in Spanish literature of the second half of the nineteenth century. It is a new term for the masters of the great realist-naturalist novel, and the *Dictionary of the Royal Spanish Academy* records it for the first time in its 1869 edition. The first literary examples of

a character that corresponds to this definition are in Prugent's article "La cursi," published in the *costumbrista* collection *Los Españoles de ogaño*, and in Ramón Ortega y Frías's novel, *La gente cursi: novela de costumbres ridículas* [Tacky People: A Novel of Ridiculous Habits] (both 1872).

8 In his conclusions, Palacio Valdés seems devastated by this pathetic spectacle. In the mentioned sketch, he perfectly describes human ambitions: "Las malas pasiones son un poderoso auxiliar en la carrera que la juventud de la Academia ha emprendido, o como decía cierto subsecretario amigo mío, 'en la política es necesario tener algunas onzas de mala sangre'. Los vergeles de la política española tienen un vivero en la Academia de la Jurisprudencia" [Bad passions are a great help to the careers that the youthful members of the Academy have undertaken, or as a certain undersecretary friend of mine said, "in politics it's necessary to have a few ounces of bad blood." The orchards of Spanish politics have a nursery in the Academy of Jurisprudence] (*Aguas fuertes* 85).

9 See, for instance, Larra's famous article *Un reo de muerte*, published in *El Mensajero*, 30 March 1835, as well as the *costumbrista* sketch *Lo que se ve con un anteojo* [What One Sees with a Lens] from the collection *Cosas que fueron* in which Alarcón meticulously follows the execution of a member of the military who has beaten a superior. In this piece Alarcón not only denounces the death penalty but also the military honour code.

10 At the very moment that the accused reaches his final destination, the place of execution, Palacio Valdés makes it clear that everything has been a dream, a nightmare: "Una mano ruda sujetó por un instante mi cabeza; un lienzo cubrió mis ojos; sentí mucha apretura en la garganta, y ... desperté. El cuello de la camisa me estaba apretando de un modo extraordinario. No hice más que soltar el botón y quedé otra vez profundamente dormido" [A rough hand held my head for a moment; a blindfold covered my eyes; I felt a great crush in my throat, and ... I awoke. The collar of my shirt was choking me in an extraordinary way. I did nothing but unbutton it and fell once again into a deep sleep] (*Aguas fuertes* 282).

WORKS CITED

La Abeja. Madrid: Imprenta de T. Jordán, 1834–6. Print.

La Abeja Española. Madrid: Imprenta de Quiroga, 1812. Print.

La Abeja Literaria. Revista de los folletines, novelas, cuentos, anécdotas, viajes, causas célebres, modas, poesías, etc. Madrid: Imprenta de Mellado, 1845–6. Print.

La Abeja Literaria, Científica e Industrial. Madrid: Imprenta del Colegio de Sordo-mudos y Ciegos, 1864–5. Print.

La Abeja Madrileña. Madrid: Imprenta de Villalpando y en la Viuda de Vallín, 1814. Print.

La Abeja. Revista política, literaria, de ciencias, artes, comercio, agricultura y teatros, historia crítica de las Cortes. Madrid: Imprenta de Sordo-Mudos, 1864–5. Print.

Álbum de Galicia. Tipos, costumbres y leyendas, con un prólogo de Antonio Cirvigo y Vorca. Lugo: Tipografía de El Norte de Galicia, 1916. Print.

Alas, Leopoldo. "*Aguas fuertes* por Armando Palacio Valdés." In Leopoldo Alas, *Clarín, Obras Completas*. Edición de Laureano Bonet con la colaboración de Juan Estruch y *Francisco Navarro*, vol. 4, *Crítica (Primera Parte)*. Oviedo: Ediciones Nobel, 2003. Print.

Alarcón, Pedro Antonio de. *Cosas que fueron*. Madrid: Pérez Dubrull, 1871. Print.

Alborg, Juan Luis. *Historia de la literatura española. Realismo y Naturalismo. La novela. Parte primera*. Vol. 5.1. Madrid: Gredos, 1996. Print.

Ayala, Maria de los Ángeles. *Las colecciones costumbristas (1870–1885)*. Alicante: Universidad de Alicante, 1993. Print.

– "El costumbrismo como fundamento de la escritura galdosiana: del tipo al personaje Torquemada." In *Actas del X Congreso Internacional Galdosiano (2013)*. Las Palmas: Cabildo Insular de Gran Canario, 2015. 119–27. Print.

– "El discurso costumbrista en los *Episodios nacionales* galdosianos." In *Estéticas y estilos en la literatura española del siglo XIX*, ed. Marisa Sotelo et al. Barcelona: Publicacions i Editions de la Universitat de Barcelona, 2014. 13–22. Print.

Ayala, Maria de los Ángeles, ed. *Madrid por dentro y por fuera. Guía de forasteros incautos*. Madrid: Biblioteca Nueva, 2008. Print.

Aza, Vital. *Las fieras del Retiro* (1873). *Madrid por dentro y por fuera. Guía de forasteros incautos*. Madrid: Biblioteca Nueva, 2008. 1:287–300. Print.

Baquero Goyanes, Mariano. "La novela española en la segunda mitad del siglo XIX." In *Historia General de las Literaturas Hispánicas*, vol. 5. Barcelona: Vergara, 1968. 53–143. Print.

Blanco García, Francisco. *La Literatura Española en el siglo XIX*. Madrid: Sáenz de Jubera, Hermanos, Editores, 1891. Print.

Bustillo, Eduardo. *El Libro azul. Novelitas y bocetos de costumbres*. Madrid: Ilustración Española y Americana, 1879. Print.

Castro, Federico. *Flores de invierno, cuentos, leyendas y costumbres populares*. Madrid, 1882. Print.

Castro y Serrano, José de. *Cuadros contemporáneos*. Madrid: Fortanet, 1871. Print.

Cejador y Frauca, Julio. *Historia de la lengua y la literatura*. Madrid: Revista de Archivos, 1917. Print.

Coloma, Luis. *Lecturas recreativas*. Bilbao: Corazón de Jesús, 1884–7. Print.

Correa Calderón, Evaristo. *Costumbristas españoles. Estudio preliminar y selección de textos.* Madrid: Aguilar, 1951. Print.

Cruz Rueda, Ángel. *Armando Palacio Valdés. Su vida y su obra.* Madrid: Talleres Gráficos "Montaña," 1949. Print.

Escobar, José. "Costumbrismo y novela: el costumbrismo como materia novelable en el siglo XVIII." *Ínsula* 546 (1992): 17–19. Print.

Las Españolas pintadas por los españoles. Colección de estudios acerca de los aspectos, estados, costumbres y cualidades generales de nuestras contemporáneas. Ideada y dirigida por Roberto Robert. Madrid: Imprenta a cargo de J.E. Morete, 1871–2. Print.

Españoles de ogaño, colección de tipos de costumbres dibujados a pluma por los señores... 2 vols. Madrid: Librería de Victoriano Suárez, 1872. Print.

Los Españoles pintados por sí mismos. 2 vols. Madrid: Boix, 1843–4. Print.

Esteban, Casta. *Mi primer ensayo. Colección de cuentos ... por ... viuda de Bécquer,* Madrid, 1884. Print.

Fontanella, Lee. *La imprenta y las letras en la España romántica.* Bern: Peter Lang Publishers, 1982. Print.

Grassi, Ángela. *Palmas y laureles.* Prologue by Carlos Frontaura. Barcelona, 1884. Print.

Herrero, Javier. "El Naranjo Romántico: Esencia del Costumbrismo." *Hispanic Review* 46.3 (1978): 343–54. Print. doi:10.2307/472418.

Hombres españoles, americanos y lusitanos pintados por sí mismos. Colección de tipos y cuadros de costumbres peculiares de España, Portugal y América, escritos por los más reputados literatos de estos países, bajo la dirección de Nicolás Díaz de Benjumea y don Luis Ricardo Fors, ilustrada con multitud de magníficas láminas debidas al lápiz del reputado dibujante don Eusebio Planas. Barcelona, [1882]. Print.

Iarocci, Michael. "Romantic Prose, Journalism, and Costumbrismo." In *The Cambridge History of Spanish Literature*, ed. David T. Gies. Cambridge: Cambridge UP, 2004: 381–91. Print.

Larra, Mariano José de. *Fígaro. Colección de artículos dramáticos, literarios, políticos y de costumbres publicados en los años 1832, 1833 y 1834 en el "Pobrecito Hablador," la "Revista Española" y el "Observador" por ...* Madrid: Imprenta de Repullés, 1835. Print.

Le Gentil, George. *Les revues littéraires de l'Espagne pendant la première moitié du XIX siècle.* Paris: Hachette, 1909. Print.

Lomba y Pedraja, José R. *Costumbristas españoles del siglo XIX.* Oviedo: Publicaciones Universidad de Oviedo, 1932. Print.

Lorenzo Álvarez, Elena de. "La primera narrativa corta de Palacio Valdés." In *Palacio Valdés. Un clásico olvidado (1853–2003)*, ed. Lorenzo Álvarez and

Arturo Ruiz de la Peña. Laviana: Excelentísimo Ayuntamiento de Laviana, 2005. 215–36. Print.
Lustonó, Eduardo de. *La capa del estudiante. Cuentos y artículos de costumbres.* Madrid, 1880. Print.
Madrid por dentro y por fuera. Madrid: A. de San Martín y Agustín Jubera, 1873. Print.
Matheu, José María. *La casa y la calle. Crónica contemporánea.* Madrid: Tello, 1884. Print.
Mentaberry, Adolfo. *Los jardines del Retiro* (1873). *Madrid por dentro y por fuera.* Madrid: Biblioteca Nueva, 2008. 1:225–64. Print.
Montesinos, José F. *Costumbrismo y novela. Ensayo del redescubrimiento de la realidad española.* Madrid: Castalia, 1960. Print.
Montgomery, Clifford M. *Early costumbrista writers in Spain, 1750–1830.* Philadelphia, 1931. Print.
Mujeres españolas, americanas y lusitanas pintadas por sí mismas. Barcelona, 1882. Print.
Mujeres españolas, portuguesas y americanas. 3 vols. Madrid, Havana, and Buenos Aires: Imprenta y Librería de D. Miguel Guijarro, editor. 1872, 1873, 1876. Print.
Navarro y Rodrigo, Carlos. *Cuadros al fresco, cuentos de todos los colores.* Madrid: J.A. García, 1880. Print.
Ortega y Frías, Ramón. *La gente cursi. Novela de costumbres ridículas.* Madrid: Imprenta Galería Literaria, 1872. Print.
Ortega y Munilla, José. *Pruebas de imprenta, cuentos y artículos.* Madrid: "La Guirnalda," 1883. Print.
– *El Salterio. Cuentos y apuntes.* Seville, 1881. Print.
Ossorio y Bernard, Manuel. *Cuentos novelescos.* Manila, 1884. Print.
Palacio Valdés, Armando. *Aguas fuertes.* Madrid: Ricardo Fe, 1884. Print.
– *Aguas fuertes.* 2nd ed. Madrid: Libreria general de Victoriano Suárez, 1907. Print.
– *Alone and Other Stories.* Trans. Robert M. Fedorchek. Lewisburg: Bucknell UP, 1993. Print.
– *El pájaro en la nieve.* Madrid: Imprenta Blas, 1918. Print.
– *El pájaro en la nieve.* Madrid: Imprenta de los Hijos de Santiago Rodríguez, 1925. Print.
– *Los Puritanos. Novela.* Madrid: Compañía Ibero-Americana de Publicaciones (S.A.), 1929. Print.
– *Los puritanos y otros cuentos.* Ed., intro., and explanatory notes in English by W.T. Faulkner. New York, 1904. Print.
Palomo, Pilar. "Galdós y Mesonero Romanos (una vez más: costumbrismo y novela)." In *Galdós. Centenario de "Fortunata y Jacinta" (1887–1987).* Madrid: Universidad Complutense de Madrid, 1989. 217–238. Print.

Penas, Ermitas. "Costumbrismo y novela: en torno a *Fortunata y Jacinta*." In *El costumbrismo, nuevas luces*, ed. Dolores Thion Soriano-Mollá. Pau: Presses de l'Université de Pau et des Pays de l'Adour, 2013. 411–23. Print.

Peño Carrero, Julián. *Cuadros y cuentos de aldea, originales de ...* Madrid: M.M. de los Ríos, 1877. Print.

Pereda, José María de. *Esbozos y rasguños*. Madrid: Tello, 1881. Print.

Pérez Galdós, Benito. *Los apostólicos. Obras Completas*. Madrid. Aguilar, 1970. Print.

– *Aquel (1872). Españoles de ogaño, colección de tipos de costumbres dibujados a pluma por los señores ...* 2 vols. Madrid: Librería de Victoriano Suárez, 1872. 2:266–74. Print.

Prugent, Enrique. "La cursi." In *Los españoles de ogaño. Colección de tipos dibujados a pluma por los señores ...* Vol. 1. Madrid: Librería de Victoriano Suárez, 1972. 256–8. Print.

Répide, Pedro de. *Madrid a vista de pájaro el año 1873. Curiosísima lámina que se publica con la explicación de todos los parajes y monumentos numerados en ella*. Madrid: Imprenta Latina, 1874. Print.

Rodríguez Chaves, Ángel. *Páginas en prosa*. Prologue by R. Blanco Asenjo. Madrid: Imprenta de Campuzano hermanos, 1882. Print.

Rubio Cremades, Enrique. "Costumbrismo. Definición. Cronología y su relación con la novela." *Siglo diecinueve* 1 (1995): 7–25. Print.

– "El costumbrismo como documentación novelesca en *Fortunata y Jacinta*." In *Galdós en el centenario de "Fortunata y Jacinta."* Madrid: Prensa Universitaria, 1989. 103–10. Print.

– "Costumbrismo y novela." *Anales de Literatura Española* 2 (1983): 457–72. Print. https://doi.org/10.14198/aleua.1983.2.21.

Salvany, Juan Tomás. *De tarde en tarde. Cuentos y novelas*. Madrid, 1891.

Sebold, Russell P. "Comedia clásica y novela moderna en las *Escenas Matritenses* de Mesonero Romanos." *Bulletin Hispanique* 83.3–4 (1981): 331–7. Print. https://doi.org/10.3406/hispa.1981.4448.

Sotelo Vázquez, Marisa. "El costumbrismo en *La Estafeta romántica* de Pérez Galdós." In *El costumbrismo, nuevas luces*, ed. Dolores Thion Soriano-Mollá. Pau: Presses de l'Université de Pau et des Pays de l'Adour, 2013. 391–409. Print.

Tarr. F. Courtney. *Romanticism in Spain and Spanish Romanticism: A Critical Survey*. Liverpool: Institute of Hispanic Studies, 1939. Print.

Valis, Noël. *The Culture of Cursilería: Bad Taste, Kitsch and Class in Modern Spain*. Durham, NC: Duke UP, 2002. Print.

Williams, Raymond. "Structures of Feeling." In *Marxism and Literature*. Oxford: Oxford UP, 1977. 128–35. Print.

3 Money, Capital, Monstrosity: Metaphorical Matrices of Realism in Antonio Flores's *Ayer, hoy y mañana*

REBECCA HAIDT

Pointing to the detailed descriptions of things and spaces in Wenceslao Ayguals de Izco's novel *María, la hija de un jornalero* [Maria, a Labourer's Daughter], Russell Sebold once asked rhetorically, "¡Santo Dios! Si esto no es realismo en 1845, ¿en qué misterioso y filosófico *quid* consistirá tan cacareado concepto literario?" [Dear God! If this is not realism in 1845, then in what mysterious and philosophical *quid* might such a vaunted literary concept consist?] (52). Yet realism's mimetic *quid* at mid-century was never just description. As Benito Pérez Galdós put it, "la novela moderna de costumbres ha de ser la expresión de cuanto bueno y malo existe en el fondo" [the modern novel of manners must be the expression of all that is fundamentally good and bad deep beneath the surface] ("Observaciones"). The nineteenth-century representation of *fondo* or *milieu*, "a moral and physical atmosphere which impregnates the landscape, the dwelling, furniture, implements, clothing ... and fates of men" (Auerbach, *Mimesis* 473), included tensions "between what is and what seems to be, between sincerity and hypocrisy, between social conventions and hidden mores" (Frey 180–1) – or what Galdós had termed the "good and bad." Decades before Galdós's observation, Mariano José de Larra had something similar in mind when he argued that *costumbrismo* requires "animación" [animation] or tensions between the depiction of (observable) reality, and allusion to what shapes reality below the surface: "el escritor de costumbres necesita ... formarse una censura suya y secreta que dé claro y obscuro a sus obras" [the *costumbrista* writer must ... develop a unique, hidden code of censure that lends chiaroscuro to his works] (4).[1] Both before and after 1845, *bueno y malo, claro y obscuro* proved to be essential concepts for the literary treatment of contemporary anxieties around rapid change and social inequities, and they became crucial to the development of *fondo* in realist poetics and techniques (Oleza 3).[2] The synergism of mass print and social critique would prove instrumental for Spanish development of a verbal registration of *milieu*.[3] Indeed, dozens of Spanish translations of Eugène Sue's works in the 1840s revealed a wide marketplace for literature (e.g., *folletín, cuadros de costumbres*) that might satisfy Spanish readers' interest in texts registering the reality of contemporary social problems (Martí-López 64–9).[4] Galdós himself published *costumbrista* articles in the 1860s, translated Dickens's *Pickwick Papers* in 1868, and admired Larra's mastery of irony (Turner, *Fortunata* 3–4), all of which point to the connectedness of his virtuosic realism with *costumbrismo* along a literary spectrum of social critique, and within a transgeneric, cross-decades market for stories about the forces shaping reality at its *fondo* (Sebold 26–7).[5]

Realism developed across decades of literary practice through interplay among metaphors, allusions, and critique, all creating a depth of meaning beyond that generated through enriched description alone. This complex use of language to create *fondo* is particularly evident in the work of Antonio Flores (1818–1865), a journalist and print entrepreneur known more as a *costumbrista*. In fact, critics may not have been sufficiently attentive to the way in which *costumbrista* discourse fits into the spectrum of realism. Having translated Sue's *Mystères de Paris* [Mysteries of Paris] in 1844, Flores admittedly positioned himself as a realist who – like others during the period – sought profitable print ventures that might also diffuse a socialist strain of commentary on contemporary problems – particularly the problems created by the rise of financial speculation and the spread of steam-powered industrialization.[6] Disenchanted with the immoralities of liberal modernity and critical of the globalized "enfermedad social" [social malady] brought by "civilización" [civilization] (for example, the critique of "progress" in his 1850 novel *Fe, Esperanza y Caridad* [Faith, Hope, and Charity], prologue, 1:xii–xiii), Flores wrote a large number of *cuadros* (scenes) focusing on money and technology in the age of steam, explicitly featuring tensions between *claro y obscuro, bueno y malo*; these later would be collected in 1863–4 into a seven-volume work entitled *Ayer, hoy y mañana o la Fé, el Vapor y la Electricidad. Cuadros sociales de 1800, 1850 y 1899* [Yesterday, Today, and Tomorrow, or Faith, Steam, and Electricity. Social Scenes of 1800, 1850, and 1899].[7] *Ayer, hoy* has been characterized as a *costumbrista* collection; but in the pages that follow, I will contend that in fact, it strongly evidences elements of realist discourse. Though his narrative techniques do not approach Galdós's magisterial "surrounding" of objects (Turner, *Fortunata* 93), in *Ayer, hoy* Flores certainly sought literary means of registering what Galdós decades later would term the "mil artificios" [thousand tricks], whether financial, political, or machine-driven, by means of which a money-obsessed society "[se] oculta su propia tristeza" [hides from its own unhappiness] (Galdós, *La sociedad* 27). I will argue here that in the central "Hoy" volumes of *Ayer, hoy*, Flores used techniques of literary realism, such as irony and metaphorical matrices, to depict in particular the *tristeza* [sadness] pervading a society transformed by money in the "siglo de vapor," or steam-driven century.[8]

Ayer, hoy is conceived as a three-part exhibition of social scenes from "Ayer" ("1800"; volumes 1–2), "Hoy" ("1850"; volumes 3–5), and "Mañana" ("1900"; volumes 6–7). Though the whole collection is plotted across the nineteenth century, the "Hoy" section in particular offers a coherent, "highly ironic and critical investigation of the liberal concept of modernity" (Ginger 210–11) and of money's negative impact on modern society at mid-century. The adjective "sociales" [social] in the collection's title (*Ayer, hoy y mañana ... cuadros sociales ...*) connotes several ideas developed with acuteness in the volumes of "Hoy": contemporary *society* as an embodiment of economic, political, and cultural changes on a national scale; the *cuestión social* [social question], which from the 1840s onward generated intersecting literatures (from novels to hygienicist and economic treatises) addressing the social and economic instabilities exacerbated by modern capitalism; and *social reality*, in the *fondo* of which Flores emphatically includes the chiaroscuro, the good and the bad, of the contemporary pursuit of money.

Little attention has been paid to Flores's emphasis on money as a figure and/or tropal nexus in the three volumes of "Hoy." But what makes *Ayer, hoy* "one of the most significant works of literature, and indeed of thought, in nineteenth-century Spain" (Ginger 220) is Flores's building of money-related *tristeza* into the *fondo* of the contemporary reality he depicts. In fact, an argument about the negative role played by money within liberal modernity is integral to the coherence of Flores's mimesis. The nineteenth-century "simulacrum of liberal modernity" (Ginger 214) arises from money's conceptualization as "a fair and precise medium of exchange between legal equals" whose motivations were "measurable and universal" (Valenze 16). The "liberal illusion" conceived money's place in the emerging capitalist economy as one "ensuring ... justice and opportunity" as the outcome of exchanges among human actors (16), a figurative playing field whose idealized "opportunities" bore little connection to the material realities of the liberal illusion: legal fictions converting individuals into societies, government programs supposedly serving the interests of all yet ultimately co-opted by local and individual greed, etc. In the *cuadro* "Placeres de sobremesa" [After-Dinner Pleasures], for example, Flores illustrates this last facet of the liberal illusion through a corrupt character's founding of a bank named "El multiplicador de las fortunas" [The multiplier of fortunes], which touts itself as an "enemigo de los despilfarros, creado en beneficio de las clases pobres" [enemy of squanders, created to benefit the impoverished classes] (292). Because their figural and tropal planes of operation mimic the abstractive qualities of money and the networked nature of capital, some of the linguistic features of realism, such as metaphor as an "agent of interrelatedness" (Turner, *Fortunata* 112), are instrumental in Flores's argument about the deformation of people and things within the illusory logic of money and free market exchange. Flores's analogical matrix is deployed across *cuadros* in an argument that spans the "Hoy" section, in which money/gold takes on the qualities of personhood and animates social relations in monstrous fashion.[9]

In the pages that follow, I will draw on some of the many *cuadros* from "Hoy" in which Flores depicts people and things (a conversation, a former monastery) within a metaphorical/analogical matrix of allusion in order to comment on the larger, hidden transformations brought by the pursuit of money and the liberal illusion. Flores uses in particular figures such as analogy, simile, hyperbole, and personification, and tropes such as metaphor and synecdoche, reinforced by a pervasive narrative irony that, as Lilian Furst put it, "point[s] to a hidden presence" (58) and "suggest[s] the potential for an alternative reading" (59) that is both inside and outside the text. Evidencing a "dimension of spatiality" built from the confrontation and interrelatedness of perceptions and presences (Turner, "Metaphors" 43) – a spatiality cultivated at the highest levels of verbal artistry in Galdós's realism – Flores's "Hoy" relates settings, characters, and conversations ironically across *cuadros* with an underlying sense of sadness in the face of money's power to deform and dehumanize.

Irony, *Figura*, and the Analogical Matrix: Capturing the *Fondo* of Money and Capital

Flores, like Larra, Balzac, and Galdós, shared in a nineteenth-century search for a narratorial "punto de vista revelador" [revealing point of view] that might give readers access to "la realidad ... desapercibida" [unperceived ... reality] (Escobar "Costumbres" 38). Yet the literary registry of the "unperceived" is reliant on multiple features of fiction's rhetoricity – beginning with "the fiction of identity" that is "fundamental of language" (Miller 40). For example, irony permits narrator and audience to realize what lies underneath or behind the reality supposedly revealed through a faithful verbal mimesis. From Quintilian onward, cultivated discourse accorded highest value to *figura* [figure], that is, "hidden allusion in its diverse forms" (Auerbach, "Figura" 26–7), achieved through techniques of semantic relatedness such as tropes. Metaphor (for example) is a figural technique that clusters "projective" relations that may overlap and link as "matrices" within different fields (e.g., mathematics, poetry) (Buchanan 83–5, 98–9). In fact, the "underlying condition" of fiction is an "imputation of reality" to the conceptual relationality made possible by figure, particularly within matrices relating analogical and metaphorical content (83–4). Writers such as Galdós excelled at fictional artistry utilizing figure; but the fact is that nineteenth-century authors from *costumbrismo* onward experimented with *figura* in registering the changing cognitive paradigm for reality (Peñas Ruiz 438).

Irony is a verbal technique suited particularly for allusion to the social disconnectedness created by the "sublimated reality" (Marx, *Capital* 1:22) of exchange relations. The device of the narrator-observer implies the possibility that the reader may not have perfect access to "reality"; thus (for example) Ramón Mesonero Romanos's *costumbrista* narratorial boast that [I] "no cuento sino lo que veo, y esto sin tropos ni figuras" [I only relate what I see, without either tropes or figures] ("La Romería" 62); or Flores's sarcastic narratorial cautioning to the reader that "nosotros no quitamos, ni ponemos, ni decimos nada" [we neither remove, nor insert, nor comment on anything] ("Placeres" 287). Indeed, narratorial irony permits the narrator to hide (from certain characters) and reveal (to the reader) "knowledge of the ongoing historical changes that are molding an entire era, and of the 'moteur social' that is producing ... changes" (Reid 19–20), such as deformed relations among persons and things. Through irony, a narrator aims to establish some distance from the hidden "social motor" deforming or undermining an illusory reality in which the other characters in the story are trapped (Miller 20). In fact, the metaphorization of *costumbrista* narrative as "sketches" or *cuadros* and *escenas* (e.g., Dickens's *Sketches by Boz*) brought into play a semantics around the narrator-observer's detachment from illusion, enhanced by verbal irony's enactment of distance as truth telling. From the 1830s onward, an essential component of the *fondo* developed by nineteenth-century writers who sought to register cultural anxieties around the "fictitious symbol" that was money (Labanyi 390) was ironic revelation (to the reader) of the illusion of love or connectedness under which characters suffer in a "modern society [that] acclaims Gold, its Holy Grail, as the glittering incarnation of its inmost vital principle" (Marx, *Capital* 1:113).

Among the most potent of conceptual relations around money-as-a-fiction are figures and tropes of the tensions between animate and inanimate, and the danger of something inanimate – money – supplanting properties of life or soul. From Aristotle's notion of usury as unnatural generation ("money being born from money") in the *Politics*, through Scholastic condemnation of speculation as an unnatural "kind of birth" (Valenze 54–5), to eighteenth- and nineteenth-century economic metaphors (such as motion and circulation) drawing on concepts in physiology to describe the workings of artificial systems, money has been conceptualized through a personification that captures tensions between normal and abnormal, animate and inanimate (Valenze 62). During the turbulent nineteenth century, literary mimesis had to address the fact that capitalism had a seemingly endless capacity to generate metamorphoses, multiplying both "forms of exchange and powerful and essentially unstable forms of representation" (Richards 69). New entities dealing in speculation and credit, the operations of new structures such as railroads and stock markets – all seemed to gain social and economic life by means of invisible flows of information and hidden networks of contacts and entities (Harrington 1) whose mystifications created unsettledness and anxiety as "the distinction between the fraudulent and the legitimate becomes problematic" (Labanyi 167).

A major contributor to nineteenth-century unsettledness around money and things was commodification, which mystified the connections between exchange relations and their social embodiment (Valenze 16). Marx used figurative language in *Capital* to convey the hidden deformative powers of money under capitalist modernity. Figures such as personification permitted Marx to impress on readers the *tristeza* inherent in relations conditioned by money's deceptive duality as both embodied (in new entities, commodities) and abstract (in value). For example, to make a point about commodification's unsettling contradictions, Marx personified linen: a length of linen "looks within" the coat that it has become and recognizes "the beautiful soul of value akin to the linen's own"; but the coat, transformed into a commodity, has lost its ability to respond or relate (that is, to "express value in relation to the linen"), as both its "beautiful soul" (the linen) and its production value (the tailoring labour that shaped it) have been abstracted (Marx, *Capital* 1:22). Marx animates, or lends a persona to, the length of linen, so as better to drive home his point about commodification's depersonalization, its transformation of soul or memory into abstractions such as "value," within relations of exchange.

Commodification, in fact, empties things of "thingliness" (Stallybrass 183), provoking a long-standing cultural unsettlement around the tensions between animate and inanimate, natural and unnatural.[10] In his example of linen and coat, Marx employs the rhetorical strategy of literary realists by taking advantage of *figura* to manipulate a "contrapuntal function of metaphor in structure," whereby an argument (that is, Marx's argument about commodification) gains force from the building-in of "overthought and underthought," or relations within a matrix, such as contrasts between human and non-human, visible and invisible, material and moral, etc. (Schorer 559–60) – or, as in Marx's example, contrasts such as the (personified) humanity of linen (overthought) contrasted with the inhumanity of a coat embodying only market value (underthought).[11]

In considering the inclusion of "overthought and underthought," it is worth recalling here Galdós's insistence that contemporary novelistic art must depict not just *costumbres*, but that which lies beneath, the *fondo*. The art of literary realism relied on the "telescopic character in words," such that a single word may stand in for and at the same time obscure the "network of relations" within semantic matrices (Buchanan 23). *Figura*, metaphor, and the logic of relation permitted realists and *costumbristas* not just to depict social and political confusions but to allude to the hidden forces motivating them (industrialization, speculation, commodification, monetization) through verbal "telescoping." One of the most effective of telescopic tropes for the monstrosity engendered under capitalism was that of the personification of money's influence and power, and the attendant dehumanization of social life. In "Hoy," Flores employs money-based metaphors of transformation, conversion, and dehumanization to telescope what Wolff calls "the inversions and fetishism of capitalist market relations" (81). The "shared metaphorical entailments" (Lakoff and Johnson 97) in Flores's "Hoy" are rooted in the conversion and transformation pervading all things in the steam-driven century: that is to say, steam comes from a conversion or transformation of water and energy into something else, and opens potentially limitless motor power, continuous output and generation. What is set in motion in an era dependent on steam's transubstantiation is a series of related or supporting conversions, displacements, substitutions, bringing into being "a social universe of alienation and exploitation" (McNally 120). Gold is converted to paper currency and credit; money is animated and acquires powers surpassing those of humans, while people have value only as potential profit centres; monasteries become factories; what seems solid is fragile ("melts into air") and on the verge of crashing. According to the "hidden logic of associative thinking" (Turner, *Fortunata* 109), these relations of conversion and transformation permit the reader to "see the unseen," and thereby to grasp the association between the abstractions of value inherent in exchange relations and the dehumanization of social values in a modernity whose freedoms are determined by market conditions.

"Fuentes de la riqueza pública" and "Humo animal": Monstrous Transformations of Credit and Capital

In "Humo animal ..." [Animal Smoke ...] and "Fuentes de la riqueza pública" [Sources of Public Wealth], Flores uses matrices of alchemy and transubstantiation to figure the transformations worked by the "piedra filosofal del negocio" [philosopher's stone of business] ("Humo" 132): in a century conditioned by transformation, steam ("vapor") can be converted to metal (iron, gold). Thus, somehow, "el oro nos sale al encuentro por todas partes" [we find gold all over the place] ("Fuentes" 234). Iron transforms into gold through capitalism's mystifications, its invisible sleights of hand, its monstrous capacity to build factories and fortunes upon intangible credit and insubstantial paper; and just as quickly, that gold can disappear through the very real likelihood of a stock market crash that will destroy businesses, families, and communities (243–4). The creations of the nineteenth century engender monstrosities that exceed human proportions, needs, or boundaries: centralization creates one set of problems, specialization another. A related conversion metaphor linked to steam within Flores's metaphorical matrix is that of smelting, of "hornos de fundición" [blast furnaces] belching out "el capitalista mónstruo" [the monstrous capitalist] and the deformations of civilization (222–3).

In "Fuentes de la riqueza pública," Flores critiques the proliferation of *sociedades anónimas* [stock corporations] in the wake of the *desamortizaciones* [disentailments] of the 1830s–1850s.[12] According to the narrator, the stock corporation is a frightening product of the alchemical powers of money, and itself sets off a chain of monstrous conversions. Expropriated properties transform from lands or buildings into invisible profits, intangible credit, projected earnings; and under the cover of "anonymous" projections, persons can engage in hidden manoeuvres for advantage over, or covert manipulation of, others in society. The monetization of a society typically ushers in frightening and disorienting confusions between persons and things, as money becomes animated with powers of life and death, and persons increasingly sell themselves as if they were things. Tracking the semantic and cultural disruptions attendant on the monetization of everyday life in eighteenth-century England, Finn (citing from Marcel Mauss's *The Gift*) observes "a constant slippage between the category of the person and the category of the thing; indeed, money that talked, that assumed humanlike personality, was a recurrent theme of English fiction throughout this era" (150). From the late eighteenth century onward, paper money and stock certificates were understood to be "a modern form of alchemy" in that paper wealth could be substituted for commodities and thus – not being subject to the material limits of the latter – acquire the capacity for infinite (and intangible) accumulation (Finn 154). Flores's development of this aspect of realist *fondo* is part of a larger whole, a deliberately connected analogical system designed to make a moral argument about liberal modernity: that is, metaphors, irony, and semantic play make it possible for the narrator to depict money's very real deformations of the human, the social, the moral.[13]

The irony of the title "Fuentes de la riqueza pública" becomes apparent as the narrator reveals that nothing is what it seems, neither "riqueza" (built as it is on shady credit, and productive as it is of *quiebras* [bankruptcies or financial crashes]) nor its supposedly "public" aspect (given that capital's operations depend on secrecy, and on constant transformations under cover of legal fictions). The use of ironic titles to telescope larger reversals of values is frequent in "Hoy." The basic metaphor of fountains permits the narrator to structure the *cuadro*'s extended allusion to, and irony around, the circulation and flow of currency and credit. Theories of political economy have found a way to unstop wealth saved by families and release it into "las fuentes de la riqueza pública" (236), which are used by *sociedades mercantiles* [incorporated commercial entities] and *industriales* [industrial entities] to "regar los sembrados económicos del positivismo matemático" [irrigate the economic crops of mathematical positivism] (236). What used to be bottled up or contained is now released to flow everywhere, as though plumbers had freed "millones de reales fontaneros" [millions of *reales*] theoretically of use to everyone in society (233–34). In an age of "ideas metálicas" [metallic ideas] of engines and iron, "el oro nos sale al encuentro por todas partes" [we find gold all over the place] (234), a centrepiece of the liberal illusion that money is everywhere accessible to everyone. Flores's narrator metaphorizes newspapers as "el Moisés del siglo XIX" [the Moses of the nineteenth century], as the papers' constant touting of new industrial societies and banks and their celebration of "el espíritu de asociación" [the spirit of association] have "completely redeemed us" (236). As Moses freed those in bondage (the narrator ironically analogizes), family fortunes have been freed by (newspaper-promoted) societies to dissolve into a speculation theorized for the benefit of all (235). Performing liquid miracles, the newspapers' call for "el espíritu de asociación" has sucked assets saved by individuals and families ("aguas perdidas" [water under the bridge], in the ironic terms of the metaphor) and converted them into paper money and stock certificates (235–6). But at the basis of the "grandes caudales" [vast fortunes] which "han hecho brotar las fuentes de la riqueza pública" [the sources of public wealth have caused to pour forth] is an illusion: by converting real gold (family assets) into paper fictions (instruments of credit, stock certificates, printed money) along a tropal axis of "release" and "flow," capital's potentially limitless substitutions of the insubstantial (paper) for the tangible (goods, labour) perform a dangerous alchemy that under the guise of "freeing the waters" (235) threatens to dissolve contemporary families, savings, and businesses.

Flores's narrator, for example, recounts the stories of the impact of this "freedom" on two members of society at mid-century. One is a *primista* (a speculating buyer who attempts to profit from unsecured bids and resales), who wins a disentailed property, then immediately re-auctions it in the name of someone else, with the resulting sale "una de las mejores gangas de la primera extracción" [one of the best jackpots of the first round of bidding] (237).[14] With the proceeds he then is able to bid on larger exclaustrated parcels; but instead of using the profits from the first sale, he buys the larger properties extensively on credit (237) so as to turn towards "otro manantial más productivo" [a more productive fountain of wealth], that of *contratista* [contractor] (237–8). As a *contratista*, the former *primista* profits from government contracts to provide food to soldiers, uniforms for prisoners, tobacco purveying, and so on (238). With the profits from contracting, "se hizo capitalista, y con su crédito y los capitales agenos [*sic*], fundó varias sociedades anónimas" [he became a capitalist, and with his own and others' capital, founded various stock corporations] (238). As a *capitalista*, the former *primista* generates profit with a dizzying speed made possible precisely because of capital's networked, abstracted circuits, and because of money's power to "free" profit from not just material or labour power but from identities and security. Flores recognized, as did Marx, that "in the realm of apparently free-floating paper assets, the line between truth and fiction, real capital and fictitious capital, seems to dissolve" (Finn 154).

"Fuentes de la riqueza pública" shows how the "sociedad anónima" is doubly metaphorical of dehumanization and transformation. On one level of figuration, the purpose of the corporation is to shelter, under one invented name, the real names of many actual investors, with the resulting conflation a legal fiction of namelessness (the "anonymous" aspect expressed through *sociedad anónima*). Thus (on a second level), the society's anonymity metaphorizes the transformability inherent in monetary abstraction itself, particularly that of credit. The claims of these societies – as advertised in newspapers – are baseless, not only because their society names are a cover or mask for the names of the members, but also because the funds they claim to have are insubstantial, since they rely on networks of credit and speculation, rather than real assets. Flores shows how the workings of capital are based in secrecy, noting that the creator gets the greatest profit by taking his cut and selling his shares before the operations of the society even begin ("Fuentes" 239). The stock market provides him some advantage, but not as much as he claims to his less intimate friends (240). Indeed, the *primista* makes false claims of greater value to acquaintances so as to drive up the stock price without any basis in actual value. Thus monetization – the driving up of value without any corresponding basis in real assets – extends along the metaphorical axis of "flow" to transform human relations, effecting an ironic regeneration of society (235) in which "sociedades anónimas," speculators whose purposes and connections (or lack of them) are hidden by the liberal illusion of the corporation, seek profits through a "formula" emblematic of "este siglo en que los nombres han sido suplantados por los números" [this century in which names have been supplanted by numbers] (237). Rather than actual people with some kind of real connection to others in a community, the "anonymous societies" that are capitalism's motor empty society of human value, instead fetishizing money and "freedom."

Flores contrasts the *primista* with an average investor less quick to take advantage of flow and freedom. Initially suspicious of paper money, this investor comes to believe that "el oro que nada le producía" [gold, which produces nothing for him] is insufficient in modernity, and that he must exchange his tangible assets for "un papel que le producía tanto" [a piece of paper that gains him so much] through projections such as the "acumulación de intereses y el interés compuesto y otras recetas mercantiles" [accumulated interest and compound interest and other mercantile prescriptions] (242). It takes this investor a long time to leave behind "el amor que hasta entonces había tenido a los retratos de Carlos III en oro" [the love he until now had felt for [King] Charles III's portraits in gold] and convert his coins into "las acciones de minas y en las de sociedades anónimas y en toda clase de papeles litografiados y llenos de jeroglíficos" [shares of mining ventures and stock certificates and every kind of paper lithographed in hieroglyphics] (242). Once he does, however, "le parecía imposible haber dudado que los hombres de tantas luces, que habían sabido inventar la del gas y la del fósforo, fuesen capaces de aumentar la producción del dinero" [it seemed to him impossible ever to have doubted that the highly enlightened men who had figured out how to develop lighting from gas and phosphorus would also be capable of ramping up the production of money] (242). Within the metaphorical matrix around "flow," the dangers of dissolution within torrential waters are associated with those of releasing gold into the "fuentes de la riqueza pública": if indeed the conversion of gold into paper money and savings into speculation are analogous to the invention of new "lights," they are as diaphanous and insubstantial as light; as easily dispersed and as lacking in solidity as gases. Thus the average investor, caught within the illusion of projected earnings, eagerly dissolves all his savings: "se hizo accionista de minas, de seguros y de ferro-carriles, tenedor de papel del Estado, y en suma, poseedor de toda clase de papel de Bolsa" [he became a shareholder in mines, insurance companies, and railroads; a holder of public bonds, and, in short, a hoarder of every kind of paper put out by the Stock Exchange] (242).[15] But just as the forces motivating progress and modernity are without substance (steam, magnetism, electricity, gas), so the conversion of gold coins into market fictions will yield results without substance: that is, "quiebras" [bankruptcies] and stock market crashes: "las quiebras, amigo lector, son la moneda más corriente en este siglo de las Corrientes de gas, de magnetismo y de electricidad" [bankruptcies, dear reader, are the most common currency in this century of gas, and of magnetic and electrical Currents] (243).

At the core of capital's power to melt, convert, erase (as Marx had said in the 1848 *Communist Manifesto*, "all that is solid melts into air") is risk, breakage, loss.[16] The most solid *comerciante* [businessman] can go to bed financially sound, but wake to find his wealth vanished; his house (that is, his business/*casa*) might seem more solid than the Escorial, but it suddenly crashes; the carriages in which he sent things are also broken without losing a single wheel – "en fin, todos son quebrados en esta época de la entereza y de la arrogancia" [as it turns out, everything is broken in this era of wholeness and arrogance] (244). As Flores noted in the *cuadro* "Humo animal," the steam-driven society "es el teatro de las grandes peripecias" [is the theatre of grand adventures] (134). But the real problem with *quiebras*, literally "breakages" or "[financial] crashes" (observes the narrator), is that loss obeys the logic of flow and dispersal too. The terrible irony of the "flow" of "public wealth" is that losses disperse just as easily as did (the illusory gains of) "riqueza": thus, the *comerciante*'s financial failure or *quiebra* also "hace pedazos a centenares de hombres y a millares de familias" [dashes hundreds of men and thousands of families to pieces] (244). By the end of the *cuadro*, we see that there is nothing actually flowing from the fountains of public wealth – or rather, what is flowing (away, in loss) is everyone's substance: that all is an endless flow of empty credit, and thus all a fiction: the customer owes the grocer, the grocer owes the wholesaler, the wholesaler owes the manufacturer, the manufacturer owes the bank, and the bank owes the shareholders, "que son ni más ni menos que los parroquianos del tendero de comestibles" [who are none other than the grocer's customers] (245). Most notably, as long as the customers don't realize that *they* are the shareholders in the bank – that is, as long as the folks on the bottom of the ladder who have nothing don't realize that the bank has nothing either; that it is a long chain of displacements and substitutions of nothingness –"no hay cuidado" [there's nothing to worry about] (245). When real relationships are voided by legal fictions such as *sociedades anónimas* and real savings nullified by the monstrous alchemy of monetization, everything can fall apart, "y es tal el estallido, que todo salta y todo se rompe, como cosa frágil y quebradiza" [and in the resulting crash everything jumps, everything falls apart, like something fragile and easily cracked] (244). Yet as long as nobody demands of anybody else that they be paid back, credit will permit investors to throw loud parties and dances, muffling "el crujir de la fábrica" [the structural creaking] (245) and dampening the sound of the coming financial crash.

In "Humo animal," Flores continues to weave into the metaphorical matrix of money's dehumanizing conversions the telescoping of larger transformations brought by industrialization and the co-opting of disentailed properties for profit. Flores contrasts two types of smoke ("humo") produced from a chimney in a disentailed property: when the property was in religious hands, the chimney produced smoke from kitchens that fed monks, cooked food for the poor, and sustained the sick (148) – the "animal smoke"; yet after conversion into property for commercial purposes, the chimney belches out smoke from struggling new industries (148–9) – or "mineral smoke." The narrator metaphorizes the contrast between yesterday's "grasa animal que se evaporaba anunciando un rancho" [animal grease evaporating in a plume of smoke, signalling a community kitchen] and the contemporary "manga de vapor mineral que pregona una industria" [blast of mine-fed smoke advertising an industrial site] (135) as "la aguja que nos señala el origen del oro" [the needle that points us towards the source of gold [i.e., money]] (135). Within the matrix around conversion, transformation, devaluation, dehumanization, "smoke" relates to "money/gold" through the alchemy of revolution and liberal modernity. Thus the new chimneys belching the transformed smoke of the *siglo de vapor* are "los hornos de fundición de las oficinas del Estado" [smelters of state offices] (149), the liberal state having replaced previous human communities and values through an alchemy effected by "la piedra filosofal del negocio, como la llaman los doctores del rito revolucionario" [the philosopher's stone of business, as the doctors of the revolutionary rite call it] (132). The rapid transformations of monkish refectories into credit, *sociedades anónimas*, projects, is a metempsychosis (135), a transport of the soul after death, such that the "rechoncha y sucia chimenea de cocina" [squat, dirty kitchen chimney] of "refectories monacales" [monastery dining halls] is transformed into "esa altísima y elegante columna" [that elegant and elevated column] typical of industrial smokestacks (135). The expressed intent of this *cuadro* is "copiar la transformación de los conventos de frailes, en cárceles o cuarteles, los refectorios monacales en fábricas de vapor y las chimeneas de sus hornos de bollos en chimeneas de hornos de fundición" [to depict the transformation of friaries into prisons or barracks; monkish refectories into steam-driven factories; and the fires that used to bake rolls into the flames of smelters] (146–7). Disentailments effectively have made *bienes nacionales* pass, not from dead hands (the "manos muertas" of religious property holdings) to synecdochic "live" ones (those of the investors supposedly bringing the economy to life) (147), but from one set of dead hands to another: "esto es, para pasar de la comunidad de los frailes a la comunidad de los bolsistas" [that is, pass from the community of friars [*manos muertas*] to the community of stockholders], whose hands hold certificates representing the "death" of communities, values, and a certain moral wealth, within the terms of Flores's critique (147).

The imagery of "dead hands" relates the personification of money to the voiding of values in persons, a moral deadness. The "obra más grande que ha consumado la revolución" [greatest achievement of this revolution] is that of having anthropomorphized money, granting it "derechos de ciudadanía, pergaminos nobiliarios, y carta blanca en suma" [rights of citizenship, patents of nobility, in short, carte blanche] (133). Indeed, money now has "carta blanca ... para que improvise nobles, y sabios, artistas y guerreros y toda clase de hombres grandes" [carte blanche ... to improvise nobles and wise men, artists and warriors, and every kind of achiever] (133).

In "Los escaparates" [The Shop Windows], Flores again personifies money: the bank note in the spectator-narrator's hand causes the objects in shop windows to jump as the money passes by; the bank note makes a "marcha triunfal" [triumphal march] past the windows as "un monarca absoluto" [an absolute monarch], "un antiguo señor de vidas y haciendas, por entre sus más fieles y más obedientes subditos" [a venerable master of lives and estates, among his most faithful and obedient subjects], or "un sultán en medio del harem de sus hermosas odaliscas" [a sultan surrounded in his harem by his beautiful odalisques] (11). But as money acquires personhood and power, the *desamortizaciones* set in motion an industrial process of demoralization, a production line for the immoral conversion and reconversion of people into whatever it is that money might make of them, whether "bolsistas" [stock investors], "banqueros" [bankers], or "capitalistas" [capitalists] ("Humo animal" 148–9). The "smoke" given off by industry in liberal modernity is that which comes from the "hornos de fundición de las oficinas del estado" [smelters of state offices] (149): the *desamortizaciones* procured deals for bankers and created manual labour for labourers to haul off the ruins of disentailed properties (148); the bankers make money off the state; and thus what used to be actual smoke from convent hearths disappears within the invisible, intangible circuits of capital and credit.

"Un convite en 1800 y otro en 1850" and "Placeres de sobremesa": Ironies of Credit and Capital

In the middle volume (volume 4) of "Hoy," Flores metaphorized contemporary periodicals as sites of production for "mentiras" [lies] within a manufacturing network made up of "los cafés, los casinos, las tertulias políticas, los círculos mercantiles, los pasillos del Congreso, la Bolsa y los periódicos" [cafés, casinos, political clubs, mercantile circles, the halls of Congress, the Stock Exchange, and newspapers] ("Fabricación" 136–7). In volume 5, however, some of the final *cuadros* of the "Hoy" portion of *Ayer, hoy* depict the networked production and dissemination of lies through banking, newspapers, and social customs such as the *sobremesa*, a practice of lingering and conversing at the table after a meal.[17] The three *cuadros* relate the narrator's story of a visit to an old family friend, Doña Eduvigis. In the three decades between 1830 and his decision, towards the end of the 1850s, to call on the now-widowed Eduvigis (a hiatus exacerbated by the political, infrastructural, and social changes that have caused so many to alter their station, appearances, and worth), the narrator discovers that Eduvigis's family and values also have changed profoundly.[18] Flores's narrator refers the reader clearly to the enormous changes wrought in the 1830s, 1840s, and 1850s by the massive transfer of property and privilege to civil (bourgeois) social spheres (e.g., the disentailments of Mendizábal and Madoz; the Ley de Inquilinato of 1842) and the reconstitution of social relations as market relations (e.g., the 1856 Company and Banking Acts, authorizing joint-stock banks to furnish funds for risky new enterprises such as railroads, while guaranteeing limited liability to shareholders whose investments might precipitate financial crisis across social sectors).[19] The 1850s in particular were marked by the injection of market mechanisms (exchange, conversion, circulation) into the civic sphere, creating a society in which things and people served the ends of commodification and capitalization (Labanyi 48). The three *cuadros* build a story about the corrupting effects of these newly expanded spheres of credit and exchange at mid-century, and their sequence structures an argument whose coherence is intensified by the spatiality and distance of irony. The first *cuadro* in the series, "Un convite en 1800 y otro en 1850" [An Invitation in 1800 and Another in 1850], establishes the spatiotemporal parameters of the story: then (1800 and 1830) and now (the 1850s); before the *desamortizaciones* and the 1856 Company and Banking Acts, and the changes following after; an age of previous innocence and one of present immorality. The second, "Una comida de etiqueta, sin etiqueta alguna" [A Formal Meal That Breaks All the Rules], lays a groundwork of irony and critique in its emphasis on a loss of moral values and social connectedness. The title of the third *cuadro* in the series, "Placeres de sobremesa" [After-Dinner Pleasures], emblematizes the reversal of semantic connotations towards which the series has been building, its narrative structured through an extended irony: the story reveals that what should have been a pleasurable *sobremesa* – an occasion for the deepening of social connectedness – is as morally and economically bankrupt as was the meal that preceded it. The *convite* and the *sobremesa* have been deformed into something dehumanized: every human transaction becomes converted into potential lines of credit.

In fact, "Placeres de sobremesa" ironizes quite specifically the social deformations attendant on the proliferation of (foreign) credit companies, the creation of new private banks, and the expanded circulation of paper money during the 1850s. The first evidence of the deformation is the *portera*'s refusal (in "Un convite") to admit the narrator on a social visit to (the now-widowed) Eduvigis, despite his clarification that he is a "visita de confianza" [family friend] ("Un convite" 261). Confused by his inability to enter as a friend, the narrator sputters "¡Supóngase Ud. que yo quiero hablar de un negocio!" [What if I were here to talk about business!] (261) – and at the mention of "business," the *portera* immediately directs him to the family's office to register with "los dependientes y el administrador y el cajero de la casa" [the employees, the administrator, and the house cashier] (262). When Eduvigis's husband was alive (the narrator recalls), the family's habits were parsimonious, private (263–7); now, their social interface is one of spending, business, and running to auctions (*subastas*) (262–3). During a conversation with Eduvigis at the *sobremesa*, the narrator learns that the family has taken advantage of disentailments, new credit mechanisms, and changes in banking regulations to gain access to a wealthy lifestyle ("Placeres" 288–91). In addition, while Eduvigis's thrifty husband took no advantage of investment possibilities opened in the 1830s and 1840s, such as purchasing disentailed religious property, becoming an administrative contractor (*contratista de suministros*) for the newly expanding government, buying papers at the Stock Exchange ("papel en la Bolsa"), or acquiring shares in mining operations (292), her lavishly spending son-in-law has now begun his own bank, "El multiplicador de las Fortunas" [The multiplier of Fortunes], which poses as an "enemigo de los despilfarros, creado en beneficio de las clases pobres, con un capital social de trescientos millones de reales" [enemy of squanders, created to benefit the impoverished classes, with a share capital of three hundred million *reales*], a fiction permitting the family to network with wider European (Italian, French) lines of credit (292–3). The son-in-law has created this bank after forming a number of industrial societies (*sociedades industriales*), whose shares were converted into shares for other societies within a constant process of circulation and transformation of values imputed to speculation on paper certificates (290). The narrator expresses to Eduvigis his incredulity at "la rapidez con que su yerno de Ud. y el señor Palestro, hacen crecer el capital, que no parece sino que trabajan sobre una pizarra con el yeso en la mano" [the rapidity with which your son-in-law and Mr Palestro grow their capital, as though they were adding on a blackboard, chalk in hand] (288). Yet the blackboard analogy relates to the narrator's later discovery that all the wealth of the bank, and indeed the family, is abstract, insubstantial: after all, reveals Eduvigis, the capital is "nominal, es decir, figurado" [nominal, that is, figurative] (289), a fiction underlying the role of the new *sociedades industriales* and private banks in transforming men with nothing into men whom others credit as wealthy. Eduvigis's son-in-law "no tenía más capital que el día y la noche" [had no capital other than daytime and night time], but through the manipulation of speculation on paper-backed *sociedades* and a credit-based bank, he now lives in luxury (292).

In Eduvigis's home, what before 1830 had been a rigorous frugality has now been replaced by expense and abundance – luxurious food, freely poured wines, ample lighting, elegant furnishings, liveried servants, and (a detail particularly capturing Eduvigis's new willingness to spend) a costly mountain of coal in the chimney: "ardía más de un quintal de carbón de piedra" [more than a hundredweight of coal was burning] ("Una comida de etiqueta" 271). The invitees to dinner reflect the importance of foreign (French) capital to the new proliferation of banks, credit, and speculation: along with Spanish names such as "the Duke of Milagro" and "the Master of Campofresco" ("el señor de Campofresco"), the guests include Baron Villiers-Ashton (British), Monsieur Saint-Philemon (French), and Señor Palestro (Italian) (273). However, the hosts' and guests' pretences to wealthy sophistication are belied by their lack of human connectedness. During the *sobremesa*, the sharp-tongued duke complains to Eduvigis's daughter Ruperta about the narrator's having attempted to be pleasant and helpful at dinner; Ruperta counters that her mother has declared the narrator to be "persona de buena clase y de mucho talento" [a person of good class with much talent] ("Placeres" 283) and hypocritically defends old-fashioned gallantry (284). But the pursuit of money has rendered the duke and Ruperta incapable of according value to a man's good character and talent. Instead, everyone who dines with Eduvigis now is valuable as a potential creditor or investor. When the duke states that he and the baron had restrained themselves from laughing at the narrator, Ruperta chides that such rudeness might have left a negative impression on "M. Saint-Philemon, que come hoy por primera vez aquí, ¿qué habría dicho?" [Mr Saint-Philemon, who is dining here today for the first time – what would he have said about that?] (283). Ruperta thus implies that she does not wish to jeopardize Saint-Philemon's potential willingness to fund the family's private banking venture. The duke reminds Ruperta that Saint-Philemon is dispensable: "por allá hay gente bourgeois de sobra" [there are bourgeois to spare everywhere] (283). For the duke's purposes within a society of exchange relations, any bourgeois is exchangeable for another, as all citizens have been converted from human beings into synecdoches of the property and finances theoretically at their disposal on the free market. Accordingly, as a person's worth resides not in her humanity but in her bank account, the duke pronounces the narrator – who has good breeding and morals, but no wealth – a barbarian ("bárbaro") (283).

During his conversation with Doña Eduvigis, the narrator of "Placeres" also overhears her son-in-law's nearby conversation with señor Palestro, an Italian engineer whose fortune the family is attempting to attract to their bank. The narrator is amazed by the two men's ease while discussing money: "tan fácil era para ellos hacer millones, con la imposición del capital, y los intereses, y la acumulación de estos y el interés compuesto, y otros cuantos trasiegos y enjuagues que hacían con el dinero" [it was so easy for them to make millions, with the initial placement of capital, and the interest, and the accumulation of interest and the compound interest, and the many other launderings and shufflings-around of the money they manipulated] (288). The outsized sums discussed and gambled in Eduvigis's home relate along figural (hyperbole, personification) and tropal (metaphors of circulation, flow, motion) axes with imagery employed in other *cuadros* (for example, in "Fuentes de la riqueza pública" and "Fabricación de rumores"). The two men are "enjuagándose la boca con centenares de millones de reales" [wetting their whistles while laundering hundreds of millions of *reales*] ("Placeres" 288). When the guests later begin gambling, the narrator sees gold "roll" or "flow" across the gaming table "como antes habían rodado los millones por los labios del amo de la casa y del señor Palestro" [just as millions had rolled from the lips of Mr Palestro and the master of the house] (296).

The distracted narrator's distancing metaphorizes the very revelation that has been building through the two previous *cuadros*: the voiding of connectedness (or, as Ginger put it, the "profoundly impersonal character") in social relations subordinated to exchange relations, expanded credit, and the circulation of paper money. As the story progresses across the three *cuadros*, the narrator realizes that hidden resources and relationships are deforming whatever it is that he seems to be observing at the *sobremesa*, a realization structured verbally through the use of hyperbole, and tropes of flow and dehumanization. The narratorial persona, himself a trope of penetrating vision, becomes someone who is both outside (observer) and inside (possessed of a demystifying awareness of what is going on below the surface), both a character at a *sobremesa* and a perceiver of the "impersonal nature" of modern social relations conditioned by exchange and profit. Flores builds into the story levels of complexity around secrets and immoral behaviour, levels which the reader is privileged to cross through analogical relatedness and ironic distancing.[20] For example, the reader is taken inside a closed meeting, privy to narratorial revelation of the motivations of those present, and offered the ironic conclusion that the *sociedades anónimas*, supposedly operating for public benefit, secretly work only for the benefit of private groups. The marked differences in Eduvigis's family across temporal distance (that is, between 1800 and 1850) resonate in the distancing effected by narratorial irony, extending the boundaries of the mimesis beyond those of description and observation. Thus, within the sarcasm of the narrator's comment that "estaba un tanto aburrido de ver tanta gente rica y no ser yo uno de ellos" [it was rather tedious to be among so many rich people and yet not be one of them] ("Placeres" 295) resonates the deeper irony exposed over the course of the *cuadro*: that the rich people in the room were rich on paper only, as such wealth is "nominal, that is, figurative" (289); that the family's private bank has no money, only the means of laying claim to instruments of credit and speculation, leading them to convert their social contacts – aristocrats, bourgeois, friends – into (dehumanized) abstractions of investment potential.

Not a man to gamble, the narrator takes his leave of the group and walks out with General Spech, who "de todos los que había allí ... me había inspirado más simpatías" [among all those present ... had struck me as the most sympathetic] (296) because of the narrator's impression that Spech shares his distaste for speculation (297). But when Spech asks "con verdadero interés" [with genuine interest] whether the narrator knows something about the house, and the narrator states simply that to all appearances they seem a very respectable family, Spech stops under a streetlight to scrutinize the narrator's face: "Yo también creo lo mismo, me dijo el general, aprovechando la luz de un farol de la calle para investigar mi semblante" [I believe that too, the general told me, taking advantage of the light of a street lamp to scrutinize my facial expression] (297–8). It is a moment in which Spech's motives for scrutiny are not clear. What is he looking for? Doubt? Spech immediately comments "no doy crédito a nada de cuanto por ahí se dice" [I don't give credit to anything said there] (298), revealing that he had been seeking, in the narrator's features, some shared complicity of doubt with regard to the family's – and the bank's – fiscal health: "habladurías, sobre si gastan demasiado en la casa, y no se sabe de dónde sale" [idle talk about whether they overspend, and nobody knows where it comes from] (298). When the narrator shrugs and says "¿De dónde ha de salir? Del Banco" [From where is it supposed to come? From the Bank], Spech becomes alarmed: "¿Ud. sabe que sale del Banco?" [Do you know that it comes from the Bank?], he asks, "algo turbado" [somewhat agitated] (298). His detectable anxiety belies his earlier claim that he neither made risky investments nor gambled, but Spech continues the prevarication: "aunque yo no tenga nada comprometido ... la curiosidad ... y en fin ... podía haber algún amigo a quien le interesara ..." [although I don't have anything committed ... just curious ... and anyway ... it could be of interest to a friend ...] (298). The narrator, sensing Spech's dishonesty, replies "secamente" [drily] that he knows nothing. The general says goodnight "con cierto aire de mal humor" [with a certain touch of bad humour], and as the narrator continues towards his own home, he cannot stop "pensando en la casa, en la mesa y sobre todo en la sobremesa" [thinking about the house, and the meal, and above all the after-dinner talk] (298).

The conversation between the narrator and Spech is a moment worthy of a realist novel. As he and Spech exchange glances under the streetlight, the narrator is no longer the observer who earlier in the *cuadro* had reminded the reader (and himself) that "we neither remove, nor insert, nor comment on anything" ("Placeres" 287): he has become a character in a *milieu*, enmeshed in the mysteries of others' motivations, aware of the hidden mechanisms by which private lives are determined by wider public life (to paraphrase George Eliot in *Felix Holt*).[21] Spech suspects, but does not know, the ironic truth: that the "house" is dependent on the Bank, an illusion of speculation and credit; that the family owns no property (292) to back their paper projections of wealth; and that if the family's lavish lifestyle is paid for by the credit lines of members (such as Spech), then the bank's solvency is a fiction. In "Un convite" the narrator had stopped himself from taking advantage of the *portera*'s loquacity to "explotar su lengua en averiguación de algunas noticias relativas a la familia" [exploit her loose tongue to confirm certain information relative to the family], ashamed of having such "ruines pensamientos" [base thoughts] (263). Perhaps the narrator did not permit himself to ask the *portera* about "certain information" because he did not want to give credence to what he ironically is forced to acknowledge as the story develops: that banks and corporations supposedly bringing free-market ("liberal") progress to the nation are secretly short-term schemes run by private speculators for their own benefit; and that what used to have value before 1830 no longer has any substance. Employing a realist strategy almost Galdosian in nature, Flores uses Spech's scrutinizing gaze, his uncertainty beneath the streetlight, as what Turner called a "metaphor of mind" (*Fortunata* 111). Within a matrix of metaphors around transformation, monstrosity, alchemy, Spech's change from open, honest man to doubting gambler embodies a fact of realist *fondo*, which is "that story-telling minds and their relations can be known, that there are down there or in there discernible truths to be 'fathomed'" (111). Much like Balzac as well, Flores utilizes irony to reveal that the impersonal character of people and things in the modern world arises from "the historically repeated lies that are producing and destroying them" (Reid 30). By the time the narrator walks pensively home in the dark at the end of "Placeres," the spatiality of the narrative has expanded towards that of the realist novel: it is, as Furst would say, a moment adumbrated by depth and meaning (42), as the "base thoughts" the narrator attempted to hide from himself are inseparable from the *tristeza* at the *fondo* of modern reality.

Conclusion

Costumbristas, just like realists, paid deep attention to what Galdós in 1865 termed "la parte musical de las cosas" [the musical aspect of things] and in 1870 would term *fondo*.[22] Tropes and figures permitted writers across the nineteenth century to make arguments by verbally telescoping the hidden workings of larger forces structuring every level of social life (that "musical aspect"); and realism particularly aimed to depict the "tristeza" from which most people tried to hide (as Galdós had observed in *La sociedad presente* 27). The complicated psyche of Spech, for example – a sympathetic prevaricator who is also gullible and motivated by vanity to pretend that he is knowledgeable – is a realist-fictional means of depicting something that throughout the "Hoy" section Flores developed metaphorically: the idea that "economic relations were constitutive of individual and collective psyches" (Gagnier 37). This is precisely what the narrator's pensive walk home following the conversation with Spech does: telescopes "a social universe of alienation" (McNally 120) into the interaction between two characters confused by the intrusion of the economic into the social, their exchange – as did much realist fiction of the second half of the century – exemplifying the social deformations brought about by the reign of money.

NOTES

1 See Haidt 17–19.

2 Galdós, *La sociedad presente*. See also Martí-López, chapter 3; and Zavala, chapter 3.

3 For more on the print and media landscapes during the period, see Andrades Ruiz; Aymes; Fontanella; and Rubio Cremades, *Costumbrismo y folletín*.

4 On socially committed/socialist/humanitarian periodical literature and its connections to realism and the realist novel, see Ferreras; Labanyi, chapter 1; Oleza; Sebold; Turner's "Introduction" in *Fortunata*; and Zavala.

5 Galdós's narrator instructs readers, "entremos de lleno en nuestro cuento" [let us enter fully into our story] ("Una industria" 62). Andrades Ruiz notes that Galdós published at least twenty-four *costumbrista* articles/*cuentos* in *La Nación* between 1865 and 1866 (5). On Galdós's admiration for, and translation of, Dickens, see Galván and Vita; Tambling; and Willem in this volume.

6 As Flores himself noted in the prologue to *Fe, Esperanza, y Caridad* (xiii). For more on Flores and Sue, see Aymes; and Benítez Claros "Antonio Flores."

7 For more on Flores and *Ayer, hoy*, see Benítez Claros, *Antonio Flores* and "Antonio Flores"; Fontanella; Ginger; Haidt; Rubio Cremades, "El costumbrismo" and *Costumbrismo*; and Zavala.

8 Discussing metaphor in *Benito Pérez Galdos: Fortunata and Jacinta*, Turner refers to the "analogical matrix" of Galdosian realism (93–4) and references Buchanan (*Symbolic Distance*) and Schorer on figural and semantic matrices. My use of "metaphorical matrices" builds on Turner's seminal insights.

9 On analogical matrices, see Buchanan, and Schorer. For Turner's magisterial analyses of metaphorical matrices in Galdós's work, see *Benito Pérez Galdós: Fortunata and Jacinta*; "La imagen metafórica"; and "Metaphors."

10 See also Wolff's analysis in *Moneybags*.

11 For more on commodification, the exchange economy, and nineteenth-century Spanish realism, see Labanyi, chapter 5.
12 For more on the disentailments or exclaustrations of this period, see Bello; Castrillejo Ibáñez; and Rueda Hernanz et al.
13 Turner observes "Galdós's use of metaphor as both an agent of moral reasoning and novelistic intention" (*Benito Pérez Galdós: Fortunata and Jacinta* 111).
14 A description of *primistas* is found in Castrillejo Ibáñez, 244–5.
15 There is a play on words around "Bolsa," which refers to both the Stock Exchange (Bolsa) and a purse or pocketbook in which to hold money (bolsa). Indeed, as a result of all his investments on paper, the average investor "no tenía un real de plata en la suya" [doesn't have a single silver coin in his purse] when the stock market crash comes (242) – with "la suya" referring back to "bolsa." My thanks to James Fernández for helping me navigate the translation of the word play here.
16 Marx, "Communist Manifesto," section 1.
17 The three *cuadros* are "Un convite en 1800 y otro en 1850," "Una comida de etiqueta, sin etiqueta alguna," and "Placeres de sobremesa."
18 The narrator specifically marvels at the changes taking place "desde el 1830" [since the year 1830] ("Un convite" 263).
19 For more on these changes, see Labanyi, chapter 1; Moro et al; and Rueda Hernanz.
20 Rubio Cremades has noted the "complejo comportamiento moral" [complex moral comportment] that Flores builds into the characters observed by his *costumbrista* narrators ("El Costumbrismo" 196).
21 "There is no private life which has not been determined by a wider public life" (Eliot, *Felix Holt* 1:70).
22 Galdós, "Una industria que vive de la muerte" [An Industry That Makes a Living from Death].

WORKS CITED

Andrades Ruiz, María Ascensión. "Los artículos costumbrista s de Benito Pérez Galdós en *La Nación* y la influencia de los mismos en sus Novelas de la Primera Época (Retrato de la sociedad madrileña del siglo XIX)." Doctoral thesis, Universidad Complutense, 2003. Print.

Auerbach, Erich. "Figura." In *Scenes from the Drama of European Literature*, trans. Ralph Manheim. Minneapolis: U of Minnesota P, 1984. 11–76. Print.

– *Mimesis: The Representation of Reality in Western Literature*. Trans. Willard R. Trask. Princeton: Princeton UP, 2013. Print.

Aymes, Jean-René. "La imagen de Eugène Sue en España (Primera mitad del siglo XIX)." In *Del Romanticismo al Realismo: Actas del I Coloquio de la sociedad de Literatura Española del Siglo XIX*, ed. Luis F. Díaz Larios and Enrique Miralles. Barcelona: U de Barcelona, 1996. Digital edition, Biblioteca Virtual Miguel de Cervantes, 2000. http://www.cervantesvirtual.com/obra/la-imagen-de-eugne-sue-en-espaa-primera-mitad-del-siglo-xix-0/.

Bello, Josefina. *Frailes, intendentes y políticos: los bienes nacionales, 1835–1850*. Madrid: Taurus, 1997. Print.

Benítez Claros, Rafael. *Antonio Flores: Una visión costumbrista del siglo XIX*. Santiago de Compostela: U de Santiago de Compostela, 1955. Print.

– "Antonio Flores y Eugenio Sue. (Notas a la novela social española)." *Revista de Literatura* 2.4 (October 1952): 265–80. Print.

Buchanan, S. *Symbolic Distance in Relation to Analogy and Fiction*. London: Kegan Paul, Trench, Trubner and Co., 1932. Print.

Castrillejo Ibáñez, Félix. "Transformaciones en los grupos sociales de compradores." *Ayer* 9 (1993): 213–51. Print.

Eliot, George. *Felix Holt, the Radical*. 2 vols. London: William Blackwood and Sons, 1866. Print.

Escobar, José. "'Costumbres de Madrid': Influencia de Mercier en un programa costumbrista de 1828." *Hispanic Review* 45 (Winter 1977): 29–42. Print. http://doi.org/10.2307/472570.

Ferreras, Juan Ignacio. *Introducción a una sociología de la novela española del siglo XIX*. Madrid: Edicusa, 1973. Print.

Finn, Margot C. *The Character of Credit: Personal Debt in English Culture, 1740–1914*. Cambridge: Cambridge UP, 2003. Print.

Flores, Antonio. *Ayer, hoy y mañana, o la Fé, el Vapor y la Electricidad. Cuadros sociales de 1800, 1850 y 1899*. 7 vols. Madrid: Mellao, 1863. Print.

– "Una comida de etiqueta, sin etiqueta alguna." In *Ayer, hoy y mañana* 5:271–84. Print.

– "Un convite en 1800 y otro en 1850." In *Ayer, hoy y mañana* 5:259–84. Print.

– "El cuarto poder del Estado." In *Ayer, hoy y mañana* 5:119–244. Print.

– "Los escaparates." In *Ayer, hoy y mañana* 5:7–21. Print.

– "Fabricación de rumores." In *Ayer, hoy y mañana* 4:135–44. Print.

– *Fé, Esperanza y Caridad*. 3 vols. Madrid: Martínez y Minuesa, 1851. Print.

– "Las fuentes de la riqueza pública." In *Ayer, hoy y mañana* 4:233–45. Print.

– "Humo animal y humo mineral o los refectorios y los talleres." In *Ayer, hoy y mañana* 3:131–50. Print.

– "Placeres de sobremesa." In *Ayer, hoy y mañana* 5:285–98. Print.

Fontanella, Lee. *La imprenta y las letras en la España romántica*. Bern: Peter Lang, 1982. Print.

Frey, John A. "Mammon's Finger in the Novels of Balzac, Zola and Gide." In *Money: Lure, Lore and Literature*, ed. John Louis DiGaetani. Westport, CT: Greenwood P, 1994. 175–83. Print.

Furst, Lilian R. *All Is True: The Claims and Strategies of Realist Fiction*. Durham and London: Duke UP, 1995. Print.

Gagnier, Regina. *The Insatiability of Human Wants: Economics and Aesthetics in Market Society*. Chicago and London: U of Chicago P, 2000. Print.

Galván, Fernando, and Paul Vita. "The Spanish Dickens: Under Cervantes's Inevitable Shadow." In *The Reception of Charles Dickens in Europe*. London: Bloomsbury, 2013. 1:169–81. Print.

Ginger, Andrew. "Modernity, Representation, and Personality in Antonio Flores's *Ayer, Hoy y Mañana* (1863–64)." *Hispanic Research Journal* 6.3 (October 2005): 209–22. http://doi.org/10.1179/146827305X58010.

Haidt, Rebecca. "Commodifying Place and Time: Photography, Memory and Media Cultures around 1850." *HIOL Debates* 3 (2011): 10–27. https://cla.stg.umn.edu/sites/cla.umn.edu/files/hiol_deb03_01_haidt_commodifying_place_and_time.pdf.

Harrington, Ralph. "Biological Metaphor and Railway Systems: Aspects of Nineteenth-Century Perceptions of the Railway." 1999. http://www.artificialhorizon.org/essays/pdf/metaphor.pdf.

Labanyi, Jo. *Gender and Modernization in the Spanish Realist Novel*. New York: Oxford UP, 2000. Print.

Lakoff, George, and Mark Johnson. *Metaphors We Live By*. Chicago and London: U of Chicago P, 2003. Print.

Larra, Mariano José de. "Panorama matritense ... Artículo segundo y último." *El Español. Diario de las Doctrinas y los Intereses Sociales* 233 (20 June 1836): 4. Print.

Martí-López, Elisa. *Borrowed Words: Translation, Imitation, and the Making of the Nineteenth-Century Novel in Spain*. Lewisburg, PA/London: Bucknell UP/Associated UP, 2002. Print.

Marx, Karl. *Capital*. Trans. Eden and Cedar Paul. I. London: J.M. Dent and Sons, 1934. 2 vols.

– "The Communist Manifesto." https://www.marxists.org/archive/marx/works/1848/communist manifesto/ch01.htm.

McNally, David. *Monsters of the Market: Zombies, Vampires and Global Capitalism*. Chicago: Haymarket Books, 2012. Print.

Mesonero Romanos, Ramón. "La romería de San Isidro." In *Obras de don Ramón Mesonero Romanos*. Biblioteca de Autores Españoles 199. Ed. Carlos Seco Serrano. Madrid: Atlas, 1967. 62–5. Print.

Miller, J. Hillis. "The Fiction of Realism: Sketches by Boz, Oliver Twist, and Cruikshank's Illustrations." In *Charles Dickens and George Cruikshank. Papers*

Read at a Clark Library Seminar, 9 May 1970. Los Angeles: Willam Andrews Clark Memorial Library, 1971. 1–69. Print.

Montesinos, José F. *Costumbrismo y novela. Ensayo sobre el redescubrimiento de la realidad española*. Madrid: Castalia, 1983. Print.

Moro, Alessio, Galo Nuño and Pedro Tedde. "A Twin Crisis with Multiple Banks of Issue: Spain in the 1860s." European Central Bank Working Paper Series 1561 (July 2013). https://www.ecb.europa.eu/pub/pdf/scpwps/ecbwp1561.pdf?968758406587846b28acdd0 39bcd1ea2.

Oleza, Juan. "La génesis del realismo y la novela de tesis." In *Historia de la literatura española. El siglo XIX*, vol. 2, ed. L. Romero Tobar. 2 vols. Madrid: Espasa-Calpe, 1998. 410–35. http://entresiglos.uv.es/wp-content/uploads/genrealism.pdf. 26 pp.

Peñas Ruiz, Ana. "Artículos de costumbres y fisiologías literarias: Espejos y espéculos de la Sociedad (1830–1850)." In *XVIII Simposio de la SELGYC (Alicante 9–11 de septiembre 2010)*, ed. Rafael Alemany Ferrer and Francisco Chico Rico. Alicante: U d'Alacant/SELGYC, 2012. 433–47. Print.

Pérez Galdós, Benito. "Una industria que vive de la muerte. Episodio musical del cólera." *La Nación*, 2 and 6 December 1865. http://www.cervantesvirtual.com/obra-visor-din/una-industria-que-vive-de-la-muerte-episodio-musical-del-colera—0/html/ffc18922-82b1-11df-acc7-002185ce6064_1.html#I_1_.

– "Observaciones sobre la novela contemporánea en España." 1870. http://www.publicacions.ub.edu/refs/indices/07749.pdf.

– *La sociedad presente como materia novelable*. 1897. Madrid: Real Academia Española, 2013. Print.

Reid, James H. *Narration and Description in the French Realist Novel: The Temporality of Lying and Forgetting*. Cambridge: Cambridge UP, 1993. Print.

Richards, Thomas. *The Commodity Culture of Victorian England: Advertising and Spectacle, 1851–1914*. Stanford: Stanford UP, 1990. Print.

Rubio Cremades, Enrique. "El costumbrismo de Antonio Flores." *Cuadernos hispanoamericanos* 355 (1980): 184–96. Print.

– *Costumbrismo y folletín: vida y obra de Antonio Flores*. 2 vols. Alicante: Instituto de Estudios Alicantinos, 1977–8. Print.

Rueda Hernanz, Germán, et al. *La desamortizción de Mendizábal y Espartero en España*. Madrid: Cátedra, 1986. Print.

Schorer, Mark. "Fiction and the 'Matrix of Analogy.'" *Kenyon Review* 11.4 (Autumn 1949): 539–60. Print.

Sebold, Russell P. *En el principio del movimiento realista: Credo y novelística de Ayguals de Izco*. Madrid: Cátedra, 2007. Print.

Stallybrass, Peter. "Marx's Coat." In *Border Fetishisms: Material Objects in Unstable Spaces*, ed. Patricia Spyer. New York and London: Routledge, 1998. 183–207. Print.

Tambling, Jeremy. "Dickens and Galdós." In *The Reception of Charles Dickens in Europe*. London: Bloomsbury, 2013. 1:191–6. Print.

Turner, Harriet. *Benito Pérez Galdós: Fortunata and Jacinta*. Cambridge: Cambridge UP, 1992. Print.

– "La imagen metafórica como vida novelable en Galdós." *Actas del X Congreso de la AIH, Barcelona 21–26 de agosto de 1989*, coord. Antonio Vilanova. Barcelona: PPU, 1992. 2:1515–24. Print.

– "Metaphors of What's Unfinished in *Miau*." *Anales galdosianos* 27–8 (1992–3): 41–50. Print.

Valenze, Deborah. *The Social Life of Money in the English Past*. New York: Oxford UP, 2006. Print.

Wolff, Robert Paul. *Moneybags Must Be So Lucky: On the Literary Structure of Capital*. Amherst: U of Massachusetts P, 1988. Print.

Zavala, Iris. *Ideología y política en la novela española del siglo XIX*. Salamanca: Anaya, 1971. Print.

PART TWO

Modernity and the Parameters of Nineteenth-Century Spanish Realism

4 The Physician in the Narratives of Galdós and Clarín

PETER A. BLY

The second half of the nineteenth century witnessed considerable advances in the natural sciences, and the impact of such changes in knowledge inevitably were reflected in the realist narratives of the times. Perhaps nowhere was this more evident than in the area of experimental medicine. By exploring the role of doctors in Galdós's 1877 novel *Gloria* and Leopoldo Alas's *La Regenta* [The Regent's Wife] (1884–5), it is possible to see that in addition to showing the growing impact of experimental medicine on society as a whole – and in particular on women – novelists such as Galdós and Clarín ultimately questioned the limits of scientific inquiry to provide effective answers to the needs of individuals.

The experimental work in physiology (by Claude Bernard in the 1850s), in bacteriology (by Louis Pasteur in 1857), and, towards the end of the century, in radioactivity (by Pierre and Marie Curie) and in psychiatry (by Sigmund Freud) contributed greatly to the improvement in people's physical and mental health. The invention of new drugs and medical equipment, such as the stethoscope by René Laënnec (in 1819) and the ophthalmoscope by Hermann von Helmholtz (in 1851), as well as the use of general anaesthesia and asepsis in surgical operations (by Joseph Lister in 1846), revolutionized the practice of medicine, no longer a largely speculative enterprise, but rather a discipline based on scientific principles. In the early part of the century, the practice had been much more primitive: after taking the patient's pulse, looking at his tongue, and listening to the case history (Collins 120; Bynum 210), the family doctor had relied largely on his experience, the so-called medical touch (Bernard 244; Hooker 58) or clinical eye (Marañón 4: 126), to make his diagnosis. This traditional approach lingered on – even despite the new advances – up to the last third of the nineteenth century, with physicians playing the roles of psychiatrist, family therapist, and drug prescriber (Rosenberg 77–8). It was considered more of an art than a science (García del Real 718), and Bernard had strongly attacked it in his seminal treatise of 1865, *Introduction à l'étude de la médecine expérimentale* (244, 356). The new type of doctor, he said, was to be an experimenter and a savant who would, through empirical experiments, discover the truth about the workings of the human body. After examination of the patient, he would move to the laboratory, which was "le vrai sanctuaire de la science médicale" [the true sanctuary of medical science] (258).[1] Indeed, the new scientific doctor was often regarded as a kind of priest, the most brilliant of whom enjoyed social and material success, becoming exemplars for others, especially those with little or no vocation (Laín Entralgo 108). The reason for this public reverence was easy to explain: with increasing success, physicians were saving more lives and alleviating people's suffering (Marañón 4:125–7; Hooker 222; Furst, "Introduction" 17). Yet for the majority of general practitioners or GPs, the profession was "far from being a money-making business" (Hooker 40), unless they had made a good marriage. Moreover, there was significant opposition from traditionalist colleagues and patients. The oversupply of newly graduated physicians, competition from charlatans, hospitals, drug pedlars, and other fraudsters, not to forget the increasing frequency of self-medication, especially by thrifty bourgeois patients who followed the advice contained in self-help books, all contributed to the precariousness of the general physician's livelihood.[2]

Spain benefited from these medical developments, albeit with some delay over which a number of commentators vented spleen from time to time (Stannard 25, 27). This was understandable, given the constant political and military upheavals the country had endured before the so-called Glorious Revolution of 1868. This event, however, did mark a real break with the past, for it opened the country to the new scientific ideas circulating abroad, with, for example, Enrique Diego-Madrazo and Alejandro San Martín introducing Lister's procedures in surgery, and the charismatic alienist, José María Esquerdo, propagating similar advanced ideas in his classes in Madrid to disciples like Tolosa Latour (García del Real 1110). Nonetheless, Esquerdo was more renowned for his brilliant rhetoric than for any original scientific discovery. Only those of the neuroscientist Santiago Ramón y Cajal, at the end of the century, were of international renown. Furthermore, if the Glorious Revolution did usher in some modernization in the teaching and accreditation of future doctors, the monitoring of standards was not commensurate, often resulting in the proliferation of false diplomas and the concomitant oversupply of physicians in the bigger cities. Positions in country towns, by comparison, especially after the amendments to the 1855 Health Law, which revoked the guarantee of contracted medical services (Zarzoso 126), were obviously less desirable, in view of the harsh physical conditions, the lower remuneration (Baroja 624), and the frequent opposition of the local political bosses and parish priests. As in other countries, personal animosities between physicians did not help the cause of scientifically based medicine (Stannard 26).

The history of nineteenth-century medicine, by its sheer importance in the lives of individuals and societies, was bound to be reflected in contemporary literature, which more or less coincided with the first big steps in the expansion of medical research, because the realists saw themselves as social scientists "engaged in a quest for truth parallel to that of their models in the sciences" of which medicine was, of course, a leading representative (Furst, *Between Doctors* 12). The realists aimed to hold up a mirror to contemporary life and capture by careful observation all its multifarious activity. Their novels had a decidedly mimetic purpose. Some of its most distinguished writers, like Gustave Flaubert and George Eliot, carried out extensive research before using medical material in their novels. For Asa Briggs, "*Middlemarch* tells us far more about the significance of medical reform than any other novel of the nineteenth century, and a great deal more than most academic monographs" (754). Realism's subsequent development into naturalism in the 1870s and 1880s through the efforts of Émile Zola solidified this trend of viewing the contemporary novel as a scientific or medical report. In fact, Zola, in his detailed commentary, "Le Roman expérimental" [The Experimental Novel] (1880), on Claude Bernard's earlier treatise, explicitly confirmed this symbiotic relationship: he enthusiastically claimed: "Le plus souvent, il me suffira de remplacer le mot 'médecin' par le mot 'romancier,' pour rendre ma pensée claire et lui apporter la rigueur d'une vérité scientifique" [More often than not, it would be enough for me to replace the word "doctor" with that of "novelist" in order to make my thoughts clear and endow them with the rigour of scientific truth] (324). The last novel of his Rougon-Macquart series, *Le Docteur Pascal*, indeed related the work of the eponymous doctor first as an old-school practising physician visiting patients in their homes and then as a researcher into his own family history in order to determine his own character as shaped by environment and heredity, the two pillars of Zola's theory of the naturalist novel. In other words, Zola the novelist-cum-physician creates in this novel a physician-cum-novelist character. Although published thirteen years after his manifesto, the action was set in the 1870s, precisely the decade covered by both *Gloria* and *La Regenta*, the two novels to be discussed in this essay.[3]

In turn, realist-naturalist novels also contributed in real life to the growth in stature of the physician, whether general practitioner or specialist surgeon, as Marañón emphatically indicates: "La literatura de la época, con Daudet, Zola, Galdós y otros muchos, contribuyó poderosamente a la magnificación del médico" [the literature of the times, with Daudet, Zola, Galdós, and many others, contributed powerfully to the extolling of the physician] (9:335). The fact was that the realist-naturalist novel, as Furst again perceptively noted, "reveals more fully than history the social realities in the dilemmas that physicians and patients alike faced in the wake of new discoveries and technologies ... [It] serves literally to flesh out medical history in crucial ways" ("Introduction" 11). One of these ways was the detailed presentation of the patient to counterbalance the prominence that the doctor enjoyed in medical histories. Of cardinal importance here was the emergence of women in the role of sick patient occupying the centre of novelistic attention and thereby giving rise to a relationship with a male doctor (Furst, "Introduction" 19). Since the medical examination generally took place within the confines of the patient's bedroom, even after hospital visits became necessary towards the end of the century, the personal and distinctive intimacies of this female space assumed importance in the realist-naturalist novels, especially with the popular deathbed scenes.[4]

However, behind that reverence shown in real life to the new male physician as the high priest of science, there also lurked an uneasy apprehension, especially prevalent in Catholic countries like Spain, that he was or could be a serious rival to the male parish priest as a repository for intimate confessions, medical or non-medical, especially from female patients (see Marañón 4:276). As Pío Baroja, like Marañón a practitioner of medicine before he became a novelist, pithily expressed at the turn of the century: "El médico ... tiene algo de cura" [There's something of the priest about the doctor] (620).[5] Both Spaniards were, in fact, foreshadowing what Michel Foucault was to explore at much greater length in the twentieth century: how the priest had ceded his previous exclusive right as the sole listener of confessions, particularly about sexual matters, to doctors and countless other professionals.[6] Yet, despite their obviously increasing competitiveness during this end-of-century period, religion and science also "reinforce each other in the struggle for control over women in bourgeois society," as Bridget Aldaraca has perceptively remarked ("The Medical Construction" 411). It is therefore not surprising that the role of the male physician as a rival confessor to the priest for women is perhaps the one that is played with greatest frequency in the realist-naturalist novel, as is the case in *Gloria* and *La Regenta*.[7] But thirty years before the latter novel, Charles Dickens, in *Little Dorrit* (1855), had suggested that in this rivalry the physician had the advantage: "Few ways of life were hidden from Physician, and he was oftener in its darkest places than even Bishop" (688). The Physician is able to penetrate beyond the surface of medical care to a deeper reality: "Many wonderful things did he see and hear, and much irreconcileable moral contradiction did he pass his life among ... where he was, something real was" (688-9). This moral vision has led Tabitha Sparks to believe that Dickens's Physician "is so close to the truth that he is outside of the story" (1–2). If so, then the final question – perhaps often unresolvable – is: can the acutely perceptive physician say or do anything to fully cure the physical and mental maladies of his female patient?

Since, as Harriet Turner succinctly indicates, Spanish realist novels (and by extension naturalist novels) share the mimetic aims of their European counterparts, it is to be expected that the figure of the physician, Zola's representative of modern research science par excellence, will appear in them with some frequency (15). This is indeed true, though not to the extent found in the English novel. Using different criteria and sampling techniques from Collins, Florencio Pérez Bautista's calculations are limited to nine realist-naturalist novelists: Galdós, Palacio Valdés, Pardo Bazán, Padre Coloma, Pereda, Clarín, Valera, Alarcón, and Fernán Caballero. Of the 140 doctors with names (there are many more unnamed), 60 are to be found in the work of Galdós, with very few to be found in that of Clarín (27). Galdós's leading position in the list of statistics reflects not only his close and lifelong friendship with many members of the medical profession (some already mentioned, such as Madrazo, San Martín, Tolosa Latour, and Marañón) but also, as Michael Stannard has recently claimed, his fascination with and knowledge of many aspects of the new scientific medicine (1).

However, Galdós's attitude towards doctors and their practice of medicine was not consistently positive. For example, in a short article, "Junio" [June], published in the same year as *Gloria*, he expresses a somewhat depressing view of the prevailing standards in medical schools despite the reforms introduced between 1868 and 1874: "Los mediquillos de veintiún años salen a tomar el pulso a la vida, con gran regocijo de la muerte" [The twenty-one-year-old new doctors come out of medical school to take life's pulse, to the great joy of Lady Death] (485). During this same period, Galdós himself was beset with chronic migraines (Bravo Villasante 16), yet he does not seem to have sought medical attention. Consequently, his presentation of the physician in *Gloria* will assume added significance. By comparison, little is known of Alas's friendships or dealings with doctors.

~

Given Galdós's pre-eminent use of medical material in his novels, it may appear at first bizarre that this study focuses on *Gloria* (1877), with a paucity of references to physicians, rather than his later masterpiece, *Fortunata y Jacinta*. Nevertheless, my selection of *Gloria* as a point of reference for *La Regenta* can be justified by a number of reasons:

1 Alas always professed a deep admiration for *Gloria* (Rubio 96).
2 The similarity in the presentation of Holy Week processions – central episodes in both novels – is not accidental (Bly 49).
3 The main story outlines are basically similar: the eponymous protagonists are young sensitive women living in provincial towns where they are strongly torn between physical attraction to men in a relationship lying outside the accepted social norms and spiritual attachment to their Catholic faith. In this sense, they are affected, in varying degrees, by the twin naturalist determinants of heredity and environment. This constant struggle produces negatives effects on their physical and mental health, which can be diagnosed as differing stages of hysteria, that mysterious illness that supposedly afflicted so many young women in the nineteenth century (Jagoe 339).[8]
4 Both novels present the different attempts of male doctors to treat this illness in female patients.
5 The two novels were published at either end, more or less, of the period 1876–85 when Zola's naturalism came to be both studied in depth and imitated, with Galdós's *La desheredada* of 1881 being regarded as the first major Spanish imitation. *Gloria* appeared one year after the first detailed reference to Zola and his work in a Spanish journal.[9]

For all of the above reasons, then, it will be my contention that *Gloria* can be viewed as a kind of precursor of *La Regenta*, with Alas clearly seeing the potential for major and extensive development of the physician's role in Galdós's novel of 1877, especially after studying publications of new discoveries in medicine and psychology in the intervening years. The doctor's first appearance in *Gloria* occurs at a very late stage in part 2. With Morton's return to Ficóbriga only exacerbating his lover's fragile recovery after childbirth, the physician is summoned to the Lantigua house on Maundy Thursday. He enters the novel all of a sudden, without any mention whatsoever of name or official position or even a physical description. He sees Gloria after lunch and orders her to take complete rest and avoid all emotional excitement (659). No details of the medical examination are given, however. Nor are we told where it took place: in her bedroom or another location. By Good Friday, as the subject of Morton's conversion to Christianity reaches a critical point, Gloria's uncle, Buenaventura, worries, though only slightly, about her health: "Pero enturbiaba ligeramente su gozo la idea de la mala salud de Gloria, que en los últimos días padecía frecuentes accesos febriles, en los cuales alternaba, con el agotamiento de las fuerzas, una actividad abrasadora y una como acumulación de vida, que a borbotones salía por los ojos, mirando, y por la boca, hablando" (671) ["Nothing disturbed his joy but the remembrance of Gloria's feeble state of health; during the last few days she had suffered from repeated feverish attacks in which extreme exhaustion alternated with fits of vehement activity and, so to speak, of pent-up vitality, which then over-flowed in her eagerly sparkling eyes and incessant stream of words" (263–4)].

On the basis of the symptoms as recounted by Buenaventura to the doctor when the two meet by chance in the street, the doctor, without any further examination of the patient in her own bedroom, ventures a prognosis, which can only be semi-medical and hypothetical: "una pintura hipotética, no muy lisonjera, del estado en que, a su parecer, debían hallarse el corazón y el cerebro de Gloria" (671) ["a hypocritical [*sic*] and by no means hopeful picture of the state in which he supposed her heart and brain to be" (264)]. The suggestion is that she is experiencing a state of acute anxiety bordering on hysteria, although the term is not used by Galdós. Certainly, mood swings were included in Charcot's precise checklist of the many and varied symptoms of hysteria (Aldaraca, "The Medical Construction" 402). The doctor – finally identified by his first name, Nicomedes – is firmly convinced that the root cause of her condition is mysticism, which, with its belief in the possibility of union with the divine nature by means of ecstatic contemplation beyond normal human understanding, falls into the realm of hypersensitivity, another of Charcot's symptoms of hysteria.[10] In fact, juxtaposing religious and medical terms, Nicomedes calls mysticism a spiritual congestion that has to be extirpated:

> Expresó, en breves palabras, su pensamiento, asegurando que la dilatación moral salvaría a la enferma, pero que la contracción la mataría. Condenó el misticismo como la más perniciosa congestión espiritual que podía sobrevenir a la enferma, y el descargo de un enorme peso del alma le pareció excelente antiflogístico. La paz, el contento y el amor humano, en su esplendente natural desarrollo, armonizado con el divino, le parecieron admirables emolientes. (671–2)

> [[And] in a few words, he stated his opinion that moral expansion and release would save the poor child, but that oppression and confinement would kill her. He denounced mysticism as the most pernicious form of spiritual congestion which could attack her, and thought the very best antiphlogistic would be the unburdening of her soul of this load; peace of mind and the full tide of human affection given a healthy and natural play, and harmonized with the divine love, were, according to him, the real balm she needed. (264)]

Nicomedes's references to house confinement (and insinuation of its remedy, withdrawal to rural seclusion or "aislamiento" for a rest, along with a good diet) and to antiphlogistic or anti-inflammatory medication recall some of the therapies for hysteria at this time (Jagoe 345; Aldaraca, "The Medical Construction" 407). They could also be construed as a rejection of the existing environment (of the Lantigua house in claustrophobic Ficóbriga), one of naturalism's determining principles.[11]

Squashed between Buenaventura's exposition of Gloria's symptoms and Nicomedes's appropriate cures is a lengthy and strange aside by the narrator describing the professional history and character of Ficóbriga's officially appointed physician. He is called an excellent and kind man. He is very wise and a veteran soldier in the battle against death, which, while a strange way to define the practice of medicine, is perhaps an apt choice at this juncture when Gloria's mental and physical health hang in the balance. To his further merit, and contrary to the contemporary professional trends, Nicomedes seems to have turned his back on medical careerism: tiring of earning good money in big cities, he has chosen to spend his last years serving in the small town of Ficóbriga.[12] In this sense, then, he appears to have been a modern research-minded doctor during his time in the big cities, but has now returned to a more traditional practice of medicine. A second reason for this retirement into obscurity is his great desire to be alone (especially in the world of nature), which he satisfies with frequent walks in the surrounding countryside, accompanied only by his beloved black dog and a blue umbrella. As a "librepensador" (671) ["Rationalist – a Materialist" (264)], Nicomedes, it could reasonably be expected, would have been committed to empirical scientific research. He is certainly something of an eccentric, an exception in this conservative Catholic village. Yet his attendance at Mass and the great affection he has for the Lantigua family, which make him an acceptable doctor to the sick Gloria, raise certain questions about his true professional and intellectual identity. To be sure, his practice of medicine in this rural environment is positively assessed by the narrator during his third and final appearance in the novel, when he is summoned to the Lantigua house on Holy Saturday. His methodology seems to accord with that of pre-1868 family doctors with their general psychosomatic approach (López Piñero et al. 262): "Era un hombre que infundía a los enfermos un espíritu de fortaleza tal, que no podía menos de influir lisonjeramente en la salud. Curaba como cualquier otro buen médico; pero sus enfermos tenían, mediante él, la fe y la devoción de curarse" (687) ["He was one of those men who can inspire their patients with such spirits and vigour as cannot fail to have a favourable effect upon their health. His practice was the same as that of any other skillful practitioner, but his patients, thanks to his personal influence, had faith and hope in his remedies" (320)].

The quotation is important for two reasons: first, it emphasizes the professional competence, albeit average, of Nicomedes. Secondly, and much more importantly, he has such a great rapport with his patients that they believe they will be cured by him. This approach, however, does not seem to have any success with Gloria, although we never see them in conversation together or during a medical examination. To the rest of her family, however, Nicomedes is able to bring some comfort with his amusing description of the young mother's symptoms:

> En sus diagnósticos empleaba las más gallardas figuras. Según él, el corazón de Gloria era un caballo desbocado; su pensamiento, un pájaro que, habiendo remontado mucho el vuelo, se había cansado y no hallaba monte en que posarse y tenía que seguir volando o dejarse caer. Sus

nervios eran una casa de fieras en la cual se hubieran abierto todas las jaulas. (687)

[He would describe the diagnosis of a case in the most whimsical figures of speech. Gloria's heart, said he, was a horse without a bridle. Her brain was a bird over-wearied by too high a flight but that could find no hill to flee to and that must continue to fly or drop; her nerves a den of ravening creatures each ready to fly out. (320)]

This verbal tour de force is duly greeted with laughter. But, as he leaves the Lantigua house, Nicomedes immediately puts aside such joking, and with the utmost seriousness confidentially informs Gloria's two uncles in layman's terms that he is alarmed by her complete breakdown: total physical and mental rest is essential if she is to survive. The only solution acceptable to Gloria would be to join Morton and her son for a life together in a rural hamlet, as Nicomedes, the loner and lover of Nature (and thereby following some of the therapies for hysteria noted earlier), would surely have prescribed, if the circumstances had not been so dire. But is his silence at this critical juncture caused by deference to the Lantiguas or by his privileged knowledge, like that of Dickens's Physician, that any escape to the countryside (however desirable in theory) would, in practice, destroy Gloria's fragile mind and body? In the end, she takes matters into her own hands: she self-diagnoses and self-medicates, as it were, by joining her baby and husband in the country, only to die in their arms. Neither the doctor of the body and mind (Nicomedes) nor those of the soul (her uncles and aunt) can cure her.

~

Like Galdós during the composition of *Gloria*, Alas suffered ill health owing to nervous disorders while he wrote *La Regenta*. "Achaques propios de la gente de pluma" [ailments proper to people of the pen] was Galdós's epistolary diagnosis of his Asturian friend (Smith and Rubio 139). But in this particular case, as Clarín was later to confess to Sánchez Calvo, his ailments drove him to write this first and great novel: "Si no tuviera estos nervios no escribiría *Regentas*" [If I did not have these nerves, I wouldn't write any *Regentas*] (Cabezas 159). Before his first novel in 1885, Alas's fiction is mostly devoid of allusions to physicians; the short story "De burguesa a burguesa" [From One Bourgeois Woman to Another] (1878) and the review of the novel *Idilio de un enfermo* [Idyll of a Sick Man] (1884) by Palacio Valdés are the exceptions.[13]

In marked contrast to *Gloria*, the figure of the practitioner of medicine appears early and often in *La Regenta* because Ana's bouts of mental and corporal illness (the result, in no small measure, as per naturalism's dogmas, of her family's medical history and own upbringing and control by others in the environment of Vetusta society) commence early in the narrative. The first appearance of doctors – unnamed and unseen residents of Vetusta – occurs in chapter 4, when the adolescent Ana is advised to take the healthy sea air at the family's cottage in the coastal town of Loreto. It is there, when her father dies before her eyes and she is experiencing her first menstrual cycle, that Ana suffers a nervous fever that proves almost fatal. Unlike Nicomedes, the unnamed doctor of Loreto explains the illness in very clear technical terms (not reproduced in the text) that lead her aunts to consider him a "mediquillo grosero" (1:280) ["that uncouth little doctor fellow" (98)]. By contrast, the language of the unnamed Vetustan doctor who treats Ana for a relapse after her eventual return from Loreto is evasive, all medical terms being eschewed. In *La Regenta* the difference in medical approaches and opinions emerges very clearly.[14]

In contrast, Don Robustiano Somoza, whose name reflects both his dress and physique, would seem to be the archetypal family doctor of pre-1868 Spain (1:512, note 3; Pérez Bautista 31). Like Nicomedes, he has excellent bedside manners, his jovial conversation playing an important part in his curing of the sick. Nicomedes is a freethinker, and Robustiano Somoza also considers himself a Voltairian, albeit an ultraconservative in politics. Unlike Galdós's doctor, however, he likes acquiring money from his practice, although he occasionally waives fees for his friends. Yet, what Alas emphasizes about him is his total intellectual emptiness: "En punto a letras, las de su ciencia inclusive, don Robustiano no podía alzar el gallo a ningún mediquillo moderno de los que se morían de hambre en Vetusta" (1:512) ["As far as his reading was concerned, including his reading in his own subject, Don Robustiano could hardly claim to be a Triton among the minnows – among the more modern Vetustan doctors, youngsters dying of hunger there" (244–5)]. If Joaquinito Orgaz could not be numbered amongst the latter, the existence of this group in Vetusta accurately reflects the contemporary oversupply of doctors.

Somoza is an intellectual fraudster, then, who, when asked for a diagnosis, utters the fashionable cliché term of the moment: "Años atrás, para él todo era flato; ahora todo era *cuestión de nervios*" (1:512) ["Years before, flatulence had been his explanation for everything, but now it was all a question of nerves" (245)]. In the Casino scene in chapter 22, Foja accuses him of quoting words and passages from a recently read medical article that he does not understand (2:300–1n9). His last line of defence is the ironic invocation of Science, as if he were its standard-bearer (Rutherford 46–7). The best example of this professional ignorance occurs when he absurdly pontificates that the imminent death of one of his patients from alcoholism should be prevented by the imbibing of more liquor!

When cliché diagnoses and banter lose their effectiveness in a complicated case, Don Robustiano generally takes his leave, delegating a subordinate to take over. His treatment of Ana follows this pattern. First, it could be suggested that, in a very real sense, Somoza sets in motion Ana's tragic marital history, since not only does he inform her aunts that their niece has been accepted back into the local nobility but he also recommends that she put on extra weight in order to become a better marriage prospect (1:287). Notwithstanding any good intentions on his part, Somoza's intervention here is naïve and short-sighted, typical of a bumbling provincial doctor. Later in the novel, his diagnosis of Ana's March attack – the medical examination is carried out in her bedroom (chapter 19) – as a typical example of *Primavera médica* (spring fever) is barely credible, given that he merely looks at her tongue and takes her pulse in time-honoured medical fashion. The high reading registered by the thermometer placed under Ana's armpit only suggests to him that Visitación's chatter is the cause of her condition, and that this high reading is not an indicator of a more serious ailment. At a loss the next morning to give Quintanar a precise identification of the illness – it could be hepatitis, gastroenteritis, nerves, or his famous *Primavera médica* – he hastily scribbles a prescription for drugs and then extricates himself wholly from the case by assigning it to his locum. His medical examinations thereafter are brief and few: he merely takes Ana's pulse after she faints at the Shrove Tuesday dinner and dance. He even refuses to answer her summons to treat her after the Good Friday procession (2:449).

Yet, for all his hilarious incompetence as a purported practitioner and mouthpiece of modern medicine, Don Robustiano is given a more serious role to play in the novel. Alas had made this very clear in his initial presentation: "Aparte la ciencia, que no era su terreno propio, don Robustiano podía apostar con cualquiera a campechano, alegre, simpático, *y hasta hombre de excelente sentido y no escasa perspicacia*" (1:512;

my emphasis) ["Leaving science aside, for science was not his forte, Don Robustiano was anyone's match at being genial, happy, amiable and, indeed, full of common sense and not at all lacking in perspicacity" (245)]. These last-named qualities are very much in evidence in his confrontation with El Magistral in the Carraspique residence in chapter 12. Rutherford shrewdly notes that this exchange is a rare example of direct speech in the novel, in which the impression given is that Don Robustiano "is speaking with unusual eloquence and verve" (64). In addition to the traditional opposition between country doctor and cleric, a personal antipathy divides the two men. Don Robustiano commits his usual verbal gaffes, to the amusement of the cleric, but his main argument that the convent of Las Salesas is not fit for human habitation puts El Magistral on the defensive, for he recognizes the truth of the accusation. Furthermore, De Pas is not sure that Robustiano is not alluding to him when he accuses a powerful cleric of forcing young girls, including the doctor's niece, Rosita Carraspique, to become novices in this convent. Family interests aside, Somoza's concern here for proper hygienic conditions in a communal institution is proper and right for a medical practitioner in the era of Pasteur, even if De Pas reckons that the convent's own doctor (unnamed) believes that there is no such problem. Carraspique's wife may think that her cousin is something of a madman, but his prescription for improving his niece's health – a stay in a village close to the sea, with good food, especially milk and meat, to eat – is the therapy that Ana had undergone after her first attack and which Nicomedes might have finally prescribed for Gloria, had he had the chance and not prevaricated. Although El Magistral and Somoza joust over the same subject in the following chapter when it is playfully raised at the Vegallanas's luncheon party, the doctor's angry outburst on leaving ("Señores, aquella niña se pudre" (1:595) ["Gentlemen, that girl is rotting away" (299)] proves prophetically true.

Somoza's locum is the model of the new scientific physician: he is young, intelligent, and eager to further his medical research even as he maintains the customary bedside manners. Taking charge of Ana's recovery in El Vivero (chapter 27) after her third and most serious hysteria attack, he is finally given a name, but only a surname (Benítez). He is a "joven de pocas palabras y muchos estudios, observador y taciturno" (2:442) ["young man of few words and much learning, observant and taciturn" (600)]. His close supervision of her recovery seems at first a resounding success. However, two important qualifications have to be made. First, the progress of the treatment is presented largely through the words of Ana herself, whether in letters to Benítez or entries in her private diary. Aldaraca believes that, in encouraging her to write, Benítez is allowing her to fashion her own inner life and forge the only real escape route from the tedium of Vetustan social life ("El caso" 57). Nevertheless, it should not be forgotten that Ana is selective both in what she writes down and then in what she reads to herself before making additions to either text. Benítez had also enjoined her to only write to him as a last resort, perhaps afraid that she would view him as a medical confessor, as she does, in whom to confide her innermost secrets. At the same time, she also writes from El Vivero to her religious confessor, De Pas. The representatives of medicine and religion are co-equal recipients of her written texts, in lieu of her oral utterances.[15]

Benítez's prescribed therapy of country living in El Vivero seems to be the appropriate naturalist alternative to organized religion, as ironically summed up in the phrase: "¡Al campo, al campo! fue el grito de salvación" (2:453) ["To the country! To the country! was the cry of salvation" (607)]. However, at the same time, does he not make a serious professional error in accepting the choice (suggested, significantly, by Álvaro) of the Vegallanas's summer retreat as La Regenta's sanatorium, especially given the somewhat licentious behaviour of previous visitors? She certainly has misgivings: "no quiso pensar en los peligros que la estancia en el Vivero podía tener" (2:455) ["she did not want to think about the possible dangers of the stay at El Vivero" (608)]. Furthermore, though his name crops up on almost every page of Ana's writings, Benítez does not seem to keep his promise of riding out from Vetusta to see and talk to her, preferring to conduct his on-going treatment from a distance.

The only visit that Benítez makes to El Vivero is of such a strange nature that it must constitute our second reservation about the initial success of his treatment of Ana. In this episode the young doctor is not given the full physical description that Somoza had received earlier. He is merely a pair of eyes and a voice in a long conversation about his patient's health, with her husband, not with her. Benítez's direct entry on stage is as abrupt and sudden as his subsequent exit. The occasion is the lunch offered on St Peter's Day by the Marqués de Vegallana, where Benítez is first encountered by the reader enjoying a postprandial cigar. This non-medical activity immediately associates him with Mesía's taste for the same habit, whose phallic connotations here are not included in Jennifer Lowe's study of the symbol.

Though his private talk on the balcony with Quintanar is a repetition of earlier confidential discussions between them about Ana's health, it becomes even more a violation of patient confidentiality when it is overheard in its entirety by El Magistral, who is pretending to read a newspaper a few feet away. This faux pas, however inadvertent, does not redound to Benítez's credit and ultimately has far graver consequences, since it determines the course of the final chapters: Fermín, now believing that his rival is with Ana on the estate grounds, sets out on a mad hunt for them in the thunderstorm that immediately bursts above the heads of the two men in conversation on the balcony. The cleric's suspicions prove false in this instance, but are realized during later wild parties at El Vivero, with Ana and Mesía finally committing adultery in the Vegallanas' town house. So, it could be argued that Benítez, through lack of expected foresight, is responsible in the long run for his female patient's final relapse, just as Somoza, his superior, had set in motion – again through a lack of common sense and foresight – the whole process of her hysterical suffering during her married life. One woman's health of mind and body is entrusted to and undermined by two licensed male physicians, just as her spiritual life is vitiated by the care of a third man, Fermín. In Alas's novel, the most sensitive of females suffers irreparably from the care of men, whatever their good intentions.

The message that Benítez wants to convey to Víctor in the balcony conversation is that Ana is not a sick person in mind, just a naturally high-spirited young woman who needs healthy physical stimulation to counteract the negative effects of too much exposure to religious observances. Benítez chooses to express the essence of his diagnosis with a Latin aphorism: "ubi irritatio ibi fluxus" (2:473) ["where there is a stimulus there is a flux" (733n10)]. Since both listeners, the intended one, Víctor, and the supposedly unsuspected one, De Pas, immediately understand its implicit sexual meaning, its use can only be construed as a stratagem – or an act of unusual maladroitness – by the doctor, to avoid stating the plainly obvious: that Ana needs a permanent sexual relationship, something of which the physician's chewing of the cigar *à la Álvaro* suggests that he knows Quintanar is not capable and others, like Mesía, are. In an even more perplexing manner, Benítez complicates this verbal reticence by looking at his wide-eyed listener "con expresión misteriosa de lástima un poco burlesca" (2:472) ["with a mysterious expression of pity mixed with mockery" (620)], a phrase of oxymoronic meaning that reflects confusingly on the young doctor's judgment.

The same strange smile and the spitting of a piece of cigar out of his mouth accompany Benítez's second and most egregious error in this conversation: he assures Víctor that Ana's new "attraction" cannot lead to anything bad for the couple, a prediction that is put immediately in doubt by the older man's exclamation of "Santa Bárbara" at the very moment the thunderstorm breaks, indicating that it is too late. Is Benítez totally oblivious of the reputation of El Vivero for erotic goings-on, as he can see with his own eyes on this occasion? Is he really unaware of Mesía's attraction to Ana? The ironic puffing on the cigar and his later fulsome praise of Ana's radiantly healthy body when she returns with her husband and Álvaro from a summer holiday (chapter 28) would suggest that he knows the truth only too well. He can see the moral background behind Ana's medical condition, and in this sense, he possesses the perspicacity of Dickens's Physician, yet he still prefers to play a dangerous game of reticence and secrecy, albeit with the good intention of saving Ana's life and, probably, her marriage. Unfortunately, this course of action stands in contrast to his otherwise admirable – in the view of Alas's narrator – application of the latest medical advances. In contrast, Robustiano, who, while generally worthy of ridicule for his medical ignorance and buffoonery, earns genuine respect for his principled stand on the matter of the sanitary conditions at his niece's convent.

The ironic consequence of the conversation in El Vivero is that Benítez has to make even greater efforts to save Ana in the aftermath of the fateful duel between Quintanar and Mesía. Confinement to her house, a course of drugs, and sessions of counselling slowly bring Ana back from the precipice of death, as she once more follows the advice of "aquel médico frío, siempre fiel, siempre atento, siempre inteligente" (2:582) ["her doctor, always cold, always faithful, always attentive, always intelligent" (704)], with his corresponding "sonrisa fría, triste" (2:589) ["cold, sad smile" (709)], which is somewhat different from the facial gestures he had made to her husband in El Vivero on St Peter's Day. His visits to her house become less frequent as Ana eventually recovers most of her strength in the warm spring weather. Presumably, he will be summoned yet again to minister to her mental and bodily needs after her collapse outside Fermin's confessional at the end of the novel.

At various times during her periods of illness at home, Ana receives medical attention or advice from both men and women in her social circle. Surprisingly, that offered by the latter seems trivial or of little merit: Visitación, for example, one summer day takes Ana's pulse only to gauge her reaction to the news of Álvaro's departure on the same train as the attractive La Ministra. Earlier, at the onset of Ana's March attack, the Marquesa de Vegallana had briefly felt her forehead and, agreeing with Somoza's fanciful diagnosis, had prescribed a medication: sarsaparilla (root beer). In contrast, the male characters who tend the sick Ana show greater concern, understandably so in the cases of De Pas and Mesía, given that they have selfish reasons for wanting her restored to good health. For Fermín, however, in contrast to Benítez's advice, physical exercise should come second to her concentration on religious devotions. When it is necessary, it should take the form of physical visits to religious places or of works of charity in the town. Whilst he had understood very clearly the underlying sexual meaning of Benítez's Latin phrase to Víctor in El Vivero, El Magistral fails – irony of ironies! – to heed fully the lesson for his own good, as he eventually rues: "olvidé lo que oí al médico de ella, olvidé que *ubi irritatio ibi fluxus*, olvidé ser con ella tan grosero como con otras" (2:557) ["I did not remember what I heard her doctor say, I did not remember that *ubi irritatio ibi fluxus*, I did not remember to be as coarse with her as with other women" (683)]. His response to Ana's betrayal of him is to treat her with utter contempt, ignoring her final efforts to effect a rapprochement. This is a far harsher punishment than the retirement to a convent that Gloria's devout aunt, Serafinita, had relentlessly urged – much to Nicomedes's disapproval – in Galdós's novel.

Mesía, on the other hand, has a somewhat clearer and more accurate understanding of Ana's temperament, although it is a typecasting of the hysterical woman common to the period: "Es una mujer rara ... histérica" (2:162) ["She's a strange woman – a hysterical woman" (412)]. After his trip to Paris he is always quoting the names of Bernard and Pasteur. He suggests for her recovery after the March attack that she should eat "carne cruda, mucha carne a la inglesa" (2:226) ["raw meat, a great deal of meat prepared in the English manner" (454)]. He even talks of the possibility of Ana undergoing a blood transfusion to counter her anaemia. He pedantically declares, as if echoing Robustiano's earlier words in the Casino, "La ciencia había adelantado mucho en esta materia" (2:226) ["Science had made much progress in this matter" (455)]. Somoza, who is present on this occasion, nods his head in approval, but it is an empty gesture, for he knows nothing of the method and is really frightened of Álvaro's medical knowledge. With his empty name-dropping, Mesía is only acting as a mirror figure of Vetusta's leading doctor. Both are medical shams. Yet, when the former's affair with Ana saps his sexual energies, it is Robustiano who, without compunction, tells him the truth to his face, in one brief sentence, introduced abruptly into the text: "Está usted desmejorado" (2:514) ["You are looking unwell" (652)]. "Doctor" Mesía may know what is best for Ana, but certainly not for himself. All of these minor "medical assistants," both male and female, project brief shafts of comic light on the contrasting expertise and practice of Somoza and Benítez. Two additional characters – again men – deserve greater attention as more prominent and serious medical assistants.

When Víctor, Ana's husband, first learns of her March attack, he is rather annoyed, as his personal routine will be inconveniently disrupted. His anticipated labour as an aide to Somoza and as a nurse to his wife with all the possibility of errors (e.g., confusing or overdosing medicines, keeping his wife bedside company, or explaining her condition to visitors) fills him with self-pity. But at least he knows what will be involved. Indeed, he informs Somoza that in his spare time in the past he has read books on medicine (which is more than Somoza, or even Mesía, have done), in particular those published in the 1870s on internal pathology by the Swiss doctor François Jacoud. But these readings ultimately nauseated him. Still, with Benítez now in charge of Ana's care, Víctor dutifully performs the daily chores of feeling her stomach and asking about "las funciones más humildes de la vida animal" (2:185) ["the lowest animal functions" (426)], the answers being logged in abbreviated form in a notebook for the doctor's information. Víctor throws himself fully into the medical tasks, preparing the medications, painting iodine on his wife's body, and, with watch in hand, timing and chronicling all the medical tests. Yet, when Ana's recovery, albeit very slow, is forecast, Víctor eagerly returns to his normal routine, with only the occasional check-up on his wife, until a subsequent relapse forces him back to nursing duties: "el médico volvió a ser un oráculo, los pormenores de alcoba negocios arduos, el reloj un dictador lacónico" (2:190) ["the doctor again became an oracle, again the details of the bedchamber were arduous chores, the watch was a laconic dictator again" (429)].

His good relationship with Benítez during Ana's March illness grows during the summer convalescence in El Vivero, where he shows a husband's understandable desire to obtain from his wife's doctor the best and most accurate medical opinion on her health. He genuinely wants to know if there will be any more sickness with which he will have to cope. Fully understanding the physician's diagnosis given in Latin, he asks the pertinent questions about whence and (especially) from whom will the new stimulation come:

"¡Perfectamente! *Ubi irritatio* ... justo, *ibi* ... *fluxus!* ¡Convencido! Pero aquí el nuevo influjo ... ¿dónde está? Veo el otro, el clero, el jesuitismo ... pero, ¿y éste? ¿quién representa esta nueva influencia ... esta nueva *irritatio* que pudiéramos decir ...?" (2:473)

["Precisely! *Ubi irritatio* ... exactly, *ibi* ... *fluxus*! I am convinced! But this new influence – where is it? I can see the other one, the clergy, jesuitry ... but what about this one? Who represents this new influence – this new *irritatio*, one might say?" (620)]

Benítez avoids a direct answer that might identify Álvaro as the obvious source, by firing off a disparate list of others, mostly of a physiological kind: "Pues es bien claro. Nosotros. El nuevo régimen, la higiene, el Vivero ... usted ... yo ... los alimentos sanos ... la leche ... el aire ... el heno ... el tufillo del establo ... la brisa de la mañana ..., etc., etc." (2:473) ["Well, it's clear enough. We do. The new regimen, hygiene, El Vivero, you, me, wholesome food, milk, air, hay, the whiff of the cattle-shed, the morning breeze, and so on" (620–1)].

The bedroom in El Vivero where husband and wife had enjoyed the summer recuperation becomes, ironically, the theatre for the medical examination of Víctor after he is mortally wounded in a duel with Mesía. Both doctors for whom Víctor has acted as domestic medical aide in their ministrations to Ana and who were witnesses at the duel now jointly certify that Quintanar is dying of peritonitis, with Somoza's prediction of the time of death once more proving inaccurate. Medical care, whether old-fashioned or scientifically modern, is, in the final analysis, powerless to prevent Víctor's death.

The one character who tries to avoid the duel and who is most distraught at the death of Víctor is his closest friend, Frígilis, hunter and horticulturist, a man familiar with both human nature and modern science. Despite these attributes, he can share blame with Robustiano for setting in motion the course of the novel in that he had encouraged the marriage between Víctor and Ana. As a nature lover, like Nicomedes in *Gloria*, Frígilis should have realized that the marriage was a mismatch from the start, given the differences of age and interests, and that it was bound to lead to a sad end. His attempts to prevent the duel are noble, but fail to take into account the noxious influence of Fermín, who convinces Víctor to defend his honour. Even after the duel, Frígilis commits the error of leaving Ana alone in the house to read Álvaro's letter after the mail has been delivered, thus precipitating her last hysteria attack. Juan Oleza observes: "pero en la misma medida en que [Frígilis] observa y constata, también deja hacer" [but to the same extent that Frígilis just observes and confirms things, he too just lets them happen] (2:593n16). This is, perhaps, a harsh judgment. Certainly, Frígilis can be criticized for not being *consistently* prescient and attentive to the drama that unfolds before his eyes and ears. However, his positive concern for Ana's health cannot be undervalued, whether when, taking her pulse after the March attack, he appears, in a somewhat oxymoronic naturalist phrase, to be "el símbolo de la salud queriendo *contagiar* con sus emanaciones a la enferma" (2:178) ["a symbol of health attempting to infect the sick woman with its emanations" (423)], or when he entreats Víctor not to discuss with Ana the matter of her affair with Álvaro, a move that would inevitably lead to her death. Like Benítez, Frígilis is well aware, given his interaction with Vetustan society, of Mesía's reputation as a Don Juan. Is it again a question of a good and insightful man (like Dickens's Physician, Nicomedes, and Benítez), who, when confronted by the moral and personal circumstances surrounding his female patient's precarious state of physical and mental health, opts for silence as the lesser of two evils?

During her convalescence in El Vivero, Ana had written in her diary that Frígilis is "el único grande hombre que conozco de vista" (2:449) ["the only great man I know personally" (604)]. In her final convalescence, Frígilis acts as Benítez's locum when he ensures that Ana sits in the brilliant spring sunshine. Then he serves as her factotum, securing the social benefits due to her as a widow. But he eventually becomes quite literally the true doctor in the house when Benítez's visits diminish; on his own initiative, he decides to sleep every night in the room beneath Ana's so that he can rush to her aid, if necessary. He is able to offer distractions with his conducted tours and tree lectures in the garden. Ana derives great comfort from considering Frígilis as "el amigo constante, el compañero de sus tristezas" (2:593) ["her constant friend, her companion in sadness" (711)]. Notwithstanding these benefits, constant companionship cannot be an effective long-term cure for Ana's condition, nor can drugs or house calls by any doctor-cum-psychologist/psychiatrist.

Is Ana, then, the only person who can doctor and medicate herself satisfactorily, as Gloria showed in the final moments of her life? Because of the series of hysteria attacks, Ana becomes somewhat of an expert in self-diagnosis. In chapter 3, after El Magistral had indicated his need for a general confession from her, she sensed the usual symptoms and felt that her first attack was near (Aldaraca, "El caso" 56): "Se tomó el pulso, se miró las manos; no veía bien los dedos, el pulso latía con violencia; en los párpados le estallaban estrellitas, como chispas de fuegos artificiales, sí, sí, estaba mala, iba a darle el ataque" (1:229) ["She felt her pulse, looked at her hands, could only see the blurred outline of her fingers, her pulse was violent; behind her eyelids little stars were exploding, like sparkling fireworks, yes, yes, she was ill, she was about to have one of her attacks" (72)]. Ana has the same ready answer – like Somoza – for any external sign that she is unwell: "Son los nervios, Quintanar" (1:467) ["Just nerves, Quintanar" (215)]. She can sum up very well for herself her basic and eternal existential problem: that incessant oscillation that Benítez had expressed with his Latin aphorism: "Quería la infeliz desechar las ideas que la volvían loca, aquellas emociones contradictorias de la piedad exaltada y de la carne rebelde y desabrida" (2:352) ["Ana wanted to rid herself of those thoughts which were driving her crazy, and those contradictory feelings of exalted piety and disgruntled rebellion of the flesh" (538)]. In this mental self-examination, she even surpasses Benítez's medical acumen: "Veía al médico muy preocupado con el *tronco* y sin pensar en los dolores inefables que ella sentía en lo más suyo, en algo que será cuerpo, pero que parecía alma, según era íntimo" (2:185) ["The doctor seemed to be preoccupied with her body and heedless of the ineffable pains deep in the very core of her being, somewhere which was no doubt part of her body but which was so intimate that it seemed like her soul" (426)]. It is noteworthy that Ana never refers to her mind or brain as the source of her deepest pains, but to her heart and soul. For that reason, she believes it is an illness that none of the doctors in Vetusta can understand. Of course, she demonstrates a different attitude after the trauma of the Good Friday procession and during her convalescence in El Vivero, when she realizes that Benítez has saved both her mind and body. Her progress as an autodidact physician-cum-budding-psychiatrist continues with the reading of the latest research publications of Maudsley and Jules Luys – a contemporary of Charcot at La Saltpetrière hospital in Paris.[16] It is almost as if Benítez is her thesis director, and that, as a dutiful graduate student, she resolutely goes through the titles on his reading list.[17] She is even able to look at the book illustrations of brains and other body organs without fear or repugnance. Similarly, after her final relapse following the duel, she recognizes the suitability of the prescribed therapy: knitting and sewing, together with the botany lectures of Frígilis, take her mind off thoughts of remorse or apprehension about the future. By the end of the novel she has come to a full understanding of the nature of her hysteria attacks and that their origins lie in the "locuras de la debilidad de su cerebro" (2:589) ["crazy imaginings of her enfeebled brain" (709)]. She self-diagnoses, but is unable to self-medicate correctly. For at the novel's close, in an act of conscious will, she forsakes the world of scientific medicine and returns to that of religion, which again spectacularly attacks her when De Pas, storming out of his confessional, ignores her.

~

The narrative space allotted to the role of physicians in *Gloria* and *La Regenta* is undoubtedly disproportionate. Only one appears – and briefly – in the closing stages of the former, whereas two licensed practitioners appear with some regularity through *La Regenta* along with a motley assortment of unnamed professionals or would-be amateurs. However, the joint study of the two novels has demonstrated that the doctors share some common attitudes: Nicomedes possesses features that are divided between Robustiano and Benítez. The first two doctors have been in the profession for a long time, pleasing their high-society patients with bedside bonhomie. But Nicomedes is no longer interested in earning consultancy fees, and whilst he feels great affection for the Lantigua family, he is not as much the doctor of the social élite as Somoza, who, despite his pretence of being "au fait" with modern medical research, has no proper understanding of its nature. In his love of the countryside and preference to be alone, Nicomedes seems to foreshadow the character of the much younger doctor, Benítez, in *La Regenta*, with whom it is probable that he also shares an interest in modern scientific medicine. Both are desperately alarmed at the mental and physical state of their respective female patients, ultimately unable, however, to cure permanently their illness of varying degrees of hysteria, not, as Aldaraca contends – "La histeria es una enfermedad que molesta a los médicos porque no tiene desenlace" [Hysteria is an illness that bothers doctors because it has no conclusion] ("El caso" 60) – but rather because there is a moral world above and beyond that of medicine, old-fashioned or new scientific.

Galdós himself makes this point most emphatically in the novel he composed immediately after Gloria: *Marianela* (1878), which, with its detailed pictures of the zinc mines at Socartes and the presentation of the eponymous heroine's family background and the squalid conditions in which she lives, could well be considered a Zolaesque naturalist novel, although it appeared a good three years before Galdós's acknowledged venture into that new novelistic landscape, *La desheredada*, was published. However, it is far from being a triumphant anticipation of what should be the paradigm of the naturalist novel after Zola's 1880 manifesto and even less of a paean of praise for the advantages of new medical discoveries. Paradoxically, it is not the anonymous narrator, but one of the novel's characters, the ophthalmologist Teodoro Golfín, who will make the most devastating critique of the real value of these new medical discoveries and procedures, when he should be – and is, for some critics (Stannard 34–5; López Piñero et al. 242) – their most eloquent defender. On his first appearance in the novel, we are told that, although of humble origins, he has risen to the top of his specialization, revolutionized earlier by von Helmholtz. He is a world-renowned researcher, who frequently travels from America to Europe to keep abreast of the latest experiments in ophthalmology (730). But at the end of the novel, after his successful operation to restore the vision of Pablo Penáguilas, he is aghast to find that it has also produced collateral damage: the self-willed death of Pablo's erstwhile companion and admirer. As the surgeon stares at Marianela's almost extinct body, "aquel libro humano de caracteres obscuros, en los cuales la vista científica no podía descifrar la leyenda misteriosa de la muerte y la vida" (773) ["that human book of obscure characters, in which scientific vision cannot decipher the mysterious symbols of life and death" (236)], Florentina, soon to be Pablo's wife, asks a very pertinent question: "¡No sabe! ... Entonces, ¿para qué es médico?" ["You do not know! ... Then why are you a doctor?" (236)]. Golfín can only half answer: "No sé, no sé, no sé ... Sí, una cosa sé, y es que no sabemos más que fenómenos superficiales" (773) ["I do not know! I do not know! I do not know! ... Yes, one thing I do know, and that is, that we know no more than superficial phenomena" (236)]. Galdós is saying very clearly in *Marianela* that medical knowledge (highly specialized in Golfín's case) explains nothing about the mysteries of human life. Modern scientific medicine has barely scratched its surface. In his final damascene moment of self-illumination, Golfín discovers the moral contradictions that lie at the heart of modern medicine. In so doing, he has advanced beyond the guarded and limited perspicacity that Nicomedes had already suggested and that was to be more evident in Benítez's regime of treatment for Ana Ozores.

Even more interestingly, in his review of *Marianela*, Clarín makes comments similar to Golfín's that are applicable to both *La Regenta* and *Gloria*. The freshness of the latter in his mind can be gauged by the way in which he notes that the mines of Socartes lie behind the hills that surround "Ficóbriga, la patria de Gloria" [Ficóbriga, the home place of Gloria] (280). Marianela, he writes, is a young woman, "soñadora como Gloria, pero ésta posee la religión cristiana, sólida e ilustrada" [a dreamer like Gloria, but the latter has a solid and learned hold of the Christian religion] (282). Then he theorizes:

> Para las cuestiones sociales, naturales, etc., etc., quizá ya el arte sirve mucho menos que la ciencia; mas para otras regiones de la vida y de la conciencia, que muchos llaman nebulosas, pero cuya realidad se impone con un *positivismo* tan palpable como las piedras, el arte es el mejor quizá (el gran arte, el que cultiva Pérez Galdós, por supuesto) que una ciencia que no lo es, si hemos de llamar por su nombre a las cosas. (287)
>
> [For matters of a social and natural kind, etc., etc., perhaps art is now not as useful as science. But for other regions of human life and conscience, which many call nebulous, but whose reality imposes itself with a *positivism* that is as palpable as any stone, art is perhaps better (like the great art that Pérez Galdós cultivates, of course) than a science which is not art, if we are to call things by their proper names.]

That is to say, art is a better instrument or medium than modern science with which to delve into the innermost complexities of the human spirit.[18]

Consequently, the literary presentation (in the form of the realist-naturalist novel) of the ultimate failure of medicine to heal the mental illnesses of individuals, especially women like Gloria and Ana, is not surprising. Furst ("Introduction" 20–1) has wisely observed:

> In contrast to the usefulness of microscopy and analytical chemistry in diagnostics, the immediate therapeutic spin-offs of laboratory science for patients were fairly small until the very end of the [nineteenth] century. Discontent with science is aptly summarized in the German slogan demanding cures not classifications ... The literary texts thus serve to modify the tendency to view medical progress in the nineteenth century in a simplistic manner. Compromises have constantly to be negotiated; concessions are demanded of both doctors and patients that neither group is prepared to make.[19]

Neither Galdós nor Alas, the former at the beginning and the latter at the height of interest in Spain in Zola's work (1876–85), could accept the naturalist credo that heredity and environment alone determined human behaviour. In the final analysis, as Eamonn Rodgers has opined, "even those writers most amenable to the influence of naturalism maintained an eclectic and independent attitude toward the movement" (132).

In the Spanish realist-naturalist novels examined in this essay, modern medicine, despite its undeniable merits, is seen to be ultimately ineffective in dealing with the physical and (especially) mental ailments (basically hysteria) of young impressionable women. When they abandon or ignore the advice of their male physician or protector and in a momentous act of self-empowerment attempt their own ideas of self-medication, they quickly succumb to death (Gloria and Marianela) or return to further suffering, both in body and mind (Ana Ozores).

NOTES

1 All translations of quotations in Spanish and French are my own, except for those from *Gloria*, *La Regenta*, and *Marianela*, which are taken from published books, and are followed, when appropriate, by the corresponding volume and page numbers.

2 Furst (*Between Doctors* 30–1) records that between 1769 and 1871 there were 142 editions of William Buchan's *Domestic Medicine*, which prescribed appropriate treatment for the maladies catalogued. Even *Mrs Beeton's Book of Household Management* provided guidance on serious medical conditions.

3 Tertius Lydgate, the doctor in George Eliot's novel *Middlemarch* (1871–2), published almost twenty years before *Le Docteur Pascal*, is another practising physician-cum-medical-researcher. His professional ambition foreshadows the enthusiasm of Zola in his manifesto: he has "the conviction that the medical profession as it might be was the finest in the world; presenting the most perfect interchange between science and art; offering the most direct alliance between intellectual conquest and the social good" (136).

4 If, at the level of medical history, the physician of the realist-naturalist novel could be photographed, as it were, employing new instruments and treatments, generally with the approval of the narrator/author, with regard to the plot, he could also discharge a number of useful roles: as intermediary between other fictional characters and their respective social circles, especially between the members of opposite sexes, or even as a principal character in his own right as a marriage prospect in a romantic story (Leavis 179). In these plot roles the physician figure himself could

come under sharper scrutiny from the narrator for any possible character shortcomings. Philip Collins's claim that "many of 42,000 novels published in Britain during the reign of Victoria contained doctors" (111) therefore serves both as an indicator of the importance of this profession in realist-naturalist fiction and a warning that no single study can address the wide variety of ways in which the figure was used in nineteenth-century novels, or the attitude of their narrators and authors to the momentous changes in the practice of medicine.

5 Or as Julia Chang has recently written, with comparable pithiness: "Doctor and priest seem to have little distinction" (317). It should not be forgotten, however, that the same role as confidential confessor had also been discharged by the physicians of earlier generations. Writing in 1849, Worthington Hooker speaks with some authority on the contemporary scene: "Most persons have the feeling that their physician is a sort of confidant, and on that ground they are willing that he should see and hear, in his daily intercourse with them, what would be improper to be seen and heard without the confidence of intimate friendship" (383).

6 "The Middle Ages had organized around the theme of the flesh and the practice of penance a discourse that was markedly unitary. In the course of recent centuries, this relative uniformity was broken apart, scattered, and multiplied in an explosion of distinct discursivities which took form in demography, biology, medicine, psychiatry, psychology" (Foucault 33).

7 It is a role fully developed in chapter 25 of Anthony Trollope's 1858 novel *Dr. Thorne*, between the eponymous doctor and his dying patient, albeit male, the industrial tycoon Sir Roger Scatcherd (331–47).

8 For the Spanish physician José María Esquerdo in 1889, "en la patología mental de la mujer [la histeria] obtiene el premio" (in the mental pathology of women [hysteria] takes the prize), according to Aldaraca ("El caso" 53). Jean-Martin Charcot, the French neurophysiologist, was the recognized authority on hysteria in the nineteenth century. The Spanish translation of his study *Lecciones sobre enfermedades del sistema nervioso* [Lessons on Infirmities of the Nervous System] appeared in 1882. Although he believed that the illness was due to damage to the cerebellum, he was never able to prove this theory, preferring to encourage the belief that the site of origin was women's ovaries – for other colleagues, it was the genitalia – from where the central nervous system transmitted it to the brain. Other theories emphasized the opposite direction: from a woman's mind, specifically her imagination, to her body "through an obscure neural process" (Showalter 14). A somewhat misogynistic theory of the last quarter of the nineteenth century, greatly disseminated by the English

psychiatrist Henry Maudsley, maintained that hysteria was caused by character defects, found especially in coquettish, eccentric, and impulsive women (Jagoe 344). Hysteria had been discussed in Spanish medical textbooks as early as 1853, when Pedro Felipe Monlau published his famous *Higiene del matrimonio o el libro de los casados* [Marriage Hygiene or the Book for the Married] (Aldaraca, "The Medical Construction" 412–13). Alone amongst Spanish physicians of the last quarter of the century, Ángel Pulido believed that hysteria was only a neurological disease, as he stated at a session of the Sociedad Ginecológica Española in 1876 (Jagoe 343), a diagnosis of which both Galdós and Alas might have been aware.

9 The article by Charles Bigot, the Paris correspondent of *Revista contemporánea,* published on 30 April 1876, introduced Zola to the Spanish reading public and discussed his latest novel, *Son Excellence Eugène Rougon* (Pattison 11). Bigot refers to Zola's "physiological" type of novel, clearly noting the importance of heredity and environment in determining his characters' behaviour. In this regard, he likens Zola's latest novel to a vast hospital clinic (Pattison 12). In the following year, the use of the label "naturalism" became widespread. In February 1877 Pedro Antonio de Alarçón employed it when talking of the contemporary French novel in his entry speech to the Real Academia Española. Two months later another Parisian correspondent, Ángel Vallejo Miranda, employed the term for the first time in a Spanish journal (Pattison 13). Both in French and Spanish literary studies of the times, the term used was generally a combination "realista-naturalista" (Pattison 14–15), as the opening lines of Emilia Pardo Bazán's extensive study of Zola's works and theory, *La cuestión palpitante* (1882–3), also amply testify (574).

10 Only twice more in his complete literary output does Galdós select this proper name for a fictional character (see *Obras completas* 6:1946–7). In ancient Eastern history, it is the name given to a Greek mathematician, a Christian martyr, and four kings of Bythnia in Anatolia. But the onomastic form sounds very close to that of "Nicodemo," an influential member of the Jewish Sanhedrin, who was drawn to Christ's teaching and assisted at his burial. It is very possible that Galdós wanted such an association to be made, given the similarities suggested between Christ's death and resurrection on Easter Sunday and those of Gloria (Bly 39). After all, the two names are only differentiated by an example of metathesis and a final phoneme change.

11 Charcot's most famous cure for hysteria was hypnosis, but there is no suggestion of this being applied to Gloria or later, with greater justification, to Ana. In 1873, a woman diagnosed with hysteria was cured at Madrid

University's Faculty of Medicine in two weeks by means of potassium bromide solutions and blasts of cold water (Jagoe 346). Perhaps Galdós read the account of this procedure or was informed of it by his medical friends.

12 Is it possible that, in this brief bio sketch of Nicomedes, Galdós has inverted that of a real-life source? García del Real (804–5) cites the case of Eugenio Gutiérrez y González, who was "médico titular" in Lamadrid, a small village close to San Vicente de la Barquera, from 1874 to 1878. Curiously enough, Galdós had travelled through this area in 1877, as reported in his travelogue, "Cuarenta leguas por Cantabria," published just before he finished part 1 of *Gloria*. Unlike Nicomedes, Gutiérrez y González had high career aspirations and in 1879 went to Paris on a year's study leave. But, unfortunately, he had to return to his rural practice. In 1880, however, through the good offices of Francisco Giner de los Ríos, a friend of Galdós and, according to Pedro Ortiz Armengol, "descubridor de la preciosa villa de San Vicente de la Barquera" [discoverer of the beautiful town of San Vicente de la Barquera] (320), he secured an appointment as a professor of histology at a research institute in Madrid.

13 In fact, Alas complained that Palacio Valdés's novel lacked spontaneity and was too brief (Dendle 147n12). The first two chapters, however, "reveal the influence of a scientific naturalism" (Dendle 53–4). Certainly, chapter 1 (101–5) presents a very detailed picture of the Madrid surgery of one of Spain's leading physicians, Dr Ibarra. This venue represents a departure from the usual house visit from a male doctor to a woman who has taken to her bed. Furthermore, the patient, Andrés Heredia, is male, not female, although two women are also waiting in the surgery for their consultation with Ibarra. Heredia, a poet, is sounded out by Ibarra with a later model of Laënnec's stethoscope, and Ibarra then taps him on the ribs after listening to the account of his symptoms. Ibarra's prescribed cure for the illness (now diagnosed as anaemia and not tuberculosis) is, significantly, a prolonged stay in the countryside – the same solution that Nicomedes refrains from openly suggesting but which Gloria very briefly effects herself in *Gloria* and which becomes an important element in the slow curing of Ana's illness in Alas's novel. As in the latter, the patient is to send in progress reports on his rehabilitation in order for his drug needs to be assessed. The usual fee is waived, because the doctor considers himself a friend and confessor of his writer patient.

14 The real "mediquillo" in *La Regenta* is Joaquinito Orgaz, a figure similar to those new graduates that Galdós had written dismissively of in "Junio" and who were so numerous in contemporary Spanish society. Joaquinito has returned to Vetusta to find not a suitable practice but a rich bride. At

no time in the novel is he seen practising medicine or even talking about it. He never gives an opinion on the nature of Ana's attacks. He is a physician in title only. His first appearance – in the Casino and as a close friend of Álvaro Mesía and Paco Vegallana – establishes his frivolous character, more given to flamenco dancing and girl chasing. The first words he utters, "yo sé más que todos ustedes" (1:340) ["Well I know more than the lot of you" (134)], suggest that the self-important neophyte is going to impart some words of medical wisdom to those present. Instead, they are only to confirm the rumour of De Pas's imminent appointment as Ana's confessor. Consequently, the association between physician and priest is made at quite an early stage in the novel. At the end, Joaquinito is brought into the narrative merely to reveal the arrangements of the duel between Mesía and Víctor. He is an empty caricature of the new scientific doctors supposedly produced by post-1868 medical schools.

15 This epistolary self-diagnosis by Ana Ozores seems to correspond to the changes that occurred in popular self-help publications in the second half of the nineteenth century. For if, on the one hand, doctors began to publish books with titles such as *Medicine and the Public* in order to explain their profession to lay people, on the other hand, patients were cultivating a type of genre that reflected their own experiences or expectations of health care, in such books as *Life in the Sick Room*, as well as keeping private diaries, journals, and correspondence (Bynum 211).

16 According to Juan Oleza, Maudsley's theories were an important documentary source used by Clarín for Ana's case (2:443n10), while Beth Wietelmann Bauer (319) claims that this allusion to Maudsley clearly signals how medical science at this time was striving to explain the relationship of the human mind and body, to be advanced enormously a decade later by the work of Freud.

17 As Chang has recently noted, "Male doctors and intellectuals alike feared women's self-empowerment through literacy, as well as the stimulation of women's delicate nerves" (314). This fear was perhaps justified, for, in Ana's case, she does stray from the strict regime of medical literature supervised by Benítez, wandering into the fantasy world of a volume she particularly likes: *Mitología ilustrada*, one of her father's books that she had brought to El Vivero during her convalescence. She is right to muse: "Probablemente Benítez condenará este afán de leer y me prohibiría la desmedida afición" (2:459) ["Benitez would probably condemn this urge to read, and forbid me to become excessively fond of books" (611)].

18 In a footnote to the 1891 edition of this review in *Solos de Clarín*, and, therefore, of retrospective significance for Alas's attitude to medicine in

La Regenta six years earlier, he states unequivocally: "Esto escribía yo [i.e., the review of *Marianela*] hace diez años, y esto creo hoy firmemente, y esto prueba que las tendencias actuales de *mis ensayos críticos y novelescos* no obedecen a modas extranjeras, sino a sentimientos y convicciones *antiguas y arraigadas*" [I wrote this [i.e., the review of *Marianela*] ten years ago, and I still believe it very strongly today. This proves the current tendency of *my critical and fictional essays* are not due to foreign fashions, but to *old and deep-rooted* feelings and convictions of my own] (287; my emphasis).

19 In another paragraph she explains, again most pertinently: "The medical episodes in nineteenth-century literary works flesh out history in significant ways by revealing the extremely erratic pace of progress, the intensity of opposition in some quarters, and the combination of often irrational factors obstructing any innovation" ("Introduction" 21). As William James quipped in the 1880s: "sickness had become a matter of microbes, not of man" (Macleod 5).

WORKS CITED

Alas, Leopoldo, "Clarín." *La Regenta*. Ed. Juan Oleza. 2 vols. Madrid: Cátedra, 2011. Print.

– *La Regenta*. Trans. John Rutherford. Athens: U of Georgia P, 1984. Print.

– *Solos de Clarín*. Madrid: Librería de Fernando Fe, 1891. Print.

Aldaraca, Bridget. "El caso de Ana O.: histeria y sexualidad en *La Regenta*." *Asceplio* 42.2 (1990): 51–61. Print.

– "The Medical Construction of the Feminine Subject in Nineteenth-Century Spain." In *Cultural and Historical Grounding for Hispanic and Luzo-Brazilian Feminist Literary Criticism*, ed. Hernan Vidal. Minneapolis: Institute for the Study of Ideologies and Literature, 1989. 395–413. Print.

Baroja, Pío. *Obras completas*. Vol. 7. Madrid: Biblioteca Nueva, 1949. Print.

Bernard, Claude. *Introduction à l'étude de la médecine expérimentale*. Brussels: Culture et Civilisation, 1965. Print.

Bly, Peter. "Semana Santa Processions As Viewed by Galdós and Alas." *Anales Galdosianos* 49 (2014): 29–54. Print. https://doi.org/10.1353/ang.2014.0006.

Bravo Villasante, Carmen. "Veintiocho cartas de Galdós a Pereda." *Cuadernos Hispanoamericanos* 250–2 (1970–1): 9–51. Print.

Briggs, Asa. "*Middlemarch* and the Doctors." *Cambridge Journal* 1 (1948): 749–62. Print.

Bynum, W.F. *Science and the Practice of Medicine in the Nineteenth Century*. Cambridge: Cambridge UP, 1996. Print.

Cabezas, Juan Antonio. *"Clarín." El provinciano universal*. Madrid: Espasa-Calpe, 1962. Print.

Chang, Julia. "Blood, Purity, and Pleasure in Leopoldo Alas's *La Regenta*." *Hispanic Review* 84.3 (2016): 299–321. Print. https://doi.org/10.1353/hir.2016.0029.

Collins, Philip. "Physicians in Victorian Fiction." In *Art and Society in the Victorian Novel*, ed. Colin Gibson. Basingstoke: Macmillan Press, 1989. Print. 111–30.

Dendle, Brian J. *Spain's Forgotten Novelist: Armando Palacio Valdés (1853–1938)*. Lewisburg: Bucknell UP, 1995. Print.

Dickens, Charles. *Little Dorrit*. Ed. Harvey Peter Sucksmith. Oxford: Oxford UP, 2012. Print.

Eliot, George. *Middlemarch*. Ed. David Carroll. Oxford: Oxford UP, 2008. Print.

Foucault, Michel. *The History of Sexuality*. Trans. Robert Hurley. Vol 1. New York: Vintage Books, 1990. Print.

Furst, Lilian R. *Between Doctors and Patients: The Changing Balance of Power*. Charlottesville: Virginia UP, 1998. Print.

– "Introduction: From Speculation to Science." In *Medical Progress and Social Reality: A Reader in Nineteenth-Century Medicine and Literature*, ed. Lilian R. Furst. Albany: SUNY P, 2000. 1–21. Print.

García del Real, Eduardo. *Historia de la medicina en España*. Madrid: Editorial Reus, 1921. Print.

Hooker, Worthington. *Physician and Patient*. New York: Arno P and *New York Times*, 1972. Print.

Jagoe, Catherine. "Sexo y género en la medicina del siglo XIX." In *La mujer en los discursos de género. Textos y contextos en el siglo XIX*, ed. Catherine Jagoe, Alda Blanco, and Cristina Enríquez de Salamanca. Barcelona: Icaria, 1998. 305–67. Print.

Laín Entralgo, P. *Doctor and Patient*. Trans. Frances Partridge. London: Weidenfeld and Nicolson, 1969. Print.

Leavis, Q.D. "The Symbolic Function of the Doctor in Victorian Novels." In F.R. Leavis and Q.D. Leavis, *Dickens the Novelist*. London: Chatto and Windus, 1970. 179–83. Print.

López Piñero, José María, Luis García Ballester, and Pilar Faus Sevilla. *Medicina y sociedad en la España del siglo XIX*. Madrid: Sociedad de Estudios y Publicaciones, 1964. Print.

Lowe, Jennifer. "Cigars, Slippers and Nightcaps: Attitudes and Actions in *La Regenta* and *Tristana*." *Anales Galdosianos* 27–8 (1992–3): 125–9. Print.

Macleod, Roy. "The 'Bankruptcy of Science' Debate: The Creed of Science and Its Critics. 1885–1900." *Science, Technology, and Human Values* 7.41 (1982): 2–15. Print. https://doi.org/10.1177/016224398200700401.

Marañón, Gregorio. *Obras completas*. Ed. Alfredo Juderías. Vols. 4, 9. Madrid: Espasa-Calpe, 1968. Print.

Ortiz Armengol, Pedro. *Vida de Galdós*. Barcelona: Crítica, 1995. Print.

Palacio Valdés, Armando. *El idilio de un enfermo*. In *Obras*. 2 vols. Madrid: Aguilar, 1959. 2: 101–68. Print.

Pardo Bazán, Emilia. *La cuestión palpitante*. In *Obras completas*, vol. 3, ed. Harry L. Kirby, Jr. Madrid: Aguilar, 1973. Print.

Pattison, Walter T. *El naturalismo español. Historia externa de un movimiento literario*. Madrid: Gredos, 1965. Print.

Pérez Bautista, Florencio L. *Sociedad y medicina en la novela realista española*. Salamanca: U de Salamanca, 1974. Print.

Pérez Galdós, Benito. "Cuarenta leguas por Cantabria." In *Obras completas*, 6:1443–57. Print.

– *Gloria*. In *Obras completas*, 4:513–699. Print.

– *Gloria*. Trans. Clara Bell. 2 vols. New York: William S. Gottsberger, 1882. Vol. 2. Print.

– "Junio." In *Obras completas*, 6:480–6. Print.

– *Marianela*. In *Obras completas*, 4:701–75. Print.

– *Marianela: A Story of Spanish Love*. Trans. Helen W. Lester. New York: Howard Fertig, 1975. Print.

– *Obras completas*. Ed. Federico Carlos Sainz de Robles. 6 vols. Madrid: Aguilar, 1968. Print.

Rodgers, Eamonn. "The Reception of Naturalism in Spain." In *Naturalism in the European Novel: New Critical Perspectives*, ed. Brian Nelson. New York: Berg, 1992. 120–34. Print.

Rosenberg, Charles E. *Explaining Epidemics and Other Studies in the History of Medicine*. New York: Cambridge UP, 1992. Print.

Rubio Jiménez, Jesús. "Introducción." "Sesenta y seis cartas de Galdós a Clarín." *Anales Galdosianos* 40–1 (2005–6): 87–131. Print.

Rutherford, John. *Leopoldo Alas. La Regenta*. London: Grant and Cutler, 1974. Print.

Showalter, Elaine. *Hystories: Hysterical Epidemics and Modern Culture*. New York: Columbia UP, 1997. Print.

Smith, Alan E., and Jesús Rubio Jiménez, eds. "Sesenta y seis cartas de Galdós a Clarín." *Anales Galdosianos* 40–1 (2005–6): 133–97. Print.

Sparks, Tabitha. *The Doctor in the Victorian Novel: Family Practices*. Farnham: Ashgate, 2009. Print.

Stannard, Michael W. *Galdós and Medicine*. Oxford: Peter Lang, 2015. Print.

Trollope, Anthony. *Doctor Thorne*. London: Penguin, 2012. Print.

Turner, Harriet. "Towards a Poetic of Realism." *Letras Peninsulares* 13 (2000): 11–23. Print.

Wietelmann Bauer, Beth. "Confession in *La Regenta*: The Secular Sacrament." *Bulletin of Hispanic Studies* 70.3 (1993): 313–23. Print. https://doi.org/10.1080/1475382932000370313.

Zarzoso, Alfons. "Poor Relief and Health Care in 18th and 19th Century Catalonia and Barcelona." In *Health Care and Poor Relief in 18th and 19th Century Southern Europe*, ed. Ole Peter Grell, Andrew Cunningham, and Bernd Roeck. Aldershot: Ashgate, 2005. Print.

Zola, Émile. *Le Docteur Pascal*. Paris: Garnier-Flammarion, 1975. Print.

– "Le Roman expérimental." In *Oeuvres complètes*, ed. Henri Mitterand. 21 vols. Paris: Nouveau Monde, 2003–4. 9:323–48. Print.

5 Travelling by Streetcar through Madrid with Galdós and Pardo Bazán

MARYELLEN BIEDER

Spain's two leading late nineteenth-century authors published short fictional works in the wake of the introduction into Madrid of one of the visual emblems of Spain's new material reality and nascent modernity, the streetcar. Benito Pérez Galdós's short novel *La novela en el tranvía* [The Novel on the Streetcar] highlighted this innovation in Madrid's urban transport. Published in *La Ilustración de Madrid* on 30 November and 15 December 1871, within six months of the inauguration of Madrid's first streetcar line, Galdós's novella continues to attract critical attention from diverse perspectives. Elizabeth Amann avers that it is "one of the earliest reactions to the experience of tram travel in Madrid" and "to the experience of collective transportation itself" (193–4).[1] Barely more than a decade after trolleys began to run along London streets, the *tramvía* [sic] *de Madrid* or *la* [sic] *tram-way* offered the capital's citizens carriages drawn by mules along rails embedded in the pavement. On 31 May 1871, the Madrid company launched its initial route from the *cocherón*, the depot and engine shed, at the far end of Serrano Street, to the Puerta del Sol; on 17 November 1871, the line expanded to extend from Sol to the neighbourhood of Pozas (Gutiérrez 88). Nearly two decades later, on 24 February 1890, Emilia Pardo Bazan's short story "En tranvía" [On the Streetcar] appeared in the Madrid newspaper *El Imparcial*. At that time, the carriages on the Serrano to Pozas line were still powered by *tracción a sangre* [animal power]; electrification of the line occurred on 4 October 1898.[2] Madrid's periodical press recorded these newsworthy moments in the history of the capital's public transportation system with illustrative engravings, in the case of the early trolley cars, and later, when electrification arrived, with photographs.[3]

Each tramcar offered passengers two rows of seats parallel to its long sides, as Galdós's novella specifies of the new conveyance: "iba provisto de dos largos asientos corridos de madera, 'asientos de vecindad,' con sus viajeros – veinte en total – sentados frente a frente" [it was provided with two continuous long wooden seats, "neighbouring seats," with passengers – twenty in all – seated facing each other] (106). Both Galdós's and Pardo Bazán's fictions take advantage of this parallel seating configuration, which allows each passenger to see all the others, by engaging all the travellers in the action of the story. Galdós's narrator/protagonist records "la hilera de caras de ambos sexos que ante mí tenía" [the row of faces of both sexes that I saw before me] and specifies "ocho narices erigidas bajo diez y seis ojos" [eight noses protruded beneath sixteen eyes], populating his tramcar with sixteen passengers out of the total capacity of twenty (10).[4] The model of the earliest trolleys depicted in Galdós's novella, *la imperial* [the imperial], had both inside seating and uncovered exterior seating, accessible by an open circular staircase at each end of the carriage.[5] Initially, a tramcar accommodated eighteen passengers on each level, but in such close, overheated contact – what Amann terms "awkward proximity" (196) – that passengers who attempted to exit the car often found themselves "tropezando con los pies y piernas de los viajeros" [bumping into other travellers' legs and feet] (Pérez Galdós 24).[6] The *imperial* with its open-air seating lasted only a short time, the cars being soon replaced as unsuitable to Madrid's climate ("El tranvía de la calle Serrano"). The Salamanca-Pozas-Salamanca line followed the route from Serrano to Paseo de Recoletos, Alcalá Street, Puerta del Sol, Mayor, Bailén, Quitapesares, el paseo de Areneros (Alberto Aguilera), and Princesa Street, before arriving in the Pozas neighbourhood; it then returned along the same tracks to the Salamanca terminal.

Thus Spain's two major realist authors each situated a story within the space of a tramcar, which serves to redefine the relationship between the denizens of the capital and their urban space and to reimagine the spatial dynamics among *madrileños* passing along the iron rails of their repetitive journey. The familiarity of the trajectory in Pardo Bazán's short story and its unexpected class dynamics replace the introduction of technological innovation that doubtless spurred Galdós's earlier novella with its dramatic counterpoint in fiction of outmoded aristocracy. This essay will align itself with a dominant thread in critical discourse, the early nineteenth-century spatial turn in literature that anticipated the practice of Spanish realist fiction and Henri Lefebvre's late twentieth-century theorization of the social production of space. It will explore the spatial discourses and practices in these stories and examine how each one ultimately positions itself in relation to realist discourse. Despite signalling the two stories' historical setting along Madrid's Salamanca-Pozas trolley line, the essay endorses Lilian Furst's affirmation of "the quintessentially fictional nature of realist narrative" (17) and her acknowledgment of realism's "sustained dialogue between reference to actuality and the textual creation of fabricated realm" (12). Furst also adopts Roland Barthes's concept of literary reality as a construction – *l'effet de réel* (19) – and Wolfgang Iser's insistence on readers' integral role in forging "an illusion of truth, whose authenticity is vouchsafed by the credibility that the text is able to evoke in readers" (17). She equates "truthfulness" in fiction with "the verbal and textual production of an impression of truth" (173) and argues that in works like the two examined here, "the presentation of place and the projection of its realness to readers exemplifies the problematic duality of realism as it at once asserts its simple artlessness yet turns out to devolve from a complex artfulness" (173).

The urban frame of both stories, contemporaneous with the date of composition, speaks to Spain's modernization process and suggests the concomitant shifting class relations within Spanish society. At the same time, both stories draw upon the discourses and characters of popular fiction, including that written for and read by women, either in a parodic move or to elicit reader identification. In highly economical fashion, each story projects three spaces: that exterior to the streetcar, the interior of the streetcar, and the narrator's interiorized thoughts or subconscious responses. Authored by a writer anchored in realism, each narrative encompasses, within its brief expanse, a meditation on the practice of realism as well as observations on contemporary Spanish society in what Michael Ugarte refers to as "urban sociology" (265).

As Harriet Turner elucidates, Galdós "sought to depict the impact of current political, social, and economic factors that jaggedly shaped everyday life," among them "the opening of railway lines, the spread of gas lighting, the construction of roads and waterways" (392). *La novela en el tranvía* offers an early example of Galdós's representation of social stratification spatially figured through architecture, with the urban trolley transporting on its trajectory real and self-consciously imagined passengers across a broad social range. Galdós's narrator/protagonist dramatizes the conflict between fictional conventions and the excesses of daily life, borrowing from the Cervantine play of fiction-rewriting-life and life-rewriting-fiction. When in 1973 Walter Oliver penned his analysis of *La novela en el tranvía*, he could assert that no previously published criticism "feels [the novella] is more than a humorous sketch" (251). As a consequence, Oliver was one of the initiators of a rich scope of critical interrogation that has addressed the novella's multifaceted relationship to *Don Quijote*. Recent criticism continues to productively analyse the novella's dialogue with Cervantes. This essay emphasizes the spatial aspects and sociological context of the practice of realism in Galdós's novella and Pardo Bazán's story, and thus moves beyond the examination of Galdós's Cervantine intertext and Pardo Bazán's sentimental swerve to acknowledge their ultimate rejection of their characters' "imagined truths."

Galdós's first-person narrator/protagonist makes the journey across Madrid from somewhere near the northern terminus of Serrano to Las Pozas, "al otro extremo de Madrid" [at the opposite extreme of Madrid] (19), and then back again; that is, from the northern edge of Madrid's urbanization to the western boundary of its development. In Pardo Bazán's much shorter piece, the narrator and fellow passengers board the tram in Sol, the centre of Madrid, and travel to the end of the same Serrano line. Galdós's trolley passes from Salamanca, a privileged upper-middle-class neighbourhood first developed in the 1860s by the Marqués de Salamanca, through the centre of Madrid to another new neighbourhood, working-class Pozas, founded by Ángel Pozas, "el promotor que levantó el barrio en 1863 con la intención de dignificar los hogares de la clase obrera, que, como demuestran los censos eran los vecinos mayoritarios: obreros, jornaleros, sirvientas y, curiosamente, militares y ferroviarios, por la cercanía de los cuarteles y del Ferrocarril del Norte" [the developer who erected the neighbourhood with the intention of dignifying the housing occupied by the working class who, as the censuses demonstrate, were the majority of the residents: workers, day labourers, servants and, curiously, military and railway employees, owing to the nearness of their barracks and the Northern Railway] ("Pozas"). In terms of class identity and social stratification, Pozas lies at the opposite pole from Salamanca not only geographically but also socially, making the trajectory a descent from élite high social standing to predominant low working-class standing.[7]

Pardo Bazán's story follows the reverse journey, starting in the multiclass conglomeration of Sol and terminating at the far end of the wealthy Salamanca neighbourhood. Both authors coordinate the spatial movements of the tram through the urban geography and class strata of Madrid. As Oliver has commented: "A very carefully structured constellation of symbols converts the '*tranvía*' into a kind of moving laboratory similar in every respect to the world at large" (254). In Deborah Parsons's conceptualization of space, Pardo Bazán's story "illustrates the ways in which the tram offered a detached refuge from the realities beyond its windows, facilitating the abstract separation of different locales, and yet was also a confined space in which any unfamiliar intrusion was particularly evident, thus disturbingly emphasizing the realities of urban difference" (66). One could argue that an "unfamiliar intrusion" occurs in both works of fiction; while Pardo Bazán highlights the class nature of the intrusion, Galdós's novella allows one set of fictional conventions to intrude into a piece framed by realist conventions. Neither author bestows names on the fictional characters, including the narrators, with one Cervantine exception in Galdós. The omission of names underscores the anonymity of urban travel, despite the awkward proximity of bodies it entails.

La novela en el tranvía

The nameless narrator/protagonist's troubling assessments of people in *La novela en el tranvía*, together with his careless disregard of and impolite behaviour towards his travelling companions, mark his view of himself and others as unreliable from the outset. As the story opens he does accept that his urgent intent to seat himself before anyone else is an egotistical impulse. Does this rudeness indicate his lack of middle-class mores or override the self-interest that characterizes the anonymity of mass-culture behaviour, such as evidenced in mass transportation? Readers coetaneous with the publication of the novella would surely have more easily processed the cultural information latent in its geographical movement and spatial practices as well as the class dynamics at work in the trolley car. One of the unexplained factors requiring reader input is the class identity of the three principal passengers: the narrator, the doctor, and the Englishwoman.

The narrator's travelling companion, a doctor, regales him non-stop with social gossip throughout their journey together. The doctor's name, Sr. D. Dionisio Cascajares de la Vallina, makes it impossible for the reader to treat him with unmitigated solemnity, even after encountering the narrator's qualifier: "es un médico afamado" [he is a renowned doctor] (2). His contradictory judgments – famous doctor and "persona tan inofensiva como discreta" [as inoffensive a person as he is discreet] (1), when the doctor palpably does not have a discreet bone in his body – lead to the narrator's improbable characterization of medicine as the doctor's "peligrosa y científica profesión" [dangerous and scientific profession] (2), a juxtaposition that appears to repeat Cascajares's own exaltation of his dubiously scientific medical practice. The narrator receives Cascajares's initial greeting with apparent gratitude and humility: "tuvo en aquella crítica ocasión la bondad de saludarme con un sincero y entusiasta apretón de manos" [on that crucial occasion he had the kindness to greet me with a sincere and enthusiastic handshake] (1), revealing the narrator's susceptibility to deferential treatment from a social superior (or someone he perceives as superior). His admiration for the doctor's "dangerous profession" leads us to doubt the doctor's proficiency or scientific training. The narrator's welcoming of Cascajares's attention, if not of his garrulousness, prepares for his subsequent attraction to the Countess's plight, which Cascajares recounts. The name "Dionisio" suggests the source of the *folletín* [*feuilleton* or melodramatic serialized fiction] that the narrator mentally elaborates around the figure of the *Condesa*. The patron of theatre and the inspiration for ritual madness, theatre, and religious ecstasy in Greek mythology, Dionysius provides motivation for the narrator's performance as he physically enacts his response to the Condesa and her presumed pursuer, Mudarra. The last names Cascajares and Vallina undermine the initial identity of the Greek god Dionysius: "cascajares" as the place where debris is thrown and "vallina," which, although not a word, evokes "valley" and such spell-checker-generated corrections as *gallina* [chicken]. In short, it is a pompous and impressive-sounding name that beneath its surface conveys little of significance, reminiscent of the doctor himself. One of the main functions of the narrator's acquaintance with the doctor, then, is to introduce the narrator's psychology and his ineluctable attraction to *folletín* melodrama, the form the doctor's gossiping inevitably takes.

Amann distinguishes between the narrator's "initial observations" of the interior of the trolley car and his later philosophizing on the passengers' comings and goings: "Imitación es esto de la vida humana, en que el nacer y el morir son como las entradas y salidas a que me refiero" [This is an imitation of human life, in that birth and death are like the entrances and exits to which I refer] (5). Amann concludes: "Where in the initial observations the tram is pure metonymy – random juxtaposition of disparate things – it now becomes a meaningful metaphor" of human life (200). The narrator of Galdós's novella carries a newspaper-wrapped package of books onto the tram and as he travels he has to contend with its awkward shape and its intrusion into the limited space available to him. At one point he gives up and sits on the books:

"Íbamos tan estrechos que me molestaba grandemente el paquete de libros que conmigo llevaba, y ya le ponía sobre esta rodilla, ya sobre la otra, ya por fin me resolví a sentarme sobre él, temiendo molestar a la señora inglesa a quien cupo en suerte colocarse a mi siniestra mano" [We were so tightly packed together that the package of books I was carrying with me bothered me a great deal, and first I put it on one knee, and then on the other, then at last I resolved to sit on it, afraid of bothering the English lady who it was just my luck to have on my left] (2). Amann's remark that "the tram is a series of signs that the passenger must decipher" (211) posits the aggravating books as one such sign requiring reader intervention. This preoccupation with books, and the narrator's awareness, in passing, of an Englishwoman, signals their significance, since books and reading set the novella's action in motion. An inveterate reader, as he admits – "Lector yo de muchas y muy malas novelas" [Reader as I am of many and very bad novels] (10) – the narrator has undertaken the journey precisely to return the borrowed books to an unspecified person in Pozas: "me dirigí a la casa donde debía entregar aquellos libros. Devolvílos a la persona que me los había prestado para leerlos" [I set out for the house where I was supposed to deliver those books. I returned them to the person who had lent them to me to read] (19). By osmosis, the unidentified books underneath him become his *libros de caballerías* [novels of chivalry], the impetus and model for the novel his mind elaborates as he travels and to which he attempts to respond dramatically, à la Don Quixote.[8] His Pozas contact and his attitude of admiration for the doctor (undermined by the narrative), as well as the tenor of his readings, raise the possibility that the narrator may perhaps be an employee in a household in the Salamanca neighbourhood, rather than a modern Alonso Quijano.

By weaving together the doctor's gossip, his own acknowledged reading of "muy malas novelas," the fragment of a *folletín* on the newsprint wrapped around his package, and the sight of an unknown man he identifies as the "mayordomo" [majordomo] Mudarra, the narrator constructs in his mind a fiction that adopts the conventions of the *folletín* or melodramatic serialized fiction that dominated the popular press from the 1840s to the early 1900s.[9] As Alan Smith formulates it, the narrator perceives "dentro de la realidad el diseño de una tremenda historieta folletinesca" [within reality the design of an outrageous melodramatic comic strip] (63) whose *folletín* plot is "un cumplido compendio de tópicos del género" [an ample compendium of the genre's commonplaces] (66). The narrator imposes the fictional plot he is mentally constructing on the trolley's interior space, transforming a routine iteration of the streetcar journey, circuitous and never-ending, into the motif of the ship of fools in which a group of people endure a seemingly directionless, unending voyage that cuts them off from the world they know ("Ship of Fools"). In Amann's phrase, the narrator comes "to see the tram as a decipherable space, as a text to be read" (212). As a result, he attempts to identify visually the characters in the text unfolding in his mind. Referring to the scrap of a *folletín* with its plan to catch a Condesa *in flagrante*, which he sets out to thwart by dramatizing the conventions of the *folletin*, the narrator lucidly signals the divide between fiction and real life: "Esto, que en la vida tiene su pro y su contra, en una novela viene como anillo al dedo" [This, which in life has its pluses and its minuses, in a novel fits one's finger like a ring] (10). At this point in the novella, he unerringly differentiates the imagined Condesa, a familiar figure from mass readership sentimental fiction popular especially among women, from his life outside the tramcar.

In the narrator's travels through Madrid, the incompatible spheres of fiction and reality begin to merge and trap innocent victims in their web. The narrator initially draws his identification of the characters in the plot he is constructing from his consciousness of his fellow passengers: "En todos los semblantes que iban sucediéndose dentro del coche, creía ver algo que contribuyera a explicar el enigma" [In all the facial expressions that followed one after the other in the tram car he seemed to see something that helped to explain the enigma] (21). Amann captures the narrator's shift from passive spectator to dramatized spectacle: "On the return trip (from Pozas to Salamanca), the narrator who until now has been a spectator, becomes himself the spectacle: 'sin duda el trastorno interior debía pintarse en mi rostro, porque todos me miraban como se mira lo que no se ve todos los días'" [without a doubt my inner turmoil must be painted on my face, because everyone was looking at me as one looks at that which one doesn't see every day] (Amann 211; Pérez Galdós 21–2). Although he fixates principally on the interior of the carriage, near the end of his return trip his gaze strays to the physical world outside the tramcar, and he incorporates into his melodrama the Madrid he sees from within the carriage: "Entraba el coche por la calle de Serrano, cuando por la ventanilla que frente a mí tenía miré a la calle ... y vi pasar a un hombre ... Mandé parar el coche, y salí, mejor dicho, salté a la puerta tropezando con los pies y piernas de los viajeros; bajé a la calle y corrí tras aquel hombre" [The car was entering Serrano Street when through the window in front of me I looked out at the street ... and I saw a man pass by ... I ordered the trolley to stop, and I got out, or rather, I leapt to the door knocking against the passengers' feet and legs; I landed on the street and ran after that man] (24). Once again, a requisite fictional convention, the capture of the villain, runs into – quite literally – quotidian reality, that is, the villain's identity as a businessman: "el antipático personaje que bauticé con el nombre de Mudarra" [the obnoxious man whom I baptized with the name Mudarra] – a man whom he did not know – turns out to be "un honrado comerciante de ultramarinos" [an honest shopkeeper] (25), the late nineteenth century's model of a modern middle-class citizen. Hence Mudarra figures the novella's tension between capitalism, emblematized by the *tranvía,* and the narrator's invocation of Cervantine and sentimental tropes. Regarding Mudarra, for Luis Fernández Cifuentes the narrator's identification of him with the villain is "an emblem of the precarious relationship between signifiers of all kinds" (296). The critic affirms: "In the world of Galdós, the fact that the supposed traitor is only – and precisely – a 'merchant' will turn out to be the key to the whole displacement of signs" (296). As Fernández Cifuentes concludes, "the failure of resemblances and physiognomical features to mean or to represent anything" conveys Galdós's mocking of "the assumptions of literary conventions" and the code of physiognomy (300). After the narrator's confrontation with Mudarra on the streets of Madrid and the subsequent restoration of the *comerciante*'s rightful identity, the narrator begins a months-long process of recovering his own social identity and sphere of action.

The narrator has interpreted a conversation between a married couple on the trolley as recounting the Countess's demise, whereas, in point of fact, in another class inversion, the couple is discussing their *lavandera* [washerwoman] (23). Smith designates the journey to Pozas as a "'prosificación' efectuada por el mero descenso social del protagonista" ["prosification" brought about by the mere fact of the protagonist's social descent] (66). This "descent" encompasses not only the geographical movement from Salamanca to Pozas but also the misidentification of the Condesa with a *lavandera* and the *mayordomo* Mudarra with a businessman as well as the shifting importance of the Englishwoman. In the tension between the aristocracy in the *folletín* and the working classes in Pozas, Galdós makes reference to historical changes in Madrid society: "the leveling of the aristocracy, with the eclipse of the divine justification of its superiority, along with the bankruptcy and dispossession of all the signs that aristocracy fostered and sustained"

(Fernández Cifuentes 292–3). Fernández Cifuentes further opines that "La novela en el tranvía" is "intent on showing the dispersion of signs that had been upheld by the aristocracy, the insufficiency of accepted codes ... and the precarious relationship between *being* and *meaning*" (294; original emphasis), an unstable dialectic that by the close of the novella the *inglesa* [Englishwoman] comes to figure.

The counterpoint in the novella to the imaginary (if textual) Condesa, around whom the narrator weaves his *folletín*, is his flesh-and-blood travelling companion, the Englishwoman, whom he first represents synecdochically by her hat and unfeelingly accuses of not avoiding the strong-arm tactics employed by the doctor to gain a seat in the trolley car: "la abolladura parcial de cierto sombrero de paja puesto en la extremidad de una cabeza de mujer inglesa, que tras de mi amigo intentaba subir, y que sufrió, sin duda, por falta de agilidad, el rechazo de su bastón" [the partial dent suffered by a certain straw hat placed on top of the head of an Englishwoman, who was trying to get on after my friend and who suffered, without a doubt from a lack of agility, his cane's rejection] (2). Indeed, from the opening lines, the narrator is anything but a gentleman, suggesting that the streetcar creates a social cocoon uncontaminated by the norms dictating proper social interaction in mixed, public society. The narrator behaves as though he were an isolated agent, not constrained in any way by the social group of passengers waiting to enter the carriage, although he attributes this egotistical behaviour to the other travellers as well: "Impulsado por el egoísta deseo de tomar asiento antes que las demás personas movidas de iguales intenciones, eché mano a la barra que sustenta la escalera de la imperial, puse el pie en la plataforma y subí" [Under the impulse of the egotistical desire to get a seat before the other people motivated by identical intentions, I grabbed the railing that supports the *imperial*'s stairs, I placed my foot on the platform, and I got on] (1). Fernández Cifuentes avers that the narrator will only recover his sanity when he "abandons *meanings* for *beings*," when "the Countess of his dreams ... is displaced in his attention by 'la irascible inglesa a quien disloqué un pie' [the irascible Englishwoman whose foot I dislocated]" as he chased after the Condesa's persecutor, the *mayordomo* (297). Having relegated the foreign woman to an obstacle that impeded the thrust of the doctor's cane at the outset of the story, he observes her individual physical reality only when his body interferes with hers, as when, having fallen asleep, "me había dejado caer sobre la venerable inglesa que a mi lado iba" [my body had fallen onto the venerable Englishwoman who sat beside me] (14), or on the return trip from Pozas, when his hasty movements in leaving the car injure her. The "fortísimo golpe en un hombro" [extremely strong blow on the shoulder] that awoke him doubtless came from the same woman.

From the start, the Englishwoman has served as the narrator's nemesis; she is the practical, material obstacle that grounds his flights of "literary" imagination as well as the recipient of his physical aggression throughout the story.[10] The narrator chooses to sit beside her on the return journey, immediately enveloping her in his tale of the Countess: "Señora, no hay duda de que la Condesa murió envenenada o asesinada" [Madame, there is no doubt that the Countess died of poisoning or was assassinated] (20). Although Oliver terms her "an almost inarticulate English lady who had the misfortune to accompany him throughout the trip" (257), her limited Spanish vocabulary embedded in English phrases perfectly conveys her sentiments and adds a further element of comic relief to the novella.

The narrator's infatuation with the story of the Countess is such that the sociological reality of an Englishwoman who speaks little Spanish and travels to Pozas and back on the streetcar, as he does, fails to attract his attention. When he enters the tramcar in Pozas for the return trip, much to his surprise, "lo primero que mis ojos vieron fue la señora inglesa sentadita donde antes estaba" [the first thing my eyes saw was the Englishwoman seated exactly where she was before] (20). Significantly, until he sees the *inglesa*, his mind has been dwelling on "la infortunada Condesa" [ill-fated Countess]. Up to the novella's closing paragraph, the narrator consistently favours the Condesa in this alternative between fantasy (the Countess) and hard-nosed reality (the Englishwoman). Fernández Cifuentes emphasizes the improbability of a Countess riding a streetcar, even one departing from the Salamanca neighbourhood: "It is essential for the story that a streetcar is no place for a Countess, not even in the paranoid view of the insane reader [narrator]" (296). Thus the narrator bases his *folletín* on an absurd juxtaposition of aristocracy and mechanized transport. The mix of passengers representing variations of the middle classes makes the carriage a "'theatre' where innumerable faces that can be observed in great detail incite interpretations," except that the *inglesa*'s face initially does not incite the narrator to any interpretation (296). Her sensible response to his increasing agitation as he loses himself in the *folletín* he is creating passes for humour, rather than corrective truth. In Fernández Cifuentes's reading, the potential for the construction of fictions is implicit in the material circumstances of the streetcar, a phenomenon that also underlies Pardo Bazán's short story, as we will see later. Alan Smith's notion of "prosificación," the replacement of the aristocracy at the centre of a fictional world by the middle class, remains a key effect of Spanish realism. The separation of the trolley from the city and from non-passengers, visible from the carriage but apart from it, makes possible the creation of an alternate reality not tested against the practices of daily life in Madrid.

Critics have effectively tied the plot elaborated by the narrator, with the Condesa at its centre, to *Don Quijote*; however, the annoying Englishwoman also figures an equally valid connection with Cervantes. An everyday, ordinary woman of a very different background from that of the narrator, she may call to mind Aldonza Lorenzo, although he never reimagines her as Dulcinea del Toboso, until perhaps in the story's final sentence, when he acknowledges: "toda la consideración que antes me inspiraba la soñada víctima [la Condesa] la dedico ahora, ¿a quién creeréis? a mi compañera de viaje en aquella angustiosa expedición, a la irascible inglesa, a quien disloqué un pie en el momento de salir atropelladamente del coche para perseguir al supuesto mayordomo" [all of the attention that previously the imagined victim [the Countess] inspired in me I now dedicate – to whom would you-all believe? – to my travelling companion on that distressing expedition, to the irascible Englishwoman, whose foot I dislocated at the moment of leaving the tramcar in haste in order to pursue the presumed majordomo] (25). The closure thus imitates the circular geography of the round trip and the narrator's verbalization of his madness in continuing to evoke the Countess and his repeated aggression towards the Englishwoman.[11] Thus the novella ends with the inversion of the *condesa-inglesa* counterpoint and initiates an infatuation with *la inglesa*, which may signal his cure or alternatively a new madness. In any event, a flesh-and-blood woman has captured his attention with her dramatized negative characteristics, not with abstract, idealized qualities. She is only "irascible" to the extent that she objects to his boorish public behaviour and lack of courtesy to women, but this negative descriptor marks her distance from the Countess exalted by narrator, doctor, and *folletín*. Oliver contends that "every time the narrator perceives a false reality, it is the irascible Englishwoman who suffers." Nevertheless, she proves to be "el único ser vivo que conservó su serenidad de esfinge en la cómica escena" [the only living being who maintained her sphinx-like serenity in the comic scene] (qtd in Oliver 258). As Fernández Cifuentes comments, "The very nature of the streetcar – once more an explicit symbol of life – only allows for unfinished fragments, fragmentary encounters, fragmentary conversations, fragmentary resemblances" (297), including the fragment of the *folletín* and the narrator's erratic interactions with the *inglesa.*

At several months' distance from the public spectacle of his attempted capture of Mudarra, the narrator invokes his experience in the novella's last lines, affirming his return to the reality the *inglesa* also inhabits: "Ha sido preciso que transcurran meses para que las sombras vuelvan al ignorado sitio de donde surgieron volviéndome loco, y torne la realidad a dominar en mi cabeza" [Months have had to pass in order for the shadows to return to the unknown place from which they emerged to drive me crazy, and for reality to dominate in my head] (25). In sum, Galdós's novella captures a fragment of contemporary life in 1871 – a tram ride – even as it veers into an updating of *Don Quijote.* Therefore, while the tram journey comes to a close, the potential for storytelling, for elaborating the story of the narrator and the Englishwoman, does not resolve itself into a conclusion, as would occur in a conventional *folletín.* Galdós's open ending confirms Oliver's dictum that the *pequeño mundo* the narrator has constructed "is representative of ordinary life rather than the heroic, larger than life world" (255); the latter is the sphere of the invented Countess. Galdós pays equal attention to the Englishwoman and immersion into the quotidian practices of the middle classes, as he jumps the narrative beyond the streetcar and into the future. Introducing a further narrative level, the narrator recognizes his authorship of this autobiographical journey, in an affirmation of his firm grasp on reality – the material objects that constitute everyday life – in the time frame beyond the story time: "como ahora creo que es pluma esto con que escribo" [as now I believe that what I am writing with is a pen] (23).

"En tranvía"

Emilia Pardo Bazán's short story "En tranvía," published two decades later, traces a one-way journey from Sol to Serrano, the last leg of the return one in *La novela en el tranvía.* As does Galdós, she employs an unnamed first-person narrator/observer who is not consistently reliable or marked by gender and hence is traditionally read as male (narrative authority being assumed to be male-gendered). In Galdós's fiction the immediate assumption that the narrator is male presents no problem, but in Pardo Bazán's case her gender identity counters the automatic association of the unmarked narrator with a male voice. Susan Lanser poses the question: "does the convention that makes the male voice normative overshadow the presence of a woman's name on the title page?" In response, she maintains that it depends on readers: "the *noted* presence of a female name" as author "signals a female narrative voice in the absence of markings to the contrary" (167; original emphasis). The attention Pardo Bazán's story gives to clothing, motherhood, and the plight of the abandoned woman passenger seems to posit a female narrator; as Susan McKenna notes, the story "details the elegant clothing worn by the majority of the passengers" (81). I would argue, therefore, that the story's discursive practice displays knowledge and affinities that the author's culture links to middle- or upper-middle-class women. Of greater significance, perhaps, is what McKenna recognizes as "the interplay of gendered values and images" in the story (80). In any event, different readings of the story will emerge depending on the gender assigned to the narrator by the reader, resulting in different social and gender dynamics between narrator and woman passenger.

Pardo Bazán contextualizes her story not only in terms of urban geography but more specifically also by season, day of the week, and hour: the Puerta del Sol on a spring Sunday following morning Mass and the collective "callejeo matutinal" [morning stroll through the streets][12] or window shopping; in short, at the Sunday mid-day lunch hour. Here the day and hour signify as much as spatial factors in determining who travels and where. The trolley bears the emotions the narrator projects on it: "¡Ah, qué alegría el domingo madrileño, qué aristocrático el tranvía [*sic*]" [Ah, what happiness a Sunday in Madrid brings, how aristocratic is the trolley]. Unlike Galdós's novella, the story invokes from the start a community of passengers who share destinations in the Salamanca neighbourhood and the common experience of Mass and/or the Sunday purchase of pastries and flowers. Nevertheless, as in the novella, the crowd "asalta" [assaults] the trolley in its attempt to board rapidly, manifesting the breakdown of middle-class decorum in mass cultural practices. This external reality, beyond the tramcar, impinges on the mood and immediate expectations of the passengers and shapes reader assumptions and responses. As a "temporary leveler of class distinctions" (McKenna 81n24), the internal space of the trolley reflects the socioeconomic conditions of central Madrid as well as, for most passengers, the practice of Christian and alimentary rituals. Michael Ugarte articulates Madrid's broader urban geographical profile, silenced by the story, noting that by 1890 Madrid had experienced: "the beginning of two phases of urban development at once: 1) rapid industrial growth and 2) the appearance of the urban rim surrounding the city: pockets of poverty brought on by emigration from rural areas" (266). Ugarte makes a fundamental point in recognizing the implications of Madrid's economic stratification, both horizontal (geographical) and vertical (by class), in this and other urban stories by the author: "Pardo Bazán's urban stories have to do with intrusions, social juxtapositions as well as ethical questions that force her readers to think about concrete urban problems and concrete solutions" (268).

Within the trolley, the seated narrator's gaze encompasses all the car's passengers in turn, focusing in particular on a baby, in preparation for the story's unexpected dénouement. Passing the children in review, she describes them in consonance with the hyperbole of the story's initial paragraphs and with an emotional enthusiasm that perhaps confirms her female voice: "¡... y qué niños tan elegantes, tan bonitos, tan bien tratados! Dan ganas de comérselos a besos" [and what elegant children, how pretty, how well treated! They make one want to smother them with kisses]. Her paean culminates in the physical impulse to run fingers through their blond hair. Almost opposite the narrator is "un bebé de pocos meses" [a baby just a few months old], characterized in detail that serves as a counterpoint to the story's conclusion and includes a significant phrase linking the child with divine approbation and purity: "irradiando luz del cielo en sus ojos puros" [radiating heavenly light in its pure eyes]. Lastly, she mentions the disruptive figure of a lower-class woman passenger whose presence negates the tramcar's cheerful air of Sunday contentment.

Contrasting with the well-dressed bourgeois passengers is the vehicle itself, "el plebeyo tranvía" [the plebeian trolley], which nevertheless "reluce orgullosamente al sol" [gleams proudly in the sun] and comports itself as if it were a fine carriage: "landó forrado de rasolis, arrastrado por un tronco inglés legítimo" [landau upholstered in satin, pulled by a pair of legitimate English horses].[13] The protean trolley, as imagined by the narrator ensconced inside, changes from *aristocrático* to *plebeyo*, depending upon its function: as a realist mechanical object of a certain age, it is undoubtedly plebeian; as a mode of transport fit for such a Sunday crowd, it mirrors their aristocratic pretensions.[14] The time, place, and tone of the story transform the space of the *tranvía* into a special manifestation of privilege. The tension between well-used, everyday technology and the refined assembly aboard it further contrasts with the passengers on other tram lines: "En vez del olor chotuno que suelen exhalar los cargamentos de obreros allá en las líneas del Pacífico y del Hipódromo, flotan en la atmósfera del tranvía emanaciones de flores, vaho de cuerpos limpios y brisas del iris de la ropa blanca" [Instead of the bad odour that the tramcars' cargos of workers customarily let off over there on the Pacific and Hippodrome Lines, emanations of flowers, a whiff of clean bodies and iris-scented breezes from linens and bedding].[15] The narrator projects the bourgeoisie's blatant prejudice against the working class, an attitude no doubt shared by the other middle-class occupants of the tram and perhaps by the story's author herself. The narrator completes her review of the passengers by imagining someone who has dropped a coin and, in retrieving it, voyeuristically contemplates the passengers' stylish, immaculate nether regions: "piececitos chicos, tacones Luis XV, encajes de enaguas y tobillos menudos" [tiny little feet, Louis XV heels, lace petticoats, and slim ankles]. These almost invisible items of dress confirm the integrity of the passengers' self-presentation, as well as the narrator's thorough perusal of her subjects that carries beyond the bounds of her gaze on the trolley. The initial realist depiction of the passengers conveyed by the narrator's gaze and assessment gives way to her interpretation of the characters' responses to the disruptive woman passenger and their invocation of the firmly embedded prejudices shared by their social class.

As in Galdós's novella, a woman figures the contrast to what appears to be the initial plot dynamic. In the face of the self-satisfied, comfortable, well-bred, well-housed, and well-fed middle-class passengers in their Sunday finery, a poor woman with a child (inevitably invoking the Virgin and Child) also boards the trolley in Sol and proves unable to pay the paltry fifteen-*céntimo* fare to the end of the line. "En tranvía" veers briefly into *costumbrismo* in the narrator's discussion of the *mantón* [shawl] worn by the *mujer de pueblo*. In this case, the metonymic *mantón* "revela la sórdida miseria, el cansado desaliento de una vida aperreada y angustiosa, el encogimiento de hambre, el supremo indiferentismo del dolor, la absoluta carencia de pretensiones de la mujer a quien marchitó la adversidad y que ha renunciado por completo, no sólo a la esperanza de agradar, sino al sexo" [reveals the sordid squalour, the exhausted despondency of an irritating and anguished life, the shrivelling from hunger, the supreme indifference to pain, the absolute lack of pretensions of the woman whom adversity has dried up and who has renounced completely, not only the desire to please, but her sexual identity]. To the narrator's inquiry about her tram stop, the destitute woman responds: "Quiá. Si voy mucho más lejos. Sabe Dios, desde el cocherón, lo que andaré a pie todavía" [No way. I am going much, much farther. God knows how long I will walk on foot from the end of the line]. The narrator's attention to clothing to establish class distinctions and define emotional states and her knowledge of at least certain aspects of lower-class living conditions prepare Ugarte's blunt acknowledgment of the geographical reality underlying the woman's journey: "This particular woman, however, will proceed on foot to the squalid outskirts of the city" (266). With a deaf ear to social and political vindications, the narrator bluntly states that the woman "padecía amarguras más crueles aún que la miseria" [was suffering sorrows more cruel even than destitution] and avers knowingly of the *pueblo*: "La miseria a secas la acepta con feliz resignación el pueblo español, siempre ageno a reivindicaciones socialistas. Pobreza es el sino del pobre, y a nada conduce el protestar" [The Spanish people accept poverty plain and simple with happy resignation, always unconnected from socialist vindications]. Despite this fatalistic philosophy, the narrator's reading of the destitute woman's physiognomy (she is a text, after all, like the scrap of newsprint Galdós's narrator reads) reveals "una cosa más terrible, menos usual en la miseria: era la desesperación" [a more terrible thing, less common in destitution: it was desperation]. This extraordinary emotion prepares the ground for the destitute woman and child to occupy the narrator's and passengers' gaze and usurp their emotions for the remainder of their journey.

The narrator derives her authority from her knowledge of Spanish cultural practices across classes and conveys both the norm and the passengers' range of responses to the unexpected woman in the tramcar, insisting on the image of virtuous citizens returning to their homes for a substantial Sunday lunch. She gazes at the mother and baby with charitable empathy and imbues her woman with a degree of subjectivity. She emphasizes the woman's fulfilment of her maternal duties, attributing to her a flawless visual performance of middle-class norms of motherhood in the presentation of her baby. The complacency of Sunday well-being falters under the enormity of such entrenched and unresolvable misery and suffering. Abandoned by her husband two months earlier – "¡Mi marido se me ha ido con otra!" [My husband has left me for another woman!] – the mother rages against her fate, ignoring her audience, caught up in the overpowering emotions of her own world, as was Galdós's narrator. Just as the gaze in Galdós's novella reverses direction at its climax, from the Condesa to the *inglesa*, Pardo Bazán's short story shifts its gaze from the passengers' fixation on the anomalous woman to the narrator's scrutiny of herself and the reactions of other passengers.

In reversing her gaze, the narrator morphs into the protagonist of "En tranvía," initially judging her fellow travellers' charity harshly, finding their small collections of coins to be a superficial response to the endemic poverty of Madrid's underclass. Not only the few words spoken by the nameless, working-class woman but her failure to voice the culturally sanctioned phrases of gratitude for the passengers' charity make her behaviour transgress their expectations (McKenna 80). In short, McKenna maintains, "she violates the traditional custom of lower-class deference to the moneyed elite" (81). The narrator's maxim characterizes the passengers' reactions to the woman – "El que da limosna es casi siempre un egoistón de marca" [A person who gives alms is almost always outstandingly selfish] – as she follows their emotional turmoil. Picking up again the *costumbrista* thread, the narrator traces the emotional upheaval that the passengers experience from spontaneous, if limited, generosity to embarrassment and public shame: "Charlando así, encubrían el hallarse avergonzados, no de la buena acción, sino del error o chasco sentimental que les ocasionara" [By chatting that way, they were covering up the fact of finding themselves to be ashamed, not of their good action, but by the emotional error or let-down that caused them to do it]. Turning her gaze inward, the narrator herself comes under scrutiny, first by herself and then by her readers. With the pious authority voiced in sentimental domestic novels, which predominantly attracted women readers, and with the firmness of righteous self-certainty, the narrator addresses the mother in the borrowed discourse of female abnegation: "Mañana el chico aprenderá un oficio y la servirá a Vd. de amparo. Las madres no tienen derecho a achicarse así mientras sus hijos viven" [Tomorrow the boy will learn a trade and he will be your support. Mothers do not have the right to let themselves be overwhelmed like this while their children are alive].[16]

If "En tranvía" takes on commonplaces of the *folletín* in assigning the worst possible circumstances to the abandoned woman, the narrator's clichéd discourse and righteous moral certitude – one day your child will be your saviour – also echo popular sensational fiction. The passengers' meaningless platitudes in the face of sociological reality have their counterpart in the narrator's attempt to forge an uplifting ethical discourse, proving her as hypocritical as the other passengers – and equally blind to the facts of the situation. When only the narrator and the abandoned woman remain on the trolley, the woman initiates eye-to-eye contact that shifts their balance of power: "volvióse y clavó en mí sus ojos irritados y secos" [she turned around and fixed on me her inflamed and dry eyes]. The story's stunning reversal comes in its final sentence, when for the first time the narrator sees the child's face and herself confronts the brutal truth: "el hijo de la abandonada era cieguecito" [the abandoned woman's son was blind]. The mother has no economic future, not even when her child matures, only the prospect of raising a permanently dependent child who can never contribute to the household. At the privileged, closing moment, the motif of "eyes" and "seeing" reaches its climax: "la mujer, agarrando a la criatura, la levantó en vilo y me la presentó ... sus pupilas, abiertas de par en par. Abiertas, sí, pero blancas, cuajadas, inmóviles. El hijo de la abandonada era cieguecillo" [The woman, holding onto to her little child, raised him up and handed him to me anxiously/uneasily ... with his pupils wide open. Open, yes, but blank, coagulated, unmoving. The abandoned woman's son was blind]. The effect of this sudden revelation is heightened by both the tenderness of the diminutive, "cieguecillo," and the contrast with the physical well-being of the other children that rode the Sunday trolley.

Pious words, self-help clichés, moral dictates, and the money collected – none of these addresses the abject destitution and hopelessness of Madrid's outlying poverty. Although the story concludes as the trolley reaches the terminal of the Serrano line, the point at which the woman and child must descend, the narrator/protagonist necessarily remains on board to transmit the standoff to readers. For mother and child this is metaphorically a journey that does not end. But why, except for narrative exigency, does the narrator continue to the terminal as a passenger? Is it the intent to bring the story to an end within the static enclosure of the tramcar? For the destitute woman, the trolley ride was a parenthesis in her life, a speaking the truth to an audience who did not want to hear her and barely listened, an attempt at catharsis via confession that still left her abandoned and far from home. For the other passengers, including the narrator, the tram ride was the modern, practical, time- and money-saving means to return home, unexpectedly converted into a confrontation with the reality of the city's despairing working class. Any conclusion to the story, beyond the words of the text, lies with its readers who, even as the narrator rejects the hypocrisy of the other passengers, may opt to reject the narrator's failed hypocritical intervention and imagine for themselves a response to Madrid's endemic poverty.

Conclusion

Galdós's novella and Pardo Bazán's story share implicit references to the growing industrialization that grounds life in modern Madrid as the turn of the twentieth century approaches. The narrators of both works, and the other passengers in the short story, attempt to create through discourse an alternative world to the oasis inside the tramcar, one that ignores the economic transformations taking place in the city, outside the trolley. Spain's old aristocracy has lost power, but as the Salamanca neighbourhood reminds us, there is a new aristocracy of wealth; this economic reality has dispossessed the underclass and pushed it farther from the centre of Madrid. These changes reflect the reality of mechanical and industrial modernity. Cervantine irony in the novella shapes the tension still gripping the narrator's mind as he veers between infatuation for his construct, the Condesa, and the physical reality of the *inglesa*, between fiction and fact. In the closing lines the Englishwoman's presence evokes the niece that greets Don Quixote on his final return home and potential reinsertion into daily life. In contrast, the echoes of irony seemingly have no place in the social consciousness and moral parameters of "En tranvía," where empathy and pathos dominate.

Both works seek a voice of sanity to impose some counterbalance to the discursive fantasies of the narrators. In Galdós this role falls to the Englishwoman; in Pardo Bazán's story, first to the narrator and then to the readers. No matter in what direction the characters of the two works attempt to highjack social reality with their iterations of *folletín* conventions, both authors ground their fictions firmly in the sociological reality of Madrid, both at the opening of their texts and, in the novella, at the end, as they continue the cultural work of expressing how Spain imagines itself through realist discourse. Amann punningly concludes of Galdós's novella that "by applying the commonplaces of the serial novel to the common place that is the tram, the narrator seeks to reduce the alienation of the modern urban experience," an alienation that Pardo Bazán's narrator cannot assuage with moral platitudes (212). Hence, the novella ends with the *rapprochement* of narrator and Englishwoman, integrating the margins into the collective social sphere, whereas the despair Pardo Bazán depicts does not submit to resolution or even to melioration. In her story the construction of a cross-class community, if only for the duration of a relatively short tramcar journey, remains unimagined and unimaginable. Her metaphorical *tranvía* is either *plebeyo* or *aristocrático*, in its human interior and physical exterior, but not an amalgam of the two. The unending repetition of the trolley journey in both texts emblematizes the dualities explored by both authors and left for their readers to resolve.

NOTES

1 Elizabeth Amann's article relates Galdós's novella to other European literary works incorporating the streetcar.
2 The electrical power plant went on line on 3 October 1898 ("El tranvía de la calle Serrano").
3 *La Ilustración Americana y Española* featured the inauguration of the mule-drawn tramcars on its cover for 15 June 1871. In the week's "Revista General," the periodical's chronicler, el Marqués de Valle-Alegre, announced that "ahora acaba de establecerse un *tram-vía,* el cual va de la Puerta del Sol al extremo del barrio de Salamanca, y muy pronto extenderá su radio desde éste hasta el de Argüelles" [a tramway has just now been established, which runs from the Puerta del Sol to the far end of the Salamanca neighbourhood and very soon will extend its radius from Salamanca to the Argüelles neighbourhood] and then thanked "la sociedad inglesa ... [que] ha introducido una mejora apreciable en la capital de España" [the English company ... that has introduced a valuable improvement into Spain's capital] (15, no. 16: 267). The use of the spelling *tramvía* continued; witness the ad placed by the Compañía General Española de Tramvías in the *Ilustración Americana y Española* on 15 November 1877 (21.42: 311). At the end of the century, *Nuevo Mundo* featured "El tranvía eléctrico" in a full-page humorous essay on 7 September 1898 with an accompanying illustrative caricature by Sileno.
4 All citations from Galdós's novella draw from the Biblioteca Virtual Miguel de Cervantes digital edition based on the *La Ilustración de Madrid* original. Page numbers correspond to a printout of the Biblioteca Virtual edition.
5 The Real Academia Española dictionary defines *la imperial* as "Sitio con asientos que algunos carruajes tenían encima de la cubierta" [A space with seats that some carriages had on the rooftop].
6 The engraving of Madrid's earliest tramcars in the 15 June 1871 issue of *La Ilustración Española y Americana* clearly shows eighteen seated passengers downstairs and a further number on the roof, specified elsewhere as an additional eighteen seated passengers. Other sources figure the car's capacity differently; for example: "32 viajeros sentados y otros 11 de pie

en las dos plataformas, accediéndose al piso superior o imperial mediante dos escaleras de caracol" [thirty-two seated travellers and another eleven standing on the two platforms, with access to the open upper or *imperial* level by means of the two circular staircases] (Gutiérrez 36).

7 Linking this essay to Susan McKenna's richly suggestive study in this volume, the principal character in each work in my essay shares characteristics with the *flâneur*, albeit a sedentary observer limited to the fixed route of the trolley's iron rails, before whom the massed ambulatory pedestrians pass as they enter and exit the car. Thus the observer of society remains positioned in the tramcar while it traverses the dichotomy of Madrid society. In accord with McKenna's definition of the *flâneur*, Galdós's narrator "treats the people he sees and the objects he observes as 'texts' for his own pleasure" (193, below).

8 The growing body of criticism on the novella has treated in illuminating detail its Cervantine elements, especially the Clavileño episode, including Oliver, Fernández Cifuentes, Smith, and, most recently, Amann, among others. The latter comments that "critics of the story have generally focused on this fiction within the fiction, emphasizing the metatextual and intertextual dimensions of the story: the narrator's confusion of the boundaries between fiction and reality, Galdós's rejection of the genre of the *feuilleton* and its melodramatic logic, and the way in which the story anticipates his later novels" (193).

9 Elisa Martí-López defines the *folletín* as "the tradition of melodramatic novel writing associated with popular and mostly female readership. More generally, *folletín* stands for commercial literature, that is, for novels created mechanically by the new publishing industry to secure a wide and immediate success among unsophisticated readers (*folletín* is thus often denounced as an example of the commodification of literature)" (65–6).

10 English characters appear in the fiction of major Spanish authors on either side of the turn of the twentieth century, among them Maud Baldwin, the daughter of a Protestant minister, in Pardo Bazán's 1890 novels, *Una cristiana* and *La prueba*. It is tempting to identify the Englishwoman in Galdós's novella as someone who lives with and works for one of the wealthy families in the Salamanca neighbourhood, perhaps as a governess. Surprisingly, critical studies have not examined the role of the *inglesa* and have also ignored her significance at the novella's close.

11 Realist fiction frequently displays a fascination with women's feet and by extension their footwear, not surprisingly, since feet were the only visible part of their lower body. Galdós develops a degree of foot fetishism in *Tormento*, *Tristana*, *La desheredada*, and other works. Chad Wright figures

among the early critics to signal the metonymic and sexual connotations of foot and shoe motifs in Galdós's fiction. What are readers to make of the feet of the Englishwoman who travels alone on public transport? Does her unconventional independence trip her up? On the outbound journey, the doctor uses his (phallic) cane to keep her in her place as he enters the car; on the return trip, the narrator dislocates her ankle in his haste to descend from the carriage. Does this bond bind her to the narrator in a loss of independence, à la Tristana? Or is the ironic Cervantine mode still in play?

12 All citations from Pardo Bazán's "En tranvía" come from the story's original newspaper publication: it appears on a single page of *Los Lunes de El Imparcial*. Hence the absence of page numbers.

13 First termed *aristocrático* and now *plebeyo*, the trolley car incarnates the mood of its passengers or perhaps that of the narrator.

14 McKenna's discussion, in this volume (193), of the dichotomous contrasting façades of the San Sebastián church in Galdós's *Misericordia* suggests the possibility of a structural counterpoint in the duality of the trolleys, which take on different passengers and social identities along their trajectory, especially in the contrast between the two ends.

15 The narrator's paean to the assembled riders ends with a reference to a housewife selecting a Sunday treat for the family – "la escogida fruta o el apetetoso dulce que la dueña en persona eligió en casa de Martinho o de Prast" [the select fruit or appetizing sweet that the lady of the house selected personally at Martinho or Prast] – and again suggests the shopping experience of a female narrator with knowledge of the best specialty shops.

16 This is a key phrase for determining which gendered identity readers assign to the narrator. Does "las madres" include the narrator, in which case she is female, or does a male narrative voice speak of "las madres" as "others"?

WORKS CITED

Amann, Elizabeth. "Reading (on) the Tram." *Orbis Litterarum* 69.3 (April 2014): 193–214. Print. https://doi.org/10.1111/oli.12029.

Fernández Cifuentes, Luis. "Signs for Sale in the City of Galdós." *MLN* 103.2 (March 1988): 289–311. Print. https://doi.org/10.2307/2905343.

Furst, Lilian R. *All Is True: The Claims and Strategies of Realist Fiction*. Durham, NC: Duke UP, 1995. Print.

Gutiérrez, Diego. *Aquellos tranvías de Madrid* ... Madrid: La Librería, 2007. Print.

"*Imperial, La.*" *Diccionario de la Real Academia Española*. Web. www.rae.es. 15 March 2015.

Lanser, Susan Sniader. *The Narrative Act: Point of View in Prose Fiction*. Princeton: Princeton UP, 1981. Print.

Manuelblas. *Tranvías de Madrid*. Madrid, 22 February 2015. Web. http://manuelblasdos.blogspot.com/2015/02/tranvias-de-madrid.html.

Martí-López, Elisa. "The *Folletín*: Spain Looks to Europe." In *The Cambridge Companion to the Spanish Novel: From 1600 to the Present*, ed. Harriet Turner and Adelaida López de Martínez. Cambridge: Cambridge UP, 2003. 65–80. Print.

McKenna, Susan M. *Crafting the Female Subject: Narrative Innovation in the Short Fiction of Emilia Pardo Bazán*. Washington, DC: Catholic U of America, 2009. Print.

Oliver, Walter. "'La novela en el tranvía': Fantasy and the Art of Realistic Narration." *MLN* 88.2 (March 1973): 249–63. Print. https://doi.org/10.2307/2907511.

Pardo Bazán, Emilia. *Cuentos completos*. Ed. Juan Paredes Núñez. Vol. 2. La Coruña: Fundación Pedro Barrié de la Maza, 1990. 97–101. Print.

– *Cuentos dramáticos*. Ed. Luis López Nieves. Ciudad Seva. Web. http://www.ciudadseva.com/textos/cuentos/esp/pardo/cuentos_dramaticos.htm. 19 April 2015.

– "En tranvía." *Los Lunes de El Imparcial*, 24 February 1890: n.p. [1]. http://hemerotecadigital.bne.es/issue.vm?id=0000670127&search=&lang=en.

– *En tranvía* (*Cuentos dramáticos*). In *Obras Completas* 23. Madrid: Pueyo, n.d. [1901].

Parsons, Deborah L. *A Cultural History of Madrid: Modernism and the Urban Spectacle*. Oxford: Berg, 2003. Print.

Pérez Galdós, Benito. "La novela en el tranvía." *La Ilustración de Madrid* 30 November 1871 and 15 December 1871.

– "La novela en el tranvía." In *La voz de la conseja, selección de las mejores novelas breves y cuentos de los más esclarecidos literatos*. Vol. 1. Ed. Emilio Carrere. Madrid: San Calleja, n.d. [1917]. 17–58. Print.

– "La novela en el tranvía." Web. http://www.cervantesvirtual.com/obra-visor-din/la-novela-en-el-tranvía. 6 April 2015.

– *Obras completas*. Ed. F.C. Sainz de Robles. 7th ed. Madrid: Aguilar, 1963. 6:16. Print.

"Pozas, el 'barrio de al lado' que desapareció." Web. http://www.somosmalasana.com/pozas-el-%E2%80%9Cbarrio-de-al-lado%E2%80%9D-que-desaparecio/. 15 April 2015.

"Ship of Fools." Web. http://en.wikipedia.org/wiki/Ship_of_fools. 15 April 2015.

Smith, Alan E. *Los cuentos inverosímiles de Galdós en el contexto de su obra.* Barcelona: Anthropos, 1992. Print.

"El tranvía de la calle Serrano." Web. https://historia-urbana-madrid.blogspot.com/2010/09/el-tranvia-de-la-calle-serrano.html. 19 November 2018.

Turner, Harriet S. "Benito Pérez Galdós." In *The Cambridge History of Spanish Literature*, ed. David T. Gies. Cambridge: Cambridge UP, 2005. 392–409. Print.

Ugarte, Michael. "The Generational Fallacy and Spanish Women Writing at the Turn of the Century." *Siglo 20/20th Century* 12.1–2 (1994): 261–76. Print.

Wright, Chad C. "'La eterna mascarada hispanomatritense': Clothing and Society in *Tormento.*" *Anales Galdosianos* 20.2 (1985): 25–35. Print.

6 Urban Hyperrealism: Galdós's Dickensian Descriptions of Madrid

LINDA M. WILLEM

In the "Nuevos viajes" [New Voyages] chapter of *Memorias de un desmemoriado* [Memories of an Absent-Minded Man], Benito Pérez Galdós tells the story of his travels through England and his pilgrimage to Westminster Abbey, where he visited the tomb of Charles Dickens to pay his respects to the "gran novelador inglés" [great English novelist] (1468). Calling him "mi maestro más amado" [my most beloved teacher] and "un santo de mi devoción más viva" [a saint of my most fervent devotion], Galdós recalls that "en mi aprendizaje literario, cuando aún no había salido de mi mocedad petulante ... me apliqué con loco afán a la copiosa obra de Dickens" [in my literary apprenticeship, when I still hadn't departed from my petulant youth ... I applied myself with a crazed eagerness to Dickens's copious body of work] (1469). These words, written in 1916, attest to the lasting influence of the English author on Galdós, who published his first article about Dickens in 1868. Praising his "admirable fuerza descriptiva" [admirable descriptive power], the young Galdós noted that Dickens does not depict the "líneas precisas" [precise lines] or "la forma exacta" [the exact form] of objects, choosing instead to describe things and places in a "modo general" [general manner] ("Carlos Dickens" 452). Galdós also observed that Dickens "no ve en el objeto más que aquella parte, aquella línea que influye en el conjunto de la escena, que añade algo a la totalidad del cuadro" [doesn't see in an object more than that part, that line that influences the overall scene, that adds something to the totality of the painting] (453). Furthermore, Galdós admired his ability to present "espacio sin límites" [spaces without limits] in which it is possible to see "innumerables objetos, sin poder examinar ninguno" [innumerable objects, without being able to examine any of them] (452).[1]

Hyperrealism is the word that John Reed and Julian Wolfreys use to classify this descriptive effect of Dickens. While in the visual arts the term hyperrealism refers to the augmentation, intensification, and overabundance of visual details used by artists to create representations of reality whose precision and perfection surpass reality itself, paradoxically Reed (in *Dickens's Hyperrealism*) and Wolfreys (in *Writing London*) employ this word to show how it is precisely the *minimal* amount of detail in Dickens's descriptions that gives the reader the impression that his fictional reality is greater than the actual reality of the physical world. Both scholars focus their attention on the way that Dickens describes London. According to Reed, Dickens's descriptions require his readers to use their imagination and knowledge of the capital to fill in the details and provide what he has not mentioned, creating a personalized mental description that is more detailed than what could have been expressed in words written by the author. Wolfreys, on the other hand, notes that Dickens's descriptions tend to consist of long lists of objects without focusing on them individually, thereby communicating to the reader a sense of the capital as infinite, larger than life, and impossible to be known or represented in all that it contains. For Reed and Wolfreys, Dickens's novelistic London is hyperreal because it *seems* more real than geographical London.

If Dickens is the writer most associated with London, the same can be said about Galdós and Madrid. The two novelists dedicated themselves to representing the capitals of their respective countries during the dynamic period of the nineteenth century. As Lilian R. Furst states in *All Is True: The Claims and Strategies of Realist Fiction*, "particularity of place is one of the cardinal conventions of the realist novel" (24), and famous locations "may be compared to a kind of anchor, which grounds the created universe of the fiction in a knowable dimension of actuality ... to which readers are able to relate" (105). Consequently, place-names such as London and Madrid "represent an open space in which readers' imagination may engage simultaneously with prior experience and with the text" (104). However, Furst stresses that the "air of reality" contained within realist fiction is not dependent upon "a literal truthfulness, in the sense of a faithful imitation of prior reality" (173), but rather, it emerges as an "impression of truth" through the interplay between the external world and the fictive one created by the author using textual strategies and narrative techniques that provide the reader with "a possible continuance of reality" instead of a "mimetic replica" of it (114). The techniques identified by Reed and Wolfreys exemplify this process of "performative pretense" (Furst 115), in which the reader collaborates with the author in the formation of "Dickens's London," and

Galdós, by using these same techniques in his *Novelas Contemporáneas*, similarly assists his readers in constructing "Galdós's Madrid." This group of novels, designated as such by Galdós himself and published between 1881 and 1889, are considered to be his most mature works of literary realism. Passages from three of these, *La desheredada* [The Disinherited Lady] (1881), *La de Bringas* [That Bringas Woman] (1884), and *Fortunata y Jacinta* (1886–7), will be cited below to exemplify Galdós's use of place descriptions that employ Dickensian techniques.

According to Reed, Dickens exhibits constraint in his descriptions of London in order to allow "his readers to participate inventively" in the formation of the city locations (20). Dickens provides the framework upon which his readers can add specific elements, thereby making the description a collaborative process in which "fiction outstrips without overstepping reality" (23). Reed cites the following paragraphs from chapter 50 of *Oliver Twist* as an example of Dickens's descriptive style:

> Crazy wooden galleries common to the backs of half a dozen houses, with holes from which to look upon the slime beneath; windows, broken and patched, with poles thrust out, on which to dry the linen that is never there; rooms so small, so filthy, so confined, that the air would seem too tainted even for the dirt and squalor which they shelter; wooden chambers thrusting themselves out above the mud, and threatening to fall into it – as some have done; dirt-besmeared walls and decaying foundations; every repulsive lineament of poverty, every loathsome indication of filth, rot, and garbage; all these ornament the banks of Folly Ditch.
>
> In Jacob's Island, the warehouses are roofless and empty; the walls are crumbling down; the windows are windows no more; the doors are falling into the streets; the chimneys are blackened, but they yield no smoke. Thirty or forty years ago, before losses and chancery suits came upon it, it was a thriving place; but now it is a desolate island indeed. The houses have no owners; they are broken open, and entered upon by those who have the courage; and there they live, and there they die. They must have powerful motives for a secret residence, or be reduced to a destitute condition indeed, who seek a refuge in Jacob's Island. (Reed 16)

According to Reed, this description appears to be detailed, but it is not. Instead of "a torrent of details," Dickens sketches an outline of the place, including just those elements that are necessary for his readers to be able to identify the type of location to which it belongs (23). This is a neighbourhood in ruin, poor and dangerous, and after identifying it as such, the readers can resort to the information they possess about such places to fill in the outline. This participation by the reader not only creates the impression of a more complete description than it actually is, but also intensifies the impact of the description. It is hyperreal because it links fictive and geographical realities through the imagination and knowledge of the reader.

"It could be argued that much of the power of the description relies on what is not there," states Reed, who contrasts this passage with the more detailed non-fictional descriptions of slum conditions that frequently were published during this era (16). Interestingly, in his book *Realist Vision*, Peter Brooks makes the same contrast, but comes to a different conclusion. Citing a highly detailed portion of Friedrich Engels's *The Conditions of the Working Class in London of 1844* as his model, Brooks faults Dickens for what he "can't do, what he avoids seeing or speaking about" (43). Brooks goes on to say that "if, in my argument, realism tends to be intensely visual, concerned with seeing and registering, and therefore has frequent recourse to the descriptive, here one could tax Dickens with a certain refusal to see, an avoidance of the inventories of the real that we normally associate with realism" (43). Indeed, it is Brooks's focus on the visual that leads him to label Dickens's descriptions as "non-representation" because they do not include all that is visible (40). But Reed is pointing out the greater power that can be achieved by combining what is stated by the narrator with what is left open for the reader to imagine.

The recent growth in the application of cognitive science to the study of literature can provide insights into how the reader's imaginative contribution functions in Dickens's descriptions of place. In his article "The Way We Imagine," cognitive scientist Mark Turner explains that the imaginative process depends upon what he calls "double-scope blending" (41–2). This is a form of conceptual integration and compression in which human beings can blend two different conceptual input arrays to form a third mental array by drawing upon the shared structure informing the two input arrays to make analogical connections. The greater the degree of difference between the two input arrays, the greater the degree of imagination needed to form the third mental array. Thus, for the reader of Dickens, the shared structure is the actual historical city, while one conceptual input array is the reader's knowledge of the city, and the other is the description of the city within the novel. Dickens's minimally detailed descriptions encourage a greater degree of double-scope blending because the reader must fill in more gaps in order to make the connections. Not only does the reader become more active, but the blend also becomes more imaginatively charged. Highly detailed descriptions lack the power of the reader's imagination. They convey clarity and specificity but leave little or no room for the reader to participate. Whereas the readers of Engels receive a more detailed account of what the narrator sees, their engagement is passive. The readers of Dickens's descriptive outline can actively add details acquired through their own experience or through their readings of non-fictional accounts, thereby "seeing" not only what the narrator relates but also what they imagine as being there.

We can see a similarity between the description of the above-mentioned neighbourhood in *Oliver Twist* and that of the slums of Madrid in chapter 6, section 2 of *La desheredada*:

> El barranco de Embajadores, que baja del Salitre, es hoy en su primera zona una calle decente. Atraviesa la Ronda y se convierte en despeñadero, rodeado de casuchas que parecen hechas con amasada ceniza. Después no es otra cosa que una sucesión de muladares, forma intermedia entre la vivienda y la cloaca. Chozas, tinglados, construcciones que juntamente imitan el palomar y la pocilga, tienen su cimiento en el lado de la pendiente. Allí se ven paredes hechas con la muestra de una tienda o el encerado negro de una clase de Matemáticas; techos de latas claveteadas; puertas que fueron portezuelas de ómnibus, y vidrieras sin vidrios de antiquísimos balcones. Todo es allí vejez, polilla; todo está a punto de desquiciarse y caer. Es una ciudad movediza compuesta de ruinas. Al fin de aquella barriada está lo que queda de la antigua Arganzuela: un llano irregular, limitado de la parte de Madrid por lavaderos, y de la parte del campo por el arroyo propiamente dicho. Este precipita sus aguas blanquecinas entre collados de tierra que parecen montones de escombros y vertederos de derribos. La línea de circunvalación atraviesa esta soledad. Parte del suelo es lugar estratégico, lleno de hoyos, eminencias, escondites y burladeros, por lo que se presta al juego de los chicos y al crimen de los hombres. (*La desheredada* 101–2)

> [The Embajadores ravine, descending from Salitre, these days starts out as a decent street. It crosses through the Ronda and changes into a cliff, lined with hovels that look as if they had been made of piles of ash. After that it is no more than a succession of trash heaps, resembling something between a home and a cesspool. Shacks and sheds, constructions which are half pigeon-coop and half pig-pen, have their foundations on the side

> of the slope. There you can see walls made from the display case of a store or the blackboard from a mathematics classroom; roofs made from nailed tins; doors that used to be on buses, and glassless windows from old balconies. Everything there is old, moth-eaten; everything is on the verge of falling apart. It is an ever-changing city made of ruins. At the end of that district is what remains of the old Arganzuela neighbourhood; an irregular plain, bordered on the Madrid side by wash-houses, and on the country side by a creek that streams its cloudy water through mounds of earth that look like piles of rubble or demolition dumps. The railway line around the city cuts through this lonely place. Part of the ground is a strategic region, filled with holes, hills, hiding places, and barricaded enclosures, lending itself to the games of children and the crimes of men].

Like Jacob's Island, this neighbourhood actually exists geographically, and like Dickens, Galdós describes it in a generalized way, without dwelling on each element. Rather, it is the *combination* of its elements that work together to communicate to the reader the *feeling* of poverty, desolation, and danger. Included in Mesonero Romanos's guidebook *El antiguo Madrid* [Old Madrid] (2:13), the Embajadores ravine was well known to the inhabitants of nineteenth-century Madrid. Consequently, Galdós was able to count on the same participation by his readers as Dickens enjoyed from his. The readers of *La desheredada* could use their personal experience as well as their memory of what they had read in newspapers, periodicals, or books to provide the details that Galdós did not include. Imitating the descriptive style of Dickens, Galdós was thus able to stimulate and control the double-scope blending process of his reading public, guiding each reader to create a personally detailed mental image of Madrid slum conditions. Dickens's "admirable fuerza descriptiva" [admirable descriptive power] that Galdós praised is in part due to the collaboration Dickens elicits from his readers in constructing representations of the city. "Dickens's London" is a fictional place that surpasses the reality of historical London because it combines elements written by the author with elements imagined and remembered by the reader. "Galdós's Madrid" is the same. Neither "Dickens's London" nor "Galdós's Madrid" is revealed through meticulously accurate descriptions of the sites it contains. In both cases, the fictional world is supplemented by the readers' familiarity with the external world, making it seem more real than reality.

In his "Carlos Dickens" essay, Galdós contrasts Dickens's "modo general" [general manner] with the "minuciosidad" [meticulousness] of the descriptions provided by the French author Honoré de Balzac. He notes that Dickens presents the reader with "un cuadro que aparece formado y compuesto de una sola pincelada" [a painting that appears formed and composed of a single brushstroke], while Balzác "hace la anatomía" [does an autopsy] of each object, "segregando todas sus partes para estudiarlas por sí solas, midiendo con impertinencia las aristas, los ángulos, contando las manchas, modelando el original con la minuciosidad y el trabajo del que traza un facsimil" [separating all of the parts to study them individually, impertinently measuring the edges, the angles, counting the stains, modelling the original with the meticulousness and effort of someone drawing a facsimile] (452–3). This stylistic difference between Dickens and Balzac relates to the fundamental distinction Wolfreys notes between Paris and London within the context of the nineteenth century. Because of Paris's redesigned orderliness, Balzac can "give us the definite sense of the city," as characterized by "the stateliness and symmetry of Haussmann's conception" (26). Indeed, because of the Haussmann plan for the renovation of Paris, the French capital became the most modern city of the world. Between 1852 and 1870 Paris experienced a physical transformation that resulted in the levelling of narrow medieval streets and the destruction of antiquated houses in order to construct new buildings and create straight streets, wide boulevards, transportation hubs, and green plazas. Writing within this rational environment, Balzac was able to view the capital as an entity that is uniform, orderly, and able to be understood as a system and as a totality. This concept of the city is reflected in Balzac's extremely detailed descriptions, which focus on each element individually and in relation to its other parts.

On the contrary, nineteenth-century London is characterized by a lack of order and unity. It is not possible to conceptualize all that it contains. Rather than a rational system, it is a great "Labyrinth, but one's perception is only part of the Labyrinth as it manifests itself. One can never see it in its totality," making it impossible to understand and grasp the city in its entirety (Wolfreys 26). Its streets and buildings, as well as the people who inhabit them, seem innumerable. According to Wolfreys, one of the ways that Dickens expresses this disordered and incomprehensible vastness is through descriptions of London that are not actually descriptions, but "lists of seemingly random elements" (146). However, since every list can only serve as a partial catalogue of all that there is in London, these incomplete listings convey "the sense of incompletion, the unendingness, the ineffability" of the English capital (25). Through the act of listing instead of describing, Dickens transforms the reality of geographical London into a fictitious place that is hyperreal in its inexhaustibility.

As an example of this technique, Wolfreys cites the description of Krook's store when Esther sees it through the shop window for the first time in chapter 5 of *Bleak House*:

> In one part of the window was a picture of a red paper mill at which a cart was unloading a quantity of sacks of old rags. In another was the inscription BONES BOUGHT. In another, KITCHEN-STUFF BOUGHT. In another, OLD IRON BOUGHT. In another, WASTE-PAPER BOUGHT. In another, LADIES' AND GENTLEMEN'S WARDROBES BOUGHT. Everything seemed to be bought and nothing to be sold there. In all parts of the window were quantities of dirty bottles – blacking bottles, medicine bottles, ginger-beer and soda-water bottles, pickle bottles, wine bottles, ink bottles ... There were a great many ink bottles. There was a little tottering bench of shabby old volumes outside the door, labeled "Law Books, all at 9d." Some of the inscriptions I have enumerated were written in law-hand ... Among them there was one, in the same writing, having nothing to do with the business of the shop, but announcing that a respectable man aged forty-five wanted engrossing or copying to execute with neatness and dispatch. There were several second-hand bags, blue and red, hanging up. A little way within the shop-door lay heaps of old crackled parchment scrolls and discoloured and dog's-eared law-papers. I could have fancied that all the rusty keys, of which there must have been hundreds huddled together as old iron, had once belonged to doors of rooms or strong chests in lawyers' offices. The litter of rags tumbled partly into and partly out of a one-legged wooden scale, hanging without any counterpoise from a beam, might have been counsellors' bands and gowns torn up. One had only to fancy ... that yonder bones in a corner, piled together and picked very clean, were the bones of clients, to make the picture complete. (Wolfreys 147–8)

Nineteenth-century Madrid also is a city in disorder, physically with its antiquated infrastructure of medieval and Renaissance streets, and socially with its inhabitants who had emigrated recently to the capital from small towns throughout Spain. Although the Plan Castro reconfigured the Puerta del Sol in 1862, widened the Paseo de Recoletos, and expanded the capital through construction to the north, east, and south, Madrid of the late nineteenth century lacked the systematic interconnectedness of the French capital. Furthermore, despite isolated demolition projects, Madrid's long-established neighbourhoods retained a labyrinthine quality that distinguished the city's interior from the grid patterns of the newly designed neighbourhoods surrounding it. The extended boundaries of the city made it more difficult for its inhabitants to conceptualize the capital as a whole. Madrid became bigger, but not more unified. Madrid of Galdós's era, like London during Dickens's lifetime, was fundamentally incomprehensible on a human scale, and Galdós frequently employs Dickens's technique of listing in his *Novelas Contemporáneas* to create the *sensation* of a city that is unlimited, unknowable, and uncontainable. Lists abound throughout the first novel of this series, *La desheredada*, and the following description in chapter 7, with Isidora examining the contents of store windows, provides a stylistic parallel to the above-cited passage from *Bleak House*:

> Aquí las soberbias telas, tan variadas y ricas ... allí las joyas que resplandecen ... más lejos ricas pieles, trapos sin fin, corbatas, chucherías ... objetos en que se adunan el arte inventor y la dócil industria, poniendo a contribución el oro, la plata, el níquel, el cuero de Rusia, la celuloide, la cornalina, el azabache, el ámbar, el latón, el caucho, el coral, el acero, el raso, el vidrio, el talco, la madreperla, el chagrín, la porcelana y hasta el cuerno ... después los comestibles finos, el jabalí colmilludo, la chocha y el faisán asados, cubiertos de su propio plumaje, con otras mil y mil cosas aperitivas que Isidora desconocía y la mayor parte de los transeúntes también ... más adelante los peregrinos muebles, las recamadas tapicerías, el ébano rasguñado por el marfil, el roble tallado a estilo feudal, el nogal hecho encaje, las majestuosas camas de matrimonio, y por último, bronces, cerámicas, relojes, ánforas, candelabros y otros prodigios sin número ... Por mirarlo todo, deteníase también a contemplar las encías con que los dentistas anuncian su arte, las caricaturas políticas de los periódicos, colgados en las vidrieras de los cafés; los libros, los cromos, los palillos de dientes, las aves disecadas, las pelucas y postizos, las condecoraciones, las fotografías, los dulces y hasta los comercios ambulantes en que todo es *a real*. (*La desheredada* 117–18)

> [Here superb cloth, so varied and rich ... there gleaming jewels ... a bit farther away rich furs, endless fine clothes, ties, baubles ... objects that combine invention and docile industry, putting to use gold, silver, nickel, Russian leather, celluloid, cornelian, jet, amber, brass, rubber, coral, steel, satin, glass, talcum, mother of pearl, shagreen, porcelain, and even horn ...

> then the fine foods, wild boar with sharp teeth, roasted woodcock and pheasant covered in their own feathers, with thousands and thousands of other tasty things that neither Isidora nor the majority of the passers-by knew anything about ... Then there were the movable pieces of furniture with embroidered upholstery, ebony inlaid with ivory, oak carved in feudal style, walnut made to look like lace, majestic double beds and finally, bronzes, ceramics, clocks, amphoras, candelabras, and other endless wonders ... To see everything, she also stopped to contemplate the gums used by dentists to announce their art, the political caricatures in the newspapers, hanging in café windows; books, picture cards, toothpicks, stuffed birds, wigs and toupees, medals, photographs, sweets, and even the wares of the street vendors where everything cost just one small coin.]

The stores in both *Bleak House* and *La desheredada* represent in miniature the disorder of the cities in which they are located. The lists of objects reflect the point of view of the two young women as their eyes jump from one object to another. In the hyperreal and infinite world of "Dickens's London" and "Galdós's Madrid," there is no time to take in and study the details. The list of objects in Krook's store does not mention the form of each bottle, or the size of each inscription, or the colour of each book cover, or the material used for each bag, or the style of each key. Similarly, the list of objects in the shop windows of central Madrid does not describe the colours of the fabrics, or the cuts of the jewels, or the designs on the upholstery, or the shapes of the ceramics, or the style of the wigs, or the inscriptions on the medals, or the people in the photographs, or the types of sweets and stuffed birds. Like their characters, Dickens and Galdós make note of each object and then go on to the next one. The lists are long, but they are not complete because neither Esther nor Isidora can see all that is within the stores. The totality of each store cannot be understood, nor can it be contained within the description, thereby reflecting the incomprehensibility and the uncontainability of London and Madrid during the nineteenth century.

In *Realist Vision* Brooks focuses on "things" and "thing-ism ... in the context of the world looked at" (16), and his discussion of Balzac's descriptions of things seen by Lucien as he walks through Paris in *Illusions perdues* [Lost Illusions] provides a useful contrast with how Dickens and Galdós describe the above-mentioned experiences of Esther and Isidora. Like Wolfreys, Brooks states that "cities are labyrinths," but unlike Dickens's London and Galdós's Madrid, Balzac's Paris is a decipherable labyrinth, "a total environment where survival depends on your ability to read the signs, penetrate the appearances" (22). Brooks shows how Lucien takes charge of his environment, noting just those objects that he needs to acquire to reach the social status he yearns to have: ravishing studs on sparkling white shirts, marvellous gloves, a deliciously inlaid cane, dainty gold cufflinks, a charming riding-crop, and a watch as thin as a coin. On the contrary, Esther and Isidora are overwhelmed by their environment. They do not view it selectively. They see "innumerables objetos, sin poder examinar ninguno" [innumerable objects without being able to examine any of them] ("Carlos Dickens" 452). For Esther and Isidora, London and Madrid are unmanageable and unknowable labyrinths, and the uncontainable urban disorder of that experience is communicated through the indiscriminate listing of the things they see.

Reality plus X is how Wolfreys defines hyperreality, with the X consisting of the *perception* of London, as felt by the characters and conveyed to the reader by the author. "Ordinary reality is the conglomeration of the houses, wharves, bricks and stucco" (8). This is reality minus X. But hyperreality includes the lived experience of those who populate the spaces of the city. By using his listing technique, Dickens is able not only to communicate the vastness and innumerability of London but also to lend varying degrees of subjectivity to those listings by employing characters as the focalizers. That is, each list of objects has the potential to give the reader a sense of how the viewing character feels about the items. In his *Novelas Contemporáneas,* Galdós frequently exploits the subjective possibilities of Dickens's listing technique, but never more so than in the lengthy description of Jacinta's walk along the Calle de Toledo [Toledo Street] in part 1, chapter 9, section 1 of *Fortunata y Jacinta,* where her experience is not just visual but auditory as well. Unlike Isidora's casual stroll, Jacinta's walk has a definite purpose and destination. She is going to Ido del Sagrario's home in search of the child whom she believes to have been fathered by her husband. With her thoughts on this goal, she at first does not register the particulars of her surroundings, seeing them just as an "imagen borrosa" [blurred image] of "las baratijas, las panderetas, la loza ordinaria, las puntillas, el cobre de Alcaraz y los veinte mil cachivaches" [trinkets, tambourines, cheap crockery, lacework, Alcaraz copper, and thousands of knickknacks] that "pasaban ante su vista sin determinar una apreciación exacta de lo que eran" [passed by her sight without her being able to determine exactly what they were] (316). In his 1868 essay, Galdós likened Dickens to a painter who "produce sus efectos con masas indeterminadas de color, de sombra y de luz, sin que os permita precisar los objetos en particular" [produces his effects with indeterminate masses of colours, shadows and light, without allowing you to specify the particular objects], and Galdós achieves a similar effect in this scene ("Carlos Dickens" 453). The narrator specifically signals the orientation of the description from Jacinta's point of view by stating that it was as if Jacinta were standing still and the route was being drawn past her like a curtain. As such, her surroundings are perceived as a jumbled mixture of sights and sounds over which she has no control. Rather than her eye moving from one object to the other, the objects (clusters of dates, strips of white lace, lumps of figs, pieces of nougat, barrels of olives, birds in cages, piles of oranges) impose themselves upon her as if hung on a mobile curtain. Indeed, this is the city in motion: unstoppable, all-encompassing, and filled with a plethora of isolated items that Galdós presents to the reader in the form of lists. Unlike the more prosperous sections of Madrid where merchandise is displayed in store windows, the goods for sale in this poorest of neighbourhoods fill the street, creating "obstáculos sin fin, pilas de cántaros y vasijas" [endless obstacles, piles of jugs and bowls] to be overcome as Jacinta's journey progresses (*Fortunata y Jacinta* 317). Since she is only aware of bits and pieces of activity around her, the pace seems frantic and the garments appear to be grotesquely distorted human figures. For Jacinta, raised in a protected middle-class environment, the Madrid slums are unfamiliar, disorienting, and frightening. The voices of the women hawking their goods seem so harsh that they hurt her ears, while her eyes are assaulted by the intensely vivid colours of the clothing on display. Eventually the urban chaos around her becomes overwhelming, and Jacinta "no miraba nada" [didn't look at anything] (318). The listing of objects becomes a list of colours: orange, vermilion, cobalt blue, green, yellow. Seen through Jacinta's "mareada vista" [dizzy viewpoint] and her middle-class sensibilities, each colour becomes associated with something negative: the screeching sound of ungreased axles, the acid taste of vinegar, the belly of a lizard, poison, tuberculosis, and sulphur (317). Finally, one colour comes to dominate, and Galdós employs an additional stylistic technique of Dickens that Reed has identified: "transparent descriptive redundancy," which is achieved through the superfluous repetition of an element (90): "telas rojas, arneses rojos, collarines y frontiles rojos con madroñaje arabesco. Las puertas de las tabernas también de color de sangre" [Red material, red harnesses, red collars and yokes with Arabian tassels. The tavern doors were also the colour of blood] (317). Thus, the lists of things and the lists of colours come together in a single impression of everything bathed in a terrifying blood-red hue.

This is Wolfreys's reality plus X. It is an *experiential* view of a street in Madrid's southern slums as lived by one of the novel's characters. If Dickens's listing technique communicates a sense of "London as a sensual and sensory plenitude of qualities" both "quotidian and exotic at the same time," here it does the same for Madrid (12). Accustomed to residing in just one portion of the labyrinth that is Madrid, Jacinta suddenly must contend with an entirely different portion of that labyrinth and all that it contains. By sharing Jacinta's perspective, the reader not only is given a list of what she sees and hears but also experiences her unease within this alien environment. Thus, Madrid is shown to be a confusing array of disparate parts, with individual neighbourhoods exceeding the comprehension of inhabitants from other areas of the city.

An interesting combination of both Reed's and Wolfreys's hyperreal techniques is seen in chapters 3 and 4 of *La de Bringas*, where the diversity and disorder of Madrid is mapped onto the Palacio Real. After speaking of the building's second and third floors as "una verdadera ciudad ... donde alternan pacíficamente aristocracia, clase media y pueblo" [a true city ... where the aristocracy, the middle class, and the common people peacefully alternated], the narrator describes his first visit to that internal urban centre, where both he and his companion, Manuel Pez, become lost in "aquel dédalo" [that labyrinth] as they search for Francisco Bringas's apartment (*Bringas* 21). This "City Palace" replicates Madrid not only socially, with its richer and poorer neighbourhoods, but also physically, with its streets, plazas, tunnels, steps, and alleys, as well as its structures – walls, doors, ceilings – that have been reconfigured through constant remodelling. And like Madrid, it is a labyrinth that cannot be envisioned as a whole. Pez laments not having a compass or "plano" [blueprint or map] to guide them (23). Instead they must depend on their previous knowledge of the palace as divided into wings in order to try to orient themselves, and they verify their position within the palace by using landmarks they view through windows. Galdós could take advantage of a similar degree of knowledge by his readers, whose familiarity with the exterior of this iconic building and its public surroundings allowed them to use their imagination to follow the generalized description of the characters' movements through it. But Galdós's readers would have had no knowledge of its interior upper floors, so the narrator provides a listed account of what the two men encounter:

> En todas partes hallábamos puertas de cuarterones, unas recién pintadas, descoloridas y apolilladas otras, numeradas todas; mas en ninguna descubrimos el guarismo que buscábamos. En esta veíamos pendiente un lujoso cordón de seda, despojo de la tapicería palaciega; en aquella un deshilachado cordel ... Hallábamos domicilios deshabitados, con puertas telarañosas, rejas enmohecidas ... Por ciertos lugares anduvimos que parecían barrios abandonados ... Subimos una escalera, bajamos otra ... Hay escaleras que empiezan y no acaban; vestíbulos o plazoletas en que se ven blanqueadas techumbres que fueron de habitaciones inferiores. Hay palomares donde antes hubo salones, y salas que un tiempo fueron caja de una gallarda escalera. Las de caracol se encuentran en varios puntos, sin que se sepa a dónde van a parar, y puertas tabicadas, huecos con alambrera, tras los cuales no se ve más que soledad, polvo y tinieblas ... Resultado: que no conocíamos ninguna parte de aquel laberíntico pueblo formado de recovecos, burladeros y sorpresas, capricho de la arquitectura y mofa de la simetría ... (*La de Bringas* 22–4)

> [Everywhere we encountered panelled doors, some recently painted, others discoloured and moth-eaten, all numbered; but on none of them did we find the numeral we were looking for. On this one we saw a luxurious silk bell cord, a remnant from the palace tapestries, on that one a frayed rope ... We found uninhabited apartments, with cobwebbed doors and mouldy iron grates ... Certain places we walked through seemed like abandoned neighbourhoods ... We went up one staircase and down another ... There are staircases that begin and don't end, vestibules or tiny plazas in which could be seen the bleached ceilings of the rooms below. There are pigeon coops where there formerly were living rooms, and parlours that once were the landing of an elegant staircase. Spiral staircases were found at various points, without being able to determine where they would end up, and walled-up doors, holes covered with wire, through which could not be seen anything more than loneliness, dust, and darkness ... Result: that we did not know any part of that labyrinthine town formed of nooks, barricaded enclosures, and surprises, a whim of architecture and a mockery of symmetry.]

The building's features convey a sense of bewildering urban discontinuity that helps to establish the metaphorical connection between this

City Palace and the equally unruly city of Madrid. The symmetrical exterior of the Palacio Real belies the unfathomable architectural "irregularidades" [irregularities] it contains and which also exist in the urban environment beyond its walls (24). Furthermore, knowledge of the building's façade is simply a partial understanding of the palace, as is the knowledge of any individual portion of Madrid. Just as a blueprint would have been useful to Pez and the narrator as they explored the unfamiliar geography of the palace's interior, so too are maps used to help both strangers and residents manoeuvre around unknown sections of the capital. But these tools are merely futile attempts by humans, both fictional and of flesh-and-blood, to control and comprehend the uncontrollable and incomprehensible immensity of Madrid. Becoming lost is inevitable. By mapping the city onto its Royal Palace, Galdós engaged the imagination and memories of his readers to fill in missing details of the narrator's route, even as he used the listings technique to show that no amount of detail is sufficient to find a way out of the maze of Madrid.

The Bringas's apartment itself further echoes the association between the Palace and the city. Each of its rooms is named after the ones in the royal chambers below, and Rosalía's sewing room, the *Camón*, parallels the displays in Madrid's shop-windows. Indeed, the narrator states that "más que taller, parecía el *Camón* la sucursal de *Sobrino Hermanos*" [rather than just a workroom, it seemed like the *Camón* was a branch office of the Sobrino Hermanos store] (84). This is Rosalía's realm, and unlike the orderliness that characterizes Francisco's control over the other rooms of the apartment, the *Camón* is as chaotic as the city that supplied the objects within it. In chapter 15 of *La de Bringas*, Galdós allows the reader to experience this disorder by describing it through Francisco's point of view when he unexpectedly enters the room:

> Había allí como unas veinticuatro varas de *Mozambique*, del de a dos pesetas vara, a cuadros, bonita y vaporosa tela que la Pipaón, en sueños, veía todas las noches sobre sus carnes. La enorme tira de trapo se arrastraba por la habitación, se encaramaba a las sillas, se colgaba de los brazos del sofá y se extendía en el suelo para ser dividida en pedazos por la tijera de la oficiala, que, de rodillas, consultaba con patrones de papel antes de cortar. Tiras y recortes de *glasé*, de las más extrañas secciones geométricas, cortados al *bies*, veíanse sobre el baúl esperando la mano hábil que los combinase con el *Mozambique*. Trozos de brillante raso de colores vivos

> eran los toques calientes, aún no salidos de la paleta, que el bueno de Bringas vio diseminados por toda la pieza, entre mal enroscadas cintas y fragmentos de encaje. Las dos mujeres no podían andar por allí sin que sus faldas se enredaran en el *Mozambique* y en unas veinte varas de *poplín* azul marino que se había caído de una silla y se entrelazaba con las tiras de foulard. (*Bringas* 84)
>
> [There were about twenty-two yards of *Mozambique* cloth, at two *pesetas* a yard, a plaid, pretty, and gauzy material that Rosalía, every night in her dreams, saw covering her flesh. The enormous strip of cloth was dragged around the room, perched on chairs, hanging from the arms of the sofa, and was spread out on the floor in order to be divided into pieces with the scissors of the seamstress, who, on her knees, was checking the paper patterns before cutting. Strips and cutouts of taffeta, in the strangest geometric shapes, cut on the bias, were waiting on the trunk for a skilful hand to combine them with *Mozambique* cloth. Pieces of shiny satin in vivid colours were the warm touches, still on the artist's palette, that the good Bringas saw scattered about, among uncurled ribbon and fragments of lace. The two women could not walk through there without their skirts becoming tangled in the *Mozambique* cloth and in the eighteen yards of navy blue poplin that had fallen from the chair and became intertwined with the strips of silk.]

Francisco's attention immediately centres on the *Mozambique* as it wraps itself around the furniture in the room, and the description of that fabric first mentions what is of primary interest to Francisco: its price. Francisco's further concentration on its length suggests his concern for the overall cost of the item, as does his notice of the other luxury fabrics (taffeta, satin, poplin, silk) and accessories (ribbons, lace). These objects are the "necessary superfluities" that Brooks cites as being vital to how Balzac's characters control their social environment. But in Galdós's description, Francisco does not see the social value of these items. He can only calculate their worth in terms of money. For Francisco, they are indeed superfluities, but they certainly are not necessary. As such, they fall into the category of ornamental objects that Naomi Schor, in her book *Reading in Detail*, argues have been associated since antiquity with the feminine, and therefore classified as trivial, insignificant, or petty, and consequently accorded an inferior status in pictorial and literary descriptions. Schor credits Balzac with validating and legitimizing ornamental objects by employing a "high density" of descriptive details in his realist aesthetic (131). Galdós also features ornamental objects in *La de Bringas,* but once again, he differs from Balzac in how he describes them. In the *Camón,* there is a proliferation of ornamental things, but not the typical Balzacian "proliferation of details" about them (Schor 44). Like the shop windows seen by Esther and Isidora, the *Camón* is described through lists of what Francisco sees as his eye moves around the room. And like the descriptions of Jacob's Island and *el barranco de Embajadores,* the reader is provided with an identifiable location type – a millinery shop – that can be used in the process of imagining a detailed picture of what Rosalía's room looks like. By focusing Francisco's attention on the costly *Mozambique* cloth, Galdós imitates how Dickens "no ve en el objeto más que aquella parte, aquella línea, que influye en el conjunto de la escena, que añade algo a la totalidad del cuadro" [doesn't see in an object more than that part, that line that influences the overall scene, that adds something to the totality of the painting] ("Carlos Dickens" 453). There are splashes of "colores vivos" [vivid colours] surrounding the *Mozambique,* but the only colour named is the "azul marino" [navy blue] of the poplin. The reader must supply the missing details, imagining not only the colours of the ribbons, lace, and fabrics but also the shapes into which the taffeta has been cut, as well as the entire physical appearance of the seamstress who is doing the cutting. Rosalía has transferred a portion of Madrid's labyrinth – its garment district – into this room, and the description conveys Francisco's confusion upon being thrust into that labyrinth. He mentally lists each object individually in an attempt to take in the totality of what he sees, but the disarray of the room, like the disorder of the city, can't be comprehended, and in Francisco's disoriented state of mind the objects haphazardly strewn about seem to be "cosas sobrenaturales o mágicas" [supernatural or magic things] (84).

For Furst, "it is the sustained dialogue between reference to actuality and the textual creation of a fabricated realm that is the distinctive hallmark of the realist novel" (12). Through the techniques identified by Reed and Wolfreys, Dickens and Galdós require their readers to actively engage in that dialogue by filling in the omitted details of descriptions and by experiencing along with the characters the uncontainability of London and Madrid suggested by long lists that merely approximate the vastness of the cities in which they are found. Both authors use their respective cities as what Furst calls "a prop in the animation of a pretense" that they carry on with their readers during "the illusion-making process" (25). Furst also stresses that "it is essential to realize that the appearance of truthfulness inherent in the illusion must necessarily (because a novel is by nature a construct made up of words) derive primarily from the effect of the words printed on the page, even while they seem to refer to an external world" (25), and as such "accuracy as a criterion for assessing the effectiveness of descriptions of place must yield to the power of rhetoric" (114). The hyperreal techniques used by Dickens and Galdós do not produce exact copies of the places they describe but rather create descriptions that leave ample room for the imaginative contribution of the reader. The vividness of these descriptions is based not only on what they include but, more importantly, on what they leave out, so that the reader can engage in double-scope blending to create and feel the *sensation* of particularity of place.

A useful contrast can be made between Reed's and Wolfreys's concept of hyperrealism and how it is traditionally conceived in the plastic arts. Visual hyperrealist representations seem more real than reality because they provide more details than the eye can normally see. They *contain* the image in all of its multiplicity. They capture the attention of the viewer, but they do not engage the imagination. The artist has already surpassed surface reality, so there is nothing to add. The hyperrealistic effect is given to the viewer to observe. The opposite process occurs with the descriptions of Dickens and Galdós. The hyperrealistic effect in their novels derives from the interplay between a minimal amount of descriptive words and the reader's personal engagement with both the text and the city. These descriptions contain gaps to be filled in a myriad of ways, none of them definitive. There is multiplicity, but not containment. The hyperrealistic effect needs to be created and experienced by the reader. "Dickens's London" and "Galdós's Madrid" are fictional realms that seem more real than their counterparts in the world because they are brought into being through techniques that use selective elements of external reality as catalysts to engage the individualized internal reality of each reader.

~

"It is universally accepted that Galdós was influenced to some degree by Dickens' work," states Timothy McGovern on the first page of his book *Dickens in Galdós*. Indeed, it is a critical commonplace to call Galdós the "Spanish Dickens," and scholars have long felt an affinity between the two authors, especially in terms of the fictional characters that they created.[2] Similarities pertaining to settings and locations have received considerably less attention, with critical commentary typically limited to brief and undeveloped observations.[3] But what the various comparisons of both characters and places have in common is their tendency to focus on content and situation rather than style. That is, *who* or *what* is described takes precedence over *how* the description is written. Consequently, characters have been discussed as social, literary, thematic, or symbolic types, or as carrying out plot actions reminiscent of Dickens's novels, and places have been compared in terms of what happens in those locations. Two exceptions are Vernon Chamberlin's article on habitual speech tags (*muletillas*) and Rodolfo Cardona's examination of "descripciones rápidas que destacan dos o tres rasgos definitivos, terminando con una conclusión" [quick descriptions that highlight two or three definitive features, ending with a conclusion] (35), but both of these stylistic devices have been discussed just within the context of characterization. Given the strong associations of Galdós with Madrid and Dickens with London, it is surprising that scholars have not explored the stylistic similarities in the descriptions of the two capital cities that served as the setting for the vast majority of the authors' novels. The techniques identified by Reed and Wolfreys provide a useful point of departure for such an undertaking, not only because they correspond to what Galdós had noted as aspects of Dickens's "admirable fuerza descriptiva" but also because those techniques are present in Galdós's own work.

Nineteenth-century realism is known for its detailed descriptions, and as realists both Dickens and Galdós traditionally have been associated with that concept. But realism is not a monolithic movement. It varied from country to country and from one writer to another. The insights presented by Reed and Wolfreys allow us to understand how the minimally detailed place descriptions of Dickens and Galdós differ markedly from the highly detailed ones of Balzac, yet they *seem* to be more detailed than they actually are because they communicate a *sense* of their respective cities even though they do not present a comprehensive image of them. This is done through generalized descriptions that elicit the reader's participation to complete them, and through long lists that evoke the infinite and larger-than-life quality of geographical London and Madrid. These *stylistic* techniques are key elements used by both authors to entice their readers into feeling the lived experience of their capital cities and collaborating in the creation of the fictional hyperreality of "Dickens's London" and "Galdós's Madrid."

NOTES

1 All translations are mine.
2 McGovern's book is the most extensive treatment of the subject. In it he bases his comparison of Dickens and Galdós on their common use of three character types – the ascetic, the miser, the *lazarillo* – as symbols that highlight the struggle between the Old Order (aristocracy and religious conservatives) and the New Order (capitalists and businessmen). Particularly insightful are his pairings of *Dombey and Son* with the Torquemada series, and of *Little Dorrit* with *Misericordia*, but he also provides substantive examples from other works by Dickens (*Barnaby Rudge, Great Expectations, The Old Curiosity Shop*) and Galdós (*La Fontana de Oro, El doctor Centeno, La loca de la casa, El abuelo*). In addition, numerous scholars have made brief comparative observations about characters. In Effie Erickson's early article, for example, *Fontana de Oro*'s *Elías* is seen as similar to Uriah Heep in *David Copperfield* or Sampson Brass in *The Old Curiosity Shop*, Pablo in *El audaz* is like the long-suffering Oliver Twist, and Alejandro Miquis is like David Copperfield (423–30). Furthermore, Erickson was the first scholar to point out the strong similarities between the Pez family of professional bureaucrats and the Barnacle family in *Little Dorrit* (427). Stephen Gilman also has mentioned several correspondences, such as Florence Dombey being the Dickensian counterpart to Isidora Rufete (111n45), and he speculates that Mrs. Boffin's journey to one of London's poorest suburbs to acquire an orphan in *Our Mutual Friend* may have been the model for Jacinta's visit to Madrid's slums in search of Pituso (218–19). Michael Nimetz considers Doña Cándida in *El amigo Manso* to be a more sinister version of Mrs Sparsit from *Hard Times* (156–7); Peter Bly sees Mr Dick in *David Copperfield* as the inspiration for Galdós's creation of old eccentrics (168); Nicholas Round cites the heraldic painter in *Misericordia* as a Dickensian grotesque (164); Gilman declares Estupiñá to be the most comically Dickensian character in *Fortunata y Jacinta* (293); José Montesinos refers to the Dickensian nature of the "personaje secondario" (216); and Linda Willem shows that a comic vignette in Galdós's reconstructed novel, *Rosalía*, contains characters and events reminiscent of Dickens's work in general and *Pickwick Papers* in particular. Most recently, Jeremy Tambling compares two *Bleak House* characters with ones in *Misericordia* and *Fortunata y Jacinta*, calling Don Frasquito "an old dandy like Mr. Turveydrop," and stating that the "richly eccentric Doña Guillermina resembles something of Mrs. Jellyby in her philanthropy" (192–3).
3 Erickson likens the Leganés insane asylum in *La desheredada* to the debtors' prisons in *Pickwick Papers* and *Little Dorrit*, and she compares

Clara's convent school in *La Fontana de Oro* to the institutions in which young David Copperfield and Oliver Twist were housed (424). Walter Pattison speculates that the burning of Newgate Prison during the anti-Catholic uprising in *Barnaby Rudge* served as the model for the burning of the Inquisition building during the Toledo riots in *El audaz* (42). Pedro Polo's school in *El doctor Centeno* resembles those in *Nicholas Nickleby* and *Hard Times* for Erickson and Pattison, respectively (428 and 163n23). Chad Wright cites the Porteño house and its contents in *La Fontana de Oro* as similar to Dickens's use of symbolic settings in such novels as *Bleak House*. A.F. Lambert draws a parallel between the *Administración* in *Miau* and the Circumlocution Office in *Little Dorrit* (47). He also joins Gilman in comparing the squalid conditions of Hampton Court in *Little Dorrit* with those found in the servants' quarters of the Royal Palace in *La de Bringas* (47 and 139n11).

WORKS CITED

Bly, Peter. *The Wisdom of Eccentric Old Men: A Study of Type and Secondary Character in Galdós's Social Novels, 1870–1897*. Montreal and Kingston: McGill-Queen's UP, 2004. Print.

Brooks, Peter. *Realist Vision*. New Haven: Yale UP, 2005. Print.

Cardona, Rodolfo. "Galdós a los 25 años: Primeras formulaciones críticas sobre la novela." In *Benito Pérez Galdós: Aportaciones con ocasión de su 150 aniversario*, ed. Eberhard Geisler et al. Madrid: Vervuert/Iberoamericana, 1996. 29–42. Print.

Chamberlin, Vernon A. "The Muletilla: An Important Facet of Galdós' Characterization Technique." *Hispanic Review* 29.4 (1961): 296–309. Print. https://doi.org/10.2307/471548.

Erickson, Effie L. "The Influence of Charles Dickens on the Novels of Benito Pérez Galdós." *Hispania* 19.4 (1936): 421–30. Print. https://doi.org/10.2307/332742.

Furst, Lilian R. *All Is True: The Claims and Strategies of Realist Fiction*. Durham, NC: Duke UP, 1995. Print.

Gilman, Stephen. *Galdós and the Art of the European Novel: 1867–1887*. Princeton: Princeton UP, 1981. Print.

Lambert, A.F. "Galdós and the Anti-Bureaucratic Tradition." *Bulletin of Hispanic Studies* 53.1 (1976): 35–49. Print. https://doi.org/10.1080/1475382762000353035.

McGovern, Timothy Michael. *Dickens in Galdós*. Bern: Peter Lang, 2000. Print.

Mesonero Romanos, Ramón de. *El antiguo Madrid: Paseos histórico-anecdóticos por las calles y casas de esta villa*. Vol. 2, Madrid: Oficinas de la Ilustración Española y Americana, 1881. Print. *Biblioteca virtual universal*, 2003. http://www.biblioteca.org.ar/libros/92799.pdf. Accessed 4 May 2013.

Montesinos, José F. *Galdós II*. Madrid: Castalia, 1980. Print.

Nimetz, Michael. *Humor in Galdós: A Study of the Novelas contemporáneas*. New Haven: Yale UP, 1968. Print.

Pattison, Walter T. *Benito Pérez Galdós*. Boston: Twayne/G.K. Hall, 1975. Print.

Pérez Galdós, Benito. "Carlos Dickens." In *Los Artículos de Galdós en "La Nación"*, ed. William H. Shoemaker. Madrid: Insula, 1972. 450–4. Print.

– *La de Bringas*. Madrid: Alianza, 1984. Print.

– *La desheredada*. Madrid: Alianza, 1983. Print.

– *Fortunata y Jacinta*. Vol. 1. Madrid: Cátedra, 1985. Print.

– *Memorias de un desmemoriado*. In *Novelas y miscelánea*, ed. Federico Carlos Sainz de Robles. Madrid: Aguilar, 1973. 1430–73. Print.

Reed, John. *Dickens's Hyperrealism*. Columbus: Ohio State UP, 2010. Print.

Round, Nicholas G. "Misericordia: Galdosian Realism's 'Last Word.'" In *A Sesquicentennial Tribute to Galdós 1843–1993*, ed. Linda M. Willem. Newark, DE: Juan de la Cuesta, 1993. 155–72.

Schor, Naomi. *Reading in Detail: Aesthetics and the Feminine*. New York: Methuen, 1987. Print.

Tambling, Jeremy. "Dickens and Galdós." In *The Reception of Charles Dickens in Europe*, ed. Michael Hollington. Vol. 1. London: Bloomsbury, 2013. 191–6. Print.

Turner, Mark. "The Way We Imagine." In *Theory of Mind and Literature*, ed. Paula Leverage et al. West Lafayette, IN: Purdue UP, 2011. 41–61. Print.

Willem, Linda M. "A Dickensian Interlude in Galdós' *Rosalía*." *Bulletin of Hispanic Studies* 69.3 (1992): 239–44. Print. https://doi.org/10.3828/bhs.69.3.239.

Wolfreys, Julian. *Writing London: The Trace of the Urban Text from Blake to Dickens*. London: Palgrave, 1998. Print.

Wright, Chad C. "Artifacts and Effigies: The Porteño House Revisited." *Anales galdosianos* 14 (1979): 13–26. Print.

7 Observed versus Imaginative Communities: Creative Realism in Galdós's *Misericordia*

SUSAN M. MCKENNA

A canny observer of contemporary manners and painter of modern-day life, Benito Pérez Galdós is, perhaps, the Spanish artist who best embodies the role of the nineteenth-century literary *flâneur*. Indeed, upon arriving in the capital for the first time, Galdós himself affirmed that walking the streets of Madrid and observing its inhabitants not only provided a fuller and more stimulating education than did any university but also supplied the philosophical, juridical, canonical, economic, political, and above all literary material for his novels.[1] In the prologue to the 1913 edition of *Misericordia*, Galdós explains that one of his most unusual characters found among a cast of thousands, Almudena Mordejai, was the product of his actions as a *flâneur*.

> El moro *Almudena Mordejai*, que parte tan principal tiene en la acción de *Misericordia*, fue arrancado del natural por una feliz coincidencia. Un amigo, que como yo acostumbraba a *flanear* de calle en calle observando escenas y tipos, díjome que en el Oratorio del Caballero de Gracia pedía limosna un ciego andrajoso, que por su facha y lenguaje parecía de estirpe agarena. Acudí a verle y quedé maravillado ... Toda la verdad del pintoresco *Mordejai* es la obra de él mismo, pues poca parte tuve yo en la descripción de esta figura. (39)[2]

> [The Moor, Almudena Mordejai, who plays such an important part in the action of *Misericordia*, was taken from real life thanks to a happy coincidence. A friend of mine, who is, like me, accustomed to strolling around the streets observing scenes and people, told me there was a ragged blind man begging on the steps of the Oratorio del Caballero de Gracia who

> seemed, by his features and language, to be a Moor. I went to see him and was amazed ... All the truth comes from the picturesque Mordejai himself – I had little to add in my description of him.]

Thus it was that, through happy coincidence, customary habits and an interest in walking Madrid's city streets came together to create one of Galdós's most original, profoundly human, at times problematic, and utterly modern characters. Alternately perceived in the text as Muslim, Christian, and Jew, Almudena fuses his three religions as easily as he combines their three cultures. He speaks Arabic, Hebrew, and Castilian, unwittingly eliding one into the other, seemingly unaware of the lexical confusion. He projects a fluid identity that is young and old, naïve and wise, real and imagined, poor and rich, kind and cruel, earthly and spiritual. He is blind and yet he sees. The plurality of Almudena's character reflects Galdós's vision of the modern city, for it, too, is bold and new, savage and beautiful. Like the spectator who derives some pleasure from his position within the crowd, Galdós also regards the urban environment with some contempt, for he is not a detached observer. Witness to the hollow morality of a bankrupt society decaying from within, the author envisions the possibility of redemption through its most humble individuals. Personified in its churches, its streets, and its characters, the city that Galdós paints is real and tangible. It is, as well, the dream world of his protagonists. Madrid on the eve of the twentieth century, like Almudena himself, is and is not African, Semitic, and European, ancient and modern, Christian and non-Christian. It is a city no longer defined by either/or but rather by both/and; that is, both observed and imagined.

This essay examines the creation of modern urban identity in Galdós's 1897 novel *Misericordia*, by reconstructing the author, his characters, and his work through the critical lens of observed imagination and creative realism. The term creative realism, deployed to analyse Galdós's fluid and ever-changing narrative techniques, identifies a trend in his writing that simultaneously exploits and explores the limitations of traditional realistic discourse while also reimagining normative forms of subjectivity. Using this framework, the essay shows how Galdós moved beyond the conventional bounds of realism to promote national regeneration and expand artistic expression.

For the contemporary critic, the word *flâneur* evokes immediate associations: Baudelaire and the ebb and flow of the seething crowd, or Benjamin and the intoxication born from long, aimless walks through the streets and arcades of Paris. In French, of course, the word *flâneur* is understood to mean stroller, idler, walker. As one who observes the spectacle of modern-day life, the *flâneur* is usually portrayed as a well-dressed man, leisurely strolling the city streets, an anonymous face in the crowd.[3] The *flâneur* treats the people he sees and the objects he observes as "texts" for his own pleasure. At the same time that he participates physically in these texts, he remains outside, contemplating the constantly shifting urban landscape as it evolves before him. While Baudelaire's aesthetic and critical visions helped open up the modern city as a space for investigation, theorists such as Georg Simmel codified the urban experience in more sociological and psychological terms.[4] Benjamin, we know, appropriated this idea of the *flâneur* as a way to think about the confluence of nineteenth-century urban conditions that coalesced to transform society from a culture of production to one of consumption. From a Marxist viewpoint, Benjamin sees the *flâneur* as a product of modern life and the Industrial Revolution as portrayed in his *Arcades Project*. For historians and literary scholars alike, Benjamin's conceptual appropriation of this Parisian type is particularly useful as it underscores the historically specific conditions of urban spectatorship that emphasized mobility, fluid subjectivity, and pleasure in the modern era. Because the city provided the arena for the circulation of bodies and goods, the exchange of glances, and the exercise of consumerism, it is almost impossible to conceive of modernity outside of its urban context. It is to Galdós's city of Madrid that we now turn – a city at once ancient and modern, traditional and transitional, real and imagined. It is a city whose urban spaces and faces signal the past, the present, and the future – a city awkwardly lurching towards modernity.

A semiotic and linguistic tour de force emphasizing multiple dualities opens the novel and introduces the reader to its multivalent structures and themes. Echoing Charles Dickens's *A Tale of Two Cities* (1859),[5] *Misericordia* begins with an ironic presentation of the Church of San Sebastián and the beggars who line up along its two principal entrances: "Dos caras, como algunas personas, tiene la parroquia de San Sebastián ... mejor será decir la iglesia ... dos caras que seguramente son más graciosas que bonitas: con la una mira a los barrios bajos, enfilándolos por la calle Cañizares; con la otra al señorío mercantil de la Plaza del Ángel" [Like some people, the parish of San Sebastián ... its church, rather ... has two faces that are surely more quaint than comely. From one face it gazes at the lower-class districts strung along Cañizares Street; from the other it scans the commercial zone of the Plaza del

Ángel] (61–2).[6] While Dickens does in fact present two cities, Paris and London, and their respective inhabitants, Galdós imagines a city within a city: the teeming masses who eke out their meagre existence on the margins of society and the upper-class parasites who feed on each other, and on the poor. The symbolic dichotomy of the novel has been studied by scholars as diverse as Robert Russell, Diane Urey, and Geoffrey Ribbans, who privilege the ambivalence of this opening sequence for its "reconciliation of opposites," "ironic duality," and "ambiguous dichotomy" (Russell 105; Urey 61; Ribbans 203). The architecture of this two-faced building provides as well the organizational structure for the novel's narrative; that is, a story constructed by and through its numerous configurations of dyads including repetitions, parallels, pairs, twins, couples, equals, opposites, and equivalents. It is a refracted, carnivalesque world where, as Russell notes, hunger becomes a blessing, blindness vision, the servant a master, madness wisdom, and illusion reality – a world where one thing is said but often means another (104–5).

In ancient Roman myth and religion, Janus, the god of doors, gates, and beginnings, is also depicted as having two faces because he looked to both the past and the future. He presided over the sowing of crops, and the Roman army marched to war through his sacred doorway, the *Ianus geminus*. Situated in the Forum, the door would remain open until the war was over and the soldiers returned home. Janus also represented the transition between primitive life and civilization, the countryside and the city, peace and war, and youth and maturity. He was worshipped at the beginning of harvest time, planting, marriage, and birth. Accordingly, Ribbans uses the conflicting dualities of the Janus motif in his reading of *Misericordia* to explore the sustained and unresolved tensions between "the contrasting forces of imagination and perceived reality" in the text (210).[7] It is the contrast between these two forces, he concludes, that will ultimately result in the novel's "profound ambiguity" (210). Strikingly, Benjamin introduces his 1939 exposé, "Paris, Capital of the Nineteenth Century," with an epigram from Maxime Du Camp that ironically compares historical study with the Roman god: "History is like Janus; it has two faces. Whether it looks at the past, or at the present, it sees the same things" (14). The ambiguity of this two-faced motif, as we will see, plays a critical role in Galdós's representation of urban identity in late nineteenth-century Spain, for it, too, presupposes the assimilation of epochs, cultures, and peoples.

Like most *flâneurs*, Galdós walked the streets of the metropolis and imagined both the city and its architecture as palimpsests where traces of heterogeneous times accumulate and can be read, like a text whose previous pages remain imperfectly erased, still partly visible in the new composition. As set forth by Andreas Huyssen, the concept of urban palimpsest serves as a trope that can tie together divergent artistic practices that have their sources in public memory. This approach offers an inventory of simultaneous and erratic faces of the urban space that change according to the instruments of its cultural representation: verbal, pictorial, architectural, etc. Galdós's Church of San Sebastián, an architectural calamity of conflicting styles and designs, exemplifies this palimpsestic construction and, at the same time, makes evident the analogous relationship of the edifice to the individual. The narrator ironically reminds us that together the two faces of the church "maravillosamente" combine the architectonic and moral character of the city of Madrid (61–2). Urey concludes her study of Galdosian irony with a reference to this textual moment: "Just as in the church of San Sebastián, the moral and architectural aspects of the novel – its meaning and its language – are 'marvelously,' but not truly, fused; for they are always ironically opposed" (63). Correspondingly, affirms José Muñoz Millanes, the architecture of a city is the "testimony par excellence of its daily life" because it registers "the vicissitudes of humankind" over time. Thus, the analogical connection that Galdós assembles here couldn't be clearer or more direct: Madrid is at once the city and its architecture; San Sebastián and its inhabitants; the rich and the poor.

The continuous bifurcation of structures, images, characters, and themes introduced in the first two paragraphs becomes, as José Schraibman has noted, a "juego de dualidades" [game of dualities] that forms the basis for the novel's "sinfonía contrapuntal" [contrapuntal symphony] (882–3). The one exception, however, is Almudena Mordejai, the character who personifies Galdós's equivocal notion of urban identity in fin-de-siècle Spain – a complex and elusive identity tied to the past, conflicted in the present, straining towards the future. We first encounter Almudena in chapter 3, when the narrator explains that, for the moment, he will only say that Almudena is blind; that he is the one beggar with whom Benina shares any confidence; and that he is an Arab from the land of Sousse, three days' journey from Marrakesh. The paragraph concludes with the narrator's imperative to "fijarse bien," counselling the reader to pay close attention. Almudena's introduction in chapter 3 is hardly coincidental. He is a unique character for many reasons, most notably because he breaks with the established binary patterns and denotes instead the more mystical number three, for he represents a fluid amalgamation of three religions, three cultures, and three languages. Moreover, Almudena is marginalized from the prevailing social order on multiple levels, being dark-skinned, Arabic, illiterate, blind, and poor. Like the Cathedral that stands adjacent to the grounds of the Royal Palace and wears his name, Nuestra Señora de la Almudena, he is a multifaceted creation whose past experiences and influences remain visible in his present-day composition.[8] He is what Robert Ricard has termed a "composite Semite:" a personification of the three great religions that once peacefully coexisted in medieval Spain (22).

The same year that Galdós published the first edition of *Misericordia*, 1897, he was also elected to the Spanish Royal Academy and delivered a commemorative speech titled "La sociedad presente como materia novelable" [Present-Day Society as Material for the Novel]. A retrospective overview of society and the state of the modern novel, Galdós's speech expressed his disillusionment with the middle classes, on whom he had pinned his hopes in the euphoric optimism of the 1870s, a time he now characterizes as lacking both direction and uniformity. Notable throughout is his use of terms signifying decay, such as disappearance, disintegration, fragmentation, dissolution, deterioration, and dispersal. Present-day society, he portends, is marked by confusion, anxiety, bewilderment, and "la relajación de todo principio de unidad" [the loosening of all principles of unity] (160). Although this chaotic environment, he continues, may have favoured, and perhaps even encouraged, literature and the narrative arts to flourish – the human imagination often blossoms in "las tristes y desoladas ruinas" [the sad and desolate ruins] – he offers no comparable advantage for society and its "antiguos organismos sociales" [antiquated social institutions] (165). Rather, these same worn structures – the church, the state, and the bourgeoisie – will receive harsh criticism in *Misericordia*, portrayed throughout the text as egocentric, ineffectual, profligate, and hypocritical anachronisms.

Any hope for society's renewal, the novel suggests, depends on the authenticity and cohesion of Madrid's under-classes, exemplified most readily by the union of Almudena and Benina, a servant who is the protagonist of the novel. Beginning and ending the story together, they are outsiders who subsist on society's margins. They inhabit a city that is evolving into the modern age, one whose changing economic relations reflect as well its shifting social structures and fluctuating subjectivities.

One of the most influential nineteenth-century novelists to examine textually Madrid's transition from a traditional society to a more modern one, Galdós routinely employed the people he met and the scenes he observed in the streets to sketch his narrative impressions. Not surprisingly, his progressive disillusionment with the Restoration, Liberalism, and the middle classes corresponds with his increasing awareness of and interest in the difficulties incurred by the masses, the common people, in whom he has now placed his hope.[9] These political and social reassessments, maintains Peter B. Goldman, become integral components in his novelistic experimentation: "re-creating social ambiguities and contradictions – as he saw them – in the world of his novels, searching for new and viable solutions" (15). All definitions, all assumptions, all categories that may have once seemed stable, including subjectivity, come into question, then, in Galdós's creatively realistic representation of Spanish society in *Misericordia*.[10]

The image of the city, its buildings, its public spaces, and its streets as a subjective construction is an important component of contemporary urban theory.[11] For example, many urban theorists posit that the presence of the street in a literary text has several implications that transcend textual space, because the text now becomes a symbolic space for the discussion of society. In her recent study of the modern Spanish novel and the role played by "la calle madrileña como espacio social" [the streets of Madrid as a social space], Sara Muñoz-Muriana begins with Galdós's *La desheredada* (1881) and *Tristana* (1892) before moving on to the twentieth century. In the modern novel, she maintains, the street serves both to structure narrative action and configure subjectivity (1). Expounding on the architectural theories proposed by Robert Gutman in "Street Generation," Muñoz-Muriana argues that the street fulfils two main social functions: the first, instrumental; and the second, expressive. The street facilitates travel between buildings and places and enables the interaction between its inhabitants. As a social institution the street fosters both movement and human interaction (7–8). She continues, "pero será en el XIX cuando esta caracterización de la calle como lugar-movimiento en el que se produce una continua estructuración y destabilización de la subjetividad del personaje cobre plena forma a nivel textual" [but it will be in the nineteenth century when this description of the street as a place-movement that produces a continual structuring and destabilization of the character achieves its full form at the textual level] (21). Expanding on this view, Leigh Mercer examines how these same urban novels constructed their public spaces to chart the shape and the growth of the bourgeois city. Public space functions as more than just decorative background in these narratives, she contends, for it is here that "writers produced the cultural imaginary of a new, complex system" (7). Shifting subjectivity and the need for reinvention, thus, are connected to and determined by the modern urban conditions and radical transformations occurring in Madrid at this time.

Characterized by "a late but then urgent modernization," Madrid at the turn of the century faced many of the same social problems and controversies experienced by its European counterparts earlier in the century (Parsons 5). Unskilled labourers from the countryside, eager to work in the expanding industries, streamed in to the ill-equipped capital. Lacking the proper social and economic infrastructure, the city struggled to keep pace with its rapidly growing population. Poverty and mendicancy became two of Madrid's most urgent problems.[12] *Misericordia* draws attention to these issues and the contemporary debates disseminating in Madrid that arose in response. In a counter-reading of *Misericordia* that takes into account the Spanish state's imposition of disciplinary regimes on its marginal and migrant subjects and the subsequent diffusion and normalization of these subjects, Hazel Gold suggests that the novel's emphasis on homelessness, vagrancy, and begging "lays bare a series of epistemological fissures, in both the social and the narrative realms, that cannot be repaired" (143). These fissures, she continues, signal not only a crisis of personal identity but also one of social authority, and they point as well to a looming crisis in national image and identity (144). By concentrating on the issues of vagabondage and urban homelessness, *Misericordia*, she concludes, "engenders a meditation on the deepening crisis of national identity that preoccupies Spain's intellectual élite at the turn of the century" (149). Confirming this reading, Teresa Fuentes Peris notes how Madrid's rapid and uneven social and economic transformation at the end of the nineteenth century exacerbated "the long-standing problem of begging in the cities – especially Madrid" (109). Underdeveloped industrial structures proved unable to absorb the rapidly expanding labour force. *Misericordia*, she affirms, examines the changing attitudes towards charity that accompanied these problems, criticizing the "arbitrary nature of categorization" that divided individuals into those who were "deserving and underserving" (110). Neither Almudena nor Benina, however, fits neatly into any of the broad categories defined during the period: respectable/non-respectable, moral/immoral, deserving/

undeserving. By condemning "bourgeois efforts" in classification and containment of those social groups deemed morally deviant and thus threatening to society, Galdós, she concludes, "disengages himself from contemporary discourses on begging and vagrancy, presenting them as bourgeois constructions aimed at the regulation of the poor" (123).

Misericordia, then, allows for neither preset categories nor fixed subjects. Even one's name, the customary signifier of individualized identity, remains in flux. Alongside Almudena, the revolving set of names assigned to each of the main characters – Benina, for example, is also called Benigna, Nina, Benigna de Casia, dama, bunita, santa, and amri – evince the breakdown of societal structures that were once considered to be both predetermined and permanent entities. This sense of flux is made spatial when the names are used to refer to places in the city itself; for example, when the novel refers to the devolving street names that depict Doña Paca's steady economic demise. These changes in spatial localization, a technique, according to L. Elena Delgado, often employed by Galdós, serve as "mapas" [maps] that identify his characters' psychological and social transitions (116). For Delgado, identity and thus subjectivity are linked to both the spatial and discursive localizations within the text: internal and external spaces that "se representan imbricados siendo los tropos geógraficos los que traducen las desviaciones de la subjetividad" [are understood as interconnected, given that the geographical tropes are what interpret any divergences in subjectivity] (111). Doña Francisca Juárez de Zapata, for example, becomes Doña Paca, as she moves from the Barrio Salamanca and a noble house in Calle Claudio Coello to progressively poorer neighbourhoods represented by the streets named Olmo, Saúco, Almendro, and finally Imperial. At the end of the novel Paca's relocation to a house on the elegant Calle Orellana functions as "a symbol of her financial solvency and her reintegration into decent society" (Gold 145).

Almudena's name also has multiple meanings and derivations. Almudena is both Spanish and Arabic, while Mordejai is Hebrew. Vernon A. Chamberlin informs us that *almudit* in Arabic means granary, but in the Susi dialect of the Berber from southern Morocco, the man who summons the faithful to prayer atop the minaret is the *'lmudden.* In Spanish the word is *almuédano* or *almuecín* (491–2).[13] Capitalist enterprise, industrialization, consumerism, and urban expansion now mark the city in which Almudena, Benina, and countless others struggle to survive. Madrid and its citizens endeavour to transform themselves in tandem with a society in rapid transition itself. Modern commerce and exchange have brought about social mobility and greater fluidity in identity formation, thus replacing the outmoded organizational structures and patterns of an earlier socio-economic order. Significantly, not one of the novel's protagonists, as Gold has so keenly observed, originally comes from Madrid (144). Benina, Gold reminds us, was born in a small town near Guadalajara; Doña Paca and Don Romualdo hail from Ronda; Ponte is from Algeciras; and Almudena, born in Ullah de Bergel, travels through several countries in Africa, the Near East, and Europe before settling in Madrid (144). In this way, the hybrid constructions of modern urban identity on the threshold of the twentieth century, Galdós suggests, rest upon a culture of commodities and mass consumers. Social cohesion is in decline; subjectivity, too, is fluid and unfixed. If modernity is an intrinsic characteristic of the urban city, then what exactly does *Misericordia*, through its narrative reconstruction of the city of Madrid and its inhabitants, tell us about modernity in turn-of-the-century Spain?

Galdós puts forward his character Almudena Mordejai, alongside his companion Benina, as a possible starting point for the renewal of urban identity in twentieth-century Madrid. A composite individual, Almudena is a recent immigrant to the city yet most likely descends from an ancient family of Sephardic Jews expelled from Spain in the fourteenth or fifteenth century. A reconciliation of three major religions as well, he is initially identified as Muslim, later describes himself as "ebibrio" (Hebrew), and then subsequently explains that he has been baptized: Joseph Marien Almudena or José María de la Almudena (239). Moreover, he insists numerous times that there is only one God and offers to marry Benina within any religious tradition she chooses before they begin their pilgrimage to the holy city of Jerusalem, equally sacred to the followers of Islam, Judaism, and Christianity. Both ancient and modern in his approach, Almudena, like Janus and the Church of San Sebastián, is at once a link to the past and a bridge to the future. Not unlike the marginal subjects in Akiko Tsuchiya's homonymous study, Almudena, and by extension Benina, question the established norms and paradigms and suggest, instead, a radical alternative to the social ambiguities and inherent contradictions of fin-de-siècle Spain. Regeneration, it appears, is now in the hands of Madrid's common people.

Much has been said about the ambiguity of the title, *Misericordia*, and its two most obvious definitions: the virtues of charity and mercy and the name of a public workhouse for Madrid's indigent population. Nevertheless, there is a third definition to consider that clearly solidifies the connection Galdós creates between the city, its architecture, his characters, and his hope for the future. *Misericordia* is also a term used by art historians to signify a narrow ledge on the underside of a hinged seat, as in a church choir stall, designed to support a person standing at rest against the upturned seat. A structural component of the choir stall, located in the innermost sanctum of the church, this misericord reinforces the idea of mutual support and assistance established by Almudena's unlikely relationship with Benina. In a world where money has become the organizing principle and human relations are commodified, Almudena and Benina not only defy the status quo but also offer some small hope for the restoration of a society in crisis. The authenticity and success of their curious alliance opens the way for future unconventional associations, unencumbered by middle-class mores and norms.

As evinced in his speech before the Academy, Galdós's belief in absolute terms is no longer possible in 1897: "la misma confusión evolutiva que advertimos en la sociedad, primera materia del arte novelesco, se nos traduce en éste por la indecisión de sus ideales, por lo variable de sus formas, por la timidez con que acomete los asuntos profundamente humanos" [the same evolutionary confusion that we notice in society, useful material for novel writing, translates to us as readers through the indecision of its ideals, the variability of its forms, the timidity with which it undertakes those matters which are profoundly human] ("La sociedad" 163). Instead, growing dissatisfaction with the failed promises of the Restoration, with an inert and ineffectual middle class, as well as with the narrative confines of realism itself lead him to seek out alternative models for national regeneration and artistic expression. Almudena and Benina together embody the possibility for something old and new, traditional and modern, European and non-European, Christian and non-Christian. Marked by a mélange of opposing characteristics and enacting, at times, a blend of androgynous roles, Almudena and Benina, like Don Quixote and Sancho, challenge conventional categories and/or definitions. They represent at once the sinner and the saint, the insider and the outcast, the domestic sphere and the world of the market, the real and the ideal: a syncretic blend of contradictory and, at times, destabilizing paradigms. Though the novel proffers no simple solutions or happy endings, it does provide some glimmer of hope originating both individually and in the confluence of these two disparate souls. Similarly interconnected and mutually illuminating, the successive ages of the city and the different historical faces of its architecture also reflect the compound complexion of its inhabitants and replicate the model for its possible regeneration. Urban identity in turn-of-the-century Madrid wears not two but many faces. For Galdós, the promise of modernity lies in the acceptance and eventual union of the city's multiple miens.

Just as Galdós reimagines contemporary society and its members in order to construct a modern urban identity, so too does he create distinctive narrative frames in which to tell their tale. Tired and worn structures and patterns from the past no longer suffice. In *Misericordia* Galdós employs a metafictional mode that expands the limits of realist narrative and calls attention to the arbitrariness of literary conventions.[14] Most nineteenth-century realist novels, as exemplified by his own *novelas contemporáneas* (modern novels), attempted to conceal their literary artifice. Nonetheless, realism's manipulation of the reader, observes Lilian Furst, can be just as adroit, though less obtrusive, than those works that insistently proclaim themselves to be just a story (102). Self-conscious commentary on the relationship between author, text, and reader, along with a reflection on the process of literary creation, plays an important role in determining the signification of the text. Indeed, intertextuality is an inherent component of the novel's metafictional dialogue. Intertexts in *Misericordia*, for example, include the individual stories related by each of the characters. Ponte recites verses of romantic drama from works such as Hartzenbusch's *Flor de un día* or Rodríguez Rubí's *La trenza de sus cabellos* to the enraptured Obdulia. Almudena interprets Hebrew prayers and songs, unintelligible to the unversed ears of those who listen. Even the characters themselves, moreover, suggest literary conventions reminiscent of other genres: Antonio, the picaresque novel; Obdulia, the romantic tradition; and Benina, the life of saints. Direct reference to Doña Guillermina Pacheco and la Pitusa, two important characters in *Fortunata y Jacinta*, effectively results in Galdós quoting himself, a self-reflexivity that evolves throughout his career. One final observation on the novel's intertextuality would necessarily include the political, social, and historical conditions in which the text was produced. Discourse, as Bakhtin reminds us, is a social interaction and cannot be understood independently of the situation that engendered it (284). History and society are themselves texts, and the author, with his own work, attempts to rewrite them. *Misericordia*, then, in accordance with the rest of Galdós's corpus, examines and critiques the very milieu – that is, late nineteenth-century Spain – that made possible society's formation and its potential reforms. Manifold expressions of intertextuality in the novel underscore the multi-tiered composition of all texts.

Breaking with realism's conventional use of the third-person narrative, *Misericordia* employs instead the first-person point of view.[15] The narrator's intrusion into the story evinces itself immediately, for he addresses his audience in the familiar *vosotros* [you] and then with the more inclusive *nosotros* [we] form within the novel's first two paragraphs. Emphasizing the veracity of his tale, the narrator momentarily editorializes with phrases such as "en esta verídica historia" [in this true story] or "casi no es hipérbole decir" [it's hardly an exaggeration to say]. He problematizes novelistic construction, noting the difficulties incurred in the accurate reproduction of Almudena's speech, "que no es fácil al narrador reproducir, por ser en lengua arábica" [which is not easy for the narrator to reproduce, as it is in Arabic] (92). Perhaps his most daring intervention involves another direct address wherein he demands active participation in the creative process from the reader. The paragraph begins with the dialectic "por desgracia o por fortuna" [unfortunately or fortunately], whereupon he tells the reader to decide for himself whether misfortune or fate determined the following outcome. Jolted from a state of passive reception to one of active determination, the reader must now take part in writing the script. Overtly self-conscious about the construction, narration, and interpretation of his story, the narrator's continuous commentary intrudes on the text itself, foregrounding the narrative acts of reading and writing.

As a result, *Misericordia* demands a reconsideration of the symbiotic connection between articulated language and creation. Contrasting the speech patterns of the rich with those of the poor, the narrator concludes that grammatical rules and etiquette observed in conversation by the rich obscure the ineffable delight experienced when speech is freely conducted, like that of the poor. The narrator describes Almudena's language as "signos, jeroglífico descifrable, oriental escritura que los oyentes entendían sin saber por qué" [symbols, decipherable hieroglyphics, an Oriental script that his listeners understood without knowing how] (148). Father Mayoral, "clérigo de mucha ilustración y humanista muy aprovechado" [a well-educated priest and studious humanist], befriends Almudena to learn more Arabic from him. Words satiate hunger, compensate misery, deceive sadness, and seduce the sceptic. "Qué consuelo para los miserables poder creer tan lindos cuentos" [What a comfort for the wretched to be able to believe such beautiful stories], exclaims the narrator (148). More spiritually nourishing than the day's sustenance, Benina's evening conversation with Doña Paca inspires the women to go on living another day. So critical to Paca's emotional well-being is Benina's colloquy that she grows annoyed with her one evening "porque no la entretenía, como otras veces, con festivas conversaciones" [because she did not entertain her as she did on other occasions with her witty conversation] (251). The repetition of Paca's emphatic "cuéntame" [tell me] throughout the text suggests the primacy of the narrative act in the novel. Language becomes the creative force that is invention through verbal articulation. Creation is contingent upon dialogue whereupon language begets reality.

Multiple storytellers and listeners inhabit the fictional world of Galdós's *Misericordia*. The beggars with whom the novel begins tell their own stories of misery and deprivation. The antiquated gallant Don Frasquito Ponte entertains the romantic Obdulia with eloquent accounts of bygone events. A more inoffensive individual never existed, we are told, nor a more useless one as well. Ponte's imagination, like his mummified body, has become sterile: "se iba quedando fósil" [[it] had been fossilizing] (163). Like Doña Paca, he revels in the glories of his past. Any attempt to fashion a present or create a future is at best ineffective. Similarly, Paca lacks creative will and depends entirely on the energy and imagination of her servant Benina. "Si yo tuviera tu talento" [if I had your talent], she tells Benina, "pronto saldría de estas trapisondas" [I would quickly free myself from these shady affairs] (189). And she later admits, "yo no sirvo para nada" [I'm useless], further underscoring the barrenness of her invention. The Delgados and Zapatas represent the parasitic society of the moribund middle class. Even the younger generation of Zapatas, Antonio and Obdulia, the former epileptic and the latter typhoidal, appear deficient when contrasted with the creative forces of Benina and, to a certain extent, Antonio's wife Juliana. Antonio fabricates stories in his rebellious youth to justify recalcitrant behaviour while Obdulia re-enacts the part of the romantic heroine, her pathetic endeavours exemplified by the conversion of cats into chamberlains and courtiers who keep vigil with her loneliness. Accordingly, the text suggests that regeneration requires cross-pollination with the fertile imagination of the pueblo.

Almudena, Juliana, and Benina personify the inventive forces originated in Madrid's working classes. To relieve the burden of Benina's worries, Almudena weaves a magical account of Samdai, the beneficent king of the underworld. His ingenious poetry inspires Benina to believe in the miraculous power of the word to fashion one's own reality: "Lo que contaba Almudena era de lo que *no se sabe*. ¿Y no puede suceder que alguno sepa lo que no sabemos los demás?" [All that Almudena was telling her was "not known." But couldn't it happen that someone might know what the rest of us don't know?] (140–1). In Benina he has found the woman of his dreams. She is beautiful because he says she is so: "una dama" [a lady] because he calls her thus. The mystery of his language, the intensity of his imagination, and the conviction with which he narrates his story comprise the operative faculties that allow him to create. Juliana is similarly endowed with productive capabilities, for she designs and manufactures not only clothing but also the will of her anaemic husband and in-laws. Juliana's fertility is, of course, most clearly manifested in her having given birth to twins. Both she and Almudena represent the fruitful conception inherent in imaginative desire. Each fashions his/her own world through verbal command; the ideal becomes the real by reason of the word.

Imaginative begetting in *Misericordia*, however, is best illustrated by Benina's narration of Don Romualdo, the charitable priest for whom she pretends to work when instead she begs at the entrance to San Sebastián. Throughout the text the narrator makes numerous references to Benina's fertile imagination and extraordinary capacity for creation. Unremitting activity miraculously generates extra hours in the day and the means to gather provisions for herself and Doña Paca. When creditors torment the impractical Paca for payment, she pleads with Benina to "inventar algo" [make something up] to produce the necessary ten *duros*. Benina's narrative of Don Romualdo is so convincing that Paca entertains the notion that she has already met him. Don Romualdo's appearance and subsequent presentation of the terms of the inheritance occasion the narrator to reflect on Benina's invention: "Le había inventado ella, y de los senos oscuros de la invención salía persona de verdad, haciendo milagros, trayendo riquezas, y convirtiendo en realidades los soñados del Rey Samdai" [She had invented him herself, and now a real person emerged from the dark bosom of her invention to work miracles, to bring riches, and to transform into reality the dream gifts of King Samdai] (295). The flaccid breasts of the ageing Benina produce the life-giving force that sustains both Ponte and the Zapatas. Just as she is "la madre" [mother] to Antonio and Obdulia during their illness, so she is the mother of and caretaker to Paca, Ponte, and Almudena in their suffering. Benina's Don Romualdo makes possible the fiction upon which Doña Paca's reality is built. As the novel progresses, the fine line between the two is subtly erased.

Misericordia's fusion of reality and fiction, reason and imagination, follows a long line of Cervantine realism. The text manifests the possibility of this convergence in the opening chapters when the narrator observes a world turned upside down and a world out of order. Dreams play an important role in fusing the imaginary with the real; as Benina notes, dreams are the work of God, so who, therefore, can determine what is truth and what is fantasy? Benina's own creation, the fictive Don Romualdo, ostensibly takes on human form in the creator's mind where "lo real y lo imaginado" [the real and the imagined] are transformed into one. The conversion is so complete that Benina believes she sees his niece, Doña Patros, on the street one evening. She later questions whether Don Romualdo is indeed the product of her invention or whether dreams exist independent of human interaction, where fiction engenders truth. Benina's self-conscious reflection on the process of literary creation further advances the metafictional dialogue intrinsic to the text's signification. Imagination forms the basis of both our fictions and our realities. Each individual, the novel suggests, crafts his/her own world on the foundations of dreams.

Ultimate power in the novel is determined by the control of language. Juliana comes to dominate both Antonio and Doña Paca by simply expressing her ideas verbally. Towards the end of the novel Juliana's rule remains uncontested for she now dominates the words of others. From the shadows, she directs Paca's conversation with Benina, "sugiriéndole por lo bajo lo que había de decir" [suggesting in a low voice all she was to say] (297). In response, Benina can say nothing, having nothing left to say. Her loss of language here evinces her demise as caretaker of the Zapata family: she who controls the word reigns. Ponte's madness is likewise the result of word power, this time in the form of verbal abuse. Tormented by rumours offensive to his antiquated and exaggerated code of honour, Ponte eventually succumbs, his death precipitated by the exclamation "ingrata" [ingrate] that he hurls upon Paca. This scene, vaguely reminiscent of Echegaray's *El gran Galeoto,* inverts the creative nature of language to its equally powerful potential for destruction. Words preside over life and death – language defines existence. Nonetheless Benina regains authority over the word in the final episode of the novel. Obsessed with the idea that her children are dying, Juliana seeks Benina's counsel. If Benina tells her that the children will not die, then Juliana will be cured of her obsession. She pleads with Benina to free her from "esta maldita idea" [this damned idea] (318); her statement alone will suffice to heal Juliana's mental anguish. Magnanimous as always,

Benina assents to Juliana's request, affirming with her word that the twins, healthy and strong, will not die. Once spoken, this simple sentence relieves Juliana's anxiety and restores her robust health. Benina the creator redeems the guilt-ridden Juliana by bestowing upon her children the life-affirming power of the word. Author of her own text once more, she recovers her command of language. Her words ordain existence.

Misericordia tells the story of linguistic begetting, novelistic construction, and societal regeneration through its critical exploration of modern urban identity. At once observed and imagined, the city of Madrid, with its streets, architecture, inhabitants, and communities, provides the setting, the structure, the human material, and the thematic framework fundamental to Galdós's self-reflexive examination of turn-of-the-century Spain. As analytical form, narrative device, and attitude towards knowledge and its social context, regeneration, Galdós suggests, in both its social and artistic forms, demands an inventive reimagining of traditional boundaries and borders, symbolically expressed in the novel as a misericord. And this insight informs as well our contemporary cultural readings of Madrid's urban spaces. Galdós's craft of fictional realism, affirms Deborah Parsons, "paralleled the illusory nature of Madrid life itself," for he questioned "any transparent representation of this urban society," even as he tried to represent and affirm it (37). "No podemos prever hasta dónde llegará la presente descomposicíon" [We cannot say how far the current disintegration of society may go], laments Galdós to the Royal Academy in 1897. But he does have faith in "el ingenio humano" [the human imagination] and, subsequently, in the potential of Art. And it is, indeed, this profoundly human capacity for invention that not only confers on Benina and Almudena their extraordinary beauty and power but also allows Galdós, the literary *flâneur*, to move beyond mere observation to the active creation of an urban imaginary. Returning once more to the 1913 prologue, Galdós illustrates this slippage between observed imagination and creative realism through his description of his encounter with the real-life Almudena: "Le llevé conmigo por las calles céntricas de Madrid donde le invité a confortar su desmayado cuerpo con libaciones contrarias a las leyes de su raza. De ese modo adquirí ese tipo interesantísimo, que los lectores de *Misericordia* han encontrado tan real" [I brought him with me through the central streets of Madrid where I invited him to fortify his worn-out body with libations contrary to the laws of his race. I thereby acquired that most interesting character, whom the readers of *Misericordia* have found to be so real] (39–40). Fact and fiction, reality and dreams, the real and the ideal continually blur in Galdós's representation of Madrid. The future of modern urban identity, then, exemplified by the novel's metafictional dialogue and its individual and textual hybridity, lies in the creative power of the word.

NOTES

1 "Escapándome de las cátedras, anduleaba por las calles, plazas, y callejas, gozando de observar la vida bulliciosa de esta ingente y abigarrada capital ... mis días se me iban en flanear por las calles" [Escaping from the lecture halls, I used to stroll through the streets, squares, and alleyways, having a good time observing the bustling life of this huge and multi-coloured capital ... my days all spent in strolling the streets] ("Memorias" 1655). See also María de los Ángeles Ayala, "Galdos, *flâneur* y peregrino por Inglaterra: La casa de Shakespeare," 182 and Soraya Sádaba Alonso, "Espacio y personajes en *Misericordia* de Benito Pérez Galdós," 64.

2 This and all further quotations from the novel are taken from Luciano García Lorenzo's 1982 edition. All translations are mine.

3 For a re-examination of the *flâneur* that explores issues of gender, see Wolff; Kuppers; and Ganeva.

4 See, for example, Simmel.

5 The first sentence of book 1 reads: "It was the best of times, it was the worst of times, it was the age of wisdom, it was the age of foolishness, it was the epoch of belief, it was the epoch of incredulity, it was the season of Light, it was the season of Darkness, it was the spring of hope, it was the winter of despair, we had everything before us, we had nothing before us, we were all going direct to Heaven, we were all going direct the other way – in short, the period was so far like the present period, that some of its noisiest authorities insisted on its being received, for good or for evil, in the superlative degree of comparison only" (3).

6 For a discussion of Galdós's use of irony, see Urey, 59–63. See also Smolen, 63–7.

7 See also Sádaba Alonso, 71–2.

8 For an in-depth discussion of the history of the cathedral and Almudena's relationship to Nuestra Señora de la Almudena, see Chamberlin; and Schyfter's chapter, "Almudena and the Jewish Theme in *Misericordia*," in *The Jew in the Novels of Benito Pérez Galdós*.

9 See Goldman.

10 In *Marginal Subjects*, an exemplary study of representations of gender deviance in the late nineteenth-century Spanish novel, Akiko Tsuchiya examines how gender deviants, by resisting normativity, not only opened up new spaces of subjectivity and agency but also undermined both the "social norms" and "the narrative conventions" that upheld such norms in "the realm of the imaginary" (27).

11 Urban geography and sociology have established the central import of the modern city, not only in understanding modernity but also in providing a conceptual framework for its analysis. Works on Madrid incorporating these approaches include Juliá, Ringrose, and Segura; Ugarte; Parsons; Baker; and Baker and Compitello. More recently, Leigh Mercer explores the idea of public space as a performative realm in her *Urbanism and Urbanity*.

12 See Bahamonde Magro; and Magnien.

13 See also Schyfter 79–80; and Gold 143–4.

14 Formative studies include Kronik; Spires; and Tsuchiya, *Images of the Sign*. See also Highfill.

15 Galdós's novels make use of an evolving and eclectic array of narrative strategies and points of view. Variations in the first-person narrative include the epistolary form in *La incógnita* (1889); novels written in dialogue such as *Realidad* (1889); and complicated narrators-characters who sometimes switch their positions in works such as *El amigo Manso* (1882), *Lo prohibido* (1885), and *Fortunata y Jacinta* (1886–7), among others.

WORKS CITED

Ayala Aracil, María de las Ángeles. "Galdos, flâneur y peregrino por Inglaterra: La casa de Shakespeare." *Anales de Literatura Española* 24 (2012): 181–93. Print. https://doi.org/10.14198/ALEUA.2012.24.11.

Bahamonde Magro, Ángel. "Cultura de la pobreza y mendicidad involuntaria en el Madrid de siglo XIX." In *Madrid en Galdós. Galdós en Madrid*. Madrid: Comunidad de Patrimonio Cultural, 1988. 163–82. Print.

Baker, Edward. *Materiales para escribir Madrid: Literatura y espacio urbano de Moratín a Galdós*. Madrid: Siglo Veintiuno Editores, 1991. Print.

Baker, Edward, and Malcolm Alan Compitello, eds. *Madrid de Fortunata a la M-40*. Madrid: Alianza, 2003. Print.

Bakhtin, Mikhail M. "Discourse in the Novel." In *The Dialogic Imagination: Four Essays*, ed. Michael Holquist. Austin: U of Texas P, 1981. Print.

Benjamin, Walter. *The Arcades Project*. Ed. Rolf Tiedemann. Trans. Howard Eiland and Kevin McLaughlin. Cambridge, MA: Belknap P, 1999. Print.

Chamberlin, Vernon A. "The Significance of the Name Almudena in Galdós' *Misericordia*." *Hispania* 47.3 (1964): 491–6. Print. https://doi.org/10.2307/336167.

Delgado, L. Elena. "Subjetividades errantes: Galdós y la localización de la diferencia." *Anales Galdosianos* 36 (2001): 111–19. Print.

Dickens, Charles. *A Tale of Two Cities*. New York: Random House, 1935. Print.

Fuentes Peris, Teresa. "A Diseased Morality: Begging and Indiscriminate Charity in Galdós's *Misericordia*." *Journal of Iberian and Latin American Studies* 8.2 (2002): 109–26. Print. https://doi.org/10.1080/1470184022000035148.

Furst, Lilian. "Realism and Its Code of Accreditation." *Comparative Literature Studies* 25 (1988): 101–26. Print.

Ganeva, Mila. "Female *Flâneurs*: Judith Hermann's *Sommerhaus, später* and *Nichts als Gespenster*." *Gegenwartsliteratur* 3 (2004): 250–77. Print.

Glannon, Walter. "Charity and Distributive Justice: *Misericordia* Reexamined." *MLN* 100.2 (1985): 247–64. Print. https://doi.org/10.2307/2905736.

Gold, Hazel. "Outsider Art: Homelessness in *Misericordia*." *Anales Galdosianos* 36 (2001): 141–54. Print.

Goldman, Peter B. "Galdós and the Nineteenth-Century Novel: The Need for an Interdisciplinary Approach." *Anales Galdosianos* 10 (1975): 5–18. Print.

Gutman, Robert. "Street Generation." In *On Streets*, ed. Stanford Anderson. Cambridge, MA: MIT P, 1978. 249–64. Print.

Highfill, Juli. "Metafiction and Beyond: Collective Consciousness in *Misericordia*." *Revista de estudios hispánicos* 40.2 (2006): 265–82. Print.

Huyssen, Andreas. *Present Pasts: Urban Palimpsests and the Politics of Memory*. Stanford: Stanford UP, 2003. Print.

Juliá, Santos, David Ringrose, and Cristina Segura. *Madrid historia de una capital*. Madrid: Alianza, 2008. Print.

Kristeva, Julia. *Desire in Language*. New York: Columbia UP, 1980. Print.

Kronik, John. "*Misericordia* as Metafiction." In *Homenaje a Antonio Sánchez Barbudo: Ensayos de literatura española moderna*, ed. Benito Brancaforte. Madison, WI: Department of Spanish and Portuguese, U of Wisconsin, 1981. 37–50. Print.

Kuppers, Petra. "Moving in the Cityscape: Performance and the Embodied Experience of the Flâneur." *New Theatre Quarterly* 15.4 (1999): 308–17. Print. https://doi.org/10.1017/s0266464x00013245.

Labanyi, Jo, ed. *Galdós*. London: Longman, 1993.

Magnien, Brigitte. "Cultura urbana." In *1900 en España*, ed. Serge Salaün and Carlos Serrano. Madrid: Espasa-Calpe, 1991. 107–29. Print

Mercer, Leigh. *Urbanism and Urbanity: The Spanish Bourgeois Novel and Contemporary Customs (1845–1925).* Lewisburg, PA: Bucknell UP, 2013.

Muñoz Millanes, José. "The City as Palimpsest." Trans. Jason Weiss. *Ciberletras,* 3 August 2000, n. pag. Web. 17 February 2015.

Muñoz-Muriana, Sara. "'Andando se hace el camino': Calle y prácticas formativas del sujeto marginal en la novela española moderna." Diss. Princeton U, 2012. Ann Arbor: UMI, 2012. Print.

Parsons, Deborah L. *A Cultural History of Madrid: Modernism and the Urban Spectacle.* Oxford: Berg, 2003. Print.

Pérez Galdós, Benito. "Memorias de un desmemoriado." In *Obras completas,* ed. Federico Carlos Sainz de Robles. Vol. 6. Madrid: Aguilar, 1951. 1655–1703.

– *Misericordia.* Ed. Luciano García Lorenzo. Madrid: Cátedra, 1982. Print.

– "La sociedad presente como materia novelable." In *Ensayos de Crítica Literaria,* ed. Laureano Bonet. Barcelona: Nexos/Ediciones Península, 1990. 157–65.

Ribbans, Geoffrey. "The Janus-Face Structure of *Misericordia.*" *Anales Galdosianos* 36 (2001): 203–18. Print.

Ricard, Robert. "Sur le personnage d'Almudena dans *Misericordia.*" *Bulletin Hispanique* 61.1 (1959): 12–25. Print. https://doi.org/10.3406/hispa.1959.3612.

Rossi, Aldo. *The Architecture of the City.* Trans. Diane Ghirardo and Joan Ockman. Cambridge, MA: MIT P, 1984. Print.

Russell, Robert. "The Christ Figure in *Misericordia.*" *Anales Galdosianos* 2 (1967): 103–30. Print.

Sádaba Alonso, Soraya. "Espacio y personajes en *Misericordia* de Benito Pérez Galdós." *Cuadernos de investigación filológica* 27–8 (2001–2): 63–79. Print. https://doi.org/10.18172/cif.2200.

Schraibman, José. "El Ecumenismo de Galdós." *Hispania* 53.4 (1970): 881–6. Print. https://doi.org/10.2307/337854.

Schyfter, Sara E. *The Jew in the Novels of Benito Pérez Galdós.* London: Tamesis, 1978. Print.

Simmel, Georg. "The Metropolis and Mental Life." In *Simmel on Culture,* ed. D. Frisby and M. Featherstone. London: Sage, 1997. 174–85. Print.

Smolen, Marian. "Las dos caras de San Sebastián: Hacia un análisis de la técnica caricaturesca en *Misericordia* de Benito Pérez Galdós." *Romance Notes* 21 (1980): 63–7. Print.

Spires, Robert. *Beyond the Metafictional Mode: Directions in the Modern Spanish Novel.* Lexington: UP of Kentucky, 1984. Print.

Tsuchiya, Akiko. *Images of the Sign: Semiotic Consciousness in the Novels of Benito Pérez Galdós.* Columbia: U of Missouri P, 1990. Print.

– *Marginal Subjects: Gender and Deviance in Fin-de-siècle Spain*. Toronto: U of Toronto P, 2011.

Ugarte, Michael. *Madrid 1900: The Capital as Cradle of Literature and Culture*. University Park: Penn State UP, 1996. Print.

Urey, Diane. *Galdós and the Irony of Language*. New York: Cambridge UP, 1982. Print.

Wolff, Janet. "The Invisible Flâneuse: Women and the Literature of Modernity." *Theory, Culture and Society* 2.3 (1985): 37–46. Print. https://doi.org/10.1177/0263276485002003005.

PART THREE

Stretching the Limits of Spanish Realism

8 Colonialism, Collages, and Thick Description: Pardo Bazán and the Rhetoric of Detail

JOYCE TOLLIVER

In August of 2016, the journalist Deborah Treisman asked the writer Tessa Hadley to comment on how she used "small cultural signifiers," such as a second-hand bright pink coat, or a particular shopping bag, to lend depth to characterization in her short story "Dido's Lament." Treisman asked, "How much do you think can be conveyed through this kind of detail?" "Almost everything," responded Hadley. "I suppose that's the whole premise of a certain kind of fiction, really, of realist fiction – that we can get at the general through the particular." She elaborated:

> ... writing is a bit like anthropology, I suppose – using all the cultural layering of detail and nuance and perception to construct a world of significance. When I'm writing a story, its world is thin, unsatisfactory, untrue, until I start to find my way to these details, those "small cultural signifiers." As these accumulate on the page, the life in the piece thickens, the details breed, and the story starts to stir.

Emilia Pardo Bazán, like today's writer Tessa Hadley and indeed like all realist writers, creates the illusion of a world through the saturated representation of details of the material world. This saturation, this "thickening," to use Hadley's phrase, is indeed remarkably similar to the work of the anthropologist as Clifford Geertz conceived of it, in his landmark essay, "Thick Description." The accumulation of these details creates what Harriet Turner describes as a sensorial "collage of space and time" ("'Why the Face of the Voice'" 216). Many of Pardo Bazán's stories teach readers about the significance of seemingly insignificant details, but it is in her essays about the colonies that she most dramatically infuses objects with meaning, mirroring the privileging of the detail that is found in Spanish realist novels. In the 1899 essay "Artículo ex-colonial" [Ex-Colonial Article], for example, her analysis of the failings that led to the loss of Spain's last significant colonies is framed by a long meditation on chocolate, on its rising price, the result of the loss of trade controls in the colonies; and on the loss of the culture of leisure associated with the empire. In "Siempre la guerra" [Always the War], Pardo Bazán's discussions of the press coverage of the 1898 war lead to the contemplation of another domestic object, the *mantón de Manila*, as a primary source of knowledge of the Philippines for many Spaniards. In this essay, inspired by Turner's lessons on "thing-ism," I examine Pardo Bazán's evocation of material details as synecdoches for a colonial rhetoric that hinges on the sense of absence and of lack, in contrast to realist *fiction's* evocation of presence and of knowledge (Turner, "The Realist Novel" 81).

Both "Siempre la guerra" and "Artículo ex-colonial" appeared first in Pardo Bazán's column, "La vida contemporánea" [Contemporary Life], which was published monthly between 1895 and 1915 in the Barcelona journal *La Ilustración Artística*. The short essays she wrote for this column usually offered reflections on a particular event or cultural phenomenon characterizing that moment in Spain. Her topics ranged from smoking and gender roles ("Columnas de humo" [Columns of Smoke]), to the noise made by automobiles ("*Teuf ... teuf*"), to the price of chocolate in the aftermath of the War of 1898 ("Artículo ex-colonial"). Taken together, the "Vida contemporánea" essays form an ethnographic study of everyday Spanish life at the end of one century and the beginning of another.[1] Pardo Bazán herself seems to have seen these articles in that way: in 1901 she gathered a selection of them for a volume of her self-compiled complete works, and published them under the title *De siglo a siglo* [From Century to Century]. Pardo Bazán's choice of title for this collection captures the moment of transition from one century to the next, from the imagined stability of the Restoration of the Monarchy in 1875 to the fragmentation and turbulence of the early twentieth century. It also evokes 1898, a year that was the fulcrum between the age when Spain could still consider itself an empire and the time when what was left of the Spanish empire would be eclipsed by the new power of the United States.

De siglo a siglo thus captures the end of empire and the beginning of a future Spain, which the author does not pretend to fully comprehend.

The collected essays suggest that the incipient post-empire age is characterized both by modernity and by Spain's resistance to cultural and economic change, as well as by both deep nostalgia and a regret over past failings. Pardo Bazán ironically juxtaposes the melancholy associated with these years with the period's concomitant frivolity. The tensions between all of these opposing tendencies, and others, are reflected in the thematic *vaivén* from essay to essay and even within some of the individual essays gathered in *De siglo a siglo*. In their focus on aspects of daily life that are representative of something particularly Spanish, they are reminiscent of Mariano José de Larra's *cuadros de costumbres*, or sketches of customs, penned a half-century earlier.[2] In this sense, some of the essays resuscitate the satirical *costumbrismo* essays of the first half of the nineteenth century. Yet they do not simply mimic the satirical gesture of Larra's *cuadros de costumbres*. Rather, in technique as well as content, they anticipate the detailed analyses of cultural practices that characterize the interpretation of cultures as it was carried out in the late twentieth century.

In particular, these essays anticipate the interpretive approach to cultural analysis that Geertz would later call, after Gilbert Ryle, "thick description." Writing in 1973, Geertz proposed that ethnography should abandon the attempt to form totalizing descriptions of cultural practices, conceiving of culture, instead, in semiotic terms. From this premise it follows that making sense of culture is a matter of "construing" complex semiotic codes:

> Believing with Max Weber that man is an animal suspended in webs of significance he himself has spun, I take culture to be those webs, and the analysis of it to be therefore not an experimental science in search of law but an interpretive one in search of meaning. It is *explication* I am after, *construing* social expressions on their surface enigmatical. (5; my emphases)

In explaining how ethnographers "construe," or make sense of, these "social expressions," Geertz refers to Gilbert Ryle's notion of "thick description." He explains Ryle's distinction between two seemingly identical acts: an involuntary twitch of the eye, on the one hand, and a wink, on the other. The difference between the two lies entirely in the construction of their meaning, which in turn rests upon the winker's intention (or the twitcher's lack of intention) and upon the correct perception of that intention. A "thin" description would simply record the physical action; a "thick" description would take into account the "public code" that allows for the transformation of the twitch into the wink (6).

Geertz compares the task of the cultural analyst to the task of the literary critic, in that both deal not with the straightforward deciphering of codes, but rather with interpretation (9). He adds that the "thick description" of anthropology that he advocates is anchored in the observation and interpretation of details; he calls his approach "microscopic" (21), explaining that "the anthropologist characteristically approaches ... broader interpretations and more abstract analyses from the direction of *exceedingly extended acquaintances with extremely small matters*" (21; my emphasis). While, for Geertz's ethnographic project, these "extremely small matters" typically belonged to cultures that were unfamiliar to his readers, in contrast to the realist novelist's practice of examining precisely those details that seemed most familiar, Geertz's explanation of "thick description" captures well the project of the realist novelist as conceived by Leopoldo Alas ("Clarín"). As Turner explains, Alas "advocates the idea of the novel as a 'reproduction' based on close observation and documentary evidence, on 'scrupulously examined details'" (Alas 127, qtd. in Turner, "The Realist Novel" 81).

Pardo Bazán's *De siglo a siglo* essays on the War of 1898 and its aftermath combine the interests of the mid-twentieth-century interpretive ethnographer with the techniques of the writer of realist fiction. The essays employ techniques used by writers of realist novels as Turner explains them. In particular, we see reflected in these essays the notion of the realist writer's "'collage' which ... made the act of writing into a nexus of experiences operating inside and outside between character, author, and reader" (Kidd 12, qtd. in Turner, "Why the Face of the Voice" 217). Kidd's image of the collage inspires Turner to analyse how, in realist novels, "the techniques of suspension, simultaneity, and spatiality all evoke the impression of a collage in which 'the face of the voice is in the hand': face and voices and hands overlap to cause ... that thin flat page to 'bulge' with the perception of 'real,' multidimensional artifacts and actions" (Turner, "Why the Face of the Voice" 217).

Turner's image of the reader's experience of realism's "bulging," "multidimensional" collages insistently calls to mind the metaphor of "thickness" that Ryle used to describe the task of the anthropologist, just as the Clarinian "'scrupulously examined details'" resonate with Geertz's evocation of the anthropologist's "extended acquaintance with extremely small matters" (21). In these essays, the "exceedingly small matters" that form the core of Pardo Bazán's analyses of larger issues often revolve around a particular object, which she reveals to be saturated with cultural meaning. Through her "thick description," Pardo Bazán thus reveals "the subtle incrustrations of intention and invention, fantasy and ideology, tradition and accident that, like a family history that can be recovered only by means of exacting genealogical research, an object carries in the train of its existence," as Jeffrey Schnapp puts it, in his essay on industrial invention (Schnapp 245).

By considering how Spaniards interact with these semiotically charged objects every day – and by considering the intersection between everyday objects and cultural practices – Pardo Bazán makes sense of the seeming incoherence of Spanish society at the turn of the century. In "Siempre la guerra" (1898) and "Artículo ex-colonial" (1899), for example, she focuses closely on two objects in particular: a Spanish shawl – or *mantón de Manila* – and a nice hot cup of really good chocolate, respectively. Each of these objects is undoubtedly symbolic of some aspect of the waning or defunct empire, but Pardo Bazán's rhetorical evocation of these and other objects goes beyond the symbolic. In these essays, she does not simply demonstrate that "the world is not simply what it is but a cipher of a higher reality" (Labanyi, "Doing Things" 227). Rather, she shows how the way in which Spaniards interacted with the *mantón de Manila* or with the appurtenances of chocolate-drinking embodied – or rather materialized – important aspects of Spain's imperial past. In her consideration of these objects as synecdoches, she again anticipates interpretive anthropology, in which, as James Clifford says, "fields of synecdoches are created in which parts are related to wholes – and by which the whole, what we often call culture, is constituted" (131).[3]

Both of the notions I have discussed so far – "thick description" and the realist's collage – lend insight into how Pardo Bazán bridges the nineteenth-century realist writer's recording of details of material life, on the one hand, and that of the twentieth-century cultural analyst, on the other. In her fictional works, she deploys a rhetoric of detail to evoke a sense of presence and of knowledge. But in her essays on the cultural effects of the war, Pardo Bazán evokes material details as synecdoches for a colonial rhetoric that hinges, not on the sense of presence and of knowledge, but rather on feelings of absence and lack.

In "Siempre la guerra," published in June of 1898, Pardo Bazán expresses a sense of colonial uprootedness, dislocation, and loss. We might expect that her commentary on the war in the Philippines would be characterized by a lament over the loss of political and economic control that comes with the end of the empire. Indeed, that sense is clearly and poetically expressed in several of the other essays that she included in *De siglo a siglo*. But in "Siempre la guerra," we find a contemplation of loss that is both more philosophical and more defeatist. The essay begins on an uncharacteristically tentative note: "Notad la importancia que de pronto han adquirido desde los últimos infaustos acontecimientos, nuestras ... ¿puede decirse *nuestras*? posesiones del Archipiélago Magallánico" [Notice how important our – can we say "our"? – possessions in Magellan's Archipelago have suddenly become with the most recent wretched events] (112).[4] Pardo Bazán's hesitation is well justified: just fifteen days before the essay was published, the Philippines had proclaimed independence, and less than a week earlier, Spain had surrendered Guam. The newspapers had been full of news about the Philippines all month, and the news accounts were often illustrated with photos of warships or Spanish or Philippine soldiers. But the articles were also accompanied by semi-ethnographic photos of supposedly typical Philippine residents – that is, not the Christian mestizo inhabitants who formed the majority of inhabitants, but rather the unassimilated Muslims or the "negritos" from the southern islands, as they were called at the time. The Philippines may have been one of the so-called overseas provinces, but the image promulgated in the press was one that insisted on the alien nature of this branch of Spain's national family.[5]

It is this sense of alienation that permeates Pardo Bazán's "Siempre la guerra." She suggests that the constant news of the war has done nothing to bring the Philippines closer. But she goes further, and wonders whether, in fact, peninsular Spaniards ever really did know anything at all about the most remote geographical area of their empire: "Manila, Filipinas, acudían rara vez a la memoria. Era una tierra pintoresca y riente, pero muy distante, perdida en las soledades del Océano; nos faltaba, por decirlo así, la noción de su realidad" [Manila, Philippines, were hardly ever on the minds [of Spaniards]. That was a picturesque, laughing land, but it was very distant, lost in the solitude of the Ocean; we didn't have any notion, really, of their reality] (113).

In fact, she argues that most peninsular Spaniards were (and her use of the past tense in the above lines is significant) aware of the existence of the Philippines only through their domestic use of material objects associated with the Archipelago. She enumerates a long series of objects that were routinely incorporated into peninsular daily life, as the only real evidence of any relationship whatsoever with the Philippine Islands:

> ... petacas de paja ... cofrecillos y muebles de laca con incrustraciones de nácar y flores y aves de brillantes colorines; cajas de sándalo ... abanicos pesados de varillas de filigrana, de plata o carey; colchas bordadas, en las cuales luce una flor extravagante, barroca e imposible; perlas y madreperlas; tejidos de nipis y cortinas de bambú ... (117)

> [... straw tobacco cases, little lacquered chests and furniture inlaid with abalone and brightly coloured flowers and birds; sandalwood boxes ... heavy hand fans with blades made of silver or tortoiseshell filigree; embroidered bedspreads sporting an extravagant flower, baroque and impossible; pearls and mother-of-pearl; *abacá* fibre weavings and bamboo curtains ...]

Of all these everyday decorative objects, the one that most eloquently reflects the history of the colonial relationship is the *mantón de Manila*. But this supposedly quintessentially Spanish garment – this perfectly folkloric accessory – has never been "typical" of Spain in the sense of being autochthonous – or, in fact, typical of anything Spanish, except for the economic bases of its colonies in southeast Asia. As Pedro Ortiz Armengol has shown, the Chinese first began manufacturing the garment for export, not to Spain, but to colonial Mexico, so it is richly steeped in a colonial legacy (216). Always manufactured for foreign consumption, it was never native to Manila, and only gradually was it adopted for use in Spain.

Pardo Bazán's revelation of the colonial appropriation of the *mantón de Manila* is reinforced in her own discourse, when she claims that not only has this garment always been made for exportation but it was made to envelop, not the desexualized body of the Filipina, but rather the shapely Spanish female body.

> ... ese trapo es ya más peninsular, más andaluz, más madrileño que asiático. Yo no me represento, envuelta en el mantón, a la mestiza del archipiélago, de rostro deprimido, chata nariz, achocolatada tez y cabello azulado y lacio, sino a la garbosa hija de Sevilla o la gaditana de quebrada cintura, cuando no a la salada chulapa del Rastro o del barrio de Maravillas (117)

> [... now that garment is more peninsular, more Andalusian, more Madridian than Asian. I do not imagine the Archipelago mestiza, with her

flattened face, her snub nose, her chocolatey colour and her limp blue-black hair wearing the *mantón*, but rather the graceful daughter of Seville, or the slim-waisted Cádiz girl, if not the saucy chula from the [working-class Madrid] Rastro or Maravillas neighbourhoods]

In contrast to Galdós's evocation, in *Fortunata y Jacinta*, of the Chinese heritage of the *mantón de Manila* (Pérez Galdós 126–9), Pardo Bazán points to the "incrustations," to use Schnapp's term (245), of cultural attitudes towards race, social class, and sexuality that are legible in the garment and that bear witness to its colonial appropriation.[6] Further, she insinuates a more subtle move of cultural appropriation: not only is the brightly coloured shawl now widely thought of as more Spanish than Asian, but its associations specifically with Andalucía, rather than Madrid, represent yet another layer of cultural and literal fabrication.

Emphasizing the constructed nature of the touristic image of Spain, Pardo Bazán mentions Carolina Otero, a dancer who was wildly popular in France at the time, performing under the name La Belle Otero.

> En el extranjero ha empezado también a saborearse el picante atractivo del mantón, y a cada viaje que hace a Madrid la famosa Carolina Otero, se lleva dos o tres de los de más ancho fleco ... para enriquecer la colección que ya posee y con la cual se engalana al ejecutar en no sé qué Folies las danzas hispano-moriscas. (114)
>
> [The piquant attraction of the *mantón* is also being savoured outside of Spain, and every time Carolina Otero travels to Madrid, she goes away with two or three of them, the kind with the longest fringe ... to add to the collection she already has, with which she adorns herself for her performances of Hispano-Moorish dances at that Folies place.]

Ironically, the popularity of Carolina Otero is further evidence of the fictional nature of the cultural meaning attached to these "Moorish-Spanish" dances and to the brightly embroidered garment associated with them: Otero was from Pontevedra, in the north; and she left Spain as a very young adult. The made-for-exportation dances of La Belle Otero were famous more because of their exotic eroticism than their Andalusian authenticity. Certainly, there was no trace of Manila in her sheer body-hugging outfits, which provided Parisians with a fantasy that embodied the "land of the castanet" in the figure of the sexually appetizing flamenco dancer.[7] For Parisians – and, more importantly, suggests Pardo Bazán, for Spaniards – the Philippine Islands, even the picturesque Philippines of the *mantón de Manila,* were always irreal, experienced only through the acquisition of exoticized objects of fantasy. In this sense, we might be tempted to say that Pardo Bazán exposes the fetishized nature of the objects: they serve as a stand-in for the colonial Philippines themselves. But, according to the author's logic, rather than allowing middle-class Spaniards to evade any recognition of the colonial realities that produced them, instead they evoke a fictional version of those realities. It is the fictional construction itself, and the hollowness at its core, that interests Pardo Bazán here.

Pardo Bazán's "thick description" of that folkloric object, the *mantón de Manila,* is a meditation not only on the loss of the Philippines as a colony but also on more abstract issues. Her exposure of the falseness of the national symbolism of that quintessential garment of Spanish femininity calls into question the stability of the notion of "local customs," and emphasizes the constructed nature of what are "authentic" national customs. By extension, notions of a fixed and universal "national character" are also undermined.

In this sense, Pardo Bazán echoes Unamuno's rejection of the costumbristic project of capturing a national spirit by collecting "retratos que solo a los parientes interesan, que en cuanto muere el padre arranca de la pared el hijo el del abuelo para echarlo al Rastro" [portraits that are of interest only to the relatives of those who sat for them, [since] as soon as his father has died, the son tears the portrait of his grandfather off the wall to throw it in the jumble-bin] (37). While she shares the *costumbrista*'s desire to document cultural practices, her aim is not to hold back the tides of time or to resist cultural change, but rather to "thicken" her readers' understanding of culturally meaningful objects and practices in order to better understand the present moment. Pardo Bazán's approach, in these essays, is in accordance with Unamuno's well-known exhortation to Spaniards to "buscar lo eterno en el aluvión de lo insignificante, de lo *inorgánico,* de lo que gira en torno de lo eterno como cometa errático, sin entrar en ordenada constelación con él" [seek the eternal in the floodwaters of the insignificant, of the *inorganic,* of that which spins around the eternal like an erratic comet, without entering its orbit] (43–4). But she goes beyond the philosopher's recognition of the place of the ephemeral in history. For Pardo Bazán, Unamuno's abstract postulation of history as the living of the present moment is a given. In fact, it forms the basis of virtually all the essays in *De siglo a siglo.* She needs no further urging to "seek the eternal in the insignificant"; she *shows* her readers how the essential – if not the eternal – is encapsulated in what Micaelita Aránguiz, the protagonist of her "El encaje roto" (Torn Lace), called "pequeñeces que significan algo" (little things that mean something) (62).

The significance of "pequeñeces," of little things – of the everyday and domestic – is dramatized sharply in "Artículo ex-colonial." This melancholy piece was published in January of 1899, only about a week after the final withdrawal of Spanish forces from Cuba. The title frames the article in terms of the national trauma, but the bulk of the article deals with a far more serious topic: chocolate. Not the adulterated, flaky stuff suddenly invading the shelves of Madrid's stores at the beginning of the first "ex-colonial" year of Spain's modern history, but the really good chocolate, the kind that was prepared in the old days, in the days of the empire. Now that Spain had lost its cash crop, even bad chocolate was suddenly hideously expensive.

Chocolate, Pardo Bazán explains at the outset of the essay, is a sort of symbolic repository of the recently deceased Spanish empire, for it is in chocolate that one can find the crystallization of "nuestras glorias y nuestras desventuras" [our glory and our misfortune] (150): "Cuando ganamos a América, revelamos al mundo el chocolate; cuando la perdimos definitivamente, lo primero que notamos en la esfera de la economía doméstica, es que el cacao se ha puesto por las nubes" [When we won America, we revealed chocolate to the world; when we lost her for good, the first thing we noticed in the realm of home economics was that cocoa is through the roof] (150). With the decline of the empire came the decline of a cultural practice, and along with it, the disappearance of a whole subset of industries related to the manufacture of the decorative pieces used to serve the national drink (151). So when Spaniards began to drink tea – *tea,* the national drink of the Anglo-Saxons, whom Pardo Bazán so despised – something was drastically wrong. As Pardo Bazán puts it, "Al invadirnos el té (el té, más sajón que chino), podemos dar por consumada nuestra anulación ante la historia futura" [With the invasion of tea (tea, more Saxon than Chinese), our future has certainly been annihilated] (150).

In contemplating the era when the chocolate trade was firmly under Spanish control, Pardo Bazán offers a nostalgic evocation of the time of the empire – even the years when the empire was in frank decline – as a more gentle, more refined, more civilized time. Referring to the ill-fated attempts to resist the imposition of the new custom of taking tea, rather than chocolate, she comments, "Se tropieza siempre con el inconveniente de que se paga chocolate y se compra fécula. Detrás del té y del chocolate hay un problema histórico: no se restaura una bebida sin restaurar un mundo, sin restaurar una época, sin restaurar una nación" [You always run into the problem that you pay for chocolate and you get starch. Behind tea and chocolate there is a problem of history: you cannot bring back a drink without bringing back a world, without bringing back an era, without bringing back a nation] (154).

"Artículo ex-colonial" is partially an attempt to do just that, to "bring back an era" – namely, that other turn of the century which comprises the reign of Carlos IV, at the end of the eighteenth and the beginning of the nineteenth centuries. In contrast with the rushed quaffing of a cup of tea, she writes, one must sit down for chocolate, preferably in, as she says, "un gran sillón de los llamados *fraileros*, con su cordobán, sus clavos de asterisco, sus brazos anchos y su asiento profundo" [a great chair, of the type called *friar's chairs*, with its cordovan leather, its upholstery nails, its wide arms, and its deep seat] (152). Pardo Bazán comments on one particularly nice "friar's chair" she has seen, which sported a little removable table, which the occupant could use to support a book or, of course, the chocolate stand (152).

Once she has evoked the image of the proper chair for chocolate, Pardo Bazán elaborates, not just on its uses, but on the rituals of daily life that would surround this fine chair, and on the fortunate gentleman who would carry out these leisurely rituals. He would rise early to go to Mass, and then return to bed – "ardid de devoto para edificar a los vecinos y no estropear la salud" [a trick the devout use to edify the neighbours without ruining their health] (152). Around eleven, he'd take a little walk and read the newspapers, then return home for a fine mid-day meal. After lunch, time for a little nap in his special chair, while he listened to "his little niece or his young wife" gently play the piano a room or so away. At four o'clock, finally, came the high point of the day, when, says Pardo Bazán, "la bandeja del chocolate venía a buscar su sitio en el avance del sillón" [the chocolate tray came to find its place in front of the chair] (153).

In this quick sketch of the cozy, privileged daily life of the chocolate drinker, Pardo Bazán does indeed manage to evoke a world and an era now past. She does so in a way that is reminiscent of Larra's evocation of the daily routine of the useless fop of "La vida de Madrid," [Madrid Life] written over a half-century earlier. Larra's "artículo de costumbres" details the narration of the sequence of non-events of the day in the life of this urban gadabout. When the narrator, Fígaro, asks him,

"And what do you do in society?" the reply is, "Nada; entro en la sala; paso al gabinete; vuelvo a la sala; entro al ecarté; vuelvo a entrar en la sala; vuelvo a salir al gabinete; vuelvo a entrar en el ecarté ... luego a casa y ¡buenas noches!" [Nothing; I walk into the parlour, I go on to the sitting room, I return to the parlour, I go into the card room, I go back to the parlour; I go out and go back into the sitting room, then back to the card room ... then, home, and time for bed!] (473).

Larra's fictional young madrileño is almost exhausting in his idleness. He dedicates the entire day to activity, yet this activity is meaningless and unproductive. The idleness of Pardo Bazán's chocolate drinker, in contrast, lacks even the useless energy of Larra's famous character. In evoking the era of the unperturbed chocolate drinker, Pardo Bazán also evokes a time of indolence, of self-satisfied somnolence, and of isolation. There is no "society" here, as there is in Larra's essay; the chocolate tray seems to float to the owner's chair of its own accord; the music wafts out of the next room for the delectation of the "señor del sillón" [gentleman in the chair], and the feminine presence creating that gentle music is, in both senses, immaterial: whether the young wife or the little niece, she is merely part of the auditory scenery.

It is not by chance that Pardo Bazán explicitly places the high point of the chocolate culture in the time of Carlos IV, that poor ineffectual soul whom Goya slyly portrayed as an idiot and a cuckold. It was, after all, only four months after she published "Artículo ex-colonial" that Pardo Bazán went to Paris and delivered "La España de ayer y la de hoy" [Spain, Yesterday and Today], the lecture that provided the origin of the term "black legend." In this address, she contrasted the "black legend" of the Conquest with what she termed the "golden legend," arguing that the "leyenda negra" of the Spanish empire had done less harm than its counterpart, the wildly idealistic evocation of Spain's glorious imperialist past, which, in 1899, was keeping even Spain's foremost intellectuals from responding with vigour and sang-froid to the economic and cultural crisis facing the nation. Her vigorous warnings of the dangers of the "leyenda dorada" place her in an ideological camp very different from that of the male writers we now associate with the so-called Generation of 98, such as Unamuno, with his dreamy evocation of a quixotic Spain.

Pardo Bazán's dedication of an essay to a subject as *apparently* frivolous as the price of cocoa, within a month after the signing of the treaty that ended the War of 1898, might seem initially to be a facetious, ironically escapist gesture. But in framing her highly political essay as a contemplation of the symbolic saturation of the everyday, Pardo Bazán could scarcely have chosen a better example than chocolate.

The word "chocolate" has its root in the Nahuatl word "txocol-atl," which Bugbee parses as water ("atl") that has been beaten – a reflection of the Aztec custom of whipping the blend of water and crushed cacao seeds to make the drink of which Moctezuma was inordinately fond, if we are to believe the account of Bernal Díaz (Bugbee 26). The codex known as the Libro de Tributos indicates that several regions of Mexico paid tributes to Moctezuma in cacao beans. Clearly, chocolate played an important part in the economic and cultural life not only of the Aztecs at the time of Moctezuma but also of the so-called Conquest. Spaniards blended the bitter cacao seeds with sugar (and, later, with various aromatic essences besides the vanilla and chiles used by the Aztecs), a culinary fad that entered the rest of Europe via France early in the seventeenth century (Bugbee 37).[8] The Spaniards developed and appropriated the exportation of cacao to the point that it soon became what Pardo Bazán calls Spain's golden fleece ("Artículo ex-colonial" 150).

The Spanish economy benefited greatly from the exportation of cacao from virtually all of northern Latin America until the Wars of Independence, by which time the Spaniards had also planted cacao trees in the Philippines. When the United States won the War of 1898, it also won the economic rights to the production of Philippine and Caribbean cocoa.[9] By that time, the Hershey Company in Pennsylvania had already begun marketing baking chocolate and chocolate-covered caramels, and civilization, as any good Spaniard knew it, was, for all practical purposes, over.[10]

In choosing chocolate as the quintessential metaphor for the Spanish empire, and for its long, drawn-out death, Pardo Bazán constructs a discourse that shifts between a colloquial, domestic register – in which she comes close to sounding like a middle-class housewife – and the more abstract discourse of the public intellectual, which was associated with the deep baritone ranges of the men of the Generation of 1898. She comments that "cocoa is through the roof" and that "you pay for chocolate and get starch" ("Artículo ex-colonial" 154); she lingers lovingly on detailed descriptions of the various styles of chocolate paraphernalia produced by Mexican and Spanish artisans. She also conjures up what she might have called the Chocolate Era by extensive enumeration of sartorial terms rarely, if ever, seen in the essays of her male contemporaries of the Generation of 1898: "Eran los tiempos del jubón, del coleto, de la valona ... de los chambergos con cintillo de pedrería; eran después los del tontillo, de la casaca ... del calzón corto, de la media de seda que dibuja la pierna torneada y nerviosa" [It was the age of jerkins, of doublets, of wide falling collars ... of broad-brim hats with jewelled bands; later it was the age of bustles, of frock coats ... of breeches, of silk stockings that showed off nervous, shapely legs] (150).

Finally, as is only fitting of the author of two cookbooks (*Cocina española antigua* [Old-Fashioned Spanish Cooking] and *Cocina española moderna* [Modern Spanish Cooking]), she dedicates a long paragraph to a detailed evocation of the sorts of sweets that were served on the chocolate tray: not the insipid little cookies of the present age, but much more elaborate delicacies made with fruits: "conservas en caja, de esas que todavía se elaboran en los conventos, y dulces de almíbar, caseros y de un sabor inolvidable. La brillante pasta de membrillo...el limoncillo amargo, la melosa guinda ... el rubio cabello de ángel" [pressed preserves, the kind they make in convents, and unforgettable homemade sweets made out of syrup. The brilliant quince paste, bitter crystallized lemon, sweet preserved cherries ... blonde-yellow angel hair] (151).

In the context of a discussion of the differences between the purity of the "real" chocolate, the chocolate of the time of "our great-grandparents" ("nuestros bisabuelos") (154), and the poor excuse for chocolate that was sold in 1899, she tells a homely anecdote:

> Unas señoras americanas muy distinguidas me regalaron un chocolate que, a la vista, parecía grosero trozo de piedra negruzca. Lo habían elaborado exactamente como lo elaboraron los aztecas antes de conocer a Hernán Cortés. No he probado cosa más rica. Y es que el chocolate no quiere adornos ni perfeccionamientos; sazonarlo es como pintar con carmín la rosa, o echar almíbar en el melón de Valencia. (154)

> [Some very distinguished American ladies presented me with some chocolate that, at first glance, looked like a crude chunk of blackish stone. It had been prepared exactly as the Aztecs used to prepare it before they made the acquaintance of Hernán Cortés. I have never tasted anything so delicious in my life. You see, chocolate does not need any adornment or polishing: to add spices to it is like painting a rose with rouge, or putting sweet syrup on a Valencia melon.]

A paragraph later, she abruptly repositions her colloquial domestic chat, switching to succinct yet abstract judgments about "el problema de España": "Nuestro menguado sino nos condena a té y pastas ... porque nos conduce a imitar, a perder lo que fue bueno de nuestro pasado, sin encontrar ni instituir lo que es óptimo en el presente de otros pueblos" [Our waning destiny condemns us to tea and biscuits ... because it leads us to imitate, to lose what was good about our past, without seeing or adopting the best things about other nations at the present moment] (154). In this way, Pardo Bazán shows us that it is precisely through the domestic – or, more exactly, through a feminine-coded "thick description" of everyday practices – that her readers can begin to fully understand the economic significance and the deeper cultural meaning of the War of 1898.

With this condensed analysis, Pardo Bazán's lament, just two sentences earlier, that "you pay for chocolate and you get starch" suddenly expands in meaning: in her reference to the deceptive adulteration of what Linnaeus termed "the food of the gods" (Linnaeus 782), her apparently trivial complaint about an inconvenience of everyday life becomes a metaphor for the nation-wide malady of loss of authenticity, loss of substance, and – in an echo of Larra – the myopia of Spain's rejection of any potentially positive influence from other nations. In marked contrast to the conservative *costumbristas* whom Unamuno so deplored, however, she leads us to question what exactly it *was* that was good about Spain's supposedly glorious past, beyond the sleepy self-deceptive tranquillity that characterized the privileged life of the "señor del sillón frailero." She laments a loss of national authenticity, but her sketch of that supposed authenticity is saturated with irony.

Pardo Bazán's focus on the details of domesticity is not just a rhetorical device, a strategy to get her readers' attention in order to discuss weightier matters. On the contrary, the housewife's lament and the intellectual's lament are mixed well in this essay – with one brief exception: "Yo creo que en España no se puede hacer cosa al derecho colectivamente: aquí sólo el individuo se afirma con cierta energía, y sólo esfuerzos aislados logran algún suceso" [I believe that in Spain it is impossible to do anything well as a collective: here, it is only the individual who takes any sort of energetic initiative, and it is only through individual efforts that anything gets accomplished] (154). She follows this suggestive statement with a self-reflexive caveat: "No pierdo de vista el chocolate en esta digresión: al contrario" [I am not losing sight of chocolate in this digression; on the contrary] (154). According to this statement, the focus of the essay is not, as its title might indicate, the loss of the colonies and the profound implications of that loss – all *that*, says Pardo Bazán, is a digression. We might be tempted to assume that, in referring to her overt social commentary as a "digression" from the foregrounded topic of chocolate, Pardo Bazán is simply speaking ironically; that, by flippantly discoursing on the value of chocolate, she is allowing her readers a moment of evasion from the oppressive consideration of Spain's "Desastre." Yet the rest of her essay demonstrates that the weighty, abstract analysis of Spain's "ex-colonial" period cannot be separated from the seemingly trivial matter of the decline in the quality of chocolate available to middle-class Spanish housewives.

She returns from her "digression" by offering a solution to the problem of bad chocolate: one must not buy the pre-packaged chocolate from the store shelves, but rather use solid chocolate and call in a "chocolatero," who has the equipment and the expertise to prepare chocolate properly in one's home (154–5). In other words, she recommends an economic boycott of bad chocolate, but also, seemingly, a return to the days of the Chocolate Era, which in turn implies a return to the home: "No es digno de tomar chocolate el que no lo hace en casa, a estilo del reinado de Carlos IV" [Anyone who does not prepare chocolate at home, as it was done during the reign of Carlos IV, does not deserve to have it], she admonishes (155).

The return to hot chocolate prepared from scratch and taken at home, then, is a return to the imperial past. Yet, as Pardo Bazán herself repeatedly reminded us, that past is ephemeral, and never was nearly half as glorious as its chocolate – which itself may be what she means when she refers to "what was good about our past" (154). After all, the only real note of life in her portrait of the eighteenth-century occupant of the *sillón frailero* is seen when "el del sillón" [the chair's occupant] takes his chocolate: "majestuosamente, a pulso, con lenta fruición voluptuosa, sepultaba el bizcocho de canela en el pocillo, lo desbarbaba y escurría en el borde, y lo alzaba después hasta la boca, sintiendo el vigor y el aroma de la americana bebida" [majestically, with a firm pulse, savouring it slowly and voluptuously, he sank the cinnamon sponge cake in the pot, tapped it and rolled it on the rim, and then raised it to his mouth, breathing in the vigour and aroma of the American drink] (153). Yet even this almost erotic pleasure is portrayed in terms perilously close to those of the languid decadence of a Marqués de Bradomín. No, the signs of vitality here seem to be limited to the chocolate itself, to "the vigour and aroma" of the American – not Spanish – drink. It is through the representation of chocolate that we hear a response to Francisco Silvela's allegation, made five months earlier, of lifelessness, of lack of virility, in the Spanish nation: Silvela's essay "Sin pulso" [Without a

Pulse] is echoed in Pardo Bazán's description of our Chocolate Era gentleman waking from his afternoon nap to take his chocolate, now "a pulso" [with a firm pulse] (153).

In "Siempre la guerra" and "Artículo ex-colonial," Pardo Bazán suggests that Spain's troubles, at the end of the empire, reach far beyond the military, beyond the government, beyond the failing economy, and into the dining rooms, kitchens, and parlours of all of Pardo Bazán's middle-class readers. Her reflections on the loss of really good chocolate, like her contemplation of the illusory nature of the *mantón de Manila*, are far from digressions. In fact, they form the very centre of her analysis of the end of Spanish empire. The *mantón de Manila* functions as a synecdoche for the constructed history of Spain's colonial relationships, in the same way that Víctor Quintanar's half-smoked cigar sums up perfectly the sexual failure of his marriage to Ana Ozores, la Regenta. In "Artículo ex-colonial" and "Siempre la guerra," as in Spanish realist novels, the "part stands for, intimates, or poses as the whole but is not, in and of itself, that whole" (Turner, " The Realist Novel" 82). As she does in her realist novels, Pardo Bazán "trick[s] out [the] larger meaning through the interplay of part and whole"; "objects become transformed into 'synecdochic close-ups' and 'metonymic setups'" (Jakobson 1115; qtd. in Turner, "The Realist Novel" 82).

Pardo Bazán practises Geertz's "thick description" through meditations on what Geertz called "extended acquaintance with extremely small matters" (21). She ties particular Spanish cultural practices, such as the leisurely drinking of the afternoon cup of chocolate, to the material objects that stand for those practices: the *mantón de Manila*, or the little piece of unadulterated chocolate. Geertz defines culture as those "webs of significance" (311) that humans spin; in like fashion, Pardo Bazán makes sense of the end of the imperial era through the webs of connections she draws between and among the objects and practices of everyday life.

Each of these practices, and each of these objects, is meaningful not just because it has come to symbolize the Spanish empire and its end, but because it *contains* the history of that empire, in the same way that each small shard of a hologram contains the entire holographic image.[11] Yet, like the hologram, whose significance lies in the fact that it captures an apparent reality that is not there, that is merely illusion, the history crystallized in the *mantón de Manila* or in the appurtenances of chocolate was itself always an illusion. Pardo Bazán retrieves these holographic shards and holds them up for her readers to see. But in doing so, she also obliges them to recognize the illusory nature of these images, to place the illusion of Spain's imperial power firmly in the past, and, ultimately, to make the frightening leap from a century that has ended to one that is just beginning, the leap *de siglo a siglo*, "from century to century."

NOTES

1 The most thorough study of the "Vida contemporánea" essays is Eduardo Ruiz-Ocaña Duenas's award-winning dissertation, *La obra periodística de Emilia Pardo Bazán en "La Ilustración Artística" de Barcelona (1895–1916).* Denise Dupont has analysed the "Vida contemporánea" essays as reflections on Spanish modernity. See also the introduction to Pérez Bernardo's edition of *De siglo a siglo*, in particular her commentary on the "crónicas del 98" (54–66).

2 Harriet Turner first suggested to me that I explore the parallels between Pardo Bazán and Larra, many years before I was able to fully appreciate how perceptive her suggestion was.

3 James Clifford elaborates on Geertz's comparison between the interpretive anthropologist and the writer of fiction: "In the predominantly synecdochic stance of the new ethnography, parts were assumed to be microcosms or analogies of wholes. This setting of institutional foregrounds against cultural backgrounds in the portrayal of a coherent world lent itself to realist literary conventions" (125).

4 All translations are my own.

5 These images mirrored the version of the Philippines' inhabitants presented to Spaniards in the 1887 Philippine Exposition held in the Retiro Park in Madrid, when model villages of un-Westernized Indigenous people were displayed in the Crystal Palace. For an in-depth study of the 1887 Exposition, see Sánchez Gómez.

6 Critical discussions of the representation in Galdós of the *mantón de Manila* and other Asian domestic objects have tended to focus on their economic significance. For example, Javier Herrero has suggested that, in *Fortunata y Jacinta*, the *mantón* is symbolically juxtaposed against the British top hat to suggest the decline of Spanish economic power and the rise of the grey industrial North (257). Labanyi notes that, while the young Barbarita is fascinated by the *mantones* and other Asian items sold in her father's store, the lack of distinction between the Arnaiz family home and their store nearly ruins the business ("Las cosas en Galdós" 405).

7 *De siglo a siglo* also contains a scathing review of H. Chatfield-Taylor's *The Land of the Castanet*. See Pérez Bernardo (57–8) and Tolliver for brief analyses of this essay.
8 Bugbee cites an uncredited translation of Brillat-Savarin's 1825 treatise "Physiologie du goût."
9 Not only would Spain no longer profit from the exportation of goods produced by its former colonies, but it also lost the economic market for peninsular exports. As an attempted partial remedy for the blow to the Spanish economy caused by the events of 1898, taxes were raised on food and drink, as well as on fuel. The so-called bread riots of 1898 were the response to these raised taxes. As Sebastian Balfour notes, housewives were "the main protagonists of nineteenth-century bread riots" (409).
10 According to the Hershey Company's website, the Hershey Chocolate Company was founded in 1894, after the owners bought chocolate-making equipment at the 1893 Columbian Exposition.
11 I am grateful to Nicholas C. Burbules for suggesting the image of the hologram, as well as for his many other helpful comments on an early draft of this essay.

WORKS CITED

Alas, Leopoldo ("Clarín"). "Del naturalismo." In *Leopoldo Alas: Teoría y crítica de la novela española*, ed. Sergio Beser. Barcelona: Laia, 1972. Print.

Balfour, Sebastian. "Riot, Regeneration and Reaction: Spain in the Aftermath of the 1898 Disaster." *Historical Journal* 38.2 (1995): 405–23. Print. https://doi.org/10.1017/s0018246x00019476.

Bugbee, James M. *Cocoa and Chocolate: A Short History of Their Production and Use*. Dorchester, MA: Walter Baker and Co., 1886. Print.

Clifford, James. "On Ethnographic Authority." *Representations* 2 (1983): 118–46. Web. https://doi.org/10.2307/2928386.

Dupont, Denise. "Lecturas de la Gran Guerra: Los últimos años de Emilia Pardo Bazán." Annual Meeting of the Modern Language Association. Boston, 5 January 2013. Conference Presentation.

Geertz, Clifford. "Thick Description: Toward an Interpretive Theory of Culture." In *The Interpretation of Cultures*. New York: Basic Books, 1973. 3–30. Print.

Herrero, Javier. "El mantón de Manila contra el sombrero de copa: Indumentaria y comida en *Fortunata y Jacinta*." In *Ideas en sus paisajes: Homenaje al Profesor Russell P. Sebold*, ed. Guillermo Carnero, Ignacio Javier López, and Enrique Rubio. Alicante: Universidad de Alicante, 1999. 255–62. Print.

Hershey's History. Website. https://www.thehersheycompany.com/en_us/this-is-hershey/milton-hershey.html#secTitle. Web. 19 November 2018.

Jakobson, Roman. "The Metaphoric and Metonymic Poles." In *Critical Theory since Plato*, ed. Hazard Adams. Irvine: U of California P, 1971. 1113–16 Print.

Kidd, Sue Monk. *The Secret Life of Bees*. New York: Viking, 2002. Print.

Labanyi, Jo. "Las cosas en Galdós/Las cosas de Galdós: Valor de cambio y valor de uso." In *VIII Congreso Internacional Galdosiano 2005*, ed. Yolanda Arencibia, María del Prado Escobar, and Rosa María Quintana. Las Palmas: Cabildo de Gran Canaria, 2009. 402–9. Print.

– "Doing Things: Emotion, Affect, and Materiality." *Journal of Spanish Cultural Studies* 11.3–4 (2010): 223–33. Print. https://doi.org/10.1080/14636204.2010.538244.

Larra, Mariano José de. "La vida de Madrid." In *Artículos varios*, ed. E. Correa Calderón. Madrid: Castalia, 1976. 464–70. Print.

Linnaeus, Carl. *Species Plantarum*. Vol. 2. Stockholm: Laurentius Salvius, 1753. Biodiversity Heritage Library. Web.

Ortiz Armengol, Pedro. *Letras en Filipinas*. Madrid: Ministerio de Asuntos Exteriores de España, 1999. Print.

Pardo Bazán, Emilia. "Artículo ex-colonial." In *De siglo a siglo*, 150–5. Print.

– *La cocina española antigua*. Madrid: Renacimiento, 1910. Print.

– *La cocina española moderna*. Madrid: Renacimiento, 1917. Print.

– "Columnas de humo." In *De siglo a siglo*, 31–6. Print.

– *De siglo a siglo*. Madrid: Administración, 1902. Print.

– "Días nublados." In *De siglo a siglo*, 53–7. Print.

– "El encaje roto." In *"El encaje roto" y otros cuentos*, ed. Joyce Tolliver. New York: MLA, 1996. 58–65. Print.

– *La España de ayer y la de hoy*. Madrid: Administración, 1899. Print.

– "El país de las castañuelas." In *De siglo a siglo*, 47–52. Print.

– "Siempre la guerra." In *De siglo a siglo*, 116–20. Print.

Pérez Bernardo, María Luisa, ed. *De siglo a siglo (1896–1901): Crónicas periodísticas de Emilia Pardo Bazán*. Madrid: Pliegos, 2014. Print.

Pérez Galdós, Benito. *Fortunata y Jacinta: Dos historias de casadas*. Vol. 1. Ed. Francisco Caudet. Madrid: Cátedra, 1983. Print.

Ruiz-Ocaña Duenas, Eduardo. *La obra periodística de Emilia Pardo Bazán en "La Ilustración Artística" de Barcelona (1895–1916)*. Madrid: Fundación Universitaria Española, 2004. Print.

Sánchez Gómez, Luis Angel. *Un imperio en la vitrina: El colonialismo español en el Pacífico y la Exposición de Filipinas de 1887*. Madrid: Consejo Superior de Investigaciones Científicas–Instituto de Historia, 2003. Print.

Schnapp, Jeffrey T. "The Romance of Caffeine and Aluminum." *Critical Inquiry* 28.1 (2001): 244–69. Web. https://doi.org/10.1086/449039.

Silvela, Francisco. "Sin pulso." *El Tiempo*, 16 August 1898. Web.

Tolliver, Joyce. "Pardo Bazán and Spain's Late Modern Empire." In *Approaches to Teaching the Writings of Emilia Pardo Bazán*, ed. Margot Versteeg and Susan Walter. New York: MLA, 2017. 93–8. Print.

Treisman, Deborah. "This Week in Fiction: Tessa Hadley on Fiction as Anthropology." *New Yorker*, 1 August 2016. Web. 25 November 2016.

Turner, Harriet. "The Realist Novel." In *The Cambridge Companion to the Spanish Novel from 1600 to the Present*, ed. Harriet Turner and Adelaida López de Martínez. Cambridge: Cambridge UP, 2003. 81–101. Print.

– "'Why the Face of the Voice Is in the Hand': On the Poetics of Realist Fiction." In *Studies in Honor of Vernon Chamberlin*, ed. Mark A. Harpring. Newark, DE: Juan de la Cuesta, 2011. 215–30. Print.

Unamuno, Miguel de. "La tradición eterna." In *En torno al casticismo: Cinco ensayos. Ensayos*. 1895. Vol. 1. Madrid: Publicaciones de la Residencia de Estudiantes, 1916. Web.

9 Embodied Minds: Critical Erotic Decisions in *La Regenta*

RANDOLPH D. POPE

In her insightful reading of Leopoldo Alas's famous novel *La Regenta* (1886–7), Harriet Turner noticed that Oviedo has been invaded and transformed by Vetusta: "La imaginaria ciudad de Vetusta, antes contemplada y conquistada por el Magistral, ahora ha conquistado a Oviedo" [The imaginary city of Vetusta, in the past contemplated and conquered by the Magistral, now has conquered Oviedo] ("Andanzas y fugas" 40).[1] The novel has escaped the library and clings to the reality from which it received its inspiration. While it is configured within parameters that owe to positivism and naturalism, I wish to reach beyond these markers to suggest an explanation for why it continues to be remarkably lifelike and not just the instantiation of a theory. To consider this uniqueness of the novel – how many other novels of that period have invaded a city? – I propose considering how decision making is vividly and illuminatingly described in *La Regenta*, in a way that corresponds well to our contemporary understanding, especially as it encompasses emotions and the body.[2]

The realist novel can be read as an example of how one can live beyond the pages of the book. It can be compared to an architect's model of a building in the sense that it considers a future realization, at least a possible one, and is not just an object for static contemplation. There is, of course, no obligation to project a future enactment in the reader's life of situations similar to the ones found in the novel, but what I am proposing here is to take as a starting point the fact that a good number of readers of realist novels find the characters, circumstances, and events in the text similar to those they know from their own lives, and, in some cases, they may gather some insight into how to live wisely, what to do and what to avoid. This should not be confused with a message from the author or moral preaching, a decanted moral code; on the contrary, most of the novels to which we return once and again dwell in paradoxes, conflictive situations, and muddled thought. They are like legal cases that make it all the way up to the Supreme Court where they can be decided one way or the other, but not always unanimously. The ending of *Fortunata y Jacinta*, for example, has provoked two radically different interpretations, on the one hand as an instance of Fortunata's angelic generosity, on the other as an example of the victimization of the poor at the hands of the very rich who are able to buy and co-opt the desired and chosen children of the lower classes, leaving them little if any choice.[3] The novel as a genre thrives on ambiguity, complexity, opaque behaviour, and puzzling situations, offering not a finished perfect model but instead a representation of how people actually live. This applies of course to what we have traditionally called high literature and not to most popular literature, where good and evil are clearly traced and situations explained according to beliefs and expectations that satisfy many readers without any deep shock or lasting interrogation. Popular literature serves well its own different purpose.

The novel, then, compared to a painting that focuses on the present, has a very strong investment in the future. Most readers keep turning pages to know what will happen, which is determined by a variety of factors, many of them unpredictable and not depending on the characters' volition, such as an act of nature, war, sickness, an inheritance, or otherwise uncontrollable events.[4] If it rains in Vetusta this may create a gloomy atmosphere that propitiates an enervating boredom where temptation can fester, but this is beyond the control of any single character and perhaps not even of the writer, since once he locates his city in northern Spain we will expect rain to be a major presence. Much is also given: the city is called Vetusta for a reason, since the characters are moving within a city plan and a venerable cathedral, as part of structuring realities that precede them by centuries. But there are also instances in which characters are called to make individual decisions. Here is where they must practise the art of living, the care of the self, and their ethical imagination, to use terms from Michel Foucault, Alexander Nehamas, and Victoria Camps.[5] There is a deep and varied tradition of systems and strategies useful for facing these crucial moments, Christianity of course being one, but Stoicism, Epicureanism, and existentialism a few of the many others. The recourse to these conceptual approaches, labelled and dutifully archived by intellectual history, distorts the experience most of us have in our daily lives, where ideas are only one factor in decision making, and decisions often appear scrambled, contradictory, complex, and confused. Phenomenology (a method and approach more than a conceptual system) and cognitive science have long insisted on the importance of the body, on our being embodied minds. This goes beyond issues of health and sickness, hereditary traits, or the range and limitations of our senses. It is a challenge to the human tendency to transform the world into ideas, divide it into objective and subjective factors, and establish the conscious mind as the ruler in charge. Here are a few quotes from Maurice Merleau-Ponty that make this point clear:

> The perceiving mind is an incarnate mind. (*The Primacy of Perception* 3)

> Scientific thinking, a thinking which looks on from above, and thinks of the object-in-general, must return to the "there is" which underlies it; to the site, the soil of the sensible and opened world such as it is in our life and for our body – not that possible body which we may legitimately think of as an information machine but that actual body I call mine, this sentinel standing quietly at the command of my words and acts. (*The Primacy of Perception* 160)

> The experience of one's body, then, is opposed to the reflective movement that disentangles the object from the subject and the subject from the object, and that only gives us thought about the body or the body as an idea, and not the experience of the body or the body in reality. (*Phenomenology of Perception* 205)

The body perceives and is alert to the world in which it is immersed, reacting and deciding often much earlier than the conscious mind becomes aware of the situation and considers it.[6] "Quietly," then, does not mean passively or undecidedly, just not signalling with language or deciding after going through a stack of syllogisms. Hunger and thirst make us aware of the body's needs with unmistakable clarity, yet quietly. A superb example of the body in practice can be found in Valera's *Pepita Jiménez*, where the seminarian Luis has a well-defined idea of what he should do with his life until he goes back home for a vacation and meets the young widow Pepita Jiménez. While he continues a debate in his mind about the comparative merit of spiritual devotion and secular life, his body reaches a quick and unequivocal decision after his hand has touched hers: "Al entrar, Pepita y yo nos damos la mano, y al dárnosla me hechiza. Todo mi ser se muda. Penetra hasta mi corazón un fuego devorante, y ya no pienso más que en ella" [When we meet, Pepita and

I shake hands, and, when we touch each other, she bewitches me. My whole being is changed. A devouring fire reaches into my heart, and from then on I think of nothing else but of her] (114). This lack of control is disturbing, so in a subsequent letter Luis will align this intense bodily communication under an effort of the will: "Cuando Pepita y yo nos damos la mano, no es ya como al principio. Ambos hacemos un esfuerzo de voluntad, y nos transmitimos, por nuestras diestras enlazadas, todas las palpitaciones del corazón. Se diría que, por arte diabólico, obramos una transfusión y mezcla de lo más sutil de nuestra sangre" [When Pepita and I now shake hands it is not as at the beginning. We both make an effort of will and transmit to each other, through our conjoined hands, all the beats of our hearts. One could say that, by devilish art, our blood is transfused and is blended up to its most subtle components] (118–19).

Subsequent events in the novel will show that "voluntad" [will] has little to do with this blood transfusion and that these are not decisions reached after any consideration. Daniel Kahneman, winner of a Nobel Prize in Economics, presents in his bestselling 2011 book, *Thinking, Fast and Slow*, a dichotomy between two systems we use for deciding, on the one hand reaching fast decisions based on instinct and emotion, on the other deciding only after careful deliberative thought:

> When we think of ourselves, we identify with System 2, the conscious reasoning self that has beliefs, makes choices, and decides what to think about and what to do. Although System 2 believes itself to be where the action is, the automatic System 1 is the hero of the book. I describe System 1 as effortlessly originating impressions and feelings that are the main sources of the explicit beliefs and deliberate choices of System 2. (21)

This is not the same as a Freudian description of the mind, with its subconscious cluttered with archives, traumas, memories, and behavioural patterns (among other shambles and relics of the past), scrutinized by the superego and haunted by the id. It is an invitation to perceive differently how we exist in the world. Of course, the new insights of cognitive science and philosophy are not discovering a new area of observation, but reconfiguring it.[7] Already Augustine in his *Confessions* superbly described the perplexity he felt at not being able to understand or control his own mind. How much, he wondered, was the mind owned by a person, when it appeared to reach its own decisions, independent from the consciousness and the will? Nietzsche startlingly and beautifully begins *On the Genealogy of Morality* thus:

> We are unknown to ourselves, we knowers: and for a good reason. We have never sought ourselves – how then should it happen that we *find* ourselves one day? It has rightly been said: "where our treasure is, there will your heart be also"; *our* treasure is where the beehives of our knowledge stand. We are forever underway towards them, as born winged animals and honey-gatherers of the spirit, concerned with all our heart about only one thing – "bringing home" something. As for the rest of life, the so-called "experiences" – who of us even has enough seriousness for them? Or enough time? (1; original emphasis)

Nietzsche was one of us, a scholar, a knower, a philologist; so his declaration that *our* (in italics, to indicate there is another) treasure of information, accomplishments, and publications neglects the experience of the rest of life and does not advance the knowledge of ourselves still rings true, at least to me. Who would have enough time? Another philosopher, Heidegger, published in 1954 a book that at first would appear to ask a trivial question, *What Is Called Thinking?* Surprisingly, though, he starts from the premise that most of us are not actually thinking, and "*Most thought-provoking is that we are still not thinking*" (4; original emphasis). His observation, which I find illuminating, indicates that we have to be invited or provoked to think by a reality that creates an opening to new understanding, where words fail us. For Luis in *Pepita Jiménez,* the unexplainable, what requires thought, comes from his hand becoming an instrument, not of writing, in which he is an expert, but of sexual attraction. His attention to this perplexity is detected by his uncle – the recipient of his letters – who, more experienced in real life, comes to understand that Luis's path is no longer a missionary's, but rather the return home of the prodigal son. What a hand can do! Here is how Heidegger puts it:

> But the craft of the hand is richer than we commonly imagine. The hand does not only grasp and catch, or push and pull. The hand reaches and extends, receives and welcomes – and not just things: the hand extends itself, and receives its own welcome in the hands of others. The hand holds. The hand carries. The hand designs and signs, presumably because man is a sign. Two hands fold into one, a gesture meant to carry man into the great oneness. The hand is all this, and this is the true handicraft. Everything is rooted here that is commonly known as handicraft, and commonly we go no further. But the hand's gestures run everywhere through language, in their most perfect purity precisely when man speaks by being silent. (16)

There are two remarkable moments in *La Regenta* in which two characters, Ana and Fermín, perceive their own bodies speaking by being silent, as a different aspect of being from their conscious, controlling mind. In the first case, Ana is preparing herself for a general confession of her life sins with her new spiritual guide, the eloquent, tall, and imposing Fermín de Pas. A book that should serve her as guide does not hold her attention:

> Dejó el libro sobre el tocador y cruzó las manos sobre las rodillas. Su abundante cabellera, de un castaño no muy obscuro, caía en ondas sobre la espalda y llegaba hasta el asiento de la mecedora, por delante le cubría el regazo; entre los dedos cruzados se habían enredado algunos cabellos. Sintió un escalofrío y se sorprendió con los dientes apretados hasta causarle un dolor sordo. (1:163)

> [She left the book upon the dressing-table and clasped her hands upon her lap. Her full-flowing brown tresses tumbled in waves over her shoulders to the seat of the rocking-chair, and spread around on to her lap; a few strands were caught between her interlocked fingers. She shuddered, and was surprised to find her teeth clenched so tightly that they ached. (64)]

Putting the book aside is followed by an apparently innocuous action – holding her crossed hands over her knees (could it be a protective crouch?) – which allows the narrator to offer us the beginning of a voyeuristic display of Ana's body, starting with her long and abundant hair. A shiver and the grinding of her teeth make her fear she may be about to have a nervous attack, as she has experienced before. She takes her pulse – a way of finding out how her body is doing – checks her vision, and concludes she is fine. She then retires to her room, crossing a threshold that suddenly looks like theatrical stage curtains, "con elegantes colgaduras de *satin* granate" (1:163; original emphasis) ["elegant drapery of garnet-red sateen" (64)]. While her bed is described as very ordinary, at its foot lies an authentic tiger skin. The narrator offers an aside to recount Obdulia's opinions about the sexless nature of the room contrasted with the sensuousness of the bedding and the beauty of Ana's body, which we are invited to admire through an echo of Obdulia, who "admiraba sinceramente las formas y el cutis de Ana" (1:164) ["sincerely admired Ana's figure and complexion" (65)]. Then, when readers are well prepared, something striking happens: Ana closes the curtains, sheds the blue gown she is wearing, and appears completely naked, even more beautiful than one of her sensuous admirers, Saturno Bermúdez, could imagine: she "apareció blanca toda, como se la figuraba don Saturno poco antes de dormirse, pero mucho más hermosa de lo que Bermúdez podía representársela" (1:165) ["stood there, white, as Don Saturn often saw her just before he fell asleep, but much more beautiful than he was capable of imagining her" (65)]. A feminine and a masculine desiring view coincide in confirming Ana's great attractiveness. She enjoys the innocent voluptuous pleasure her body affords her: Ana "abrió el lecho. Sin mover los pies, dejóse caer de bruces sobre aquella blandura suave con los brazos tendidos. Apoyaba la mejilla en la sábana y tenía los ojos muy abiertos. La deleitaba aquel placer del tacto que corría desde la cintura a las sienes" (1:165) ["[Ana] drew back the bedclothes. Without moving her feet, she let herself fall face downwards, arms outspread, upon the silky softness of the sheets. She rested her cheek on the bed, keeping her eyes wide open. She took great delight in that tactile pleasure, which ran from her waist to her temples" (65)].

Her body experiences a pleasure, "aquel placer del tacto," which pleases her, "la deleitaba," in what is a striking observational internal distance that insulates Ana from any responsibility for this enjoyment. It just happens. Her conscious mind drifts away now, as she lies naked on her bed, to her preparation for confession and the memories of how as a child she missed having a mother. She is presented as longing to be loved, desiring.

A parallel scene allows us to see Fermín's own struggle between his conception of his professional self and the demands of his body:

> Estaba desnudo de medio cuerpo arriba. El cuello robusto parecía más fuerte ahora por la tensión a que le obligaba la violencia de la postura, al inclinarse sobre el lavabo de mármol blanco. Los brazos cubiertos de vello negro ensortijado, lo mismo que el pecho alto y fuerte, parecían de un atleta. El Magistral miraba con tristeza sus músculos de acero, de una fuerza inútil. Era muy blanco y fino el cutis, que una emoción cualquiera teñía de color de rosa ...
>
> Mientras estaba lavándose, desnudo de la cintura arriba, don Fermín se acordaba de sus proezas en el juego de bolos, allá en la aldea, cuando aprovechaba vacaciones del seminario para ser medio salvaje corriendo por breñas y vericuetos; el mozo fuerte y velludo que tenía enfrente, en el espejo, le parecía un *otro yo* que se había perdido, que había quedado en los montes, desnudo, cubierto de pelo como el rey de Babilonia, pero libre,

feliz... Le asustaba tal espectáculo, le llevaba muy lejos de sus pensamientos de ahora, y se apresuró a vestirse ... (1:409–10; original emphasis)

[He was naked from the waist up. His powerful neck seemed even more powerful now, because of the strain put upon it by his tensed position as he leaned over the white marble wash-basin. His arms, like his broad, powerful chest, were covered with fine black curly hair; they were the arms of an athlete. The canon looked sadly at his muscles of steel, charged with useless power. His complexion was pale and delicate, the slightest emotion tinging it rose-color ...

As Don Fermín washed, he recalled his prowess at skittles, back in his home village, where he had always made the most of the opportunities offered by holidays from the seminary to go half savage, running through rocky scrub in the high hills. The brawny, hairy young fellow before him in the mirror somehow seemed like a lost alter ego which had stayed behind in those hills – naked, as hairy as the King of Babylon, yet free, happy. He was alarmed by this sight, which carried his thoughts far away, and he dressed hurriedly. (232–3)]

The fright his body causes him, "le asustaba tal espectáculo," splits him into the conscious, supposedly controlling self and the "*otro yo,*" which can be covered, hidden, but not ignored. The evocation of Fermín's vacations from the seminary reminds us of Luis Vargas, who was fortunate not to continue his career as a priest and to find Pepita when he could still change his path.[8]

Ana Ozores has been a faithful wife to an uninspiring husband with whom apparently she has not even consummated her marriage. We can assume that there are many reasons for her fidelity, among them religious values, social mores, and even an appreciation for her slightly goofy, yet kind husband. When the town's Don Juan, Álvaro Mesía, an able politician, bachelor, and successful seducer, sets his sights on her, Ana is determined to resist him, and so she does during many long chapters, to the exasperation of some of her friends who would like her to fall from virtue, as they already have. But on a day when Ana would appear to be especially fortified because she has just been to confession, has had an inspiring conversation with her spiritual advisor in the Cathedral, and is returning home after having enjoyed a time of meditation in the countryside, she meets Álvaro. To a rather flirtatious remark from Ana, Álvaro replies with what could appear to be a formulaic and lukewarm observation about how attractive she can be for anyone.

What Ana wants to hear is how attractive she is to him, to Álvaro, as she had up to now taken for granted. Could she have been mistaken? "¿Nada más que ilusiones?" (1:363) ["just illusions?" (201)]. Was this all just dreams of seduction, but nothing more? Since Ana allows herself to enjoy temptation but does not yet wish to transgress into adultery, this brush-off from Álvaro shakes her deeply. How to know precisely what Álvaro feels? Language is proving not to be transparent, univocal. But it is not the only way to convey information, and in love affairs it tends to be secondary to a deeper connection of the body. We can remember here that all the confusion the young seminarian Luis suffers in *Pepita Jiménez* dissolves instantly when he shakes hands with the young widow.

Ana now has an idea, a very corrosive one: "La idea de que Mesía nada esperaba de ella, ni nada solicitaba, le parecía un agujero negro abierto en su corazón que se iba llenando de vacío" (1:364) ["The idea that Mesía expected nothing from her, and asked for nothing, gave her the sensation that a black pit had opened in her heart and was being filled with nothingness" (201)].

There are several points worth highlighting in this brief sentence. First is that being in society is to be framed by a horizon of expectations, some of them explicit while many others are implicit, expected to be recognized and obeyed even if at times prudently unacknowledged. Various thinkers have considered this point relatively recently, for example Althusser, with his concept of interpellation, which illuminates how the production of self happens mostly by internalizing a very strong ideology of how to live correctly.[9] Ana's desirability came from her beauty. Not being attractive any longer would therefore be significant to her understanding of being: "un agujero negro," and thus an emptiness in her heart, in her body, is not an exaggeration. From a different point of view, Merleau-Ponty, as mentioned earlier, has described with minute precision the significance of each one of us being above all and first of all embodied. Interacting with reality, conceiving reality, can only happen through our being a body.

Before exploring this further, let us consider how we could expect this decision scene to continue. There could be a monologue or soliloquy as we could find in an Unamuno novel or a play by Calderón. Ana could imagine a conversation with her confessor or shuffle the stack of admonitions she has received against an illicit affair. Yet this is not the choice of the writer, who follows a double path. Through Flaubertian indirect free speech we peek into Ana's thoughts, which reveal disquiet and frustration at being deprived of the heroic possibility of resisting the seducer's temptation. Then, from an interior point of view we are taken to an exterior one: Álvaro notices in her words and her voice that she has been shaken: "En la voz de la Regenta, en el desconcierto de sus palabras, notó que le había hecho efecto la sequedad de la vulgarísima galantería" (1:364) ["In Ana's voice and confused words he noticed that she had been affected by the dryness of his banal compliment" (202)]. What is surprising here is that Ana's incoherent words are not reproduced, as if this encounter were sliding beyond words to a tremor in the voice and an unhinging of logic or syntax. Álvaro, of course, has been defined as "materialista," so through him the materiality of the body's performance is perceived and stressed. While we are not told about any verbal conclusions Ana may have reached, the body has been transformed, since Álvaro observes that her eyes are on fire and she is blushing: "al mirarla a su lado con llamas en los ojos y carmín en las mejillas" (1:364) ["he glanced at Ana walking by his side with fire in her eyes and crimson in her cheeks" (202)]. We do not need to go back to Ovid to decipher these bodily messages, but both belong to the uncontrollable and to what lies beyond the reach of consciously desired behaviour; "do not blush" is a nonsensical command because it cannot be obeyed. If there were any doubt about the fact that we are witnessing a deep shift in register, the experienced and calculating seducer is also thrown off his prepared plan and his body is also affected:

> Anita sentía seca la boca; para hablar necesitaba humedecer con la lengua los labios. Lo vio Mesía que adoraba este gesto de la Regenta, y sin poder contenerse, fuera de su plan, *natura naturans*, exclamó:
>
> —¡Qué monísima! ¡qué monísima!
>
> Pero lo dijo con voz ronca, sin conciencia de que hablaba, muy bajo, sin alarde de atrevimiento. Fue una fuga de pasión, que por lo mismo importaba más que una flor insípida, y no era una desfachatez. Podía tomarse por una declaración, por una brutalidad de la naturaleza excitada, por todo, menos por una osadía impertinente, imposible en el más cumplido caballero. (1:364–5)

> [Anita's mouth was dry, in order to speak she had to moisten her lips with her tongue. Mesía noticed this action, one which he adored, and, unable to restrain himself, departing from his plan, natura naturans, he exclaimed: "How lovely! how lovely!" But he said it in a hoarse, hushed voice, hardly aware that he was speaking, and without showing any disrespect. It was

an escape of passion, and therefore of more consequence than any insipid compliment, and not impertinent. It could be taken for a declaration of love, for the foolish blunder of a man whose blood had been stirred, for anything except a shameless piece of effrontery – of which a perfect gentleman could never be guilty. (202)]

Everything here speaks about unleashing and displacement, much as the narrator tries awkwardly to reincorporate the event into the proper and correct behaviour for a gentleman. Álvaro cannot restrain himself; he goes beyond his plan, his voice becomes hoarse, and his passion escapes him. Most radical is the affirmation that he was not conscious of what he was saying, "sin conciencia de que hablaba." How then can this be a space for a logical, considered reflection? And this has been, as the narrator makes clear, a crucial day.

Ana fingió no oír, pero sus ojos la delataron, y brillando en la sombra, buscando a don Álvaro que había retrocedido un paso en la obscuridad, le pagaron con creces las delicias que aquellas palabras dejaron caer como lluvia benéfica en el alma de la Regenta.

—Es mía—pensó don Álvaro con deleite superior al que él mismo esperaba en el día del triunfo. (1:365)

[Ana pretended not to hear, but her eyes betrayed her. Shining in the shadows, searching for Don Alvaro, who had stepped back in the darkness, they repaid with interest the delight which his words had poured into her soul like a beneficial shower of rain.

"Yes," thought Don Alvaro with a pleasure even greater than that which he had anticipated he would feel on the day of triumph. (202)]

The eyes have a will of their own and betray their owner: "sus ojos la delataron." A decisive moment, then, resolved in the profound depths of the embodied mind.

The situation, though, continues unresolved, since Ana is determined to keep Álvaro at an enjoyable yet safe distance and is drawn more and more into the circle of the Magistral, who offers her the possibility of exploring mystical experience, for which she has ability and insight, an aspect of her that should not be forgotten or diminished.[10] It will take some alcohol and the conviviality of a lunch at the Marquis's Vetusta home to make evident to the three members of the love triangle how they are falling deeper and deeper into passions that are surprising to their rational selves. The following quote is essential to understand how the narrator is setting up the disarray that will follow. Ana has just heard that Don Fermín is declining to join them in the country house where she and her friends are planning to go:

> El don Fermín, que ya tenía las mejillas algo encendidas por culpa de las libaciones más frecuentes que de costumbre, se puso como una cereza cuando vio a la Regenta mirarle cara a cara y decir con verdadera pena:
>
> —Oh, por Dios, no sea usted así, mire que nos da a todos un disgusto; acompáñenos usted, señor Magistral ...
>
> En el gesto, en la mirada de la Regenta podía ver cualquiera y lo vieron De Pas y don Álvaro, sincera expresión de disgusto: era una contrariedad para ella la noticia que le daba la Marquesa. (1:507)

> [And Don Fermín, whose cheeks were already flushed from drinking more than usual, turned the color of a cherry when the judge's wife looked him in the eyes and said with heartfelt sorrow: "Oh, please, don't be like that, you'll make us all so sad, you know. Come with us, Don Fermín." In the look on her face anyone could see (as both De Pas and Don Alvaro certainly saw) a sincere expression of sadness – the marchioness's news had upset her. (302)]

Once again we see that Ana betrays her feelings through the body with gestures and her look. This time we get to hear her words, of which perhaps the first is the most important: "Oh," just an expression of an emotion that does not find its words, perhaps frustrated desire, wounded pride, truncated joy, or disappointment. Here she was about to go to the country house with all her friends, next to her husband and flanked by these two handsome and admired men! But the Magistral, prudently, is begging off ... It is not the words only, though, that impact Don Fermín, but something he sees – "vio a la Regenta mirarle cara a cara" [he saw the Regent's wife look at him face-to-face] – and a feeling he perceives – "con verdadera pena" [with true sorrow]. The impact of non-verbal communication is clearly brought out by the narrator's noting that Fermín is frightened by the emotion caused by Ana's gesture, more than by her words.

His reaction is not one that could be wished, planned, or desired, given the circumstances: he blushes intensely – "se puso como una cereza" [turned the colour of a cherry]. Darwin devoted an entire chapter to the phenomenon of blushing in *The Expression of the Emotions in Man and Animals*, calling it "the most peculiar and the most human of all expressions" (309).[11] He provides a physical description: "The reddening of the face from a blush is due to the relaxation of the muscular coats of the small arteries, by which the capillaries become filled with blood" (309), and then proceeds to wonder about the fact that by a direct bodily stimulus we can relatively easily cause laughing, weeping, or trembling from fear, but not blushing. The mind, he affirms, must be affected. Yet, what control does the mind have over relaxing the muscular coats of small arteries? Darwin observes that "blushing is not only involuntary; but the wish to restrain it, by leading to self-attention actually increases the tendency" (310). We can notice here the difficulty he experiences when wishing to place the origin and agent of this reddening of the face while he still wants to see "the mind" and "the body" as neatly separated, with the rational mind in control.

In his detailed and fascinating exploration of blushing, Darwin investigates whether this phenomenon is limited just to the face and neck, finding reports of more general bodily reddening, and he inquires about geographical and racial distribution of this behaviour, concluding that "the facts now given are sufficient to show that blushing, whether or not there is any change of color, is common to most, probably to all, of the races of man" (320). The point, of course, was to establish it as a universal experience that would distinguish humans from animals and reveal an important aspect of social behaviour and evolution. While it is possible to blush when alone, the embarrassment increases when the person who experiences blushing is aware it cannot be hidden from anyone observing: "Under a keen sense of shame there is a strong desire for concealment. We turn away the whole body, more especially the face, which we endeavor in some manner to hide" (320). The Magistral cannot hide. Curiously, the text indicates only that Ana has betrayed herself into an open revelation: "En el gesto, en la mirada de la Regenta podía ver cualquiera y lo vieron De Pas y don Álvaro, sincera expresión de disgusto." Anyone can see Ana's displeasure, and we can assume that anyone can also see Fermín's blushing.

Who or what is responsible for such an involuntary action? Darwin examines some causal triggers for blushing, not unsurprisingly noting that "no happy pair of young lovers, valuing each other's admiration and love more than anything else in the world, probably ever courted each other without many a blush" (327). Part of Fermín's emotion, then, may come from his enjoyment of Ana's admiration, but another factor may also intervene in causing this cherry-red condition, a recognition of his guilt – his relationship with Ana has slid unwittingly from confessor and spiritual guide to lover – and the thought that others may notice this improper behaviour: "It is not the sense of guilt, but the thought that others think or know us to be guilty which crimsons the face" (Darwin 332). This would explain why he is frightened by how pleased he is by Ana's admiration and by his bodily response. There is a previous and revealing moment in which blushing plays a role, when Fermín is at home and receives a letter from Ana. Doña Paula, observant as ever to protect her son from any scandal, notices that Fermín does not read the message, and he senses her vigilance:

> Don Fermín hubiera deseado a su madre a cien leguas. No podía ocultar la impaciencia, a pesar del dominio sobre sí mismo, que era una de sus mayores fuerzas; ansiaba poder leer la carta, y temía ruborizarse delante de su madre. "¿Ruborizarse?," sí, sin motivo, sin saber por qué; pero estaba seguro de que, si abría aquel sobre delante de doña Paula, se pondría como una cereza. Cosas de los nervios. Pero su madre era como era. (1:413–14)

> [Don Fermín wished his mother a hundred leagues away. He could not hide his impatience, in spite of the self-control which was one of his greatest strengths, for he longed to read the letter but was afraid he might blush in front of his mother. "Blush?" yes, without reason, without knowing why; but he was certain that if he opened the letter in Doña Paula's presence his face would turn the color of a cherry. It was just nerves. But his mother was his mother. (235)]

This is a concise description of the nature of blushing: an uncontrollable revelation, not of the conscious mind, of what would fall under the dominated "sí mismo," but of a nervous condition, "cosas de los nervios."[12] Blushing in front of his mother is a reduction of the man to the child, and a more stereotypically feminine rather than masculine form of behaviour.[13] Considering how disturbing blushing is for him, the first detailed description the narrator gives of the Magistral becomes significant.

> De Pas no se pintaba. Más bien parecía estucado. En efecto, su tez blanca tenía los reflejos del estuco. En los pómulos, un tanto avanzados, bastante para dar energía y expresión característica al rostro, sin afearlo, había un

> ligero encarnado que a veces tiraba al color del alzacuello y de las medias. No era pintura, ni el color de la salud, ni pregonero del alcohol; era el rojo que brota en las mejillas al calor de palabras de amor o de vergüenza que se pronuncian cerca de ellas, palabras que parecen imanes que atraen el hierro de la sangre ... En los ojos del Magistral, verdes, con pintas que parecían polvo de rapé, lo más notable era la suavidad de liquen; pero en ocasiones, de en medio de aquella crasitud pegajosa salía un resplandor punzante, que era una sorpresa desagradable, como una aguja en una almohada de plumas. Aquella mirada la resistían pocos; a unos les daba miedo, a otros asco; pero cuando algún audaz la sufría, el Magistral la humillaba cubriéndola con el telón carnoso de unos párpados anchos, gruesos, insignificantes, como es siempre la carne informe. La nariz larga, recta, sin corrección ni dignidad, también era sobrada de carne hacia el extremo y se inclinaba como árbol bajo el peso de excesivo fruto. (1:9–10)
>
> [De Pas did not use cosmetics. His face, with its white sheen, looked more as if it were stuccoed. In his cheeks, which were just prominent enough to give his face strength and character without making it ugly, there was a tinge of red, with an occasional tendency towards the color of his bands and his hose. It was not cosmetics, or the rosy color of good health, or a sign of drinking; it was the red which rises to the cheeks in the warmth of loving or shameful words, attracting like magnets the blood's iron ... The most striking feature about the canon theologian's eyes, which were green with speckles that looked like grains of snuff, was that they seemed as soft, smooth and clammy as lichen; but sometimes a piercing gleam would shoot out from them – an unpleasant surprise, like finding a needle in a feather pillow. Few people could bear that look. Some were frightened by it, others were disgusted; but if anyone were bold enough to withstand it, the canon lowered his eyes, and veiled them with their broad, heavy lids, which were as meaningless as flabby flesh always is. There was too much flesh, too, towards the tip of his long straight nose, which was neither well-proportioned nor distinguished, and drooped like a tree under the weight of an excess of fruit. (26)]

The recovering stucco-like quality of his complexion and the thick curtain of his eyelids hide and protect his passionate nature. One should note the presentation of Fermín's body as a mechanical object, iron attracted by a magnet, matter congested by orgasmic thoughts. Much later in the novel, as he enjoys Ana's invitation to join her in the excursion to the country house, the Vivero, "De Pas sentía unas dulcísimas cosquillas por todo el cuerpo al oír a la Regenta; y sin pensarlo se inclinaba hacia ella, como si fuera un imán" (1:517) ["De Pas felt the most delightful tingling sensation all over his body when he heard these words and, not thinking what he was doing, he leaned towards Ana as if attracted to her by magnetism" (309)]. Fermín is noticing his body react, and the narrator stresses the involuntary nature of this reaction by observing that it was done "sin pensarlo."[14]

The rather disproportionate nose, long and hanging as if weighed by fruit, is as clear a phallic symbol as the telescope he holds in his hand. We are later informed that his mother's nose is similar to his: "La nariz, la boca y la barba se parecían mucho a las del Magistral" (1:413) ["Her nose, mouth and chin were identical to those of her son" (234)], not unexpected given her resolute nature. Fermín's face has a hint of the redness that comes from love or shame, but also from passionate thought. This last occasional change in his face's colour would be appropriate to his profession as an orator and polemicist, being flushing and not blushing. When Doctor Somoza visits Ana, who is sick in bed, he takes her temperature and, noticing it is very high, becomes irate: "Se puso el doctor como una cereza" (2:112) [The doctor turned the colour of a cherry], an appropriate behaviour for a man with a "torvo ceño" [terrible frown] and who speaks "with enojo" (2:112) [with anger].[15] But Fermín's blushing in front of Ana and Álvaro is of a different nature, unwanted and indiscreet. It is somewhat ironic that in a novel called *La Regenta,* neither Ana nor most people around her can ultimately rule over their emotions and reasonably consider the consequences of their behaviour. While the effect of nerves has been very well described and studied for Ana, it has been seen mostly in the critical moments of sickness, and it has not been studied for other characters or at times of more normal social intercourse.

It may not be simply coincidental that cherry is the colour associated with a scandalous widow who attempts, unsuccessfully, to seduce the Magistral. We see the "falda de color cereza de la siempre llamativa Obdulia Fandiño" (1:479) ["the cherry-colored skirt of the ever-showy Obdulia Fandiño" (279)], and "el cuerpo gentil, color cereza, de Obdulia, que desde allá abajo parecía querer tragar al buen mozo en los abismos de los grandes ojos negros" (1:482) ["the appealing form of the cherry-attired Obdulia, who, from where she sat, seemed to be trying to swallow the handsome priest down into the depths of her large black eyes" (282)]. The same sensuous colour appears, suggestively, in the episcopal palace.

> El Magistral dejó atrás el zaguán, grande, frío y desnudo, no muy limpio; cruzó un patio cuadrado, con algunas acacias raquíticas y parterres de flores mustias; subió una escalera cuyo primer tramo era de piedra y los demás de castaño casi podrido; y después de un corredor cerrado con mampostería y ventanas estrechas, encontró una antesala donde los familiares del Obispo jugaban al tute. La presencia del Provisor interrumpió el juego. Los familiares se pusieron de pie y uno de ellos hermoso, rubio, de movimientos suaves y ondulantes, de pulquérrimo traje talar, perfumado, abrió una mampara forrada de damasco color cereza. De lo mismo estaba tapizada toda la estancia que se vio entonces y que atravesó De Pas sin detenerse. (1:438)
>
> [The canon walked through the entrance hall, which was large, cold, bare and not very clean, crossed a square courtyard where there were a few scrawny acacias and some flower-beds containing wilted plants, climbed a staircase, the bottom flight of stone and the rest of half-rotten chestnut, and at the end of a corridor enclosed with rubblework and narrow windows came to an ante-room in which the bishop's familiars were playing at cards. The arrival of the vicar-general interrupted their game. The familiars stood up and one of them, a handsome blond man whose movements were smooth and undulating, and whose vesture was immaculate and perfumed, opened a door covered with cherry-colored damask. The walls of the chamber which now became visible, and through which De Pas passed without a pause, were lined with the same material. (252–3)]

That sensuousness and even voluptuousness are present here in this effeminate priest who removes this cherry-red screen can remind readers of the young altar boy Celedonio, introduced in the first chapter, in whom "se podía adivinar futura y próxima perversión de instintos naturales" (1:100–1) ["a perversion of natural instincts could be foreseen in the near future" (25)]. He will close the novel kissing Ana after she faints when threatened by the Magistral. Then, too, Fermín leaves without stopping, but not without first performing a startling gesture:

> El Magistral se detuvo, cruzó los brazos sobre el vientre. No podía hablar, ni quería. Temblábale todo el cuerpo; volvió a extender los brazos hacia Ana ... dio otro paso adelante ... y después, clavándose las uñas en el cuello, dio media vuelta, como si fuera a caer desplomado, y con piernas débiles y temblonas salió de la capilla. (2:536)

> [The canon theologian stopped, lowered his arms and held them in front of his body, one wrist over the other. He could not talk; nor did he wish to talk. His whole body was shaking, again he stretched his arms towards Ana, he took another step forwards – and then digging his finger-nails into his neck he turned on his heel as if he were going to collapse, and on weak, wavering legs stumbled out of the chapel. (715)]

He cannot speak, and his body shakes; he stretches his arms towards Ana – to attack her or to embrace her? – and then attempts briefly to strangle himself, walking away on shaking and weak legs, the former Hercules rejecting and punishing his body as he reintegrates himself into his churchly functions. This is his final decision and, like so many of the other crucial ones we encounter in the novel – our list of examples could have been much longer – taken on the fast and bodily track.

Harriet Turner observed that the novel about Vetusta has taken over Oviedo, entered back into life, reintegrating itself to where it came from. What I have attempted to show here is that one of the reasons for its vitality is that the way in which the novel describes decisions is not the result of positivism, naturalist philosophy, or pre-Freudian intuition, even if it may agree with them in part, but something much deeper and scarcer, precise observation of experience and of the embodied mind, fully validated by our present understanding.

NOTES

1 All translations are mine, except for those of *La Regenta*, where I quote Rutherford's translation.

2 The bibliography on *La Regenta* is vast and mostly admirable, and I owe much to it after many decades of teaching this novel. My approach here is slightly different, mostly from a phenomenological angle and profiting from the many scientific revelations of cognitive science. The conflictive "voices" in Ana's mind have been connected authoritatively to hysteria and mysticism by Jo Labanyi in "Mysticism and Hysteria in *La Regenta*." What Labanyi identifies as "the otherness of self" (43) I am seeing here, at a more basic level, as Clarín's insightful and subtle description of the normal condition of the human mind.

3 Harriet Turner in *Benito Pérez Galdós: Fortunata and Jacinta* takes the side of an angelic Fortunata, insightfully demolishing Guillermina's reputation as *santa*: "*La santa* dismisses the gift of the child as a *rasgo* – merely

an impulsive act – whereas *la diabla* knows her generous gift redeems both herself and her rival. Redemption lies beyond the narrower religious faith of Guillermina, who fails to perceive that *la diabla* is, as she claims, angelic" (91–2).

4 Joan Ramon Resina in "Ana Ozores's Nerves" writes that "Ana's fall is narratively overdetermined ... This is not the genealogical determinism of Zola, but it is nonetheless one that stresses the individual's dependence on his or her milieu" (246). I share this conviction, believing that Clarín's approach does not derive from a programmatic approach, but from fine observation of realities that mostly continue to be active today.

5 Foucault spoke in many of his works about the "techniques and procedures for directing human behavior" and how "the problem of self-examination and confession" was connected to "government" ("On the Government of the Living" 81). I have found Nehamas's *The Art of Living* instructive about the connection between philosophy and actually living a life. Camps in her admirable *La imaginación ética* examines how the individual, when faced with real decisions in a particular life, finds little comfort in abstract philosophical guidelines.

6 The complexity of how decisions are made has been illuminatingly studied by cognitive science and is well described by Antonio R. Damasio in *Descartes' Error*, where he proposes, "We are, and then we think" (248). The temporal priority of some bodily reactions to conceptual perception, evaluation, and decision has been slightly misunderstood, in my opinion, in the otherwise learned and splendid introduction to Luisa Elena Delgado, Pura Fernández, and Jo Labanyi, *Engaging the Emotions in Spanish Culture and History*, where it states that "this temporal grid risks giving the impression of a teleological linear process, in which the destiny of affect (body) is to end up producing an emotion (mind)" (6). The point is that this priority reveals that there is a way in which the body speaks before it becomes conceptual thought. Of this we are not usually conscious, but Clarín saw it and wrote about it most insightfully.

7 In *Retrieving Realism* (here referring to the philosophical opposition of realism versus idealism), Hubert Dreyfus and Charles Taylor insist on taking into account the non-verbal and preconceptual, including a "pre-understanding." In many cases we know our way around the world in a "nonconceptual" way, where "language isn't playing any direct role" (50). "Ordinary coping isn't conceptual" (51). They conclude that "phenomenologists and neuroscientists are converging on a nonmentalistic account of situational skillful coping" (51). For how this amplified range of our

decisions affects how we evaluate decisions, see Mark Johnson's *Morality for Humans*, where he states: "One of my main theses in this book is that moral deliberation is a complex form of human problem-solving that emerges from our embodied visceral engagement with our world and then reconstructs that world through a projective imaginative process that can be both affect-laden and reasonable" (93).

8 Beth Wietelmann Bauer's excellent article "Novels in Dialogue" examines the connection between these two novels: "Like Luis Vargas, Fermín de Pas exhibits pride, rhetorical prowess, and frustration and embarrassment over the restrictions that clergical decorum places upon masculinity" (104). What I am adding here is that the conflict is not only between libido and a frail or false mysticism but also between different regions of the embodied self. It should be noted that at the end of *Pepita Jiménez* Luis is somewhat nostalgic about what his life could have been as a saintly priest: "Luis no olvida nunca, en medio de su dicha presente, el rebajamiento del ideal con que había soñado. Hay ocasiones en que su vida de ahora le parece vulgar, egoísta y prosaica, comparada con la vida de sacrificio, con la existencia spiritual a que se creyó llamado en los primeros años de su juventud" [Luis never forgets, immersed in his present happiness, the debasement of the ideal with which he had dreamt. There are times in which his life now seems to him vulgar, egotistical, and prosaic compared with a life of sacrifice, with that spiritual existence to which he thought he had been called in the early years of his youth] (275).

9 Althusser describes how production needs to reproduce the relations of production, one of them being the production of ideological subjects and the mechanisms of recognition. Thus, "an individual is always-already a subject, even before he is born," and "before its birth, the child is therefore always-already a subject, appointed as a subject in and by the specific familial ideological configuration in which it is 'expected' once it has been conceived" ("Ideology and Ideological State Apparatuses"). Clarín devotes many pages of his novel to providing a dense description of what is socially "expected" of Ana Ozores.

10 Harriet Turner wisely highlights the very real desires of several characters, which are no less sincere because they remain unrealized: "Ana, Víctor y don Fermín no pueden nunca realizar la aspiración que sienten por algo nuevo y bello" [Ana, Victor, and Don Fermin cannot attain what they aspire to, something new and beautiful] ("Andanzas y fugas" 38). Our tendency to value undermining and irony has led us often, in my opinion, to a lack of understanding of the complexity of our self where contradictory or disparate feelings and concepts can coexist.

11 Darwin's amazingly perceptive, lively, entertaining, and elegant chapter examines blushing as non-conscious behaviour with great detail and continues to be relevant. The article on blushing in Gregory and Zangwill's *Oxford Companion to the Mind* does little more than paraphrase Darwin, concluding that "Although all this was said well over a century ago there is little to add now, apart from its detailed physiology, to Darwin's comments on blushing" (98).

12 Mary Ann O'Farrell in *Telling Complexions* provides many excellent examples of instances of characters blushing. I am not convinced, though, by her theoretical framework, which sees blushing in novels as a form of Foucauldian social control and a somatic confession, "a mechanism, that is, the workings of which forward the grander social work of legibility and manners" (110), or that – "in seeming involuntarily and reliably to betray a deep self – blushing assists at the conversion of legibility into a sense of identity and centrality" (5). I prefer to see blushing as an unruly revelation, really involuntary, since confession implies a willing agency that is precisely absent in blushing.

13 Pamela Gilbert's lecture "'A Mild Erection of the Head'" provides an accessible and clear outline of how science and blushing were intertwined in nineteenth-century England, noting that blushing was considered more seemly for women and children than for men.

14 Schmeichel and Inzlicht begin "Incidental and Integral Effects of Emotions on Self-Control" with what could be a description of Fermín's predicament, the conflict between the spontaneous unthought and the cautions of self-control: "Probably most human behaviors are impulsive. This seems especially likely to be true for infants and children, who are only beginning to develop the capacity to override impulses. But even for healthy adult humans who are presumed to have a fully developed capacity for self-control, impulsive or automatic behaviors predominate" (272).

15 The scene is dramatic:

> Somoza volvió a las ocho de la noche; a pesar de la primavera médica, no estaba tranquilo; miró la lengua a la enferma, le tomó el pulso, le mandó aplicar al sobaco un termómetro que sacó él del bolsillo, y contó los grados. Se puso el doctor como una cereza ... Miró a Visita con torvo ceño y echándose a adivinar exclamó con enojo:
>
> -¡Estamos mal! ... Aquí se ha hablado mucho... Me la han aturdido, ¿verdad? ¡Como si lo viera ... mucha gente, de fijo ... mucha conversación! (2:113)

[Somoza returned at eight o'clock that evening. In spite of "spring fever" he was uneasy; he looked at his patient's tongue, felt her pulse, took a thermometer from his pocket, told her to put it under her arm, and observed the degrees. Then he turned as red as a cherry, scowled at Visita and, relying on guesswork, exclaimed in anger: "We're in a bad way! There has been a great deal of chattering here." (421)]

WORKS CITED

Alas, Leopoldo. *La Regenta*. Ed. Gonzalo Sobejano. 2 vols. Madrid: Clásicos Castalia, 1981. Print.

– *La Regenta*. Trans. with an introduction by John Rutherford. Athens: University of Georgia Press, 1984.

Althusser, Louis. "Ideology and Ideological State Apparatuses (Notes towards an Investigation)." 1970. https://www.marxists.org/reference/archive/althusser/1970/ideology.htm.

Bauer, Beth Wietelmann. "Novels in Dialogue: *Pepita Jiménez* and *La Regenta*." *Revista de Estudios Hispánicos* 25 (1991): 103–21. Print.

Camps, Victoria. *La imaginación ética*. Barcelona: Seix Barral, 1983. Print.

Damasio, Antonio R. *Descartes' Error: Emotion, Reason, and the Human Brain*. New York: Avon Books, 1994. Print.

Darwin, Charles. *The Expression of the Emotions in Man and Animals*. 1872. New York: Philosophical Library, 1955. Print.

Delgado, Luisa Elena, Pura Fernández, and Jo Labanyi. *Engaging the Emotions in Spanish Culture and History*. Nashville: Vanderbilt UP, 2016. Print.

Dreyfus, Hubert, and Charles Taylor. *Retrieving Realism*. Cambridge, MA: Harvard UP, 2015. Print.

Foucault, Michel. "On the Government of the Living." In *The Essential Works of Foucault 1954–1984: Ethics, Subjectivity and Truth*, vol. 1, ed. Paul Rabinow. New York: New York Press, 1997. 81–5. Print.

Gilbert, Pamela. "'A Mild Erection of the Head': The Meaning of the Blush in Nineteenth-Century Britain." https://vimeo.com/125855251. Web.

Gregory, Richard L., and O.L. Zangwill. *The Oxford Companion to the Mind*. Oxford: Oxford UP, 1998. Print.

Heidegger, Martin. *What Is Called Thinking?* Trans. J. Glenn Gray. New York: Harper and Row, 1968. Print.

Johnson, Mark. *Morality for Humans: Ethical Understanding from the Perspective of Cognitive Science*. Chicago and London: U of Chicago P, 2014. Print.

Kahneman, Daniel. *Thinking, Fast and Slow*. New York: Farrar, Straus and Giroux, 2011. Print.

Labanyi, Jo. "Mysticism and Hysteria in *La Regenta*: The Problem of Female Identity." In *Feminist Readings on Spanish and Latin-American Literature*, ed. L.P. Condé and S.M. Hart, Lewiston, NY: Edwin Mellen P, 1991. 37–46. Print.

Lewis, Michael. "Self-Conscious Emotions: Embarrassment, Pride, Shame, and Guilt." In *Handbook of Emotions*, 3rd ed., ed. Michael Lewis, Jeannette M. Haviland-Jones, and Lisa Feldman Barrett. New York: Guilford P, 2008. 742–56. Print.

Merleau-Ponty, Maurice. *Phenomenology of Perception*. Trans. Donald A. Landes. London and New York: Routledge, 2012. Print.

– *The Primacy of Perception*. Ed. James M. Edie. Evanston: Northwestern UP, 1964. Print.

Nehamas, Alexander. *The Art of Living: Socratic Reflections from Plato to Foucault*. Berkeley: U of California P, 1998. Print.

Nietzsche, Friedrich. *On the Genealogy of Morality*. Trans. Maudemarie Clark and Alan J. Swensen. Indianapolis and Cambridge: Hackett Publishing Co., 1998. Print.

O'Farrell, Mary Ann. *Telling Complexions: The Nineteenth-Century English Novel and the Blush*. Durham and London: Duke UP, 1997. Print.

Resina, Joan Ramon. "Ana Ozores's Nerves." *Hispanic Review* 71.2 (2003): 229–52. Print. https://doi.org/10.2307/3247189.

Schmeichel, Brandon J., and Michael Inzlicht. "Incidental and Integral Effects of Emotions on Self-Control." In *Handbook of Cognition and Emotion*, ed. Michael D. Robinson, Edward R. Watkins, and Eddie Harmon-Jones. New York: Guilford P, 2013. 272–90. Print.

Turner, Harriet. "Andanzas y fugas por espacios vetustenses." In *El espacio en la narrativa moderna en lengua española. Coloquio internacional Universidad Eötvös Loránd, Budapest, 12–13 de Mayo de 2003*, ed. Gabriella Mensczel and László Scholz. Budapest: Eötvös József Könyvkiadó, 2003. 34–41. Print.

– *Benito Pérez Galdós: Fortunata and Jacinta*. Cambridge: Cambridge UP, 1992. Print.

Valera, Juan. *Pepita Jiménez*. Madrid: Imprenta de J. Noruega a cargo de M. Martínez, 1874. Print.

Västfjäll, Daniel, and Paul Slovic. "Cognition and Emotion in Judgment and Decision Making." In *Handbook of Cognition and Emotion*, ed. Michael D. Robinson, Edward R. Watkins, and Eddie Harmon-Jones. New York: Guilford P, 2013. 252–71. Print.

10 María Zambrano on Women, Realism, and Freedom

ROBERTA JOHNSON

Spanish philosopher María Zambrano (1904–1992) drew heavily on literature in her theoretical writing. Her central philosophical notion *razón poética* [poetic reason], embodied in literature, posits a soul [*alma*] or emotions that mediate between the interior and the exterior realms of the person. Zambrano herself did not write many works that could be considered pure literature (a play titled *La tumba de Antígona* [Antigone's Tomb] and the autobiographical novel *Delirio y destino* [*Delirium and Destiny*]),[1] but her philosophical essays contain highly literary, even lyrical, passages. She also wrote a number of essays of literary criticism and theory. Zambrano believed that a Spanish philosophical tradition, long considered non-existent, could be found in Spanish literature beginning with *Don Quijote*.[2] She distinguishes herself from her male forerunners – Unamuno, Azorín, Baroja – in her appreciation of nineteenth-century realism, especially that of Benito Pérez Galdós. In fact, José Luis Mora notes that Zambrano established Galdós as a predecessor to Unamuno and Ortega.

Janet Pérez has studied in some detail what María Zambrano's ontology and metaphysics owe Ortega and Unamuno and how she differs from them.[3] Less considered is how Zambrano's aesthetics or literary theory diverges (especially in its references to gender) from those of other important Spanish writers from the early twentieth century. As a champion of realism, Zambrano differs from her masculine forebears and contemporaries. In the context of her intellectual grandfathers Unamuno and Azorín, her philosophical father Ortega, and her brothers of the Generation of '27 (among them vanguard novelists such as Antonio Espina and Benjamín Jarnés), her aesthetics, which exalt Galdós's realism and his female characters, are audacious. Realism allows for an ethical position not found in European modernism or in

Spanish aesthetics that correspond to that modernism – those of the so-called Generation of '98 and the vanguards (Generation of '27) of the 1920s.[4] Realism fosters an identification between the reader and a physical world that the '98ers and the vanguardists avoided in their novelistic practices and against which Ortega argued in his *La deshumanización del arte* [The Dehumanization of Art 1925].[5] The purpose of the present essay is to show how Zambrano's recuperation of the national philosophical-novelistic tradition is at the same time the creation of a personal philosophical voice that incorporates qualities Zambrano especially associated with female characters both in the *Quijote* and in Galdós's *Fortunata y Jacinta, Misericordia,* and *Tristana*. We will see that, although Zambrano did not write an entire book on the novel in general or on a particular novel or novelist (as did Unamuno, Azorín, and Ortega y Gasset on the *Quijote*), her articles on the novel as a genre served as a laboratory in which she explored ideas that appear later in her books – *El sueño creador* [Creative Dreams] (1955), *El hombre y lo divino* [Man and the Divine] (1955), *Persona y democracia* [Person and Democracy] (1956–8), and *Claros del bosque* [Clearings in the Forest] (1977).[6] The essays on the novel were written primarily between 1938 and 1948, the period in which Zambrano was in the process of forming her mature ideas on being, reality, dreams, time, and liberty via poetic reason. José Luis Mora notes that Zambrano refers to the novel (especially those of Galdós) "en momentos de intensidad y compromiso. Es decir, cuando está dando las primeras formas a su pensamiento" [at moments of intensity and special dedication. That is to say, when she is just forming her ideas] (Mora, "Un nombre de mujer" 1). By thinking about the *Quijote* and the Galdosian novel over an extended period of time, from 1937 to 1970, Zambrano developed ideas on liberty, time, dreams, reality, and being in the presence of the other,[7] and she herself became increasingly liberated and self-sufficient in her own life as she analysed the lives of female characters in realist novels.

When Zambrano first began writing on the novel in the mid-1930s, she was married to Alfonso Rodríguez Aldava and militated for a Republic in Spain with articles in the journal *Hora de España* [The Spanish Hour]. There she published "La reforma del entendimiento español" [The Reform of Spanish Understanding] (1937), centring on the figure of Don Quixote, and an essay on Galdós's novel *Misericordia* [Charity] (1938), which initiates her meditation on Galdós. In a second period, Zambrano was exiled in Mexico, where she wrote *Poesía y pensamiento en la vida española* [Poetry and Thought in Spanish Life] in 1939. In a third period, which began in 1940, she moved to the Caribbean – Cuba and Puerto Rico – where she gave the lecture "Mujeres de Galdós" [Galdós's Women] in 1942. The fourth period began with her mother's death (1946) and her separation from her husband (1948). In 1946 Zambrano took charge of her semi-invalid sister Araceli, with whom she lived in various locations – Paris, Cuba, Rome, and La Pièce, France, where Araceli died in 1972. In this last period Zambrano wrote several works focused on the novel: "La ambigüedad de Cervantes" [Cervantes's Ambiguity] (1947), "La ambigüedad de Don Quijote" [The Ambiguity of Don Quixote] (1948),[8] "La mirada de Cervantes" [Cervantes's Gaze] (1947), "Lo que le sucedió a Cervantes: Dulcinea" [What Happened to Cervantes: Dulcinea] (1955), *El sueño creador* [The Creative Dream] (first version 1955), "Misericordia: La obra de Galdós" [Misericordia: Galdós's Work] (1958–60), and "Tristana" (1970). As Zambrano moved physically and temporally away from the Republican Spain (1931–9) she had defended so passionately and became personally and professionally independent, she increasingly emphasized the theme of liberty, a liberty achieved by female novelistic characters within a realist milieu.

For Zambrano the novel, unlike classical tragedy, embodies human liberty and independence. She notes that the protagonists' existence in each genre differs, especially in terms of their self-consciousness: "El centro de la novela, como el de la tragedia, es el protagonista; la diferencia entre ellos estriba en el modo como están situados ante su propia vida, ante sí mismos. El protagonista de tragedia se ignora a sí mismo y, se precipita en su acción como la única posible; no ha elegido. El de novela, antes que consistir en lo que es o es a medias, se constituye en lo que pretende ser" [As in tragedy, the protagonist is at the centre of the novel; the protagonists differ in the way they are situated with relation to their lives, with relation to themselves. The tragic protagonist is unaware of him- or herself, and rushes into his or her action as though it were the only possible one; he or she has not chosen. Before becoming what he or she is or partially is, the novel's protagonist is what he or she wants to be] (Zambrano, *El sueño creador* 106). The novelistic character invents him- or herself by means of his or her own *novelería* [novel writing]; thus "el suceso que trae consigo la novela y el novelar es la libertad antes que el ser" [the event the novel brings to light and novel writing is freedom before being] (106). This freedom is achieved in a real social world. As Ana Bundgård points out, "Zambrano describe detalladamente el 'tejido social' de la novela" [Zambrano describes the "social fabric" of the novel in a detailed manner] (356).

The novel – a narration that supposes a chronology – is also the genre that provides the most opportunities for considering time, the time in which freedom is effected. As Zambrano indicates in her essay "La actitud ante la realidad" [The Attitude towards Reality] from 1965, "El tiempo hace posible que la realidad total se fragmente, que podamos atender sucesivamente a ella, que entre ella y la conciencia humana haya una comunicación, un contacto y una distancia, el tiempo nos liberta de la realidad haciéndonos posible que tratemos con ella y tratar para el hombre es conocer y actuar. Realidad-tiempo-libertad es la ecuación del despertar" [Time makes it possible for total reality to fragment so that we can attend to it successively, and there can be communication between reality and the human consciousness, a contact and a distance. Time frees us from reality, making it possible for us to deal with it, and dealing for man [humanity] is to know and act. Reality-time-liberty is the equation of awakening] (66). Thus Zambrano's essays on the novel are less interested in the historical (the focus of many male writers when they address the nature of the novel) in order to concentrate on the contemporary (and thus the future). María Luisa Maillard notes that Zambrano insisted on treating the novelistic genre "por ser un género contemporáneo, nacido de la afirmación de la individualidad renacentista y el que responde de forma emblemática a un mundo despojado de la servidumbre de los dioses y reducido al horizonte de lo humano" [because it is a contemporary genre, born of the Renaissance affirmation of individuality, and it is the genre that responds in emblematic form to a world that has eliminated servitude to gods and reduced it to the human horizon] (111). The emphasis on the contemporaneous does not exclude a consideration of the past. As Mora observes, both Galdós and Zambrano saw in the novel a "género que sin renunciar a la referencia histórica ... nos permite una relectura del pasado, es decir, sacar una lección moral donde había fracaso en el campo de la acción política. Consigue, pues, la novela principalmente que no perdamos de vista la unidad establecida sobre otros parámetros y nos obliga, además, a creer en que la salvación es posible" [genre that, without renouncing historical references, allows us to reread the past, that is to say, to take a moral lesson when there has been a failure in the political arena. The novel mainly helps us keep sight of the unity established over other dimensions and in addition obliges us to believe that salvation is possible] (Mora, "Un nombre de mujer" 127–8).

If the treatment of time in the novel is gendered, so is the approach to reality. The reality of the novels Zambrano examines is often feminine, even in the *Quijote*, whose protagonist is masculine. Without a doubt Zambrano identified with the female subjectivity of the women characters she has selected as vehicles to develop a philosophy of human liberty. Such an identification between character and author arises when Zambrano treats the character and the author of the *Quijote* as a single entity in "Lo que le sucedió a Cervantes: Dulcinea," and she comments in *El sueño creador* that "la libertad que se revela ambiguamente, es una especie de juego de espejos entre personaje y autor. Los personajes de novelas padecen y actualizan el sueño de la libertad" [the liberty that is revealed ambiguously is a kind of play of mirrors between character and author. Novelistic characters suffer and bring to life the dream of liberty] (106). Mora correctly observes that "el personaje Nina-Zambrano habla ya consigo misma de sí misma" [the character Nina-Zambrano talks to herself about herself] (Mora, "Un nombre de mujer" 73).[9] Her physical situation in the material and temporal world, which is communicated via the senses (light, for example) and the passions (love and pain), facilitates the personal identification with the female character.

As Antonio Risco points out, nineteenth-century realism created "la posibilidad de transformación de la naturaleza, de la sociedad y del hombre mismo por el acto" [the possibility of transforming nature, society, and man by means of action] (41). Zambrano follows in Azorín's footsteps when she affirms realism as an important Spanish tradition. As early as 1912 in *Lecturas españolas*, Azorín posited a realist tradition in Spanish thought and culture: "teníamos en España una tradición antigua de realismo en nuestra novela picaresca" [in Spain we had a long tradition of realism in our picaresque novel] ("Galdós" 797). And Azorín, as Zambrano would do later, emphasized the uniqueness of nineteenth-century realism (especially in Galdós), what he calls its "trascendencia social" [social transcendence], the "sentido en el artista de una realidad superior a la realidad primera y visible, a la relación que se establece entre el hecho real, visible, ostensible, y la serie de causas y concausas que lo han determinado" [artist's sense of a reality that is superior to the first and visible reality, the relationship that is established between the real, visible, ostensible fact and the causes that have determined it] ("Galdós" 797). According to Azorín, Galdós studied "no sólo las cosas en sí, como hacían los antiguos, sino el ambiente espiritual de las cosas" [not only things in themselves, as did the ancients, but the spiritual ambience of things], and he believed that Galdós helped to form a national consciousness: "ha hecho que la palabra *España* no sea una abstracción, algo seco y sin vida, sino una realidad ... ha hecho vivir España con sus ciudades, sus pueblos, sus monumentos, sus paisajes" [he made the word *Spain* a reality rather than a dry, lifeless abstraction ... he made Spain live with its cities, its towns, its monuments, its landscapes] (Bundgård 798). Although none of the members of his generation, or Azorín himself, followed Galdós's realist aesthetic, Azorín believed that his generation absorbed the vision of Spain that the great novelist projected. In one of his articles on the Generation of '98, Azorín observed that "[Galdós] aparece silenciosamente, con sus ojos chiquitos y escrutadores, con su mirada fría y escrupulosa; aparece viéndolo todo, examinándolo todo ... iba, paso a paso, dándonos sus libros repletos de menuda realidad; las nuevas generaciones fuimos acercándonos, solidarizándonos, compenetrándonos con la realidad. En adelante, la tragedia de España había de saltarnos a los ojos; nuestro espíritu estaba ya fuertemente aferrado a ella. Habíamos *visto*; lógica, fatalmente, había de surgir el lamento y la indignación" [Galdós appeared silently with his small, scrutinizing eyes, with his cold scrupulous gaze; he saw everything, examined everything ... Little by little he gave us books full of minute detail; the new generations were approaching, forming a solidarity, entering into reality. Then, Spain's tragedy leapt in front of our eyes; our spirit was strongly tied to it. We had *seen*; logically, fatally, lament and indignation arose] (qtd in Pérez López 196–7).

If what Azorín says of the impact Galdós had on his own generation is true, María Zambrano inherited this tradition.[10] Azorín and Zambrano differ, however, on the concept of dreams. Azorín seems to agree with Galdós's comment about Spain's slumbering state: "'Su sueño – añade – es como de ancianidad y niñez combinados, juntos en reposo inocente.' Ese sueño duerme España entera: Galdós novelista; Galdós, en más de cien volúmenes, ha trabajado por que despierte y adquiera conciencia de sí misma" ["His dream – he adds – is that of old age and childhood combined, together in innocent repose." All Spain dreams this dream: Galdós the novelist. In more than one hundred volumes, Galdós laboured to make Spain wake up and acquire consciousness of itself] ("Galdós" 799). As we will see later, dreams in Zambrano project much more towards the future than towards the past and the present. And, of course, Azorín's female characters do not have the liberating vision that Zambrano finds in Galdós's. In fact, none of the writers of the Generation of '98, of Ortega's generation (the Generation of '14), or of the vanguard (Generation of '27) created memorable female characters.[11]

José Ortega y Gasset, Zambrano's teacher and "mentor," scarcely mentions Galdós in his vast work. Ortega was especially hostile to realism, and perhaps for that reason he was not interested in writing about the novelist.[12] Zambrano, however, finds a positive value in the realist novel in which life "ha triunfado" [has triumphed] over ideas, especially in Galdós's novels. While Ortega despised what he called the "puros hechos" [pure facts] and lack of ideas in realism, Zambrano believed that the Spanish realist tradition revealed the hidden history of Spanish philosophy ("La actitud" 465). Ortega is even harsher when he speaks about realism in painting, because, according to him, in realist art one does not have to invent anything: "Ahí están las cosas, aquí está el lienzo, paleta y pinceles. Se trata de hacer pasar las cosas que están ahí al lienzo que está aquí ... Realismo es entonces la negación del arte, dígase con todas sus letras" [Things are there, and the canvas, the pallet, and the brushes are here. It is a question of bringing the things over there to the canvas over here ... Thus realism is the negation of art, not to put too fine a point on it] (Ortega, *OC* 1:568).

What the male writers did not understand or what did not interest them was that realism contains the possibility of changing personal or social reality. It does not just repeat its "things." María Zambrano can be allied with other women writers of the first third of the twentieth century – Blanca de los Ríos, Sofía Casanova, Carmen de Burgos, Concha Espina, Margarita Nelken, and Federica Montseny – in finding in a realist aesthetic a means of approaching Spanish reality (above all that of women) in order to change it, quite a different goal from that of Azorín, Unamuno, and Ortega, who were searching for the eternal essence of the Spanish nation in order to dissect it.[13] What differentiates Zambrano from the other Spanish women writers of her time is that instead of writing socio-political realist novels as they did, she theorized about realism and its importance for understanding personal and national reality. However, Zambrano did demonstrate a talent for narrative in *La tumba de Antígona* (although ostensibly a drama, it has many narrative passages) and in the "delirios" she placed at the end of her autobiographical novel *Delirio y destino*. And like the other Spanish women writers of her era, she emphasized female subjectivity in her narrative works.

Zambrano's essays on Galdós were published about the same time as those on *Don Quijote*; in fact, nearly all of them refer to both Galdós and Cervantes.[14] One notes a similar trajectory in her approach to the two writers in different periods of her life and work, which begin with a consideration of what the great Spanish novels can reveal about the essence of Spanish being and end with what they can tell us about the individual human being (mostly women). Zambrano's first writings on Cervantes and Galdós, published in *Hora de España* in 1937 when it was becoming clear that the Republic was losing the Civil War, seek a kind of Spanish *intrahistoria* [eternal national essence] that would vindicate the suffering Spanish people. "La reforma del entendimiento español" [The Reform of Spanish Understanding] (*Hora de España*, September 1937) situates the origins of a Spanish philosophical tradition in the concept of failure as set out in *Don Quijote*, "la aceptación realista resignada y al par esperanzada, del fracaso" [the realistic, resigned (and at the same time hopeful) acceptance of failure] (*El sueño* 97). In this article, one finds the roots of Zambrano's existential philosophy in the notions of *convivencia* [living together] and dependence on the "other" (as witnessed in the relationship between Don Quixote and Sancho), a concept she developed more extensively in her exile period.

The article begins with Don Quixote and ends with *Fortunata y Jacinta*, a novel by Galdós, especially focusing on the figure of Fortunata as a repository of the Spanish national spirit. Zambrano finds in Fortunata or transfers to her some of Don Quixote's outstanding qualities. She even decides that Fortunata is superior to Don Quixote because "en su grandeza le resbalan todos los fracasos ... guarda una idea *entre sí* que es toda su vida Idea [possibly a reference to Ortega, who did not believe that novels contained ideas], por lo demás, tan divinamente humana, tan noble como la alta categoría de su maternidad" [in her greatness, all her failures roll off her back ... she keeps an idea to herself, which is that her whole life is a divinely human Idea, as noble as the elevated nature of her maternity] (*El sueño* 102). Both Galdós and Cervantes find the Spanish will in "las capas populares, a la base misma virginal de nuestro pueblo, firme voluntad que ya no sueña con asuntos tan altos como los de Don Quijote, sino que confundida con el instinto es vocación maternal en la Divina Fortunata" [the virginal popular stratum of our people, firm will that no longer dreams of high matters as Don Quixote did, but which is bound up with instinct as is the maternal vocation in the Divine Fortunata] (*El sueño* 103). Differing from Unamuno, Azorín, and Valle-Inclán, or the vanguardists, in her essays on the novel, Zambrano focuses on the subjectivity with which Galdós endows his female protagonists, a subjectivity that allows them to assume control over their own lives and destinies, to dream themselves.

The second of Zambrano's articles on the novel published in *Hora de España* in 1938 focuses on Galdós's *Misericordia*. Here, as in "La reforma del pensamiento español," Zambrano finds Spanish essence in the protagonist Benigna, "la pureza popular ... la tradición verdadera que hace renacer el pasado, encarnarse en el hoy, convertirse en el manaña" [the popular purity ... of the true tradition that makes the past be reborn, become incarnate in today, and become converted into tomorrow] (*El sueño* 141, 144). Zambrano finds the Spanish approach to realism in *Misericordia*, just as she did in *Don Quijote*: "entre nosotros, la mente no ha sido despegado de las cosas, de la vida, o violencia alguna, por apetito alguno de poder, y la vida ha triunfado siempre" [our minds have not been detached from things, from life; there has been no violence occasioned by a desire for power] (127). However, she avers that *Misericordia* goes beyond *Don Quijote* in the desire to reveal the reason behind Spanish unreason. The Galdosian novel establishes the independence of things (or of the material world) when faced with the human mind: "se cree que las cosas *son* ... el saber es una función de la mente humana que se apoya en la garantía de que las cosas tienen en sí mismas un ser que les pertenece" [one believes that things *are* ... knowing is a function of the human mind that depends on the guarantee that things in themselves have a being that belongs to them] (141). Benigna moves among things, and thus she "es la tradición verdadera que hace renacer el pasado, encarnarse en el hoy, convertirse en el mañana ... Libre como un pájaro, se sobrepone a todo ... Crea la libertad" [is the true tradition that makes the Spanish past return, reincarnate itself in today, and convert itself in tomorrow ... Free as a bird, it dominates everything ... It creates liberty] (144–5). Although Don Quixote is also the author of himself, he is not the author of his freedom from things, because things lead to his failure. In this respect, Benigna is superior to Don Quixote, because she carries out her liberty in a material world in concrete time (which exists alongside intrahistorical time);[15] "El tiempo real y concreto en que lo histórico y lo innominado se traban reflejándose mutuamente, el tiempo con ritmo imperceptible en que transcurre lo doméstico agitado todavía por lo histórico, es el tiempo real de la vida de un pueblo que lo sea en verdad, es el tiempo de la novela de Galdós" [Real, concrete time in which the historical and the unnamed interweave, reflecting each other mutually; time with an imperceptible rhythm in which the domestic, which is still moved by the historical, is the real time of the life of a people that is really a people, is the time of Galdós's novels] (122). Zambrano's time, which includes not only the past and present as does intrahistory, also encompasses the future, and thus liberty.

In 1939, in Mexican exile, Zambrano gave some lectures published as *Pensamiento y poesía en la vida española*. Ana Bundgård discovers that in these lectures Zambrano began to evolve towards a less nationalistic and less intrahistorical philosophy. Many of Zambrano's ideas expressed only a year after the *Hora de España* articles are very similar to those I have just outlined – that Spanish realism is "un estilo de vida – una manera de estar plantado en la existencia – no es una teoría – irreducible a sistema ... una forma de tratar con las cosas, de estar ante el mundo" [a style of life – a way of being planted in existence; it is not a theory; it is not reducible to a system ... a way of treating things, of being in the world] (*Obras reunidas* 277, 280). Now Zambrano probes more deeply the idea of the person's corporality among things – the physical sensations in relation to matter – an idea that will seal the association between women, the physical world, and the novel while she developed an analysis of being-in-the-world through the novel. In her 1939 lectures, there is a cult of material charged with creative energy. For Zambrano, *Don Quijote* is a novel protagonized by things, "la magnificencia de las cosas más humildes" [the magnificence of humble things] – roads, inns, trees, lowly creatures, "a las que el tema trágico no ha podido anular – y por ende es una novela realista" [which the tragic theme has not been able to annul, thus it is a realist novel] (286). To Cervantes Zambrano adds Galdós and Ramón Gómez de la Serna as novelists of things. In her Mexican lectures Zambrano already introduces some nuances that are important when she develops the existentialist strain of her philosophy – her focus on the human way of being – in the 1950s and 1960s. The "huella del hombre, huella que es posible por esa cercanía o entrañamiento en que el hombre ha vivido con ellas" [man's trace, a trace that is possible because of the closeness or intimacy in which man has lived with them] (286) penetrates the world of things. Entering into a relationship with material is to enter light, and this light opens the path to the future.

While analysing Spain's historical situation in the nineteenth century in *Pensamiento y poesía en la vida española*, Zambrano creates an interesting paradox by placing women and the family at the centre of the period's *morada vital* [vital home]. According to Zambrano, in the nineteenth century energetic and adventuresome Spain became "doméstica" [domestic], "profundamente reaccionaria" [profoundly reactionary]; Spaniards were "dispuestos a quedarse en casa para siempre" [willing to remain at home forever] (*Obras reunidas* 344). She interprets this shift in the Spanish spirit both positively and negatively. On the one hand, she employs terms like "impone su tiranía absorbente" [imposes its absorbing tyranny] (344) to describe the hegemony that the family exercised in the nineteenth century. Spanish life is *cercada* [enclosed] and *envuelta irremisiblemente* [irremissibly surrounded]: "La fuerza mayor que en la vida española se desarrolla es la de impedir, la de detener, la de retener" [The major force developing in Spanish life is to impede, stop, restrain] (344). Women are the instrument of these forces: "impiden marchar, le impiden, si se hace falta, ser" [they impede movement, or, if need be, they impede being] (345). However, at the same time, the family, women's realm, is "un mundo poético donde todo ímpetu es amansado, donde toda furia es calmada y deshecha, en lo doméstico" [a poetic world where all initiative is tamed, where all fury is calmed and undone in the domestic] (345). Zambrano cites Santa Teresa when observing that "entre los cacharros ... anda el espíritu, el pobre espíritu que ennoblece tanto a los cacharros que a veces desfallece entre ellos" [the spirit, the poor spirit, wanders through the kitchen wares, so greatly ennobling those wares that sometimes it faints among them] (345).

In spite of this evident lowering of the Spanish spirit into nineteenth-century domesticity, Galdós's novels provide the historical memory that was interrupted by the Civil War: "El mundo que con tanta realidad nos presenta es el mundo de la tradición, de la que queda. En él aparece a través del delirio y el disparate [precisely what Unamuno did not like about Galdós], para nuestro consuelo, la única continuidad de la vida española, la unidad verdadera de España" [The world that he presents to us with so much reality is the traditional world, or what is left of it. In it appears the continuity of Spanish life, Spain's true unity through delirium and insanity] (Zambrano, *Obras reunidas* 350). This continuity and consolation of the Spanish tradition appears in more concentrated and significant form in the characters of Fortunata and Benigna, "dos gigantescas figuras de mujer que encarnan las dos fuerzas cohesivas y creadoras a las que nada ha podido abatir: la fecundidad y la misericordia" [two giant female figures that embody the two cohesive and creative forces that nothing has been able to overcome: fecundity and charity] (350). If, in the nineteenth century, women were limited in energy and national force through their domesticity, in the twentieth century, and above all in the postwar era, women in the Galdosian novel now can be understood as a "fuerza inmensa, inagotable, de la fecundidad, de la fecundidad humana lindante con la fecundidad de la Naturaleza; tan insobornable como ella, tan inocente y poderosa como ella ... la vocación irrefrenable de la maternidad, elevada a acto sagrado por el que la vida se sobrevive siempre" [immense, inexhaustible force of fecundity, human fecundity with Nature's fecundity; as incorruptible, innocent, and powerful as she is] (350). Thus Fortunata, who was Don Quixote's sister in "La reforma del entendimiento" of 1937, in the post–Civil War era has been transformed, thanks to her maternal impulse, into an "arrolladora fuerza que todo lo vence" [overwhelming force that conquers everything] (350).

Pensamiento y poesía en la vida española ends with a section on Azorín, whom Zambrano calls a Spanish mystic, because he presents Spain as suspended, stopped, in domestic time. She takes up this theme again in *El sueño creador* [The Creative Dream] of 1955, when her thought about female literary figures has progressed quite a bit beyond the identification of Fortunata and Benigna with Spanish materialism. In 1955 Zambrano introduces the notion of dreaming as a means of female (and human) liberation; it is of personal significance that Zambrano relates this liberation to the rejection of matrimony. Her answer to Azorín's domestication of Melibea in "Las nubes" [The Clouds] (perhaps his best known *estampa* [sketch] from *Castilla* of 1912) is revealing. At the beginning of the piece, the narrator announces that "Calisto y Melibea se casaron – como sabrá el lector si ha leído *La Celestina* – a pocos días de ser descubiertas las robozadas entrevistas que tenían en el jardín ... Viven ahora marido y mujer en la casa solariega de Melibea; una hija les nació que lleva, como su abuela, el nombre de Alisa" [Calisto and Melibea got married – as the reader knows, if he has read *La Celestina* – a few days after their secret meetings in the garden were discovered ... Husband and wife now live in Melibea's family home; they have a daughter named Alisa, like her grandmother] (Azorín, *Castilla* 159). Readers of *La Celestina* will be very surprised by Calisto and Melibea's having settled into domestic tranquillity, since Calisto's death when he fell from the ladder that took him over the wall into Melibea's garden and her subsequent suicide are two of the most memorable literary events in Spanish Renaissance literature.

In *El sueño creador*, María Zambrano reminds us of the domestic turn that Azorín gives Calisto and Melibea's tragic love story, and she refutes what she calls Azorín's "poética rectificación" [poetic rectification] (*El sueño* 96). Zambrano argues against various ethnic-religious theories about why Calisto and Melibea did not marry that circulated in the 1940s, including Américo Castro's suggestion that Melibea's Jewish family history would have impeded her marriage to a Christian Calisto. Zambrano prefers to believe that Melibea had asserted her will in not marrying Calisto. In Zambrano's view, Calisto is a stereotypical Renaissance gentleman, and Celestina is a meddler, "conciencia de la época" [conscience of the period]. Melibea has a dream; she is "la portadora de algo original, extraño, irreductible a los cánones de ésa y de toda época ... No era nupcial el sueño que visitó a Melibea, que de haberlo sido, habría habido nupcias aun en la muerte. No era de casarse el sueño" [the bearer of something original, strange, and irreducible to the canons of this or any period ... The dream that visited Melibea was not nuptial; if it had been, there would have been a wedding even after death. Her dream was not a dream of marriage] (98). According to Zambrano, Melibea's dream is a "sueño iniciático y de creación" [initiating dream of creation] (101), ultimately, a "sueño de libertad" [dream of liberty] (105).

"Mujeres de Galdós" [Galdós's Women], a lecture Zambrano gave in 1942, which was published as an article in the same year, reveals the important place that female characters had assumed in her thought: "Galdós es el primer escritor español que introduce valientemente las mujeres en su mundo. Las mujeres, múltiples y diversas, las mujeres reales y distintas, 'ontológicamente' iguales al varón. Y esa es la novedad, esa la deslumbrante conquista. Existe como el hombre, tiene el mismo género de realidad; es lo decisivo. Es lo primero que teníamos que ver" [Galdós is the first Spanish writer to valiantly introduce women into his world. Multiple and diverse women, real, different women that are "ontologically" equal to men. And this is the innovation, this the brilliant conquest. These women exist like men; they have the same type of reality; that is the decisive factor. It's the first thing we have to understand] (130). By the time she wrote this essay, Zambrano had already left Mexico and was residing in Cuba and Puerto Rico, where she began a more independent life, finally separating from her husband and receiving a boost in her philosophical career from her contact with the group of young poets associated with the journal *Orígenes*.[16] The group included José Lezama Lima, who would be an important intellectual friend for the rest of her life. It is also noteworthy that in Cuba Zambrano had a rather tempestuous relationship with fellow Spanish exile Gustavo Pittaluga, about whose book *Grandeza y servidumbre de la mujer* [Women's Greatness and Servitude] she wrote a review article. In that review she notes that with positivism and the

Industrial Revolution, women finally assumed a position on the same level of reality as men, and she comments on the way women manage to change their circumstances. Zambrano believes that Pittaluga is right when he says that men foresee and women have presentiments: "El hombre pretende conocer para dirigir; la mujer, presintiendo, opera desde dentro, logrando modificar el curso de los acontecimientos del modo más profundo" [Men want knowledge in order to lead; women, having presentiments, work from inside, modifying the course of events in a more profound way] (Zambrano, "A propósito" 146). But she criticizes the author because, in his treatment of the history of women and his analysis of women's situation in biblical times and the Middle Ages, "no nos ofrece una fe última, un porvenir para la mujer, en que no aparece lo que la mujer vaya a ser en esta difícil etapa de su historia que coincide con la mayor turbiedad histórica que se haya conocido" [he does not offer women a lasting faith, what women are going to be in this difficult period of their history, which is the most turbulent we have ever known] (147). As in so many other essays, she emphasizes the future over the past.

"Mujeres de Galdós" continues by confirming that Galdós's female figures are vastly better than those of Cervantes, who, Zambrano believes, did not produce any significant women characters (129). Zambrano argues that instead of creating a real woman, Cervantes invented the ideal Dulcinea, "es decir un sueño" [that is to say, a dream] (129). She also criticizes Cervantes's "masculinismo tan extremo por no ofrecer espacio a la mujer" [extreme masculinism because he did not make a place for women] (129). Galdós, however, gives women like Fortunata and Benigna the most active roles, and what is more, a man (at least for Fortunata) "es poca cosa" [isn't much] (Zambrano, "A propósito" 134). The revised and augmented essay titled "Las mujeres en la España de Galdós" [Women in Galdós's Spain] (included in *La España de Galdós* [Galdós's Spain]) contains some of the same ideas expressed in a slightly different language: "Quizás de todo este universo galdosiano lo que encarne más cumplidamente la fierza de la misma realidad sea, precisamente, la mujer" [Perhaps what best incarnates the fierceness of reality in the Galdosian universe is precisely the woman] (Zambrano, *La España* 186). Here again she compares Galdós's "real" woman to Cervantes's ideal woman. On this point Zambrano is in agreement with Concha Espina, who in her *Mujeres del Quijote* (1916) criticized Cervantes for not creating more realistic women: "No llegan todas las del *Quijote*, si ha de decirse la verdad escueta, al punto sazonadísimo de realidad humana y perfección artística en donde resplandecen algunos ejemplares masculinos, aún sin contar los del Hidalgo y su escudero" [If we are to tell the absolute truth, not all the women in the *Quijote* reach the seasoned point of human reality and perfection of some of the masculine examples, not counting the Nobleman and his squire] (Espina 26). Even so, Espina pardons the author of the *Quijote,* because, she says, Cervantes did not have the opportunity to know as many illustrious women as he did outstanding men. In *Mujeres del Quijote* Espina dedicates an entire chapter to certain female characters (Marcela, Luscinda, Dorotea, Zoraida, Clara, Quiteria, la duquesa, Ana Félix, Teresa Panza, the housekeeper, and the niece), and she endows each one with a much more developed role and discourse than they have in Cervantes's novel. Zambrano does not follow Espina's model, preferring to focus on Galdós, a novelist who had created memorable women.[17]

In 1960 Zambrano continued to believe that Galdós was the first Spanish novelist to introduce women that are ontologically equal to men, but now she augments her analysis, calling the women *desheredadas* (disinherited) who show unlimited resistance in the face of adversity through a creative, liberating force. For example, in her desire for maternity Fortunata is of heroic stature, and Benigna, "en sus humildísimos menesteres, ha alcanzado la creación, pues saca de la nada lo que su ama, pobre señora, necesita no sólo para sustentarse sino para el mantenimiento de su dignidad de desheredada que va a heredar de nuevo; de 'cesante' de la herencia" [in her humble duties, has achieved creativity because she snatches what her mistress, poor woman, needs not only to survive but to maintain her dignity as a disinherited person who is going to inherit again; she is the dispossessed of her inheritance]. For Benigna, everything is a product of divine creation, the entire world with its pains and tricks; life with its daily struggle is a blessing in her hands. For this illiterate woman, the entire universe is stamped with the marks of divine creation (Zambrano, *La España de Galdós* 203). This creative activity is a source of liberty: "Fe y poesía contemplativa y activa salvada en su renacer constante por el pueblo ... Y, al mirar, se sienten libres, libres y enteros, como la luz de ese cielo purísimo que se alza sobre ellos. Misterio último de la vida española, donde la historia se detiene; misterio del puro ser, de la quietud y de la actividad confundidas. De una pureza creadora, tanto como humanamente es posible" [Faith and contemplative poetry saved by the people in its constant renewal. And upon looking, they feel free, free and whole, like the light of that pure sky rising above them. Ultimate mystery of Spanish life where history stops; mystery of pure being. Of the mingling of quietude and activity. Of creative purity as much as is humanly possible] (204).[18]

In the meantime Zambrano had written "La ambigüedad de Cervantes" and "La ambigüedad del Quijote," key essays in her 1965 work *España, sueño y verdad*. For Zambrano ambiguity is rooted in the human being and thus in the novel, the most human literary genre and the one that "plantea el enigma de la libertad" [puts forth the enigma of liberty] (*España, sueño y verdad* 36). Here one can see the importance of Zambrano's contact with French existentialism between 1946 and 1948 when she lived in Paris with her sister after her mother's death.[19] For example, we find the beginnings of a consideration of the notion of liberty in the article on *Misericordia* of 1960. These articles on the *Quijote* from 1947 and 1948 may have been preliminary studies for *El sueño creador*, since they contain ideas that Zambrano developed in that book, especially the difference between tragedy and the novel and the novel as a dream or invention of oneself. These articles represent an advance over "Mujeres de Galdós" in some respects. Now the dreamed woman – Dulcinea – gives Don Quixote freedom; she liberates him from history: "¿No está en Dulcinea el secreto? ¿No está ella acaso encantada también? ¿Separada, absoluta, reducida a esencia, a idea, llevada al mundo de la quimera, ella que es viviente realidad?" [Isn't the secret in Dulcinea? Isn't she perhaps also enchanted? Separated, absolute, reduced to an essence, an idea, carried off to the world of chimera, she who is the living reality?] (*España, sueño y verdad* 41). Such liberation can be of ambiguous value, since, as Zambrano reminds us, Cervantes did not understand women's materiality, or their subjectivity, or their existence as did Galdós. At the end of the essay Zambrano concludes that "Dulcinea sola y blanca se consume" [Alone and white, Dulcinea is consumed] (42).

When Zambrano writes on the *Quijote* again in 1955 in an article titled "Lo que le sucedió a Cervantes: Dulcinea" [What Happened to Cervantes: Dulcinea], instead of criticizing the Quixotic invention of the ideal woman Dulcinea, she focuses on Aldonza Lorenzo, the real woman behind the invented one. This change in perspective affords Zambrano the opportunity to emphasize the importance of women and love in the *Quijote*. She finds in Aldonza Lorenzo "la fiereza de la misma realidad" [the fierceness of reality itself] that she had associated with Benigna of *Misericordia* and Galdós's female characters in general. Thus she combines Unamuno's interpretation, which concentrates on the characters, and Ortega's, which centres on the author Cervantes. Her commentary completely fuses the protagonist and the author. The woman – Dulcinea – is the inspiration for both Cervantes and Don Quixote, and she exercises the same influence on the two: "No le había sucedido nunca aquella revelación, aquella entrevista en un instante único. Pero, ¿con quién? No podía él, Miguel de Cervantes, preguntárselo siquiera porque no había caído en la cuenta – felizmente – de que la literatura se había presentado a su alma y vivía en ella bajo figura de mujer, bajo especie, más bien, puesto que no la veía" [That revelation, that conversation, had not occurred to him in one single instant. But, with whom? He, Miguel de Cervantes, couldn't even ask, because, happily, he had not realized that literature had presented itself to his soul, and he lived in it by means of the figure of woman, by means of a species, since he did not see her] (*España, sueño y verdad* 44). According to Zambrano, Cervantes, like Don Quixote, is tangled up in his love and thus he is not free, unlike Aldonza, who is reality. Aldonza shares many of Benigna's characteristics in *Misericordia*: she "nada tenía de sombra" [had nothing shadowy about her]; in her, "todo era preciso, estaba, estaba sí, siempre; más que existir, estaba" [everything was precise; she was there; she was always there; rather than existing, she was there] (47). Although "el uso de los sentidos consigue una cierta desmaterialización de ciertas corpóreas realidades" [the use of the senses achieves a certain dematerialization of some corporal realities], this did not occur with Aldonza, who "seguía estando ahí, con la brutalidad del hecho, sin más, como un hecho irreductible, pues que nunca se despojaba de nada; una fiera sin caverna. Una realidad sin ese hueco de que todo lo real parece emerger" [continued to be there, with the brutality of the fact, as an irreducible fact, that never let go of anything; a beast without a cave. A reality without the hollow from which all that is real seems to emerge] (47).

The man (Cervantes–Don Quixote) comes up against reality – woman – that resists him: "Cometió el error de insistir; nunca se había encontrado así frente a un hecho. Y el hecho era una mujer; era algo horrible. Acostumbrado a ensoñarlo todo, como estaba, empujándolo hasta el confín del horizonte invisible, acabando por hundirlo en él, no podía resignarse ... Aquello le resistía totalmente" [He committed the error of insisting; he had never found himself faced with a fact. And the fact was a woman; it was horrible. As he was accustomed to dreaming everything, pushing it to the end of the invisible horizon, ending up sinking it in the horizon, he could not resign himself ... That resisted him completely] (*España, sueño y verdad* 47). For Zambrano, then, the woman as material and the woman as liberty fuse, because liberty resides in the confrontation with reality. Woman takes him to reality – the world that resists – and thus he achieves liberty: "Y entonces acabó por sentirse libre, libre de su amor, y entrevió, al fin. Fue un desprendimiento; sintió que se le desprendía el corazón, que se quedaba en las puras entrañas como un ser que no ha vivido nunca" [And then he felt free, free of his love, and he finally saw. It was a liberation; he felt as though his heart released him, as though he was left with his pure entrails [passions] like a being that has never lived] (40). Through the encounter with a woman "nació ya hombre" [he was born already a man] (40), and in that revealed horizon, things began to happen to him again, but since he was free, he could transform them, not to his liking, but according to the law of his entrails, so that, free also, they wanted to cry and laugh. And everything that was asleep in him woke up, began to live according to its law. He did not need to forget his works already written; they were his daughters that were running around there, and now they made him happy; now everything served him, even Aldonza, the real woman, and all the girls, his sisters who were grown up and more had served him. A strange pity spilled over them and over himself (49). Zambrano argues that Don Quixote's, and by extension Cervantes's, experience of reality, the clash with reality in the form of woman, has been a transforming and liberating experience. Notably this reflects Zambrano's own clash with reality in the failure of the Republic and her subsequent exile.

Zambrano continues her emphasis on women's materiality, corporality, and reality in "La obra de Galdós: *Misericordia*" [Galdós's Work: *Misericordia*], the first article in *La España de Galdós* (1960), and here her notion of woman as reality achieves its fullest expression. Zambrano asserts that Benigna is an advance over Don Quixote, because Cervantes's protagonist only stopped being a tragic figure at the end of the novel: "Más [*sic*] sucede que bajo el personaje novelesco, a veces, se dé el estar viviendo una tragedia, como parece ser le pasaba a Don Quijote, que se diría ser un personaje de tragedia al que se le da el tiempo. Y así, apura su tragedia en novela, hasta quedarse en lo que de verdad era, Alonso Quijano el Bueno, que probó serlo así en toda su verdad. Y al fin, ya libre de tragedia y novela, se nos revela su persona" [But sometimes the novelistic character is living a tragedy, as seems to be what happened to Don Quixote; one could say he is a tragic figure who is endowed with time. And thus his tragedy is poured into a novel until he ended up as who he really was, Alonso Quijano el Bueno, and he proved to be him in all his truth. And finally, free from tragedy and novel, he reveals his person to us] (*La España de Galdós* 38).

By contrast, Benigna does not seem to be a fictional character: "empieza su peregrinar donde Don Quijote lo acaba, mas sin reconocerse, como si nunca se hubiera soñado a sí misma y que su historia, como se verá, sea la historia de alguien que se adentra en la verdad y en la vida habiendo estado desde el principio en ella" [she begins her peregrination where Don Quixote leaves his, but without recognizing herself, as if she had never dreamt of herself and her story; as we will see, it is the story of someone who gets inside truth and inside life, having been in it from the beginning] (Zambrano *La España de Galdós* 38). Benigna is the centre of the novel and she undoes what Zambrano calls the novel writing of the other characters – the lady of the house, her daughter Obdulia, and their friend Frasquito Ponte. And as the centre, Benigna "es humanamente un camino, una apertura, un lugar de comunicación" [is humanly a road, an opening, a place of communication] (34). Thus she is the opposite of Don Quixote, who transforms everything he sees into a novel – characters and people, places, landscapes, things, the dust of the roads, the light of dawn, the love of a simple woman. Whereas "Nina solamente vive ... la vida" [Nina only lives ... life] (Zambrano, *La España de Galdós* 34). In other words, Benigna is reality in the existentialist sense of the word – she creates her own existence by living it; she does not live a prior essence, while the characters that surround her (as in the case of Don Quixote) are fantasy, novelistic, because they invent a life that has nothing to do with the material world.

Here Zambrano expresses most explicitly the aforementioned idea that liberty is carried out in time, "esa absoluta necesidad de tiempo, de un tiempo propio que la vida en su correr precipita, ese asfixiarse en el tiempo" [this absolute necessity of time, of one's own time that life precipitates, this being asphyxiated in time] (*La España de Galdós* 54), in a solitude that is the "foco y principio de su libertad" [focus and beginning of [one's] liberty] (53, 54). According to Zambrano, Galdós presents us with confusion, avidity, the proliferation of life and its desire for corporality. She notes that this quality has been called "realism," as has practically everything Spanish.

"*Tristana*" (written in 1970, but published much later) is Zambrano's last article on Galdós. This article masterfully summarizes all the themes related to Galdós's female characters that Zambrano touched on in earlier essays. She finally confronts directly the scorn that male authors manifested for Galdós's "garbancismo" [garbanzo bean-ism – interest in daily life] at the beginning of the twentieth century. She defends the novelist's style, which Unamuno had so harshly criticized, pointing out that *Tristana* was written with great care. The style is so tight and clean throughout the work, she asserts, that some passages seem like polished metal (*La España de Galdós* 148). Zambrano's interpretation of the protagonist Tristana could be called (although Zambrano would have denied it) completely feminist. She notes that Tristana does not have access to her past, because what has happened to her in her life (her orphanhood and dependence on a guardian who takes sexual advantage of her) has closed off her future (152).

Zambrano believes that the problem with the characters in this novel is that "el tiempo se había cuajado con la amenaza de cristalizarse para quebrarse luego un día" [time had gelled, threatening to become brittle and perhaps break one day] (*La España de Galdós* 152). The guardian (later husband) Don Lope, like an old Don Juan, thought he was free and did not respect any woman, while Tristana was bound to him. But Zambrano argues that in the end it is Don Lope who is bound up while Tristana is free, because she awakens in time with the desire for independence, the desire to be. Her awakening is rooted in love, in feeling, in sentiment: "Se dio a querer ser alquien, y a querer hacer algo para ello. Mas lo importante era ser, y cuando el ser se aparece de este modo a alguien, adquiere en seguida una calificación, ser es ser independiente" [She wanted to be someone, and to do something to achieve being. The most important thing was to be, and when being occurs to someone in this way, it immediately acquires a qualification; being is being independent] (158). At this point Tristana encounters Horacio, and she sees herself in the other: "El ver del amor es el ver de la revelación" [Seeing from love is the seeing of revelation] (160). Linking Galdós's character with her earlier analysis of *La Celestina*, Zambrano argues that this is the moment Tristana achieves liberty: "Tristana en esto como Melibea, cayó en la confusión tras de aquel instante privilegiado de libertad en que le vio, a él" [In this Tristana, like Melibea, fell into confusion after that privileged moment of liberty in which she saw him] (161), and like Melibea, Tristana does not wish to marry, "quería liberarse a sí misma" [she wanted to free herself] (166).[20]

It is not hard to see in this interpretation of Galdós's late novel and all Galdós's novels that Zambrano addressed, as well as in her references to women in the *Quijote* and other works of Spanish literature, a mirror of Zambrano's own life story – the extraordinary story of a woman born at the beginning of the twentieth century (1904), when few Spanish women could read or write, much less attend the university. As she herself writes in the article on *Tristana*: "todavía las mujeres no frecuentaban las aulas ni estaban llamadas a las profesiones intelectuales; no podían ser más que 'genios' o, a lo menos, geniales, y mejor esto último" [women could not yet attend classes or aspire to intellectual professions; they could only be "geniuses" or, more likely, merely "genial" (Sánchez Gey 172)]. Like Benigna in *Misericordia*, María Zambrano dreamt herself and became an original philosophical thinker through her own heroic efforts.

NOTES

1 One of the few works by Zambrano to be translated into English in its entirely (by Carol Maier).

2 Zambrano is not the first Spanish thinker to look to the Spanish novel (especially the *Quijote*) for philosophical inspiration. Miguel de Unamuno (*Don Quijote y Sancho*), José Martínez Ruiz ("Azorín") (*La ruta de don Quijote*), and José Ortega y Gasset (*Meditaciones del Quijote*) employed Cervantes's novel as a vehicle for exploring the essence of the Spanish soul, but Zambrano differs from the male authors in the focus and eventual development of her thought about and from the novel. Zambrano compares Unamuno's and Ortega's approaches to the *Quijote* in "La ambigüedad de Cervantes" [Cervantes's Ambiguity] and "La ambigüedad de Don Quijote" [Don Quixote's Ambiguity], included in *España, sueño y verdad* [Spain, Dream and Reality], and in the process reveals her own difference from the two. Her main point, to which I will return later, is that Unamuno focuses on Don Quixote, while Ortega concentrates on Cervantes. In her book *Más allá de la filosofía: sobre el pensamiento filosófico-místico de María Zambrano* [Beyond Philosophy: On María Zambrano's Philosophical-Mystic Thought], Ana Bundgård (307–42) studies in detail Zambrano's treatment of the *Quijote* and that of Unamuno and Ortega.

3 Zambrano herself points to affinities between Galdós and the generation that followed him in terms of their ideas on what the novel accomplishes philosophically: "Cuando el desarraigo entre la conciencia y la realidad, entre el deseo y la realización, entre las palabras y las cosas se hace más evidente; cuando en definitiva, la falta de sentido es patente y el mundo se nos va de las manos, la literatura y, más concretamente, la novela ha mostrado ser un instrumento de deconstrucción y

restauración. Por eso Galdós la sacó de sus cenizas literarias, porque hay realidades y situaciones que no pueden ser conceptualizadas a secas, ni siquiera analizadas metódicamente y porque sólo pueden ser conocidas a fuerza de ser vividas y viceversa. En definitiva, la novela es el único género capaz de asumir ese doble camino. El esfuerzo gigantesco por lograrlo constituye hoy la mejor vigencia y actualidad de Pérez Galdós, precursor en varios de estos aspectos de Unamuno y Ortega" [When the break between consciousness and reality, between desire and its realization, between words and things becomes more evident; when, definitively, lack of sense is evident and the world slips through our fingers, literature, and more concretely the novel, has shown itself to be an instrument of deconstruction and restoration. For that reason, Galdós rescued it from its literary ashes because there are realities and situations that cannot be conceptualized on their own, or even analysed methodically because they can only be known by being lived and vice versa. Definitely, the novel is the only genre able to take on this double route. The gigantic effort to achieve it constitutes today the vitality and currentness of Pérez Galdós, in several ways a precursor to Unamuno and Ortega] (qtd in Ramirez 132).

4 Although María Zambrano's embracing realism runs parallel to the narrative practices of such Spanish fiction writers of the early twentieth century as Carmen de Burgos, María Martínez Sierra, Margarita Nelken, and Concha Espina, interestingly Zambrano did not engage with them in her essays on realism. Please see my *Gender and Nation in the Spanish Modernist Novel* for an analysis of what I call the "personal realism" of these writers, following terminology employed by Raymond Williams. Zambrano did not consider herself a feminist, even though her texts on women, like those of the other authors mentioned, certainly could be considered to reveal a feminist message.

5 Goretti Ramírez emphasizes the divergence between Zambrano's aesthetics and that of the vanguards, noting that in contrast to the "deshumanización" of art, Zambrano proposes an "*humanización* del arte" [humanization of art] (172).

6 *La España de Galdós* is a compendium of Zambrano's essays on Galdós written in different periods with different purposes and orientations. Each subsequent edition of the book (1960, 1982, 1989) contains new essays, and any study that focuses on the development of Zambrano's thought must situate the individual essays at the moment they appeared rather than approach the compilations as books (*La España de Galdós* [1960] and *España, sueño y verdad* [1965]).

7 Zambrano's last published article on Galdós, "Un don del océano: Benito Pérez Galdós," which appeared in *Las palabras del regreso (Artículos periodísticos, 1988–1990)*, is from 1986, but by that time her philosophy was essentially established.

8 The two articles on ambiguity initiate *España, sueño y verdad* of 1965, and they are often cited as though they had been written in that year. Now, thanks to the valuable bibliography of Zambrano's articles compiled by Goretti Ramírez, we know that "La ambigüedad de Cervantes" was published in *Sur* no. 158 (December 1947): 30–44, and that "La ambigüedad de Don Quijote" was published under the title "Le mythe de D. Quijote" in *La Licorne* no. 3 (Fall 1948): 199–206.

9 Bundgård also makes the identification "Nina-Zambrano," elaborating on the topic in significant detail (351, 352, 378).

10 Bundgård confirms this observation: "En el libro *España, sueño y verdad*, vuelve la escritora el [*sic*] tema del *Quijote*, en esta ocasión desde un enfoque filosófico, inscribiéndose sin titubeos en la tradición de los pensadores españoles de la llamada generación del 98" [In the book *España, sueño y verdad*, the writer returns to the theme of the *Quijote*, this time from a philosophical vantage point, inscribing herself in the tradition of the Spanish thinkers of the so-called Generation of '98] (313).

11 For a detailed discussion of the female characters created by Unamuno, Ramón del Valle-Inclán, Azorín, Pío Baroja, Gabriel Miró, Ramón Pérez de Ayala, Benjamín Jarnés, and José Díaz Fernández, see my *Gender and Nation*.

12 "La muerte de Galdós" [Galdós's Death], which Ortega published unsigned in *El Sol* on 15 January 1920, pronounced Galdós a genius as compared to Campoamor (damning with faint praise!) (Ortega, *OC* 3:30). This is Ortega's only comment on Galdós *per se*; the remainder of the article is devoted to lamenting that there were no official honours rendered to the novelist on his passing. Ortega's *Ideas sobre la novela* [Ideas on the Novel] (1925) does not mention Galdós or any other Spanish writer, except Cervantes (the *Quijote*). His examples of novelists in this essay are mostly foreign – Dostoyevsky, Proust, Stendhal. In *Meditaciones del Quijote* Ortega says that *realismo* is a "terrible, incómoda palabra" [terrible, uncomfortable word] (Ortega, *OC* 1:372) and that there is a lack of tension in the realist novel because "el ideal *cae* desde poquísima altura" [the ideal *falls* from a very short height]; the nineteenth-century novel will not last because it contains "la menor cantidad posible de dinamismo poético" [the least possible poetic dynamism] in contrast to the *Quijote*, "cuya tensión es inagotable" [whose tension is endless] (*OC* 1:399).

13 Again I direct attention to my *Gender and Nation* for a discussion of the work of Spanish women writers of generations prior to and contemporaneous with Zambrano.
14 Almost invariably when she wrote on *Don Quijote*, she included a reference to Galdós in order to comment on the female characters. See Mora, "Maria Zambrano," for a comprehensive analysis of Zambrano's writings on *Don Quijote*.
15 *Intrahistoria* and *la tradición eterna* were concepts that especially Unamuno and Azorín developed in the latter part of the nineteenth century and early twentieth century that draw on the German idea of *volksgeist* or a permanent essence of a people. In the quotation, Zambrano provides a good definition of the concept.
16 See Bundgård (152–67) for an illuminating discussion of the reasons for Zambrano's transfer from the Universidad San Nicolás de Hidalgo in Morelia, Mexico, to the Universidad de La Habana.
17 Ramírez (55n7) mentions Concha Espina's other work on *Don Quijote* (*Don Quijote en Barcelona* [1916]) in relation to Zambrano's *La agonía de Europa* (1945). She notes that both Espina and Zambrano see in Don Quixote the possibility of spiritually regenerating Europe.
18 Another interesting difference between Zambrano's articles on Galdós's female figures from 1942 and 1960 is that the last one eliminates the references to Cervantes as "extremamente masculinista" [extremely masculinist].
19 See my "María Zambrano's Ideas on Being and Jean Paul Sartre."
20 Juana Sánchez-Gey observes the role passion plays in uncovering reality as revealed in Zambrano's interpretation of *Tristana*: "Tristana vivió sin realidad hasta que vio a Horacio. La realidad estaba allí, pero no había sido descubierta porque si el amor requiere conocimiento, es ante todo generador de sabiduría" [Tristana lived without reality until she saw Horacio. Reality was there, but it had not been discovered because, if love requires knowledge, it is above all a generator of wisdom] (489).

WORKS CITED

Azorín. *Castilla*. Ed. Inman Fox. Madrid: Espasa Calpe, 1991. Print.
– *Escritores*. Madrid: Biblioteca Nueva, 1956. Print.
– "Galdós." In *Lecturas españolas, Obras completas*. Madrid: Espasa Calpe, 1998. 2:797.

– "La generación de 1898." *Clásicos y modernos*, 2:902. Quoted in Manuel María Pérez López, *Azorín y la literatura española*. Salamanca: Universidad de Salamanca, 1974. 196–7. Print.

Bundgård, Ana. *Más allá de la filosofía sobre el pensamiento filosófico-místico de María Zambrano*. Madrid: Editorial Trotta, 2000. Print.

Cruz Ayuso, Cristina de la. "María Zambrano y la *Misericordia*: Una aproximación a la obra de Galdós." *Aurora* 1 (1998): 124–31. Print.

Espina, Concha. *Mujeres del Quijote*. Madrid: Renacimiento, 1916. Print.

Johnson, Roberta. *Gender and Nation in the Spanish Modernist Novel*. Nashville: Vanderbilt UP, 2013. Print.

– "María Zambrano's Ideas on Being and Jean Paul Sartre." *Anales de la literatura española contemporánea* 40.1 (2015): 173–201. Print.

Maillard, María Luisa. *María Zambrano. La literatura como conocimiento y participación*. Lleida: Edicions de la Universitat de Lleida, 1997. Print.

Mora, José Luis. "María Zambrano: Cervantes y la reforma del entendimiento español." *eHumanista/Cervantes* 3 (2014): 661–74. Print.

– "'Misericordia' en 'La España de Galdós.'" In *Filosofía y poesía*. Madrid: Fundación Rielo, 1994. Print.

– "Un nombre de mujer: *Misericordia*. Galdós en la inspiración zambraniana." In *María Zambrano. Raíces de la cultura española*. Madrid: Fundación Rielo, 2004. 119–46. Print.

Moreno Sanz, Jesús. *La razón en la sombra: Antología del pensamiento de María Zambrano*. Madrid: Siruela, 1993. Print.

Ortega y Gasset, José. *Obras completas*. Vol. 1. Madrid: Revista de Occidente, 1963. Print.

– *Obras completas*. Vol. 3. Madrid: Revista de Occidente, 1962. Print.

Pérez, Janet. "La razón de la sinrazón: Unamuno, Machado, and Ortega in the Thought of María Zambrano." *Hispania* 82.1 (1999): 56–67. Print. https://doi.org/10.2307/346062.

Pérez López, M.M. *Azorín y la literatura española*. Salamanca: Universidad de Salamanca, 1974. Print.

Ramírez, Goretti. *María Zambrano, crítica literaria*. Madrid: Devenir Ensayo, 2004. Print.

Risco, Antonio. *Azorín: la ruptura con la novela tradicional*. Barcelona: Alhambra, 1980. Print.

Sánchez-Gey, Juana. "Acerca de la mujer [Tristana]: El Galdós de María Zambrano." In *Actas del Quinto Congreso Internacional de Estudios Galdosianos (1992)*, vol. 1. Las Palmas de Gran Canaria: Ediciones del Cabildo de Gran Canario, 1995. 485–93. Print.

Williams, Raymond. "Realism and the Contemporary Novel." *Partisan Review* 24 (1959): 200–13. Print.

Zambrano, María. "La actitud ante la realidad." In *El giro posmoderno*, ed. José Rubio Carraceo, *Philosophica Malacitana*, sup. no. 1 (1993): 66. Print.

– *Delirium and Destiny*. Trans. Carol Maier. Albany: State U of New York P, 1999. Print.

– *España, sueño y verdad*. 2nd ed. Barcelona: EDHASA, 1982. Print.

– *La España de Galdós*. Madrid: Endymion, 1989. Print.

– "Mujeres de Galdós." *Asparkía* 3 (1994). Print.

– *Obras reunidas*. Madrid: Aguila, 1971. Print.

– *Las palabras del regreso. (Artículos periodísticos, 1988–1990)*. Ed. Mercedes Gómez Blesa. Salamanca: Amarú Ediciones, 1995. Print.

– "A propósito de la 'grandeza y servidumbre de la mujer.'" *Aurora* 1 (1999). Print.

– *El sueño creador*. Madrid: Ediciones Turner, 1986. Print.

PART FOUR

The Challenges of Genre: Spanish Realism beyond the Novel

11 Writing (Un)clear Code: The Letters and Fiction of Emilia Pardo Bazán and Benito Pérez Galdós

CRISTINA PATIÑO EIRÍN
TRANSLATION BY MARY L. COFFEY

In realist fiction, then, uncertainty is more than a constant. It is the very muse ...
Harriet Turner, "'Silent Writing'" 408

Realist authors have often turned to the epistolary form, given that its potential for expressing individual subjectivity offers a means to explore the psychology of sociability, intimacy, and desire. This is particularly true of nineteenth-century Spanish realists. Notably, the letters of authors during the realist-naturalist period, constructed out of the bits and pieces of their lives and their creative desires, flow down to us through tangled channels, as uncertain as they are suggestive.[1] Although personal letters are increasingly considered a legitimate literary genre (Muñoz Molina, Rodríguez Marcos), it is also true that this documentary heritage has suffered from the inclement winds of history, even more so than other, less reserved forms of evidence. The private space of intimacy, now so exposed, becomes expurgated or even annihilated in the process of sketching out a biography or identifying a particular mindset. The possibility of transmission becomes even more difficult with the increased passage of time, until we might consider the safeguarding of correspondence, especially those letters of a particularly intimate nature, somewhat miraculous. Out of a desire to remember a loved one, out of admiration, or out of unconditional love for a male correspondent, the letters of many writers have been saved by women – lovers, wives, sisters, or daughters – who acted as executors and who decided when and how to bring such letters into the public eye, becoming authentic "estructuras supervivientes" [surviving structures] (Caballé, "El arte epistolar") of a type some critics have actually characterized as "egoísta" [egotistical] (Molina Foix 34).[2]

In effect, the postal service has been a propitious space for communication between the sexes, and it has converted the feminine side of this communicative space into the fundamental recipient, because of that quality traditionally associated with women as guardians of feeling, as a place from which emotions emerge and return. By virtue of the fact that intellectual superiority historically has been defined as masculine, and that the feminine has been devalued by identification with social, familial, and individual habit – given that we are dealing with particularly and ontologically individual phenomena – the majority of the letters that have survived are written by men. This is, in part, because women were their inheritors, because they accepted the fundamental value of the men, often to the detriment of themselves, and because their own letters were often lost owing to the carelessness of men or the desire – on the part of men as well as the women themselves – to have their letters erased from posterity. In this way we have come to know the letters that Dylan Thomas wrote to his wife but not the letters of Louise Colet to Flaubert.[3] Nor do we know the letters of Vera Nabokov to her husband, since she decided herself to destroy them (Nabokov 38, 40). There are numerous examples in which only the male voice has been recorded in history.

Yet it has happened, in other cases, that men have preserved the letters of women, and it is in these cases where we find ground for the most interesting speculation. To what can we attribute the fact that these letters were not torn up and thrown into the fire? For what reasons were they bundled up and kept, despite successive moves from residence to residence, or despite frequent housecleaning (work not done by men in any case), or despite the selective process associated with the fickle spin of the wheel of emotional fortunes? Was it the positivist design, so deeply rooted in the nineteenth-century being and so indispensable to the zeal with which realism faced the invitation to mimesis, that stimulated the desire to preserve them?

Without being able to provide valid answers to these questions, we can still see that there is a marked tendency on the part of human beings to maintain the tangible evidence of intimate experiences: the golden ringlet of a lover, the faded fragrance of a dried flower, and – perhaps with greater motivation, given its incandescence, its portable nature, its ability to powerfully evoke the past and, ultimately, to explain or justify its own evolution and misfortune – the love letter. Locked away in a chest, tied up with twine, tucked within a secret drawer of an old mahogany cabinet, this document serves as witness and is the only surviving proof of a moment that refuses to fade away, or at least is not allowed to fade away. That love letter documents a particular high point in a life, even if it cannot illuminate others.

In the case of Emilia Pardo Bazán (1851–1921) and Benito Pérez Galdós (1843–1920), despite the considerable scholarship on their romantic relationship (Ávila Arellano, Clemessy, Freire López, Ortega, Ricard, Romero Tobar), there is hardly a written trace of the friendship and intense love he felt towards her, or evidence of the letters that she received from him. This loss of his letters and the loss of his voice are impossible to overlook.

These pages are in pursuit of the erased tracks of those encounters that, thanks to the postal service, were able to take the shape of a dialogue about which we only know one half. The passage of time has exercised on the publicity-averse Galdós a type of poetic justice, one that has expunged the trail of letters directed to his beloved Emilia, highlighting his propensity towards silence, his elusive moods in expressing his most intimate feelings, and an expansiveness that he preferred to grant exclusively to the women in his universe of fiction. Of what Galdós took from lived and experienced reality, from lived and experienced love, there are no doubt obvious signs in his creative production, muted by the workings of fiction, yes, but nonetheless perceptible to the seasoned reader. That other end, the necessary blurring of the vehement and passionate correspondent that he must have been, given the tenor of what Pardo Bazán writes, produces the effect of betting on an epistolary monologue in which only one of the lovers, specifically the woman, presents the various reasons and delirious moments of a shared love taking place in the four corners of a Madrid that lurks, coerces, spies upon, and punishes their clandestine meetings. But the monologue is no more than a mirror image – in the same way that a novel can mirror both reality and imagined truth, the principal theme of this anthology – that reflects telltale evidence and the sinuous nature of writing that plays with the rhetorical artifice of semantic ambiguity and the elusive allusion (or the allusive elision) of the vital literary game in which both correspondents were masters, above all in the use of ellipsis.

This essay will try to throw some light on the dark rooms and letter boxes that served as joyful hiding places for the bodies and the imaginations of two of the greatest writers of world literature. The first section, "Intertextual/Intratextual Dialogue," provides a brief outline of the correspondence itself. Next, through the presentation of two heretofore unpublished documents, signed by Pardo Bazán's confessor, I address the functioning mechanisms of what we might call "self-righteous vigilance" ["el acecho biempensante"] as an incentive or hindrance. The first and more lengthy letter by Father Castellanos serves as proof, perhaps the most exhaustive we have ever seen, of the pressure exerted on Pardo Bazán, in view of her less than exemplary behaviour. It is a recriminatory letter that explicitly condemns her way of living and warns her of the severe harm caused to her children and her good name. The conclusions that can be reached by this essay's last section, entitled "Quitando letras y letras" [Removing Letters and Letters], builds on a quote from Galdós's novel *La revolución de julio*, "'Quitando letras y letras' ... un lenguaje encriptado, el juego de la literatura" ["Removing letters and letters" ... an encrypted language, the game of literature]. In other words, meaning in this case is constructed through a set of oblique references that engender, in essence, a game of coding and decoding.

Intertextual/Intratextual Dialogue: Reading and Hermeneutic Reciprocities

The ebb and flow of letters between Emilia Pardo Bazán and Benito Pérez Galdós continues to spark numerous comments and glosses, but none have been able to ignore that it is a mutilated correspondence. Such circumstances do not prevent the fact that the collection of epistolary evidence available from only one of two hearts involved, in this case Pardo Bazán, has aroused an interest that longs for the ability to reconstruct the diastolic beat that gave rise to the systolic. Metaphors of this type are often employed to illustrate that the lack of evidence on one side does not necessarily convert the known declarations of the other side into a self-absorbed monologue. And yet, the letters of a relationship as intense as that shared by Galdós and Pardo Bazán, despite the absence of the letters written by him, run the risk of becoming a simulacrum of communication without corroboration or support, as if the letters constituted a kind of ledger, a series of self-exploratory exercises in which the "I" divides and becomes an imagined "you," absent and true only in abstraction, lacking the tangible trace of paper as a present physical entity. Building off of Harriet Turner's exploration of the power of metaphor to create the appearance of reality, that amputated correspondence, a true work of art of double ellipsis, means much more in the context of realism-naturalism, at a time when everything aspires to be explicit, to be named and enumerated, classified, recorded, and totalized without leaving anything in the inkwell, nothing with the potential to be fictionalized ("La imagen metafórica" 1523).

It therefore makes perfect sense that a reader would be irresistibly drawn to filling in the blanks, to performing the task of putting the pieces together, according to the bias or slant of the letter writer's pronouncements. The language that remains is neither insufficient nor incomplete, since it imposes the tone and reach, the stamp of the author, the temperament, and the style of the preserved wording. It allows one to intuit, through luminous and fertile metaphors – a type of Trojan horse of realism-naturalism that Zola himself did not entirely purge, letting a vast range of emotions penetrate his writing – that both interlocutors were writing, in the syncopated language of an already fragmented correspondence, the novel of love they never published.

In her analysis of the correspondence between Galdós and Pardo Bazán, Francisca González Arias distinguishes two parallel epistolary forms: the public, whose themes and tone corresponded to the authors' roles as literary colleagues, and which also served to divert attention from the other epistolary form, which she defines as private (172). She errs, however, in claiming that their friendship began in 1883, at the famous banquet in Madrid in honour of Galdós (González Arias 170). In fact, Pardo Bazán did not attend. Pardo Bazán's involvement came in the form of a telegram, sent from La Coruña, in which she declared that it was time to honour all Spanish literature and in particular the master of the renaissance of the Spanish novel.[4] *El Imparcial* of 27 March, in "Manifestaciones en honor de Pérez Galdós" [Demonstrations in Honour of Pérez Galdós], states that the speech of the Canarian author, who himself would only arrive at the banquet when desserts were being served, was read by one of the guests, and goes on to detail the content of the telegram sent by Pardo Bazán, including the *lapsus*, quite curious, apparently attributable only to the newspaper headline.

> Coruña-Madrid. Benito Pérez Galdós. Felicita á Vd, y ofrece testimonio de admiración y respeto. Emilio [*sic*] Pardo Bazán
>
> [Coruña-Madrid. Benito Pérez Galdós. Congratulate you and offer testimony of admiration and respect. Emilio [*sic*] Pardo Bazán.]

This telegram must, therefore, be included in the corpus of epistolary writings that both writers were to exchange, despite the fact that the two did not know each other personally at that time. Galdós could not have dreamt of a better way of concealing his intimacy than the story to which either history or he himself contributed: a cartography of silence. As can be inferred from Pardo Bazán's own letters, Galdós himself felt compelled to demand the return of some of his missives, a request to which Pardo Bazán only partially acquiesced (Bravo-Villasante 12).[5] The recently published volume of Galdós's correspondence, which raises the number of letters signed by him to 1170, testifies, among other things, to the will of the author to complete his legacy with a collection of his letters (*Correspondencia* 12), and this factual verification certainly entails a contradiction with respect to his love letters, or, in the words of Emilia Pardo Bazán, "los desordenados movimientos afectivos" [disordered affective movements] (*Cartas a Galdós* 39). As is known, only one letter written by the author of *La desheredada* and addressed to Pardo Bazán has survived. It is dated 5 March 1883, and it is certainly not a love letter. Written to thank Pardo Bazán for the public support she expressed in anticipation of the banquet to be held on 26 March 1883 in Madrid in Galdós's honour, the letter employs a style and diction that indicates that Galdós considers the author of *La cuestión palpitante* [The Burning Question] to deserve respect for her critical insight.[6] Much remains unknown and unclear with respect to their relationship, but how might we attempt to reveal it?

That the epistolary history written by his partner, which totals ninety-two letters (González Arias 169), did not suffer the same fate is due not so much to the vagaries of chance to preserve it as to a desire to preserve those testimonies of their private affair, an eagerness to safeguard letters written from the perspective of an inalienable "I," one endowed with a personal intensity that Emilia Pardo Bazán could never adopt in her literary works. There is no doubt about the intense power of her epistolary pen.

Reading and transcribing these letters, attempting to reconstruct the avatars of an intermittent, discreet, and, indeed, clandestine relationship, punctuated by assignations and break-ups subsequently softened by forgiveness, can produce a reading that only recognizes the variations of the flame of love, its flare-ups and conflagrations. Many readers have embraced that form of reception and have attributed to the loquacious lover what can only have come from the silent partner. On the other hand, without even trying, one could not paint a more attractive canvas from a literary point of view, one which is so capable of turning the writers into characters, given that they themselves refashion their own identities through the use of names that endow them with a semi-fictional status. It is worth remembering the modern aesthetic efficiency of epistolary literature and even the epistolary novel that both authors knew and practised so well. Not in vain does the language of love participate in the foundation of the "I" and "you" as "we," isolating that relationship from everything else. Emilia and Benito form inextricable discursive areas for the profane. Precisely because the purpose of these letters was only to be read by the other, and to avoid the competitive demands of the world, we cannot completely transcend our awareness of being intruders in that immensely private world. No one but the two of them could fully understand, or will fully understand, their secret codes, their expressive obliquity, their uncertainties.

Nonetheless, it is the task of the specialist to attempt to decipher the secret codes through accessing the creative keys of these two singular authors. Given the tendency of both Pardo Bazán and Galdós to document their own lives, they themselves served as manufacturers of their own public personae. But the *galdosista* or the *pardobazanista* cannot turn to the same resources when trying to find the hermeneutics of the more circumspect epistolary documents. It is true that one can benefit from recognizing the connections between their letters and their fictional texts, the patterns of their creativity so firmly tied to the world they lived in, and the myriad testimonies from themselves or those who knew and worked with them. But the ruses they engaged in, the winks of complicity they exchanged with relish, the most intimate moments that ultimately gave way to reproaches or silences, we will not be able to fully calibrate. There will always be passages, terms, and gaps that we cannot fill in with all their circumstantial sense. The letters of these two great writers deserve a critical edition, a desideratum that, while not impossible in strict terms, does not cease to be necessary and feasible, with the exceptions marked, given that one half of the set remains missing.[7]

The Moralist's Advice: A Brake or a Spur to Action?

The letter that Father Castellanos, Pardo Bazán's former Franciscan confessor, addressed to his parishioner, dated April 1890, makes clear what the consequences might be for a woman caught in such a situation. We are faced with the evidence – the fear that their love letters might be intercepted – and thus the sinuous and encoded nature of their discourse, elusive and metaphorical, echoes their permanent state of alert.

The fact that this letter was a part of a bequest to the Fundación Lázaro Galdiano by the author herself, alongside the manuscript of her early novel, *Aficiones peligrosas* [Dangerous Passions], reveals the degree of friendship she had developed with Lázaro Galdiano, the book collector and her companion in her travels to Arenys de Mar during the period of her relationship with Galdós (Patiño Eirín, "La aventura catalana").[8] The publication in 1889 of her novel *Insolación (Historia amorosa)* [Sunstroke (A Love Story)] with its dedication – "A José Lázaro Galdiano, en prenda de amistad" [To José Lázaro Galdiano, in pledge of friendship] – a full year before the date of the Franciscan friar's letter to his former penitent only adds to the propitious context in which the novel became a key element of the naturalist scandal when it was published and then read, paradoxically, as an autobiographical key to the life of its author.

It is a contradiction to marry Zola's aesthetics with the supposed confession of a secretive love affair between Emilia and Benito, one which reached its apex of sincere passion between 1889 and 1890 (Bravo-Villasante 10). Indeed, it seems unlikely that the germ of the storyline came from that experience, as evidenced by another letter to Galdós in which Pardo Bazán already reveals the idea and writing in progress for the novel about the widow of Andrade in advance of her excursion to Arenys (Patiño Eirín, "La aventura catalana"; Thion Soriano-Mollá 19–21). Quite another thing is that the escape with Lázaro would likely have been present in her mind during the correction of the galley proofs, in which process the author minimizes the gravity of Asís Taboada's errors (Penas Varela 33–5). As an epicurean reaffirmation, in *Insolación* the will to secure the right to the pleasure of love persists. Indeed, not only does it not stop, it prevails. This torrential confession of desire, punctuated by the guilt that lurks, leaves in the readers, both men and women, the traces of a drive that will ultimately be satisfied. How would Galdós have read this exultant, undoubtedly direct work, despite the refractions of the stern and puritanical narrator, so endowed with powerful functions as an implicit author, so emboldened and accusing?

Though Pardo Bazán had not yet received Father Castellanos's emphatically recriminatory letter, a collection of moral accusations which before had been disconnected and disjointed, coming from various circles, now gathered in megalithic fashion, the challenging attitude of the author who considered herself a *feminist militant* emerged clearly, without ambiguity, playing with the autobiographical fallacy. She tested, deliciously and dangerously, the discretion of the Catalan hosts who entertained her on arriving in Barcelona to see the Exposición

Universal of 1888. Hers was undoubtedly a strong personality that would have ignored, in any case, any command that did not emerge from her own will.

Pardo Bazán does not use the epistolary mode in her 1889 novel set in Madrid. To have done so, she would have run the risk of committing a sin so immediate, so autobiographical, that her honour, perhaps considered more spotless than one might think, would have been compromised. Instead she opts for the use of a female first person, something not very common in her novels and stories, as a mediating and preferential factor with readers, and she does this at the expense of a narrative urge that frames and corrects without attenuating its own strength. We do not know if the author of *Un viaje de novios* [A Honeymoon] considered the possibility of defining the personality of the widowed Marchioness of Andrade by other narrative means, for example by being the transmitter and receiver of letters, and not just flirtatious notes, which could have been possible if the letter was not presented as private and secret. But it is true that Galdós, in his fictions, did so with greater assiduity and with an eye to moulding his feminine creatures of that period of transition, *par excellence*, from the naturalist decade of the 1880s in Spain to the decade that closed out the century with its Russian airs and its decadent symbolism. Ana Baquero Escudero has noticed that the presence of the epistolary intensifies in Galdós's production after 1890, increasing the degree of his narrative invisibility, to the point of producing completely epistolary novels such as *La incógnita* [The Unknown] (practically monodic in its construction from the letters that Manolo Infante sends to Equis) and *La estafeta romántica* [The Romantic Letterbox], which offers a great polyphonic variety "en la que sin duda destacan con luz propia las voces femininas" [in which the female voices undoubtedly stand out] (165). It is also worth noting the woman's epistolary writing in *Tristana* that attracts the interest of the narrator of Galdós's 1892 novel, to the detriment of the male lover's correspondence, which is silenced and whose information we only obtain through the letters of the female character. As Baquero Escudero rightly contends, Tristana's letters are fictional and solipsistic in so much as they are born of an amorous passion that creates them, and they in turn blur the image of the lover, an invented entity that personifies one's own loving vision (168). In other words, the focus is placed on the inner torment of the protagonist in such a way that precise chronological dating no longer matters. We are in the realm of the ahistorical. The wreckage of the epistolary exchange between Galdós and Pardo

Bazán says nothing else, as if the ultimate destiny of that exchange was to establish the autotelic eloquence of love in her and the silences and reticences in him, an invented yet transitive being. The elusiveness of Galdós seems to have won the game by becoming a soul without voice, solely entangled in the resonant echoes of the female expression, a perspective that grants privilege.

We must take as a given, nonetheless, the vehement epistolary exuberance of Galdós's writing addressed to Pardo Bazán. She herself, who will not translate it into fiction, on account of its being untransferrable, credited the distinctive quality of her own lexical richness, among other things, by referring to his novels and not to his personal letters, whose heartbeat we nevertheless perceive in her description of his style:

> En esto también Galdós es exuberante, y de todo se prenda, y todo lo recoge, y a todo le encuentra su interés peculiar. En su estilo hay dos cualidades de primer orden: la personalidad y la vibración íntima, reflejo de su sensibilidad de artista. Lo que falta es música y ritmo: a Galdós se le conoce que no hizo versos de muchacho, y que nunca lee sus cuartillas en alta voz, *gueulant*, como decía Flaubert. (Pardo Bazán, "Ángel Guerra" 1103–4)
>
> [In this Galdós also is exuberant, and everything is caught, and everything is collected, and everything finds its peculiar interest. In his style there are two qualities of the first order: personality and intimate vibration, reflecting his sensibility as an artist. What is missing is music and rhythm: Galdós is known not to have written poetry as a boy, and he never reads his pages aloud, *gueulant*, as Flaubert used to say.]

Pardo Bazán kept her letters and tried to preserve them, undoubtedly because they were the love letters of her life. We know that she collected her drafts, books, and papers with the order and dedication of an archivist, that she dedicated library shelves to certain authors and their place of origin, Portuguese authors for example, and that "en los cajones que guardan mi correspondencia, [había] numerosas cartas que tienen ya el valor de autógrafos porque ¡son tantos los ilustres que murieron, empezando por el simpático Oliveira" [in the drawers that hold my correspondence, [there were] numerous letters that already have the value of autographs because so many illustrious ones died, beginning with the sympathetic Oliveira!] (*La obra periodística* 1:464). But unlike the Canarian author, and in the name of the laws of realist fiction, without the co-intentionality that such fiction demands, she did not use these letters to create literature.

On the other hand, what would Emilia Pardo Bazán, a woman who had just lost her beloved father and was experiencing at the time a passionate affair with the author of *La desheredada,* have thought of her confessor's reprimand, which contains the sort of argumentative strategems that can be found in both sacramental entreaties and blackmail? Could it have caused her to feel the deep, lacerating impression that its Franciscan author undoubtedly wanted to inflict upon her? If not, given that there was no marital reconciliation after the abandonment of the lover as the letter called upon her to do, is her non-compliance to be attributed to making a firm decision or, rather, to the impossibility of going back? How can we make sense of the date of this letter filled with disapproval and pressures without accounting for the events expressed in others? Did Galdós know of this reprimand, more perhaps than did Lázaro, who was also her lover, though only in passing, and to whose archives the letter came at last? And her mother, and her aunt, at whose behest this diatribe might have been sent? Did Emilia Pardo always act alone? The letter's assertive potential, its subjective unity – in Kierkegaardian terms – suggest this is the case.

Two Unpublished Letters: Admonishment and Intimacy

Appended to this essay are transcriptions of Father Manuel Castellanos's two letters to Emilia Pardo Bazán, both of which are archived at the Lázaro Galdiano Foundation of Madrid.[9] Given Lázaro's love for manuscripts and bibliographic treasures, Pardo's decision to make him the executor of these documents served to guarantee the survival of this epistolary testimony. In addition to the transcription itself, I have added additional notes, modernized the spelling, and indicated references for most abbreviations. Consisting of four pages of tight and angular lettering organized on squared sheets covered on both sides, and signed by the Franciscan Father Manuel Castellanos (Cuenca, 1843–Santiago de Compostela, 1911), the first letter exhibits very neat handwriting, with particular care in the stroke of the capital letters, which seem copied from a previous draft. The paragraph structure denotes a calculated expository order, conscious in its hierarchy. The censorious argument develops indeed towards a crescendo. Father Castellanos follows a pattern that increasingly reveals his belief that he must make headway into the conscience of Emilia Pardo, a woman who, we should not forget, explicitly professes the Catholic faith. The letter not only appeals to the present well-being of her family, defined as seriously compromised, but also to the memory of those who are absent. It refers to the recent death of Pardo Bazán's father, so beloved and missed by his only daughter, and to the way in which Pardo Bazán's two daughters in particular will be labelled by society on account of the flirtations of a mother whose behaviour – both in terms of her affairs of the heart and her literary undertakings – might endanger the matrimonial hopes of Blanca, first, and Carmen, afterwards.

It is difficult to know what effect the reading of this blunt petition, framed as it was within a close and confidential relationship, had on Pardo Bazán. We all know the ascendancy of those priests who served as confessors to women and who, by virtue of this ministry, gained access to the most hidden recesses of the feminine consciousness in a privileged way, to the point of taking possession of it and ruling its behaviour by reprimanding, warning, instructing, punishing. One need do no more than imagine her subjected to that omnipotent power, wounded by its claws, or impelled to change her way of life by what many today would call intolerable pressures and threats. The letter's harsh judgment of both Pardo Bazán's published work and her affairs of the heart, at a moment of great weakness for her, after the painful loss of her father, and the fact that the author of *Insolación* kept this document underscore even more the condemnatory tenor of the text, framed as an ultimatum, intended to provoke tears of contrition and the repentence of a woman *comme il faut*. Yet perhaps the letter caused for the reader (or readers, given that she might have shared it with Galdós and certainly at some point shared it with Lázaro) only slight discomfort, a programmed indifference, or even an outright disdainful rejection on the part of those defined as unworthy sinners. It was assumed that Emilia Pardo Bazán had to face the contradiction of being Catholic without acting as such according to her orthodoxy, and that this apparent incoherence might perhaps cause her some bewilderment, above all, when those around her did not understand or approve of her mode of behaviour. But the existence of documents of the type examined here, and the April 1890 letter's degree of explicit and radical condemnation elevated to a consciousness for whom the memory of the sacrament of confession necessarily had to erode and injure, can only lead us to think of the determination of a woman who tried to act according to other dictates – her own – that did not stultify her desire to live freely or to love whomever she chose.

The second letter from Father Castellanos, also from the Lázaro Galdiano Foundation, is of lesser interest with respect to the relationship between Pardo Bazán and Galdós, but it serves to establish the close link between the confessor and his former penitent – his "buena Emilia" – offering more detail with regard to the tone and quality of their relationship. It is worth remembering that this former confessor had already been mentioned in Pardo Bazán's "Apuntes autobiográficos" [Autobiographical Notes] in a very revealing passage about his formative role, as a spiritual guide, with access to the most intimate details of her childhood, like her own father: "en mis once ó doce años de niña criada sin amistades ni más compañía que la paterna, con confesor prudente y trato continuo de gentes formales, cabía bien poca malicia" [in my eleven or twelve years as a child raised without friends or company other than my parents, with a prudent confessor and the continuous company of formal individuals, I harboured little malice] (Pardo Bazán, "Apuntes" 19–20). She would have to acquire it later, already aware that she had to assume responsibility for and claim an inalienable right to her own conduct. "Yo necesito mi propia estimación, perdida desde hace año y medio ... que murmure de mí el universo entero, pero que yo me juzgue bien. Y el caso es que cada día también te quiero más" [I need my self-esteem, lost for the last year and a half ... let the whole universe gossip about me, but let me judge myself as good. And the fact is that every day I love you more], she writes to Galdós on 3 December 1889 (Pattison 23–4). Months earlier, on 28 September of the same year, from Paris, she had confessed to him:

> Hemos realizado un sueño, miquiño adorado: un sueño bonito, un sueño fantástico que a los 30 años yo no creía posible. Le hemos hecho la mamola al mundo necio, que prohíbe estas cosas; a Moisés que las prohíbe también, con igual éxito; a la realidad, que nos encadena; a la vida que huye; [y] a los angelitos del cielo, que se creen los únicos felices, porque están en el Empíreo con cara de bobos tocando el violín ... Felices, nosotros. (*"Miquiño mío"* 145)
>
> [We have made a dream come true, my beloved little boy: a beautiful dream, a fantastic dream that at the age of 30 I did not believe possible. We have taken them all for a ride, the foolish world, which forbids these things; Moses, who forbids them too; reality, which shackles us; the life that flies by; [and] the angels of heaven, who think they are the only happy ones because they are in paradise with foolish faces playing the violin ... Happy, we.]

"Quitando letras y letras": Coded Language, the Literary Game

The codes of fiction, as Pardo Bazán liked to say, prevailed, and Galdós, like Pardo Bazán, knew how to monetize an empirical record of his experiences. The epistolary exchange formed part of his vital and literary metabolism. His 1903 historical novel, *La revolución de julio* [The Revolution of July], part of the fourth series of the *Episodios nacionales* [National Episodes], is a case in point. In the novel, two characters, Virginia and Leoncio, are attempting to escape the conventional world, against the will of her parents, and as part of their escape they have devised new names for themselves, Mita and Ley. This break represents the beginning of a life of their own in pursuit of love, a wild life that others do not understand. At one point Pepe Beramendi, the protagonist of the fourth series, asks Virginia what these new names signify.

> — ... Ni mi mujer ni yo hemos podido desentrañar el significado de tu nombre salvaje. ¿Qué quiere decir *Mita*?
> — Tonto, el amor tiene lengua de niño para abreviar los nombres. Al declararnos libres, quisimos olvidarnos de cómo nos llamábamos ... Él me decía *mujercita* ... y quitando letras y letras, vino a parar en *Mita* ... Yo, sin saber cómo, convertí el Leoncio en *Ley*. Los salvajes, ya lo sabes, se comen las sílabas ... (101).

> ["... Neither my wife nor I have been able to unravel the meaning of your wild name. What does Mita mean?"
> "Fool, love has a child's tongue to abbreviate names. When we declared ourselves free, we wanted to forget how we used to call ourselves ... He used to call me a little woman ... and by removing letters and letters, he came to Mita ... I, without knowing how, turned Leoncio into Ley [law]. Savages, you know, devour syllables."]

Beyond the letters that Pardo Bazán and Galdós bothered to conceal, it is the letters that posterity erased, that have been lost and perhaps will never appear, that make this intimate communication in a puzzle difficult to assemble. A Galdós always reluctant, reticent, was someone that his contemporaries did not stop to qualify in this sense. Galdós was not just the "great Argonaut" and "don Vasco di Gama" [*sic*] of his peers, the discoverer of worlds and winner of the Golden Fleece,[10] but rather and perhaps above all a man silent and self-absorbed in his creation, in need of that separation for daily and constant work. The revealing words of another of his correspondents, José Ortega Munilla, written ten years before the author's affair with Pardo Bazán, ponder the precious and rare quality of his epistolary exchanges, richer still because of their scarce and precarious nature:

> Queridísimo amigo: acabo de leer su grata epístola que agradezco tanto más cuanto que *es proverbial su odio a servirse del correo* (Madrid, 16 October 1879) (Nuez and Schraibman 187; my emphasis)
>
> [Dear friend, I have just read your gratifying letter, which I appreciate all the more due to the fact that *your hatred of using the mail is proverbial*]

Precisely because of this, the preserved remains, which no longer belong to the secrets of the protagonists or their families because they have become public documents, appear clothed with a double literary aura. The first is implicit in the very ontological fictional configuration of the epistle, a pre-existing mould or framework that places us within a space conducive to imagination and self-invention. The second comes from the manifest desire to reclaim the confessional discourse by means of the alternative movement of the tropes, the compressive mechanisms of metaphor and the expansive ones of metonymy, so magnificently studied for their implications in Galdós by Harriet Turner ("La imagen metafórica" 1523). In these formulations, simultaneously deep and playful, the nineteenth-century narrators excelled, both in their work and in life. Moreover, they imagined truths and, by doing so, transformed them into literature, that second degree of reality, that transcended reality. Recognizable to them, this other reality has ceased to be so to us, who see it as veiled and realistic at the same time. As Alfonso Reyes pointed out, "Conforme esta conversación a distancia camina de lo íntimo a lo público, se va volviendo cada vez más un objeto literario, y al fin acaba por serlo tanto que ya solo es carta por el nombre" [As this conversation from a distance moves from the intimate to the public, it becomes more and more a literary object, and in the end it becomes something that it is only a letter by name] (xi).

Did the correspondents know that their letters would become an archaeological deposit of amorous-penitential mindsets? What would be given to the public with the passage of time? Would the letter writers have approved? To quote the last line of one of Galdós's epistolary and novelistic masterpieces, *Tristana*, "Tal vez" [Maybe]. They might have suspected and even encouraged their publication, since they did not consign their letters to the pyre or give orders for others to do so. Literary writing monopolized their expressive longings, but not exclusively. In other words, they were men and women of letters even when they did not believe themselves to be so; they simply could not be anything less. They built their respective "I" taking advantage of the word, the persistence of the word, and they did so within the short distances of love. As many times as they thought they were invisible, they gave opacity to their exchanges, but they did not watch over them entirely, they did not bury them or destroy them. Those words made too much sense, they had feeling, and they could not be erased. Affairs of the heart, so banally sublimated and so frequently reviled, occupied their waking hours, and although they could both then and now be treated as vicarious (*Primum vivere* ...), they knew that the heart of their art obeyed their designs, which were the driving force of the sun and the stars since Dante. Following this concept, when reviewing *Tristana* in 1892, the same year of its publication, Pardo Bazán refutes the censure of some of its critics.

> Muchísimas novelas, de las mejores que conozco en la literatura universal, son de trama excesivamente sencilla. Aquí, el decir de una novela que "apenas tiene asunto" suele envolver una censura disimulada, como si calificasen ya de anodina o inocente la obra. Protesto contra este sentido, y protesto más fuerte aún contra otra especie que no diré que echó a volar, pero sí que adoptó sin distingos mi buen amigo el señor Altamira: la de que no tienen miga los asuntos amorosos, o al menos no tienen tanta como los sociales, políticos, filosóficos, religiosos, científicos, económicos, etc. Si ahondamos (y ahondar es ley), *los asuntos amorosos, diría yo que tienen más miga que ningunos. En el modo de tratarlos, es decir, en la habilidad, ingenio y felicidad del autor, está el toque*. Por otra parte, en la cuestión de asunto también hay que distinguir cuidadosamente entre el asunto interno y externo, entre lo que *acontece* y lo que *permanece*, entre lo que se ve y lo que se esconde, pero pueden adivinar los iniciados ... (Pardo Bazán, "Tristana" 79–80; my emphasis)

> [Many novels, of the best I know in world literature, have an exceedingly simple plot. Here, the saying that a novel "hardly has a subject" usually involves a disguised censorship, as if they described the work as innocuous or innocent. I protest against this idea, and I protest even more strongly against another of its kind, of which I will not say that it took wing, but that my good friend Mr Altamira adopted it without discernment: that

there is no substance in love affairs, or at least they do not have as much substance as those matters which are social, political, philosophical, religious, scientific, economic, etc. If we delve deep (and to go deep is law), I would say that matters of the heart have more depth than others. The key lies in the way of treating them, that is to say, in the skill, ingenuity, and happiness of the author. On the other hand, it is also necessary to carefully distinguish between internal and external matters, between what happens and what remains, between what is seen and what is hidden, but the initiated can guess ...]

Obiter dicta, for the minutiae of clandestine encounters and details experienced with the audacity of adventurers persecuted and proscribed for religion and for all that happened with their obligations, one can refer to the external. For all that is indelible, that remains – "the secretive, inner world of feeling, thought and perception" – there is the enigma (Turner, "The Poetics of Suffering" 229). Referring to that famous scene from *El Burlador de Sevilla* [The Trickster of Seville] in which the king discovers Don Juan with Isabela and asks who they are, the response is only the short phrase, very elusive, but essential: "A Man and a Woman ..."

APPENDIX: FATHER CASTELLANOS'S LETTERS TO EMILIA PARDO BAZÁN

[1r]
J[esus]h[ominem]s[alvator].[11]
S[eño]ra[.] D[oña][a] Emilia Pardo Bazán
Santiago, Abril de 1890.[12]

Mi buena Emilia: Encarecidam[en]te la suplico me haga el obsequio / de leer con detención esta epístola, escrita por quien muy de veras la quiere en el / divino Corazón de nuestro común Salvador Jesús.

Al pasar por esa de vuelta de mi viaje deseaba hablarla de un asunto / que a usted más que a otro alguno importa; empero la circunstancia de permanecer tan / pocas horas en su casa, y el ser tan reciente / la muerte de su buen Padre (q.s.g.h.);[13] / y por otra parte el / haber notado hace tiempo lo poco o nada que usted aprecia los consejos / de su antiguo confesor, no obstante el gran interés que siempre tuve de su bien, hicieron-/me desistir por entonces de mi propósito, aplazándolo para ocasión más oportuna. Des-/de entonces ni un solo día, ni un instante ha pasado sin que recuerde mi propósito, / a cuyo cumplimiento me creo obligado por la caridad que la tengo y el vivo deseo que / siempre he tenido de su bien.

No puede usted dudar, mi buena Emilia, que más de una vez y en diversas for-/mas Dios Nuestro Señor, que es grande y rico en misericordias, la llamó pulsando a / su corazón con aquellos medios suaves y bondadosos, que son efecto de su misericordia, / y que sin hacer uso de los medios de castigo y del rigor, la llamaba con amor y la invitaba con dulzura para que del todo volviera usted hacia su Padre y Redentor. En alguna / ocasión no solo sintió y conoció usted este tierno llamamiento, sino que llegó a dar pú-/blico testimonio de él, y algunas buenas almas que en Jesucristo la quieren, se forja-/ron la ilusión de haber llegado el momento de su conversión a Dios.[14] ¡Oh, si hu-/bieran permanecido siempre aquellos sentimientos que experimentó su corazón / el primero de Enero de 1888 bajo las bóvedas del Vaticano![15]

Sin tratar de profundizar en los ocultos e insondables designios de Dios, / ni en la admirable economía que su Providencia observa con el hombre en orden / a su salvación, no dudo afirmar, fundado en el testimonio de la Escritura y / Santos Padres, que ordinariam[en]te llama Dios primero al hombre por esos dul-/[2v]ces y suaves medios de bondad y clemencia; pero cuando los de dura cerviz o incircun-/ciso corazón rehúsan obedecer a estos suaves llamamientos y desprecian los medios bon-/dadosos que les depara el Señor, ¡ah! entonces Dios, antes de hacer uso de su justicia, llá-/males, sí, pero es por medios más terribles y temibles; por medios en los que se deja ver / ya no sólo la misericordia, sí que también la justicia.

Ahora bien ¿será temerario suponer que la prematura y en gran parte / inesperada muerte de su buen Padre es el medio de terror y espanto con que Dios la / llama nuevamente ya que no hizo usted caso alguno de las suaves inspiraciones que re-/cibió su corazón, de los consejos que la dio su confesor, de los buenos ejemplos que usted ha / visto en otros, etc. etc.? No, mi buena Emilia; en manera alguna puede llamarse / temeraria esta suposición, sino que preciso es confesar hallarse conforme con la doctrina / católica, y por consiguiente con la sana y recta razón. Dios, pues, como bondadoso Pa-/dre, primero nos llama con actos de bondad y clemencia, y después con actos de ri-/gor mayor o menor según sus sabias determinaciones y conforme a los admira-/bles fines de su Providencia.

Si, mi buena Emilia; la muerte de su Papá la considero como nuevo, pero / terrible llamamiento que Dios hace al corazón de usted; a ese corazón hasta el presente / cerrado a la inspiración divina; y creo más, que si su Papá es capaz de alguna pena / la tiene y no pequeña al ver que en este mundo dejó una hija única en un estado / anormal y poco edificante. Desde la tumba, apenas cerrada, sale una triste y lasti-/mera voz que pide y ruega a usted ponga término al estado en que se halla. ¡Ah! si usted / supiera cuánto pedí al Señor me concediera la gracia de llegar a la Coruña antes / que su Papá expirara! Si yo hubiera tenido tanta dicha, hubiera hecho algunas re-/flexiones a su buen Padre, próximo ya a comparecer ante el Juez de vivos y muertos, / cuando principian a conocerse las cosas como son en sí y se va a leer el libro de las / grandes y exactas cuentas; entonces aquel venerable anciano, con el fin de reparar / en lo posible la parte que hubiera podido tener en la culpa de su hija, o el débil / esfuerzo que hiciera para evitarla, entonces, digo, no dudo que dejaría escrita una peti-/ción, una súplica para la hija amada de su corazón; súplica compendiada en / estas palabras: "Hija mía, no lleves con deshonor al sepulcro las canas de tu [3r] Padre; únete a tu Esposo. Este es mi testamento". Si tal hubiera sucedido,[16] si su buen Padre / la dejara por escrito este encargo, ¿se hubiera usted negado a cumplirlo? Ciertamente que no, y / el suponer lo contrario estimo sería injuriarla. Ahora bien, lo que sin duda la hubiera di-/cho su Padre a tenerla delante en aquel terrible momento, se lo dice ahora, invo-/cando el nombre siempre respetable de quien la dio el ser, un ministro, aunque / indigno, de Jesucristo; una persona que cree amarla más que otra cualquiera des-/pués de su Madre e hijos; su antiguo confesor, en fin, que no deja de hacer por su bien / cuanto puede dentro de su esfera.

Recuerdo, mi buena Emilia, que hablando con usted ha ya tiempo sobre esta dese-/ada unión, me dijo: "Por ahora es imposible; sólo podrá tener lugar cuando se / verifique algún importante acontecimiento en la familia, como por ejemplo, el / casamiento de Blanca". Este acontecimiento importante ¿no ha llegado ya? En / vez del alegre casamiento de Blanca ¿por qué no ha de ser el lamentable y triste / de la inesperada muerte de su Padre? ¡Pobre Padre! no pudo ver a su hija úni-/ca en aquellos supremos instantes; no pudo darla el último adiós, y entró / en la eternidad sin despedirse de quien tanto quería, por quien tanto clamaba / y suspiraba, y por quien tanto hizo y trabajó toda su vida. Y esta circunstancia,[17] / el no ver el Padre a la hija, ¿fue un castigo que Dios quiso ejecutar en el Padre, / en la hija, o en ambos a dos? ¡Qué remordimiento para usted, mi buena Emilia! / "Y Emilia ¿cuándo viene?

¿Vendrá pronto Emilia?" Así decía miles de veces / el moribundo y amante Padre, que al fin expiró sin tener el consuelo de ver a / la tan suspirada hija. ¿Se borrará de la mente de usted esta circunstancia?[18]

¡El casamiento de Blanca! No sabemos quién llegará allá,[19] y aunque to-/dos ustedes lleguen a la edad núbil de Blanca, bien podrá renunciar al casamien-/to esta cándida niña, estudiando en la escuela de la que sus Padres fueron ma-/estros. Además, ¿quién se casará con sus hijas? ¿Una persona buena? Mucho / lo dudo; pues cualquiera temerá que en las hijas se reproduzca el ejemplo de / la Madre; y si por desgracia se casara con ellas un calavera de buena fami-/lia, entonces, pobres niñas y desgraciado destino. Jaime, Blanca y Car-/men la han de pedir cuenta, y tal vez aun en esta vida misma, de lo que / [4v] viendo están. Estos tres ángeles no pedirán la razón ni el motivo del estado en que se / hallan sus Padres;[20] pero en su corazón y entendimiento lo sentirán y lo juzgarán / como una mancha, que cayendo en los que les dieron el ser, viene de rechazo a ofender / a los hijos que no tuvieron culpa.

En fin, mi buena Emilia, yo quisiera ver en usted un poquito de interés / para reflexionar sobre el poco edificante espectáculo que está usted dando; tanto más / escandaloso cuanto más conocida es usted. Muchos la admiran por su erudición; algunos / la compadecen por su desgracia conyugal y por algunos de sus escritos poco mo-/rales; muy pocos la aman, pues el corazón humano naturalmente rechaza cier-/tas cosas, así como la sociedad tiene también justas exigencias; y por último, sólo su / antiguo confesor la dice tan terribles y amargas verdades. Yo, pues, no tanto la ad-/miro cuanto la quiero en Jesucristo, y porque en el Señor la amo, la escribo esta epís-/tola, y por el mismo divino Salvador, que por todos nosotros murió, la suplico dé / cabida en su corazón a la voz de Dios; vénzase a sí misma, y trate de unirse a su / Esposo para que cese el gran escándalo que hasta el presente se ha dado.[21] Comprendo / que algún trabajo la costará el vencerse; pero sólo cuesta mucho lo que mucho vale; / por mucho que dure la violencia que debe hacerse, siempre será cuestión de pocos / días, y en cambio el fruto de tan santa resolución no tendrá fin, siguiéndose / una grande paz a su corazón e inmensa tranquilidad a su conciencia, de las / que ciertamente no puede gozar ahora. Hágalo usted por Dios, por la memoria de su / buen Padre, y por el honor de usted y de sus hijos.

Ínterin, mi buena Emilia,[22] reflexione usted en el contenido de esta po-/bre carta, escrita por su antiguo confesor a los pies del Crucifijo, yo quedo ro-/gando a ese divino Salvador para que no se malogren en usted los frutos de su dolo/rosa pasión y acerba muerte, y dé usted un día de gloria a los que de veras la quie-/ren, entre los cuales se cuenta el primero, no lo dude, su afectísimo amigo

S. S. y C.[23]
Fr[ay]. Manuel P[adre]. Castellanos.
M. O.[24]
[Rúbrica]
II.
Santiago 24 El Padre Castellanos,
franciscano

Mi querida Emilia: Dios me-/diante me embarcaré mañana con 22 / religiosos más. Pida al Señor tengamos / un viaje feliz.- Carmen me va a dar / un disgusto mayúsculo, pues me voy / a ir con las ganas (que son grandes) de / bautizarle el niño o niña que dé a luz. / Veo que es muy mala matemática. / Calcula mal.- Hoy pienso verla y / le daré el encargo de usted.- Celebro estén / ya en Meirás y deseo que les aproveche / la estancia en la aldea.- Escríbame / a Chipiona y hábleme del asunto / referente a San Francisco.- Viajé des-/de Padrón a esta con el Padre Fita.- Me gus-/tó mucho.- Puede usted suponer lo / ocupadísimo que estoy estos días.- Di-/ga a Papá que cuando fui a Villagarcía / llevé y entregué a Carolina los 5000 / reales.- No puedo más.- Recuerdos / a toda la familia y ya sabe que le a-/precia muy de veras su afectísimo amigo
Padre Castellanos
[Rúbrica][25]

NOTES

1 This essay forms part of research project FFI2016-80516 (AEI/FEDER, UE).
2 There is a considerable body of scholarship on the epistolary and also on the epistolary and gender. Apart from Janet Altman's classic study *Epistolarity*, Linda Kauffman's *Discourses of Desire*, and the volume *Epistolary Histories* by Amanda Gilroy and W.M. Verhoeven, scholars such as Ángeles Encinar, Ana Rueda, Ana Caballé ("La autobiografía escrita por mujeres"), and Ana Baquero Escudero have made important contributions to the study of the epistolary genre and gender in the Spanish context.

3 It was Flaubert's niece, Caroline Franklin-Grout, who until 1926 refused to authorize the disclosure of Louise Colet's letters, and "anciana pudorosa, condenó a la hoguera las misivas de Louise a su tío, pues ofendían su sensibilidad" [a modest old woman, she condemned to the fire Louise's letters to her uncle, as they offended her sensibilities] (Malaxecheverría 9).

4 See the "Revista de Madrid" in *La Ilustración Artística*, 23 March 1883, 2, and "El banquete a Pérez Galdós, El homenaje," in *La Época*, 27 March 1883, 1.

5 That Galdós would have requested a return of all his letters is plausible if we keep in mind his 22 June 1892 letter to Concha Ruth Morell, his later lover, to whom he wrote after she asked for his permission to use one of his love letters to make a name for herself in the theatre. The request unleashes his mistrust, and he dogmatically and decisively states, "No sé cómo se te ha ocurrido tal disparate. Porque las cartas de amor no se enseñan" [I don't know what gave you such a crazy idea. Because one doesn't show love letters to others] (*Correspondencia* 252). Approximately three days earlier, Galdós had written to Morell, "¿Apostamos a que no has hecho lo que te dije de romper las cartas? Si no lo has hecho, hazlo por favor, no seas descuidada; aprende a vivir. Cuando contestes di si has roto los papeles ... Romperás las cartas, y esta principalmente" [Shall we bet that you have not done what I told you about ripping up the letters? If you have not done it, please do it, don't be careless; learn to live. When you write back tell me you have torn them up ... Rip up the letters, and this one in particular] (*Correspondencia* 252).

6 Galdós's letter maintains a strict formality of expression: "'una dama y escritora como V.' – Soy de los primeros y más vehementes admiradores de sus escritos" ["a lady and author such as yourself" – I am among the earliest and most vehement admirers of your writing] (*Correspondencia* 96).

7 See, in this regard, my review of *"Miquiño mío." Cartas a Galdós*.

8 I am indebted to the Foundation for its generous assistance and its permission to publish these letters.

9 Both letters can be found in the Foundation's files for Emilia Pardo Bazán; the first is labelled L1 C20-1 and the second labelled L1 C20-2.

10 Armando Palacio Valdés addressed two of his letters to Galdós in this way: "Mi querido amigo y grande argonauta" and "Mi querido amigo don Vasco di Gama [*sic*]" (Nuez and Schraibman 120, 115).

11 Abbreviation for the Greek name of Jesus, in reference to Christ. It is his monogram, also called a cristogram. In addition, it can appear as IHS (Jesús del Hombre Salvador).

12 The love affair between Pardo Bazán and Pérez Galdós, "sin duda, estaba aún vigente en 1890" [without a doubt was still ongoing in 1890] (González Arias 170). It is worth noting that in the final decade of the century, both authors are imagining novels and short stories that deal with amorous relationships and their difficulties. It is significant how Pardo Bazán names her novelistic diptych: Ciclo de Adán y Eva.

13 Que santa gloria haya.

14 The expression is a strong one: the penitent has lost her faith and must return to the fold, must turn to God.

15 Pardo Bazán had written about her pilgrimage to Rome in *Mi Romería* (1888).

16 The assumption on which the Franciscan Father works is formulated in terms of literal direct discourse attributed to Doña Emilia's father. The words of Doña Emilia will also be adduced below, as if her confessor had recorded her sequence accurately.

17 Pardo Bazán did not arrive in time to see her father alive.

18 The cruelty with which he makes this argument is clear. It is here that the letter reaches one of its highest levels of harassment, of moral torture.

19 At the time of the letter, Pardo Bazán had three children: Jaime, age fourteen; Blanca (Nieves), age eleven; and Carmen, age nine.

20 The reference is to their *de facto* separation and affairs outside of marriage.

21 By way of circumlocutions, tinged with euphemisms, the letter directly names "the great scandal" in which its recipient finds herself.

22 Father Castellanos employs this appellation eight times in the letter, a fact not lacking irony. Pardo Bazán's library contains various titles by Castellanos.

23 This abbreviation constitutes the only opaque place in the transcribed text. I propose, however, the following hypothetical explication: "Su Seguro Servidor y Confesor (o Consejero)."

24 Likely an abbreviation for "Ministro de la Orden."

25 This second letter makes clear the degree of familial trust enjoyed by Father Castellanos, who serves almost as a secretary to José Pardo Bazán and is accustomed to frequenting the family home in Meirás. The Carmen mentioned in this letter is not one of Pardo's daughters.

WORKS CITED

Acosta, Eva. *Emilia Pardo Bazán. La luz en la batalla. Biografía*. Barcelona: Lumen, 2007. Print.

Altman, Janet. *Epistolarity: Approaches to a Form*. Columbus: Ohio State UP, 1982. Print.

Ávila Arellano, Julián. "Doña Emilia Pardo Bazán y Benito Pérez Galdós en 1889. Fecunda compenetración espiritual y literaria." In *Actas del IV Congreso Internacional Galdosiano*, vol. 2. Las Palmas de Gran Canaria: Cabildo Insular de Gran Canaria, 1993. 305–24. Print.

"El banquete a Pérez Galdós. El homenaje." *La Época*, 27 March 1883, 1. Print.

Baquero Escudero, Ana L. "El artificio epistolar en la narrativa galdosiana." In *La voz femenina en la narrativa epistolar*. Cádiz: Universidad de Cádiz, 2003. 164–9. Print.

Bravo-Villasante, Carmen. *Vida y obra de Emilia Pardo Bazán. Correspondencia amorosa con Pérez Galdós*. Madrid: Magisterio Español, 1973. Print.

Caballé, Ana. "El arte epistolar."*Mercurio* no. 174 (October 2015): 6–7. Print.

– "La autobiografía escrita por mujeres. Los vacíos del estudio de un género." In *Las mujeres escritoras en la historia de la literatura española*, ed. Lucía Montejo Gurruchaga and Nieves Baranda Leturio. Madrid: UNED, 2002. 141–52. Print.

Clemessy, Nelly. "Unas cartas de Emilia Pardo Bazán a Benito Pérez Galdós." In *A Further Range: Studies in Modern Spanish Literature from Galdós to Unamuno*, ed. Anthony H. Clarke. Exeter: U of Exeter P, 1999. 136–44. Print.

Encinar, Angeles. "La narrativa epistolar en las escritoras españolas actuales." In *Mujeres novelistas en el panorama literario del siglo XX*, ed. Marina Villalba Álvarez. Cuenca: Ediciones de la Universidad de Castilla La Mancha, 2000. 33–50. Print.

Freire López, Ana María. "Introducción." In *Cartas a Emilia Pardo Bazán (1878–1883)*. A Coruña: Fundación "Pedro Barrié de la Maza, Conde de Fenosa," 1991. 5–15. Print.

Gilroy, Amanda, and W.M. Verhoeven. *Epistolary Histories: Letters, Fiction, and Culture*. Charlottesville: U of Virginia P, 2000. Print.

González Arias, Francisca. "Diario de un viaje: las cartas de Emilia Pardo Bazán a Benito Pérez Galdós." In *Textos y contextos de Galdós*, ed. Harriet S. Turner and John W. Kronik. Madrid: Castalia, 1994. 169–75. Print.

Kauffman, Linda S. *Discourses of Desire: Gender, Genre, and Epistolary Fiction*. Ithaca: Cornell UP, 1986. Print.

Malaxecheverría, Ignacio. "Prólogo." In Gustave Flaubert, *Cartas a Louise Colet*. Madrid: Ediciones Siruela, 1989, 2003. Print.

"Manifestaciones en honor de Pérez Galdós." *El Imparcial*, 27 March 1883, 2. Print.

Molina Foix, Vicente. "El género egoísta." *Mercurio* no. 174 (October 2015): 34. Print.

Muñoz Molina, Antonio. "Un latido de cartas." "Babelia." *El País*, 23 May 2015. 2. Print.

Nabokov, Vladímir. *Cartas a Véra*. Ed. Olga Vorónina and Brian Boyd. Trans. Marta Rebón and Marta Alcaraz. Barcelona: RBA, 2015. Print.

Nuez, Sebastián de la, and José Schraibman, eds. *Cartas del archivo de Galdós*. Madrid: Taurus, 1967. Print.

Ortega, Soledad. *Cartas a Galdós*. Madrid: Revista de Occidente, 1964. Print.

Pardo Bazán, Emilia. "Ángel Guerra." In *Obras completas*, ed. Harry L. Kirby. Madrid: Aguilar, 1973. 1093–1105. Print.

– "Apuntes autobiográficos." In *Los Pazos de Ulloa*. Barcelona: Daniel Cortezo y Cía, Editores, 1886. 5–92. Print.

– *Cartas a Galdós (1889–1890)*. Prologue and edition by Carmen Bravo-Villasante. Madrid: Ediciones Turner, 1975. Print.

– *Insolación (Historia amorosa)*. Madrid: Cátedra, 2001. Print.

– *"Miquiño mío." Cartas a Galdós*. Ed. Isabel Parreño and Juan Manuel Hernández. Madrid: Turner Noema, 2013. Print.

– *La obra periodística completa en "La Nación" de Buenos Aires (1879–1921)*. Vols. 1 and 2. Ed. Juliana Sinovas Maté. A Coruña: Diputación de A Coruña, 1999. Print.

– *Obras completas*. Ed. Harry L. Kirby. Madrid: Aguilar, 1973. Print.

– "Tristana." *Nuevo Teatro Crítico* 2.17 (May 1892): 77–90. Web. http://www.cervantesvirtual.com/obra-visor/nuevo-teatro-critico--40/html/02958176-82b2-11df-acc7-002185ce6064_80.html.

Patiño Eirín, Cristina. "La aventura catalana de Pardo Bazán." In *Del Romanticismo al Realismo*, ed. L.F. Díaz Larios and E. Miralles. Barcelona: Universitat de Barcelona, 1998. 443–52. Print.

– Review of *"Miquiño mío." Cartas a Galdós*, ed. Parreño and Hernández. *La Tribuna. Cadernos de Estudos da Casa-Museo Emilia Pardo Bazán* no. 9 (2012–13): 379–88. Digital edition available at Realacademiagalega.org. Web.

Pattison, Walter T. "Two Women in the Life of Galdós." *Anales Galdosianos* 8.8 (1973): 23–31. Print.

Penas Varela, Ermitas. Introducción. In Emilia Pardo Bazán, *Insolación (Historia amorosa)*. Madrid: Cátedra, 2001. Print.

Pérez Galdós, Benito. *Correspondencia*. Ed. Alan E. Smith, María Ángeles Rodríguez Sánchez, and Laurie Lomask. Madrid: Cátedra, 2016. Print.

– *La revolución de julio*. In *Obras completas*, vol. 3: *Episodios nacionales*, ed.

Federico Carlos Sáinz de Robles. Madrid: Aguilar, 1941. Print.
"Revista de Madrid." *La Ilustración Artística*, 23 March 1883, 2. Print.
Reyes, Alfonso. "Estudio preliminar." In *Literatura epistolar*, ed. Ricardo Baeza and Alfonso Reyes. Barcelona: Océano, 1998. v–xxiii. Print.
Ricard, Robert. "Cartas a Galdós y cartas de Galdós." *Anuario de Estudios Atlánticos* no. 11 (1965): 163–91. Print.
Rodríguez Marcos, Manuel. "Primero el epistolario, luego la biografía." *El País*, 27 June 2015. Print.
Romero Tobar, Leonardo. "Valera y Pardo Bazán en sus epistolarios." Cuadernos Hispanoamericanos no. 670 (April 2006): 65–75. Print.
Rueda, Ana. *Cartas sin lacrar: la novela epistolar y la España ilustrada, 1789–1840.* Madrid: Iberoamericana-Vervuert, 2001. Print.
Thion Soriano-Mollá, Dolores. *Pardo Bazán y Lázaro. Del lance de amor a la aventura cultural (1888–1919).* Madrid: Fundación Lázaro Galdiano-Ollero y Ramos, 2003. Print.
Turner, Harriet S. "La imagen metafórica como vida novelable en Galdós." In *Actas del X Congreso de la Asociación Internacional de Hispanistas, Barcelona 21–26 de agosto 1989*, coord. Antonio Vilanovo. Barcelona: PPU, 1992. 1515–24. Print.
– "The Poetics of Suffering in Galdós and Tolstoy." In *Studies in Honor of Gilberto Paolini*, ed. Mercedes Vidal Tibbits. Newark, DE: Juan de la Cuesta, 1996. 229–42. Print.
– "'Silent Writing' and the Power of Form in *Anna Karenina and Fortunata y Jacinta*." In *Prosa y poesía: Homenaje a Gonzalo Sobejano*, ed. Christopher Maurer, Jean-François Botrel, Yvan Lissorgues, and Leonardo Romero Tobar. Madrid: Gredos, 2001. 407–18. Print.

12 "Volvía Galdós triunfante": *Fortunata y Jacinta* on Stage (1930)

DAVID T. GIES

Some attention has been focused on the film and TV adaptations of Galdós's realist masterpiece, *Fortunata y Jacinta*,[1] but surprisingly little has been paid to an early twentieth-century stage adaptation of the same work. One understands why. While film and TV open themselves to extended narratives (space and time) – that is, a film camera can move through bourgeois interiors, follow characters from place to place, and swoop over vast cityscapes, and television can allow for multiple hours across evenings or even weeks – the stage is excruciatingly more limiting both spatially and temporally. That does not mean, of course, that a stage representation cannot move spectators imaginatively into other worlds, but it does present unique challenges both to the author/adaptor and to the stage director. One would think that Galdós's sweeping narrative is simply too large, too all-encompassing, and too emotionally complex to be reduced to a two-hour spectacle.

Yet, in 1930 the great actress Margarita Xirgu – in a daring and perhaps foolhardy adventure – brought *Fortunata y Jacinta. Variante escénica de algunos pasajes de la famosa novela de Galdós, dialogada y refundida en siete cuadros (tres actos)* to the stage. The piece, written by Antonio Soler, M. Díez G. de Amarillas, and E. López Alarcón, extracted, as the title suggests, several scenes from the "novela famosa" [famous novel] and brought them to life on 16 October 1930, at the Teatro Español. Xirgu worked in tandem with Cipriano Rivas Cherif, who served as artistic director for the company, and with Salvador Bartolozzi as the scenic and costume designer: "Salvador Bartolozzi, casado con Magda Donato, colaboró con Rivas Cherif desde 1920 hasta los años del exilio mexicano ... En *Cómo hacer teatro* recuerda los figurines y decorado de la *Fortunata y Jacinta* de Galdós" [Salvador Bartolozzi, married to Magda Donato, collaborated with Rivas Cherif from 1920 until the years of the

Mexican exile ... In *How to Make Theatre* he remembers the costumes and set of Galdós's *Fortunata y Jacinta*] (Aguilera Sastre 64). Xirgu was not only a recognized star in the theatre, but she had also already performed in several of Galdós's plays such as *Marianela, La loca de la casa,* and *Santa Juana de Castilla* (Gil Fombellida 170).

"Foolhardy" is not an inaccurate adjective to apply to this artistic endeavour. Galdós's novel (in its original Spanish) is notoriously long (nearly 400,000 words), even exceeding the already lengthy standards of the day for realist novels, such as Dostoyevsky's *Crime and Punishment* (212,000 words), Melville's *Moby Dick* (210,000 words), or Dickens's *Bleak House* (358,000 words). Galdós himself transformed several of his novels into stage versions – *Realidad* (1892), *La loca de la casa* (1893), *Gerona* (1894), *Doña Perfecta* (1896), *El abuelo* (1904), and *Casandra* (1910) – and other playwrights dramatized various of his prose pieces, such as *El equipaje del rey José* (by Ricardo José Catarineu and Cristóbal de Castro, 1903), *La familia de León Roch* (by José Jerique, 1904), *Marianela* (by Serafín and Joaquín Álvarez Quinteros, 1916), *El audaz* (by Jacinto Benavente, 1919), and *Tormento* (by Antonio Soler, 1924). Nonetheless, Spain's most famous late nineteenth-century novelist never dared to tackle his own most famous novel. How could such an extensive narrative be reduced to the confines of a 13,000-word stage play, a synthesis that would decrease the novel to a mere 3 per cent of its original length?

Little is known about the three adaptors of the work. The lead author, Antonio Soler – the only one of the three authors mentioned in Gómez García's *Diccionario de teatro* – enjoyed a career as a playwright and collaborator, writing now-forgotten pieces such as *Los sucesos de la semana,* or *¡Cuentan de un sabio que un día ...!* and *El dulce himeneo* (these last two in collaboration with Manuel Fernández Palomero). With Diógenes Ferrand he wrote *El reducto del Pilar;* with Eduardo Gómez Cereda, titles such as *Los gatos, Los hombres serios, Imposible l'hais dejado, M'hacéis de reír don Gonzalo, La muñeca ideal,* and *Los sabios de Grecia;* with Gómez Cereda and Rafael Calleja, *Maese Fígaro;* with Emilio Múgica, *El príncipe celoso;* and finally, with Nicanor Puga, *La historia de España.* One of Soler's collaborators, Enrique López Alarcón, is known to have staged plays entitled *La tizona* (16 October 1931), an adaptation of Lope's *Fuenteovejuna* (30 January 1932), *La maravilla de Efeso* (17 May 1933), *Romance caballeresco* (30 September 1933), and *Los majos del Perchel* (27 February 1935) (see McGaha). Soler had worked with Manuel Díez G. de Amarillas in 1924 on a five-act rendition of *Fortunata.*[2]

The writers and actress/producer hedged their bets right from the start, by advertising the piece as a "variante escénica" [scenic variation] of "algunos pasajes" [some passages] of the novel. How could it be otherwise? The three-act play is divided into seven "cuadros" [tableaux], a structural arrangement popular since the eighteenth century and used extensively in the nineteenth (see García Lorenzo):

1 Acto Primero, cuadro primero. La compra del Pituso;
2 Acto Primero, cuadro segundo. Doña Lupe la de los Pavos;
3 Acto Segundo, cuadro primero. El convento de las Micaelas;
4 Acto Segundo, cuadro segundo. El marido y don Juan;
5 Acto Tercero, cuadro primero. Severiana y Mauricia "la Dura";
6 Acto Tercero, cuadro segundo. Guillermina virgen y fundadora;
7 Acto Tercero, cuadro tercero. Maxi reside en las estrellas.

The titles of the scenes seem arbitrary, and are presented on the published title page of the play only; they are not repeated as each section begins in the text, nor can one extract from the stage directions the exact content of the scene. Presumably, spectators in the theatre would not see these designations, although readers of the printed version would have the opportunity to do so. The scenes take place, respectively and in this order, in the dining room of the Santa Cruz family home; in Maxi's study (with doors leading to Nicolás's and Lupe's rooms); in the visitors' lounge at the Micaelas convent; in Fortunata and Maxi's apartment living room; in the tenement house where Severiana cares for Mauricia; in the dining room of Doña Guillermina's house; and finally, in Fortunata's new abode in the Cava de San Miguel. All are interiors, which filter out Galdós's extraordinary cityscapes, leaving the play with a more hermetic feel and the viewer with a more focused attention span.

The following description gives one an idea of the time sequencing and space allocations of the play, and suggests the authors' desire to maintain the "realist" nature of Galdós's novel. Rivas Cherif remembered his reaction to Bartolozzi's scenic design and costume work:

> Porque si nuestra intención es otra que la de ese realismo concreto, podemos hacer todo lo contrario. El excelente dibujante Bartolozzi me hizo para el Español los figurines del vestuario y el decorado de la *Fortunata y Jacinta* de Galdós, novela realista; pero que a la distancia de los años transcurridos desde su publicación a su adaptación a la escena, admitía

> y aun exigía la contemplación de ironía simpática con que hojeamos una ilustración anticuada. Bartolozzi *pintó* en perspectiva levemente caricaturesca, apenas con esa punta de humorismo que no sólo no excluye la emoción, sino que la produce hasta el enternecimiento, pintó muebles en alguna escena cuya brevedad hubiera dificultado con las mutaciones el ritmo de la representación; pero él fue el encargado igualmente de dibujar los que ex-profeso se hicieron utilizables y de bulto, acomodados a la pompa de los polisones y el vuelo de levitas y capas. (292–3)
>
> [Because if we intend to do something other than recreate that exact realism, we can do precisely the opposite. The excellent draftsman Bartolozzi designed the costumes and the set at the Teatro Español for Galdós's *Fortunata y Jacinta*, a realist novel; but the time that has elapsed from its publication to its adaptation for the stage allowed and even demanded that we adopt the charming irony with which we look at an old illustration. Bartolozzi *painted* with a slightly caricaturesque perspective, with that light touch of humour that, far from excluding emotion, even produces tenderness. For some brief scenes, his design called for furniture that would have made the scene changes difficult and affected the rhythm of the performance; but he also intentionally designed furniture to suit the stateliness of bustles and the swishing of frock-coats and capes.]

One unusual, and unexplained, detail: the authors set the play in 1890, a date very specifically noted in the first stage description ("Muebles y detalles de la escena, del año 1890" [Furnishings and scenic details, from 1890]).

The issue of adaptation from one medium to another has been hotly debated in literary circles during the past fifty years. Current theories seem to want to "sever" the connection between the "source" and the resultant work (Cardwell 1). Today we draw primarily from film studies in order to problematize "the dialogic relation among texts" (Hutcheon xii), although literary critics tend now to reject the privileging of the "source" as inherently better or superior. Yet one wonders how, in the case of a novelist of the depth and scope of Galdós, his source text could not be inherently better/richer/more complex, although, as Cardwell argues, a resultant adaptation is, if nothing else, "unique" ("and by its unique nature gives rise to forms of artistic expression distinct from those in other media" 44).

Cutting and reducing the novel to 3 per cent of its length (a "surgical art" in Abbott's apt phrase (108)) meant the elimination of most of the narrative's more reflective passages, particularly as the novel reaches its climax. Hence, gone is most of the political discourse, the musings on the Restauración, and the information about the generals. Also cut is Juan Pablo Rubín's flirtation with Carlismo, as are Pater, Quevedo, Pedernero, Ramsés (Villaamil), and the discussions at the various tertulias, including the uproar (a "zipizape ... de lo más célebre" [a first-class row] as Galdós called it) (736). The adaptation likewise suppresses the musings on anticlericalism, religion, politics, banking, and commerce that are interwoven into the novel. Gone is Maxi's inspirational plan – "Yo no soy más que un precursor de esta doctrina" [I am merely a precursor of that doctrine (866)] – as are Moreno-Isla's reflections on returning to London and his ultimate death. Suppressed is Fortunata's interior dialogue/argument with Juanito (897) and scenes that move Fortunata's mental crisis towards resolution, such as her conversation with Aurora about Fenelon and Juanito (876–8) or their discussion about Juanito's possible infidelity (900). Such scenes would of course be difficult to dramatize, as would Maxi's hyperrational thoughts on Fortunata's whereabouts (922–7). The authors choose instead to highlight moments of more dramatic tension. Galdós's prose carries the "temporal narrative" (Elliott 18), while the scenes from the play are asked to carry not only some of that same narrative but also visual and auditory cues that might enhance (or distort) the spectator's experience. That is, the audience might experience a literary moment more fully through this live interpretation/adaptation (Barnette calls this "adapturgy"). As Hutcheon notes, "The difficulties of dramatizing such verbal elements as irony, ambiguity, metaphor, or symbolism pale in comparison with the problems faced by the adapter who has to dramatize what is *not* present" (71).

The authors have little interest in recasting Galdós's grand narrative in a new light, or in telling his urban family romance from a different perspective, nor, according to Breen, do they need to be faithful to the novel. "There is no obligation on the part of the interpreter to respect the author's intentions" (Breen 114), a thought echoed by Barnette when she claims, "The very nature of adaptation is flexibility" (148). Yet for some, reduction means loss. The newspaper *La Esfera* confronts the challenge head on:

> ¿Para qué plantear nuevamente el viejo problema de la adaptación teatral de las novelas? Cuando se pensaba que novela y drama eran géneros no sólo distintos, sino antitéticos, y se oponía como sus respectivos caracteres esenciales el análisis y la síntesis, ese problema, aunque aparentemente

> irresoluble, podía tener interés; pero cuando los años y los conceptos más amplios del arte nos han traído tantos dramas sintéticos y tantas comedias analíticas, la discusión genérica carece de sentido, y en todo caso podría discutirse específicamente la posibilidad de adaptación escénica de una novela determinada.
>
> Puesta la cuestión en este terreno, difícilmente señalará nadie como modelo de novelas adaptables *Fortunata y Jacinta*, de Galdós; y sin embargo, es evidente que una adaptación de esa magna obra ha logrado en el Teatro Español el favor del público. Claro está que en esa adaptación no aparece íntegra – ¿y cómo podría aparecer? – la novela de Galdós ...
>
> [Why bring up the old problem of the adaptation of novels to the theatre yet again? When it was believed that the novel and the theatre were not only completely different, but antithetical, genres, and that their respective essential characteristics, analysis and synthesis, were diametrically opposed, that problem, although apparently irresolvable, was still of interest; but now that the years and broader concepts of art have brought us so many synthetic dramas and so many analytical comedies, this discussion of genre makes no sense, and in any case one could specifically argue for the possible theatrical adaptation of a specific novel. Put that way, no one would recommend Galdós's *Fortunata y Jacinta* as a candidate for adaptation; and yet, it is evident that the adaptation of that major work has managed to win over the public at the Teatro Español. Obviously, in that adaptation Galdós's novel does not – how could it? – appear whole.]

This confirms Mittell's observation that "Novels that rely upon descriptive prose or the voice of a narrator as a defining element pose more of a challenge in adaptation" (29), a challenge that looks back to what G.E. Lessing identified in 1766 as the temporal/spatial dichotomy (chapter 18). The critic for *El Imparcial* recognizes the same problems:

> Los comentarios amables, sugeridos por el estreno de obras dramáticas inspiradas en novelas famosas, forzosamente adquieren aspecto de lugar común, porque la disparidad entre "novela" y "teatro" es manifiesta y vulgar. No así las diferencias entre una novela y su escenificación, con ser tan hondas, y tan diversos sus procedimientos, que el comediógrafo más experto titubea y vacila, cuando intenta llevar al teatro, el enorme bloque de una novela analítica, descriptiva, ampliamente ambientada y construída a trazo lento.

La trama es abrumadora. Ingrata. Es preciso depurar la trama minuciosa de la novela hasta llegar a la acción sintética, desbrozando el material inerte, que en el teatro estorba. Arrancar de la línea sinuosa de cada personaje, sus caracteres de "ser vivo"; estudiar movimientos y desarrollo en sentido rectilíneo, para crear la "situación" teatral, alada, transparente y eficaz ... y todo ello, conservando, incólume, la emoción original de la novela, sus figuras capitales, tendencias y finalidad. Improba tarea, con más posibilidades de error que de acierto ...

[Kind comments, prompted by the debut of dramatic works inspired by famous novels, necessarily become clichés, because the gap between a novel and a play is obvious and commonplace. But that is not so with respect to the yawning differences between a novel and its staging, because their approaches are so diverse that even the most experienced dramatist hesitates and wavers when he attempts to bring the enormous slab of an analytic, descriptive, richly set, and slowly constructed novel to the theatre. The plot is overwhelming. Unforgiving. One needs to reduce the detailed plot until achieving a synthesis of its story, clearing away any inert material, that in the theatre just gets in the way. Pluck out of each character's sinuous story line whatever makes them a "living being"; study movements and development in a straight line in order to create the soaring, transparent, and compelling theatrical "situation," and all the while maintaining the original emotion of the novel unscathed, its main shape, tendencies, and meaning. A daunting task, with a greater probability of failure than success.]

Writing in *El Sol*, Enrique Díez-Canedo simply refuses to comment on "una vez más, las acostumbradas consideraciones acerca de lo difícil que es transplantar un asunto de la novela al teatro" [once again, the well-known reflections on the difficulty of moving a novel's business to the theatre] (17 October 1930). Boyum states it clearly: "The rhetoric of fiction is simply not the rhetoric of film, and it's in finding analogous strategies whereby the one achieves the effects of the other that the greatest challenge of adaptation lies" (81).

Of course, suppression, elimination, and cutting are not the only strategies that transform this full, rich novel into a multi-character, description-free dialogue on stage. What Harriet S. Turner has called Galdós's "metaphors of mind" – that is, a prose style redolent of analogy and metaphor – necessarily disappears, or, rather, shifts from the prose of the text to the imagination of the spectator. Where a novel "tells" a story, a play is called upon to "show" it (Hutcheon xiv). Turner also writes of "imagistic progressions," which perhaps lend themselves more to the creation of a dramatization of the work. "When describing realism in the novel Galdós stresses neither fact nor fiction but likeness/comparison. His avowed aim was not to depict an object but to *surround* it, so to speak, by establishing dialectical patterns that build a sense of character, sketch in dot-images or formulate imagistic progressions" (93).

We might ask, then, to what extent do the authors capture (or not) the spirit and essence of Galdós's masterpiece? First, we note that most of the major characters from the novel make an appearance at one time or another on stage: we meet Fortunata (played by Margarita Xirgu), Jacinta, Juanito Santa Cruz, Doña Guillermina, Mauricia "la Dura," Lupe, Papitos, Doña Barbarita, Sor Natividad, Sor Marcela, Maximiliano Rubín, Aurora Samaniego, Severina, Plácido Estupiñá, Don Nicolás, Don Baldomero, Ido del Sagrario, Moreno Isla, and seven other secondary characters. The authors necessarily suppress the complex and rich background information provided by Galdós in the first three chapters of the book, although the characters he highlights there – Doña Barbarita, Estupiñá, and Juanito – are foregrounded in the play's crowded first act. Estupiñá has the first words in the play (in the novel, the first direct intervention is given to Don Baldomero), where he and Barbarita talk about Juanito as the rascal he was prior to his marriage to Jacinta: "tuvo sus trapicheos" [he had his adventures] (Soler et al. 3). When the couple enters the dining room, Juanito is painted in a few bold strokes as particularly spoiled and babied by his wife, who uses an accumulation of diminutives to speak to and about him, or which appear in the stage directions inserted by the adaptors ("hijito," "abandonadito," "mujercita," "camisita," "santita," "comidita," "riquín," "golpecitos").[3] Juan responds in kind: "(*Como chiquito mimoso.*) Tu nenito" [(*Like a spoiled child.*) Your baby] (4). Juanito, with an admirable economy of words, is immediately characterized as the dependent, childlike man who dominates the novel.

The first scene exuberantly packs in a host of characters and crowds them all on stage. Besides the above-mentioned Estupiñá, Barbarita, Jacinta, and Juanito, the audience is introduced to Ido del Sagrario with his "ropa prehistórica" [prehistoric clothing] (5), Moreno Isla, Don Baldomero, and Guillermina, all supplying information drawn from various places in the novel. In addition, we are introduced, through indirect reference, to José Izquierdo and then to Fortunata herself. We quickly learn of Jacinta's desire to have a child (her "manía" [obsession], a word used here as well as numerous times in the novel), for which they have waited some ten years: "Que es [una camisita] para un muñeco de carne y hueso. ¿No podemos nosotros tener uno?" [It's a tiny shirt for a real-life doll. Can't we have one?] (5); of Ido's obsession with the sale of serial novels and with his wife's supposed adultery; of Guillermina, the "beatific" "rata eclesiástica" [ecclesiastical rat] (9); of Barbarita's talent for shopping; and of the suspicion that there exists a bastard child belonging to Juan (10).

One of the most memorable scenes of the novel, of course, remains Juan's first glimpse of Fortunata, as she emerges from the apartment at 11 Cava Baja sucking on a raw egg. In Galdos's striking rendering of the scene, Juanito asks Fortunata:

> —¿Qué come usted, criatura?
> —¿No lo ve usted?—replicó mostrándoselo—. Un huevo.
> —¡Un huevo crudo!
> Con mucho donaire, la muchacha se llevó a la boca, por segunda vez, el huevo roto, y se atizó otro sorbo.
> —No sé cómo puede usted comer esas babas crudas—dijo Santa Cruz, no hallando mejor modo de trabar conversación.
> —Mejor que guisadas. ¿Quiere usted?—replicó ella, ofreciendo al Delfín lo que en el cascarón quedaba.
> Por entre los dedos de la chica se escurrían aquellas babas gelatinosas y transparentes. Tuvo tentaciones Juanito de aceptar la oferta; pero no: le repugnaban los huevos crudos.
> —No, gracias. (Galdós 475)
>
> ["What are you eating, child?"
> "Can't you see?" she replied, holding it out. "An egg."
> "A raw egg!"
> Gracefully, the girl raised the cracked egg to her mouth for a second time, and slurped it again.
> "I don't see how you can eat that raw slime," said Santa Cruz, failing to find any other way to keep the conversation going.
> "Better than cooked. Would you like some?" she replied, offering the Delfín what was left in the shell.
> Through the girl's fingers dripped that gelatinous and filmy slobber. Juanito was tempted to accept the offer; but no: raw eggs made him gag.]

This first meeting would seem to have been an easy and logical scene for the adaptors of the novel to tackle, given its dramatic punch, its erotic subtext, its lively dialogue, and of course, its consequential centrality to all that follows in the novel. Yet they choose a completely different approach. Instead of staging the encounter between the future lovers, we hear about it in hindsight in a dialogue between Jacinta and Guillermina, a reduction of dramatic tension clearly noted by the reviewer from *El Imparcial*: "Y se sucedían las escenas, en cada una de las cuales se 'refería' mucho y 'sucedía' poco, languideciendo así, rápidamente, la acción escénica" [And scene followed upon scene, in each of which much was "told" and little "happened," and thereby the scenic action quickly wilted] (17 October 1930).

What is more, a different moment of high drama, the honeymoon trip, which might have provided another opportunity to bring erotic tension to the stage, is also simply recounted in hindsight. The authors conflate the two scenes in one short dialogue:

> GUILL: Pero ... ¿estás tu segura de que ese niño es hijo de Juan? ... ¿Te ha confesado él? ...
> JACIN: Todo. Yo sabía que antes de casarnos había tenido un ... un ...
> GUILL: Un lío, hijita, un lío; llámalo por su nombre.
> JACIN: Una vez quería yo conocer todo su pasado ...
> GUILL: Eso es muy de mujer. Sigue.
> JACIN: Mientras nuestro viaje de novios, le hice cantar de plano, sobre todo una noche en que un inglés le hizo beber en Sevilla más manzanilla de la cuenta. Me dijo que la había conocido en casa de Estupiñá, cuando Plácido estaba enfermo. Una tarde fue Juan a visitarle y encontró a aquella mujer en la escalera sorbiendo un huevo crudo ...¡Vamos, que enamorarse de una mujer que sorbe huevos crudos! ... (Soler et al. 10)
>
> [GUILL: But are you sure that child is Juan's son? Has he confessed to you?
> JACIN: Everything. I knew that before we married he had an ... an ...
> GUILL: An affair, child, an affair; call it what it is.
> JACIN: At one point I wanted to know everything about his past ...
> GUILL: That's a very womanly thing. Continue.
> JACIN: On our honeymoon, I made him confess, particularly one night in Seville when an English guy in a bar made him drink a little more sherry than normal. He told me he met her in Estupiñá's house, when Plácido was ill. One afternoon Juan went to visit him and he met that woman in the stairwell sucking on a raw egg ... My! Imagine falling in love with a woman who sucks raw eggs!]

What we have in this conflation, then, are not only two major scenes from the novel, one folded into the other, but also Jacinta's emotional reaction to the raw egg incident (which reflects, of course, the disgust she expresses in the novel: "Un huevo crudo ... ¡Qué asco—exclamó Jacinta escupiendo una salivita" ["A raw egg ... How disgusting!" exclaimed Jacinta, spitting out some saliva] (Galdós 483).

The two women, Guillermina and Jacinta, continue to "set the stage" by discussing Fortunata, her brief residence in Izquierdo's home, and the shocking fact that she is "Cambrí ... de cinco meses" [five months pregnant]. This word ("cambrí) is Galdós's term: "El último a quien vi fue Izquierdo; le encontré un día subiendo la escalera de mi casa. Me amenazó; díjome que la *Pitusa* estaba *cambrí* de cinco meses ... *¡Cambrí de cinco meses ...!*" [The last person I saw was Izquierdo; I ran across him one day going up the stairs of my house. He threatened me; told me that *Pitusa* was five months pregnant ... *Five months pregnant ...!*] (Galdós 495). That is, the adaptors transfer a dialogue that took place between husband and wife in the novel into one between wife and friend. This allows them to build suspense. As Jacinta attempts to convince Guillermina that the child belongs to Juan, Juan returns to the stage, and the audience then witnesses a tense confrontation between Juan and Jacinta. She extracts from her husband not only information about Fortunata but also a seeming confession that the child is his, a quick denial – "Te juro que no. ¿Sabes de quién es ese niño? De una hijastra de Pepe Izquierdo que se llama Nicolasa" [I swear it's not true. Do you know who that kid belongs to? To the stepdaughter of Pepe Izquierdo named Nicolasa] (Soler et al. 14) – and then the real confession, in the presence of his mother and father, that Juan and Fortunata did indeed have a child who had died some three years before. His parents will not be "abuelos todavía" [grandparents yet] (16), and Barbarita and Jacinta break down in tears. The first scene comes to an emotional close.

The playwrights strive to reduce some of the novel's plot devices and extended narrative moments to brief scenes fit for the stage. Such economy – "síntesis" [synthesis] and "sintética" [synthetic] are the words used in several of the reviews – forced the adaptors to think clearly about the narrative arc of the work, and to make difficult choices about what to keep and what to discard: "La labor de transportar a la escena la famosísima novela era, pues, tan tentadora como ardua, difícil y temerosa ... han sabido [los adaptadores] conservar a la versión escénica ... los más sobresalientes valores artísticos, por lo menos aquellos de más evidente carácter dramático" [The job of moving this famous novel to the stage was, well, as tempting as it was hard, difficult, and daring ... the adaptors have managed to preserve in their stage version ... the most outstanding artistic values [of the novel], at least those that have the most evident dramatic flavour] (*La Libertad*, 17 October 1930). Turner points us towards the outside/inside nature of some of Galdós's prose, an observation that might help us understand how the novel (outside) morphs into the play (inside): "Outside, things change; inside, they remain the same" (35).

Where Galdós allowed himself the luxury of a long, poignant, and well-paced ending for the novel, the stage version opts for a vertiginous finale. In fewer than several hundred words at the play's close, the following events tumble out: Maxi tells Fortunata of Juanito's new girlfriend (Aurora), Fortunata pays Maxi to shoot said girlfriend, Fortunata decides to give her newborn son to Jacinta, and Maxi goes insane, crumpling "en gran abatimiento" [dejectedly]. "Desciende lentamente el telón" [The curtain slowly descends] (Soler et al. 68). Notably, the emotional power of the novel's ending dissipates in the rush to conclude the play; it shifts the pathos to Maxi, thereby diluting the promise of the narrative's title: "Dos historias de casadas" [Two Stories of Married Women].

Madrid was buzzing with theatre activity in the fall of 1930. While Xirgu was preparing for *Fortunata y Jacinta*'s debut at the Teatro Español, several other plays captured the public's attention. At the Teatro Fontalba, the Álvarez Quintero brothers' hit comedy, *Mariquilla Terremoto*, enjoyed continuing success. What is more, Carmen Díaz, the star of the Quintero brothers' play, earned a two-page spread in the 11 October issue of *La Esfera*, which gushed over "la garbosa arrogancia, la elegante y estatuaria apostura, el donaire y las bellas facetas de una joya escénica de tantos quilates como Carmen Díaz" [the proud haughtiness, the elegant and statuesque bearing, the grace and gorgeous facets of a scenic jewel of so many carats as is Carmen Díaz]. Díaz, who took over the part from Catalina Bárcena, had previously made the cover of *Estampa. Revista Gráfica y Literaria de la Actualidad Española y Mundial* (7 October) and would subsequently get another two-page notice in *Mundo Gráfico* (15 October), making it difficult for Xirgu to compete. The 17 October 1930 edition of *La Esfera* notes that Pedro Muñoz Seca's comedy, *El padre Alcalde*, was playing to "extraordinario éxito" [extraordinary success], after a hugely successful run through the provinces, at the Teatro Infanta Isabel, while others – Muñoz Seca's *La perulera* at the Teatro Comedia, *El alcalde de Zalamea* at the Teatro Calderón, *Papá Gutiérrez* (by F. Serrano Anguita) at the Teatro Alkazar (an "éxito clamoroso" [clamorous success] with "desfile de modas" [fashion show] thrown in), *Las brujas* ("enorme éxito" [huge hit]) at the Teatro Avenida, *Las pobrecitas mujeres* at the Teatro Cómico, and a "revista de éxito formidable" [a formidably successful revue], *El cine sonoro*, at the Teatro Fuencarral – competed for the public's attention and money. Xirgu herself was still starring in performances of Tirso's *La prudencia en la mujer*, which ran at the Teatro Español through 15 October; while she debuted in *Fortunata y Jacinta* on the evening of 16 October, she had one final performance of *La prudencia* to give on the afternoon of 17 October.

Somewhat oddly, in the section "La semana teatral" [Theatre Week] of *Estampa* (14 October 1930), we read mentions of *Mariquilla Terremoto* and *El padre Alcalde* (among others), but no mention of *Fortunata y Jacinta*. There is, however, a story, with a photograph, of the "inauguración de un monumento a Galdós" [inauguration of a monument to Galdós] in Las Palmas, the work of the sculptor Victorio Macho; another photo appears in *Mundo Gráfico* on 1 October 1930. Finally, on 21 October 1930, *Mundo Gráfico* publishes a photo of the actress: "He aquí a Fortunata, la heroína de Galdós, con su pañuelo a la cabeza y su mantón 'alfombrao', perfil madrileñísimo felizmente incorporado por Margarita Xirgu" [Here is Fortunata, Galdós's heroine, with her headscarf and "carpeted" shawl, a very Madrid-like profile happily embodied by Margarita Xirgu]. This is followed by a mention of the play itself.

> La cantera dramática de Galdós es inagotable. Llega ahora a la escena *Fortunata y Jacinta*, obra que, acaso, señala el ápice del género en el acervo novelístico del coloso. La adaptación presentaba dificultades notorias. Los Sres. Soler, Amarillas y López Alarcón han logrado vencerlas con singular reverencia para el texto original, del cual se nutre, casi en su totalidad, el diálogo. Personaje de raros claroscuros psicológicos, pese a su aparente simplicidad, es la figura de Fortunata, personificada por Margarita Xirgu con todos los cambiantes y tornasoles que demandan las vicisitudes espirituales de la infortunada mujer. Merece, asimismo, especial mención en la labor de los intérpretes el donoso desgarro madrileño de la señorita Pacheco y la notable caracterización del Sr. Maximino. El ilustre Bartolozzi, autor de los figurines y del decorado, ha estilizado los pormenores escénicos, alusivos a la época, con fina y certera intuición del ambiente. La combinación de cortinas y forillos es un alarde de sencillez y de gracia, que acredita el gusto y la maestría del artista.
>
> [Galdós's dramatic quarry is inexhaustible. *Fortunata y Jacinta*, a work that probably marks the apex of the genre in the novelistic oeuvre of this

> literary colossus, has now come to the stage. The adaptation presented major difficulties. Soler, Amarillas, and López Alarcón have managed to overcome them with notable reverence for the original text, from which the dialogue is taken almost completely. A character of rare psychological shadings, in spite of her apparent simplicity, Fortunata is brought to life by Margarita Xirgu with all of the reflections and iridescence that the spiritual vicissitudes demand of this unfortunate woman. One should mention as well Miss Pacheco's witty Spanish [Madrilenian] brazenness and Mr Maximino's notable characterization. The illustrious Bartolozzi, author of the sketches and sets, has stylized the scenic details, evocative of the period, with a refined and accurate intuition for the atmosphere. The combination of curtains and stage backdrops is a display of the simplicity and grace that underscores the good taste and expertise of the artist.]

Complicating matters for Xirgu and her company was the death of the great actor and impresario Fernando Díaz de Mendoza (María Guerrero's husband). News of his illness in Vigo hit the Madrid papers one day after *Fortunata*'s debut ("Don Fernando Díaz de Mendoza sufre un ataque de hemiplejía, siendo su estado de extrema gravedad") [Don Fernando Díaz de Mendoza has suffered a stroke and his condition is extremely serious] (*La Época*, 17 October 1930); he died three days later.

The play ran for twenty performances, about average for a new play at the time (see Vilches and Dougherty) and was taken seriously by the critics. Notices in Madrid's major newspapers – *ABC, El Debate, La Época, El Heraldo de Madrid, El Imparcial, La Libertad, El Sol*[4] – appeared the very next day, 17 October (a ninth review was published in *La Esfera* a week later, on 25 October), and they were mixed. Most praised the work, both of the adaptors and of the actors. One reviewer, J.G. Olmedilla, writing in *El Heraldo de Madrid*, laments what is lost in this adaptation, not merely because of the reduction in length, but because "por inteligentes y fielmente devotos que sean sus adaptadores, Galdós es impar e incopiable" [no matter how intelligent and faithful the adaptors might be, Galdós is singular and impossible to copy]. Yet he praises the authors' ability to "ofrecernos una versión teatral, verdaderamente moderna, sintética, de hoy, de un tema y unos caracteres de otro tiempo y otro autor" [offer us a truly modern and synthetic version for today's times of a theme and characters from another time and another author]. From his point of view, the reduction/adaptation is a bona fide success: "No se echa de menos en el espectáculo antecedente ni explicación alguna para la mejor comprensión de los personajes y sus tribulaciones.

Y no pesa ninguna escena. Ni se entibia el interés en ningún momento. Ni se encuentra un detalle indigno de la gran obra matriz" [One does not miss background information or any explanation for the better understanding of the characters and their tribulations. No scene is boring. Nor does one's interest flag at any moment. Nor can one find any detail unbecoming of the great work that gave it birth.] Another critic, writing in *El Imparcial*, asks, "¿Habrán logrado los autores de la adaptación escénica de *Fortunata y Jacinta* sustraerse a las dificultades y peligros – que dejo señalados a vuela pluma –, inherentes en su arriesgada intentona? ¿Habrán acertado a transplantar la famosa novela?" [Have the authors of the scenic adaptation of *Fortunata y Jacinta* managed to avoid the difficulties and dangers – that I mention here in passing – inherent in their rash attempt? Have they managed to transplant the famous novel?] His answer is clear:

> Volvía Galdós triunfante. Volvía empujando al tropel de criaturas encontradas en su bien amado rincón madrileño, y el público, ansioso de oírlas y de verlas agitándose con vida propia sobre el escenario, sentía emocionada impaciencia ... Luego, poco a poco, el soplo frío de la desilusión recorrió la sala. ¿Por qué se escamoteaba el parangón magnífico de Fortunata y Jacinta, base inmortal de la obra? Desaparecía, entre nieblas, la visión madrileña, se esfumaban personajes episódicos y disminuía la talla de otros centrales. Tan solo permanecía en pie "Fortunata", sostenida por el aliento poderoso de Margarita Xirgu, y, más al fondo, el centelleo de algunos rasgos de "Maxi Rubí", el pobre loco, amorosamente estudiado por Alfonso Muñoz. Y se sucedían las escenas, en cada una de las cuales se "refería" mucho y "sucedía" poco, languideciendo así, rápidamente, la acción escénica.
>
> [Galdós returned triumphant. He returned driving the mob of creatures found in his beloved corner of Madrid, and the public, keen to hear and see them come alive on the stage, felt excited, impatient ... Then, little by little, the cold breath of disappointment swept over the hall. Why conceal the magnificent relation between Fortunata and Jacinta, the immortal base of the work? The vision of Madrid disappeared in the fog, episodic characters faded out, and the importance of other central characters was diminished. The only one left standing was Fortunata, held up by the powerful spirit of Margarita Xirgu, and, on a deeper level, the sparkle of some features of "Maxi Rubi," the poor crazy man, lovingly inhabited by Alfonso Muñoz. And scene followed upon scene, in each of which much

was "told" and little "happened," and thereby the scenic action quickly wilted.]

Jorge de la Cueva, writing in *El Debate*, felt the same way, lamenting the loss of continuity and the jumping around ("se anda a saltos") that created a work that was not only immoral but also (his word) "peligrosa" [dangerous] (cited by Gil Fombellida 173). The author does not elaborate on his belief that this adaptation is "peligrosa," although the putative immorality of Fortunata and Juanito, when presented live and on stage, would certainly provoke moralists to resist such representations (as they always did).

The reviewers in general praised Margarita Xirgu's work, underscoring it as "una verdadera maravilla de realidad, de expresión y de vida" [a true marvel of reality, expression, and life] (Manuel Machado, writing in *La Libertad*, 17 October 1930), a performance that "se manifiesta con toda la pujanza de su abolengo escénico" [reveals itself with all the vigour of its scenic lineage] (*La Época*, 17 October 1930). *La Época* went so far as to defend Xirgu against "estos detractores de ahora que suponen a la insigne actriz amanereada y decadente" [those detractors today who claim the distinguished actress to be mannered and decadent], one of whom might have been the anonymous reviewer from *La Esfera* (25 October 1930), whose criticisms, perhaps for having had a full week to gestate, are more focused. It is telling that not once is Margarita Xirgu's name mentioned in his piece.[5] Also telling are the criticisms that reveal that some of the characters are "demasiado esfumados" [too vague] – in particular, Fortunata's rival Jacinta ("la borrosa rival" [the indistinct rival]), who in the play takes a secondary role to Xirgu's Fortunata: "*Fortunata y Jacinta*, en su variante escénica, es más bien *Fortunata* sola" [*Fortunata y Jacinta*, in its scenic version, is really *Fortunata* by herself] (Enrique Díez Canedo in *El Sol*, 17 October 1930).

At Fortunata's funeral, Segismundo tells Ponce that Fortunata's life was so rich and intriguing that "había allí elementos para un drama o novela" [it had the makings of a play or a novel] (Galdós 977). The stage version of *Fortunata y Jacinta* was enjoyed in its day, but then doomed to be forgotten (Díez Canedo complained of "cierta violencia congestiva" [a certain congestive violence] in the forced synthesis). It hardly brought Galdós back "triunfante" – certainly not to the theatre – as the author of the review in *El Imparcial* claimed. Spectators did not have the luxury to "pasear por las calles sin rumbo fijo, a la ventura, observando y pensando" [stroll along the streets without a fixed plan, as

12.1 Nicolás Rubín (Alejandro Maximino), Papitos (Pilar Muñoz), Fortunata (Margarita Xirgu) (*La Esfera*, 25 October 1930).

luck would take them, observing and thinking] (Galdós 919), one of the great pleasures given to the readers of Galdós's grand narrative. And while it is undoubtedly true that "an adaptation's double nature does not mean ... that proximity or fidelity to the adapted text should be the criterion of judgment or the focus of analysis" (Hutcheon 6), this stage adaptation at the least succeeded in reminding Madrid's public that one of the country's national treasures, a novelist whose brand of realism fell briefly out of favour in the first decades of the twentieth century, did indeed "[volver] triunfante" to reclaim his place as a vibrant and essential touchstone of Spanish literature. Adapting a novel to the stage is a "fraught transposition" (Hutcheon 36), but one that even Díez Canedo hoped might provoke viewers to "sacar del estante los cuatro tomos originarios, a entrarse en aquellas dos mil páginas prodigiosas" [take down from the bookshelf the four volumes of the original, and enter into those two thousand prodigious pages] (*El Sol*, 17 October 1930), not, when all was said and done, an entirely unworthy objective.

APPENDIX: CONTEMPORARY REVIEWS OF *FORTUNATA Y JACINTA* (1930)

A. *La Época* (17 October 1930)

Con ser mucho el mérito de los adaptadores de la joya galdosiana y magnífica la interpretación que ofrece el conjunto que dirigen Margarita Xirgu y Rivas Cherif, es evidente que el éxito de la jornada de anoche en el Español fue debido principalmente a la "mise en scène."

Si la ejecutoria artística de Salvador Bartolozzi no tuviese ya el más amplio refrendo, esta su labor en *Fortunata y Jacinta* serviría para acreditarle como una de las primeras figuras de la escenografía. La plástica de aquella época en todos sus matices se manifiesta con tal propiedad en *Fortunata y Jacinta*, que este solo hecho es aliciente bastante a producir el incentivo de conocer la adaptación de la obra, lograda con tanto acierto por los señores Soler, Amarillas y López Alarcón.

Han luchado estos señores por eludir el pie forzado de la languidez, que tanto perjudica el trasplante de la novela a la escena, y bien que el propósito ha sido labrado. En primer término con la fluidez del diálogo, que no llegó a pesar, y con la subdivisión de los tres actos en siete cuadros que renueva constantemente la atención del espectador.

La interpretación, repetimos, merece los más cumplidos elogios. Margarita Xirgu en la escena de amor con Juanito Santa Cruz y en la que cierra la obra, la muerte, dio el mentís más rotundo a estos detractores de ahora que suponen a la insigne actriz amanerada y decadente. El arte de la Xirgu, en estos momentos que señalamos se manifiesta con toda la pujanza de su abolengo escénico.

Admirable Julia Pacheco en el desgarro chulapo de su papel, que evoca la madrileña castiza de los barrios bajos, que ha dado paso a la tanguista adulterada de estos días.

Mereció Alfonso Muñoz cerrado aplauso en una de las escenas más culminantes de la obra. Es el suyo un papel de grandes dificultades, vencidas todas con fortuna por el notable actor. El cura que desempeña Alejandro Maximino es un tipo estudiado a conciencia y, cuidado en detalle. Muy graciosa Pilar Muñoz en la "Papitos".

Por esta somera referencia de los tres aspectos de la representación de *Fortunata y Jacinta* se infiere que el conjunto ofrece características enaltecedoras. El público, nunca remiso en dar su aprobación cuando así lo advierte, no desentonó un momento. Aplaudió al finalizar todos los actos, y en algunos pasajes con sincero entusiasmo. Llamó a escena a los adaptadores y rindió homenaje a la memoria del insigne Don Benito.

J. Morales Darias

B. *El Heraldo de Madrid* (17 October 1930)

Más que *Fortunata y Jacinta,* debería llamarse esta serie de viñetas escénicas al margen de la novela galdosiana, *Fortunata, mártir y madre,* por ejemplo, o *Fortunata* simplemente, como acaso más le hubiera gustado a Galdós. La figura de Jacinta, que en la novela es la mitad necesaria a la armonía en contrarios, apenas si en la versión teatral de López Alarcón, Amarillas y Soler es una sombra abocetada entre los trazos firmes y vigorosa de Fortunata, Maximiliano Rubín y La Dura – excelente creación de Julia Pacheco, que le valió un triunfo personal bien marcado.

Esto no es un reparo, sino una sencilla observación. Ni uno puede esperar sentir al propio Galdós redivivo en una adaptación ajena – porque, por inteligentes y fielmente devotos que sean sus adaptadores, Galdós es impar e incopiable – ni, puestos en este plano de expectación, podría defraudarnos en modo alguno la meritísima labor de Soler, López Alarcón y Amarillas. Encuentro de todo punto excelente su tarea. Más que por un vano afán – que no parecen haber sentido – de mixtificar un "pastiche" galdosiano, precisamente por el designio opuesto, que creo ver patente en su "variante escénica": el de ofrecernos una versión teatral, verdaderamente moderna, sintética, de hoy, de un tema y unos caracteres de otro tiempo y otro autor. La sombra de D. Benito está allí entre sus criaturas, pero su garra un poco ingenua, como todo lo grandioso, ha sido estilizada hábil – y respetuosamente – por unos escritores de talento, que saben construir y sobre todo eliminar lo que sería superfluo o recargado en una lámina, en una ilustración escénica, como antes he dicho que me parece cada cuadro de la *Fortunata y Jacinta* estrenada anoche, por Margarita Xirgu en el Español.

No se echa de menos en el espectáculo antecedente ni explicación alguna para la mejor comprensión de los personajes y sus tribulaciones. Y no pesa ninguna escena. Ni se entibia el interés en ningún momento. Ni se encuentra un detalle indigno de la gran obra matriz.

En cuanto a la presentación – dirigida por Bartolozzi en decorados y vestimenta – no cabe hacer sino elogiarla sin reservas. Lo mismo que la interpretación, de todo punto cuidada y respetuosa. Destacaron en ella, pariguales, la ilustre primera actriz Margarita Xirgu y el primer actor Alfonso Muñoz, personalmente ovacionado en dos finales de acto, por su certera visión del enclenque protagonista, el desdichado Maxi. Margarita Xirgu ha estudiado con gran amor el tipo de Fortunata, y, sobre todo, en las escenas de feminidad desgarrada o apasionada maternidad, estuvo de todo punto admirable. El público la ovacionó con largueza, así como a los adaptadores. En el numeroso reparto distinguiéronse también Josefina Santaularia, Pascuala Mesa, Eloísa Vigo, Mimí Muñoz, José Bruguera, Fernando Venegas, José Cañizares y Alejandro Maximino, que alcanzó otro merecido triunfo en el papel de sacerdote.

Al fin de la representación, entre grandes aplausos a todos, tuvo que hablar Alfonso Muñoz, en nombre de Margarita Xirgu y de los adaptadores, para dar las gracias y dedicar el fervor de tanto aplauso a la sombra insigne del genio.

J. G. O[lmedilla].

C. *El Imparcial* (17 October 1930)

Los comentarios amables, sugeridos por el estreno de obras dramáticas inspiradas en novelas famosas, forzosamente adquieren aspecto de lugar común, porque la disparidad entre "novela" y "teatro" es manifiesta y vulgar.

No así las diferencias entre una novela y su escenificación, con ser tan hondas, y tan diversos sus procedimientos, que el comediógrafo más experto titubea y vacila, cuando intenta llevar al teatro, el enorme bloque de una novela analítica, descriptiva, ampliamente ambientada y construida a trazo lento.

La trama es abrumadora. Ingrata. Es preciso depurar la trama minuciosa de la novela hasta llegar a la acción sintética, desbrozando el material inerte, que en el teatro estorba. Arrancar de la línea sinuosa de cada personaje, sus caracteres de "ser vivo"; estudiar, movimientos y desarrollo en sentido rectilíneo, para crear la "situación" teatral, alada, transparente y eficaz ... y todo ello, conservando, incólume, la emoción original de la novela, sus figuras capitales, tendencias y finalidad.

Ímproba tarea, con más posibilidades de error que de acierto, cuyo peligro y dificultades suelen ser insuperables para el novelista, cuando se obstina en realizarla, enamorado de su obra y seducido por la boga del libro sembrador de fervores en el público.

La obra teatral, si ha de ser fecunda, exige visión inicial determinante, con imperativo categórico, de su destino. Los novelistas que, por admirable potencialidad cerebral pudieron ser, al mismo tiempo, autores dramáticos, suministran prueba plena de esa inevitable diversidad de orígenes y de realización. Aquellas de sus obras "pensadas" y engendradas para vivir la vida de teatro, aun cuando por motivos puramente circunstanciales (compromiso editorial, carencia de teatro idóneo, etc.), adoptaran, para salir a la luz pública, apariencias de novela, conservaron perpetuamente las características de su germinación recobradas con brío avasallador, algún día pudo el autor devolverles su prístina forma.

En cambio, aquellas otras concepciones del propio autor realizadas al correr de las páginas del libro, pocas veces lograron perenne lozanía al trasplantarse sobre las áridas tablas del escenario. En su transformación habían perdido el suave aroma del ambiente, las ciclópeos muros de la construcción y las habilidades de observación y análisis.

En el frondoso teatro de Galdós y de sus adaptadores – y ninguno [*sic*] otro podría servirnos mejor en este caso – , abundan los ejemplos de ambos tipos de obra: *El abuelo, Realidad, La loca de la casa, Doña Perfecta, Electra, La de San Quintín, Los condenados, Voluntad, Alma y vida, Sor Simona, Marianela, Zaragoza, Gerona, El audaz,* etc.

Renuncio a subrayar las que fueron escritas por Galdós "pensando" en el teatro, y las que, ni él, ni sus adaptadores, lograron aclimatar en la escena. La cultura del lector suple esta digresión en gracia a la brevedad.

¿Habrían logrado los autores de la adaptación escénica de *Fortunata y Jacinta* sustraerse a las dificultades y peligros – que dejo señalados a vuela pluma – , inherentes en su arriesgada intentona? ¿Habrían acertado a trasplantar la famosa novela?

Con esa interrogante mental acudieron anoche al Español cuantos devotos de Galdós y de Margarita Xirgú caben en la espléndida sala, y ... comenzó la representación, acogida con interés y contento extraordinarios.

Volvía Galdós triunfante. Volvía empujando al tropel de criaturas encontradas en su bien amado rincón madrileño, y el público, ansioso de oírlas y de verlas agitándose con vida propia sobre el escenario, sentía emocionada impaciencia ... Luego, poco a poco, el soplo frío de la desilusión recorrió la sala. ¿Por qué se escamoteaba el parangón magnífico de Fortunata y Jacinta, base inmortal de la obra? Desaparecía, entre nieblas, la visión madrileña, se esfumaban personajes episódicos y disminuía la talla de otros centrales. Tan solo permanecía en pie "Fortunata", sostenida por el aliento poderoso de Margarita Xirgu, y, más al fondo, el centelleo de algunos rasgos de "Maxi Rubí", el pobre loco, amorosamente estudiado por Alfonso Muñoz.

Y se sucedían las escenas, en cada una de las cuales se "refería" mucho y "sucedía" poco, languideciendo así, rápidamente, la acción escénica.

Pero aquí es preciso recordar, para ser justos, que los autores de *Fortunata y Jacinta*, al rotular su obra "variante escénica de algunos pasajes de la famosa novela", procedieron con honrada sinceridad. Dándose cuenta de la imposibilidad del traslado total de la novela al teatro redujeron sus aspiraciones a dibujar lo que ahora se llama "estampas literarias" de unos cuantos pasajes de *Fortunata y Jacinta*, y justo es consignar que lo han logrado.

Y aunque solo fuera por haber evocado respetuosos la sacra memoria galdosiana, los señores Soler y Amarillas, merecerían el aplauso unánime que el público tuvo a bien tributarles. En cuanto a López Alarcón, maestro en todas las artes del teatro, si necesitase de nuevos títulos meritorios, habríalos obtenido por este formidable trabajo.

En cuanto a la interpretación, como antes dejo apuntado, permanece en pie, sobre la obra, culminante y soberana, la de "Fortunata", por Margarita Xirgu, que, supliendo con su talento mutilaciones y lagunas impuestas por la redacción teatral, supo exteriorizar todos sus manías: inferioridad mental, feminidad ingenua, apasionamiento sexual e infinito goce materno...cuantas complejidades paradógicas forman aquel estupendo estudio de mujer. Seguramente, así la "vio" Galdós, y al suponerlo, dejo tributado el mayor elogio a la insuperable creación de esa gran actriz.

Julia Pacheco, graciosa chulapona. Correctas, Santaularia, Mesa, Vigo y las hermanas Muñoz.

Alfonso Muñoz afortunadísimo en toda la obra, y muy justos Maximino y Bruguera.

Cuidada la postura en escena, y atinadísima alguna de las decoraciones, y perfectos los trajes sobre figurines del exquisita artista Bartolozzi.

Terminada la representación, Alfonso Muñoz, en nombre de adaptadores y comediantes, dedicó los aplausos recibidos a la mayor gloria de Galdós.

Luis París.

D. *La Libertad* (17 October 1930)

Si hubiera que citar un solo título entre toda la ingenia obra de Galdós como el más alto, característico y representativo de esa misma obra, siempre habría que llamar a Galdós el autor de *Fortunata y Jacinta*.

La labor de transportar a la escena la famosísima novela era, pues, tan tentadora como ardua, difícil y temerosa.

Llenos de una gran buena fe, y sobre todo de un ferventísimo amor a Galdós y a la maravilla de realidad y de honda poesía de la vida española que es *Fortunata y Jacinta*, Enrique López Alarcón – gran poeta – y sus compañeros los excelentes escritores Soler y Amarillas emprendieron y realizaron el temerario y honroso paso.

Ya el hecho de llevar al teatro *Fortunata y Jacinta* merece bien de las Letras y viene a enriquecer noblemente la dramática española.

Pero a ello hay que añadir el notable acierto de los adaptadores, que han sabido conservar a la versión escénica de *FJ* los más sobresalientes valores artísticos, por lo menos aquellos de más evidente carácter dramático.

El decorado, de Bartolozzi, es algo verdaderamente artístico, que viene a mostrar no sólo con justicia expresiva la obra, sino a sugerir de modo admirable el ambiente.

La creación de Fortunata en escena por la señora Xirgú es una verdadera maravilla de realidad, de expresión y de vida, sobre todo en los momentos álgidos de pasión y de desesperada ternura.

Muy bien Josefina Santaularia en la Jacinta; Pascuala Mesa, en la Doña Lupe; archibién Julia Pachelo, en la Mauricia, y bien en los respectivos papeles Pilar y Mimí Muñoz, y entre ello, Alfonso Muñoz, José Bruguera y Alejandro Maximino.

El público aplaudió encantado todos los actos y cada uno de los cuadros.

M[anuel]. M[achado].

E. *El Sol* (17 October 1930)

Pido al lector que me dispense si esperaba encontrar aquí, una vez más, las acostumbradas consideraciones acerca de lo difícil que es trasplantar un asunto de la novela al teatro. Bastará que recuerde los límites en que necesariamente se ha de encerrar una acción dramática, y no ya la amplitud que es propia del género novelesco, en abstracto, sino la rica humanidad que se mueve en las demás páginas de *Fortunata y Jacinta*, páginas tan conocidas de todos, que su recuerdo va unido a una porción de circunstancias del vivir madrileño, hasta tal punto, que lo vivo y lo fingido por el autor llegan a confundirse en las revueltas de la memoria.

Fortunata y Jacinta es uno de esos libros de plenitud que son corona eterna de un escritor; no hubiera compuesto Galdós otra novela, y por ello sería par de los mayores en su patria y en su tiempo. La adaptación o "variante escénica" que han llevado a la escena del Español los Sres. Soler y Amarillas, ya conocidos como adaptadores de alguna otra novela galdosiana, asistidos ahora por un hombre de la experiencia y gusto de Enrique López Alarcón, tiene por precedente el arreglo o "versión escénica" en cinco actos que los dos primeros publicaron en *Los Contemporáneos* (cuadernos del 13 y 20 de noviembre de 1924), y que, reducida a cuatro actos, estrenó en Valencia la compañía Díaz-Artigas.

La "variante" ahora estrenada se divide en siete cuadros, repartidos en tres actos. Cuadros breves, en los que entran situaciones no aprovechadas en la antigua adaptación y que concentran mucho las escenas y recortan los diálogos de aquélla. Concentran demasiado tal vez. El que conozca bien la novela – y el que esto escribe acaba de leerla de nuevo, sin perder párrafo, llevado de maravilla en maravilla y saliéndose de su primer propósito, que consistía en hojear e ir recordando – advertirá en el trabajo de condensación, sobre todo en el cuadro último, el de la muerte de Fortunata, cierta violencia congestiva; encontrará demasiado esfumados algunos caracteres, todos los de la familia Santa Cruz, sin excluir a Jacinta, y sin duda falseado el de Guillermina, esto es, primado de esa aureola de santidad sugerida por Galdós con inaudita lucidez, sin el menor énfasis.

Para resumir la impresión que estos siete cuadros producen no encuentro comparación más adecuada que la de una edición provista de ilustraciones. Parece que va el espectador enterándose de lo que ocurre por las ilustraciones y no por el texto. Y no me refiero a la plástica – notabilísima, en que Salvador Bartolozzi ha sabido encontrar el carácter de época, trayendo la acción unos años más acá de los tiempos en que Galdós la sitúa, sin mengua de su sentido, pero sin que se vea del todo la necesitad del traslado – , sino a la parte literaria, obligadamente rapsódica. En ella se ve amor a Galdós, gracia en el corte, y se respira sobre todo un aroma que mueve a sacar del estante los cuatro tomos originarios, a entrarse en aquellas dos mil páginas prodigiosas.

Fortunata y Jacinta, en su "variante escénica", es más bien *Fortunata* sola. Se va siguiendo de lejos el camino de pasión de esa criatura nacida en la mente de Galdós con todos los atributos de la humanidad; la mujer extraviada porque fue lo que los otros quisieron que fuese, vuelta siempre al primer amor, engrandecida por la idea de la maternidad y purificada por el rigor del destino. Margarita Xirgu supo expresar, singularmente en una frase, insuperablemente sentida, cuando revela su desamor por Maxi, y en las dos escenas, de amor con Juanito

Santa Cruz y de arrebato frente a Jacinta, así como en su gesto y actitud junto a la cuna del hijo, cuando le cree amenazado por Rubín en el cuadro último, la condición bravía de la heroína galdosiana. Josefina Santaularia, en la borrosa rival; Julia Pacheco, admirable en el desgarro de Mauricia "la Dura"; Pilar Muñoz, la gracia misma en la "Papitos"; Alfonso Muñoz, Bruguera, Maximino, se destacaron entre los intérpretes.

De los aplausos con que el público acogió casi todos los finales de cuadro, muy expresivos en algunos, el primer actor hizo, al final, dedicatoria al autor glorioso de *Fortunata y Jacinta*; pero ya en uno de los primeros cuadros salió a corresponder a los plácemes uno de los adaptores, en representación, sin duda, de la colectividad.

E. Díez Canedo.

F. *La Esfera* (25 October 1930)

¿Para qué plantear nuevamente el viejo problema de la adaptación teatral de las novelas?

Cuando se pensaba que novela y drama eran géneros no sólo distintos, sino antitéticos, y se oponía como sus respectivos caracteres esenciales el análisis y la síntesis, ese problema, aunque aparentemente irresoluble, podía tener interés; pero cuando los años y los conceptos más amplios del arte nos han traído tantos dramas sintéticos y tantas comedias analíticas, la discusión genérica carece de sentido, y en todo caso podría discutirse específicamente la posibilidad de adaptación escénica de una novela determinada.

Puesta la cuestión en este terreno, difícilmente señalará nadie como modelo de novelas adaptables *Fortunata y Jacinta*, de Galdós; y sin embargo, es evidente que una adaptación de esa magna obra ha logrado en el Teatro Español el favor del público.

Claro está que en esa adaptación no aparece íntegra – ¿y cómo podría aparecer? – la novela de Galdós, que es tal vez, entre todas las maravillosas producciones del maestro, la que más hondamente penetra y más lejos busca los motivos de conducta de cada personaje; pero aún sin eso, quedando cada figura dramática como una silueta y borrados tantos personajes secundarios – enormemente avaloradores de los principales – y tanto aparente episodio más claramente explicativo de la acción, el drama de *Fortunata y Jacinta* es un drama entero y verdadero, que, comparado con otros muy aplaudidos, vence con mucho en la comparación; porque aún conserva de la novela original fuerza y pasión en los caracteres e interés emotivo, por añadidura, en la acción.

"Fortunata", y más aún "Jacinta", y, como ellas, "Maximiliano", "Doña Lupe", "Mauricia *la Dura*", "Juanito Santacruz" y, en suma, todos los personajes, tienen en la novela, naturalmente, más fuerte complexión y más acusada fisonomía.

Todos están allí admirablemente definidos, con aquella portentosa seguridad de trazo con que Galdós vestía el natural en sus novelas; pero precisamente porque allí tienen ese enorme rigor, aunque la adaptación escénica los esfume, por necesidades del género dramático que, aun prescindiendo de todas las unidades, ha de encerrarse en estrechos límites de tiempo y de espacio, tienen aún fuerza suficiente para que las siluetas se destaquen y se tengan de pie, recias y fuertes, con la solidez del natural de que fueron copiadas.

En eso, como en todo, la novela galdosiana es como una cantera inagotable, pletórica de materiales, que, aun utilizados sin la maestría suprema de su creador, dan siempre la sensación estética suficiente para que se impongan como obras verdaderamente artísticas.

Esto ocurre con la versión escénica – variante de otras anteriores – de *Fortunata y Jacinta*. Las figuras principales resultan para los conocedores de la novela como copias indecisas, desvaídas; pero, aun así, tan sólidas como las de muchos dramas y comedias generalmente aplaudidos, y aún se lo parecen más a los que no tienen, por no haber gozado el deleite de la lectura, aquel insuperable término de comparación.

A éstos, en cambio, y en castigo a su culpa – y no es venial la de no haber leído *Fortunata y Jacinta* – , habrán de parecerles demasiado planas y borrosas aquellas figuras del ambiente de "Jacinta" que aparecen en el primer cuadro, innecesariamente tal vez, porque en el drama no sirven, como en la novela, para definir y explicar las figuras de "Juanito Santacruz" y de su esposa. Para que ese cuadro tuviese la eficacia analítica de los caracteres que podría dar a la "Jacinta" del drama el relieve de que carece y a "Juanito Santacruz" una personalidad escénica a que no se acusa, sería necesario que ese cuadro no fuera una sucesión de escenas cortadas de modo excesivamente lenormandiano en el bloque de la novela, sino un verdadero cuadro construído con los materiales de esas mismas escenas, y de algunas más, con unidad de composición.

Así resulta el cuadro segundo. "Doña Lupe", la de los pavos; "Don Nicolás Rubín", "Papitos" y "Mauricia *la Dura*" llevan de tal modo, grabado con tanta fuerza, el sello galdosiano, que aun esfumadas por la adaptación, que nos la muestra sólo en un momento de su proceso evolutivo, y deformadas, a veces al menos, por la interpretación, son aquellas mismas figuras vivas que nos deleitaron tantas veces cuando, reiteradamente, leímos la novela.

El cuadro tercero, las escenas en el convento de las Micaelas, resulta empequeñecido, incluso por la reducción del decorado; "Mauricia *la Dura*" desaparece de escena cuando su figura tendría un máximo interés dramático y nos falta la luz cálida del patio, bajo el sol que aún nos parecería poco para poner el cuadro escénico a la altura del capítulo de la novela, copiado de un aire libre de Sorolla.

En los cuadros restantes, hasta siete, los adaptadores han procurado ir directamente a la acción. Cada uno de ellos está hecho para mostrar un momento culminante de la novela. El cuarto, la traición de "Fortunata", y el enloquecimiento de "Maximiliano", impotente ante la pareja traidora; el quinto, el encuentro entre las dos enamoradas de "Santacruz"; el sexto, para que "Fortunata" exponga las ideas galdosianas que anteponen la maternidad a toda otra sanción del vínculo y que la misma "Jacinta" tiene en lo subconsciente, por lo menos; y el séptimo, para llegar, con la muerte de "Fortunata" junto a la cuna de su segundo hijo, al desenlace, que, por la precipitación con que los arregladores han querido hacerlo, tiene en algún momento un matiz melodramático.

Sería inútil discutir si esos momentos son, en realidad, los más interesantes de la novela. De *Fortunata y Jacinta* podrían darse aun muchas y muy diversas versiones escénicas. Los autores de la estrenada ahora nos han dado la suya. En otras aparecerían otras figuras y otras escenas, y se parecerían más a las que creó Galdós: "Guillermina", "Estupiñá" y el mismo "Ido del Sagrario", a quien, para conocerle bien, sería necesario buscar en otras novelas de Galdós. Tal vez la imprecisión de esas figuras es defecto que debe ser señalado; pero, en el fondo, y sin que hagamos ninguna aplicación – y menos a los autores de la versión estrenada ahora – de las adaptaciones escénicas de novelas magnas, podría decirse también: "calumnia, que algo queda"; y si la novela es como *Fortunata y Jacinta*, de Galdós siempre quedará mucho, y por lo menos el deseo de leer o releer la novela.

La interpretación de una obra semejante no puede nunca convencer a quien por amorosa lectura, reiterada, de la novela, tenga ya dentro de sí, por una creación interna, imágenes firmes de los personajes, tanto más fuerte cuanto más conocida la obra total de Galdós, en que los personajes viven diversos momentos de su existencia en novelas diferentes.

Por mi parte, no confrontaré las imágenes mostradas por los actores del Español con las forjadas por mí; todo lo más a que podría llevarme esa confrontación sería a decir que no hay igualdad, ni a veces semejanza, entre unos y otros. Pero, ¿cómo demonstrar que las mías son las exactas?

Para pensarlo, habría yo de creerme infalible; y Dios me ha liberado de ese error.

En cuanto a la escenografía, tal vez hubiera sido mejor situar la versión en la época de la novela; pero como ésta resulta, en cuanto a las figuras por lo menos, vistosa, y en cuanto al decorado habría que discutirle desde un punto de vista general, no cabe aquí ese análisis.

Si fuese cosa de reparar en detalles, habría que pedir la desaparición rápida de un velador, con su florero y todo, que aprece pintado en uno de los telones.

NOTES

I would like to thank Carmen Menéndez Onrubia and Gustavo Pellón for their generous help while I was preparing this study.

1 The 1980 TV series, directed by Mario Camus and starring Ana Belén, ran for some 10 hours (600 minutes in 10 episodes) (http://www.rtve.es/television/fortunata-jacinta). An earlier theatrical release (1970), directed by Angelino Fons, ran for 132 minutes.

2 *Fortunata y Jacinta. Versión escénica en cinco actos, de la novela del mismo título de Benito Pérez Galdós*. Published in *Los Contemporáneos* 16.825–6 (13 and 20 November 1924). According to Díez Canedo (in his review in *El Sol*), a reduced version of that play was performed in Valencia by the Díaz-Artigas company.

3 The words "abandonito," "comidita," "santita," "camisita," and "riquín" never appear in Galdós's novel. This infantilization of the couple continues throughout the first scene.

4 Gil Fombellida mentions the reviews in *El Heraldo, La Libertad, El Sol, El Liberal, El Debate*, and *ABC* (172).

5 While the review is not signed, it is followed in this issue of *La Esfera* by two photos, then a review of Benavente's *Gente conocida*, signed by Alejandro Miquis, who could possibly be the author of the criticism in question.

WORKS CITED

Abbott, H. Porter. *The Cambridge Introduction to Narrative*. Cambridge: Cambridge UP, 2002. Print.

Aguilera Sastre, Juan, and Manuel Aznar Soler. *Cipriano de Rivas Cherif y el teatro español de su época (1891–1967)*. Madrid: Publicaciones de la Asociación de Directores de Escena, 1999. Print.

Barnette, Jane. *Adapturgy: The Dramaturge's Art and Theatrical Adaptation*. Carbondale: Southern Illinois University Press, 2017. Print.

Boyum, Joy Gould. *Double Exposure: Fiction into Film*. New York: Broadway Books, 1985. Print.

Breen, Robert S. *Chamber Theater*. Evanston, IL: Wm. Caxton, 1986. Print.

Cardwell, Sarah. *Adaptation Revisited: Television and the Classic Novel*. Manchester: Manchester UP, 2002. Print.

Díez-Canedo, Enrique. *El Sol*, 17 October 1930. Print.

Elliott, Kamila. *Rethinking the Novel/Film Debate*. Cambridge: Cambridge UP, 2003. Print.

La Época, 17 October 1930. Print.

La Esfera, 11, 17, and 25 October 1930. Print.

García Lorenzo, Luciano. "La denominación de los géneros teatrales en España durante el siglo XIX y el primer tercio del siglo XX." *Segismundo* 5–6 (1967): 191–9. Print.

Gil Fombellida, María del Carmen. *Rivas Cherif, Margarita Xirgu y el teatro de la II República*. Madrid: Fundamentos, 2003. Print.

Gómez García, Manuel. *Diccionario del teatro*. Madrid: Akal, 1997. Print.

El Heraldo de Madrid, 17 October 1930. Print.

Hutcheon, Linda. *A Theory of Adaptation*. New York: Routledge, 2006. Print.

El Imparcial, 17 October 1930. Print.

Lessing, Gotthold Ephraim. *Laocoön: An Essay upon the Limits of Painting and Poetry*. 1766. Trans. Edward Allen McCormick. Indianapolis: Bobbs-Merrill, 1962. Print.

La Libertad, 17 October 1930.

McGaha, Michael D. *The Theatre in Madrid during the Second Republic*. London: Grant and Cutler, 1979. Print.

Mittell, Jason. *Narrative Theory and Adaptation*. New York and London: Bloomsbury, 2017. Print.

Pérez Galdós, Benito. *Fortunata y Jacinta*. In *Obras completas*, ed. Federico Carlos Sainz de Robles. 8 vols. Madrid: Aguilar, 1970–1. 5:447–981. Print.

Rivas Cherif, Cipriano de. *Cómo hacer teatro. Apuntes de orientación profesional en las artes y oficios del teatro español*. Valencia: Pre-Textos, 1991. Print.

Sánchez-Trincado, José Luis. *Galdós*. Caracas: Elite, 1943. Print.
El Sol, 17 October 1930. Print.
Soler, Antonio, M. Díez de Amarillas, and E. López Alarcón. *Fortunata y Jacinta. Variante escénica de algunos pasajes de la famos anovela de Galdós, dialogada y refundida en siete cuadros (tres actos).* Estrenada en el teatro Español, de Madrid, el 16 de octubre de 1930. Madrid: Prensa Moderna, 1930. First published in *El Teatro Moderno* 6.273 (15 November 1930): 1–68. Print.
Turner, Harriet S. *Benito Pérez Galdós: Fortunata and Jacinta*. Cambridge: Cambridge UP, 1992. Print.
Vilches, María Francisca, and Dru Dougherty. *La escena madrileña entre 1926 y 1931. Un lustro de transición*. Madrid: Fundamentos, 1997. Print.

13 When Reality Is Too Harsh to Bear: Role-Play in Juan Marsé's "Historia de detectives"

STEPHANIE SIEBURTH

Juan Marsé's short story "Historia de detectives" presents four adolescent boys who play at being detectives in postwar Barcelona, following people down the street and attempting to discover their predicaments under the Franco regime. The boys' fathers are jailed or otherwise absent, and other male adults on the Republican side whom the boys encounter on the streets have given in to despair; one of them will commit suicide before the end of the story. In this case, reality is too unremittingly terrifying, sordid, and depressing to confront directly. The movies (principally *film noir*, but also cowboy movies and others) provide the boys with plots and role models to imitate as they follow people through the city.

Marsé rewrites *Don Quijote* as he creates his young male characters whose imaginations have been formed by the movies and who actively imitate them. As we will see at the end of the chapter, Marsé's turn to Cervantes in 1987 has much in common in its structure, techniques, and purpose with the turn to Cervantes in the 1870s and 1880s by the great realist novelists. In analysing Marsé's story, I will follow Harriet Turner's emphasis on Cervantes, and on Américo Castro's prologue to the *Quijote,* as essential to an understanding of realism. Castro asserts that Cervantes's approach to reality was not about the characteristics of objects, not an answer to the question "What *is* this?" but rather an exploration of mental activity: "What force outside [a person] is affecting his inner consciousness and moving it to action?" (Castro 78). He borrows a term from the fourteenth-century don Sem Tob, called "la fazienda," or the "'inner doing' of consciousness" (Turner, *Fortunata and Jacinta* 9).[1] The major force moving Don Quixote to action is the act of reading; books "incite" him

(Castro 99), instilling him with bravery and desire for adventure. I will explore a similar psychological process as it occurs in Marsé's boys, who are trying to create themselves by imitating brave male detectives. Realism here refers to the representation of mental activity, including the workings of the imagination. But I will also be exploring the idea of realism as both an imitation of real spaces and a rewriting of literary texts. Like many realist novels, this story is a compelling representation of an external reality, in this case postwar Barcelona, with its identifiable streets, stores, and cinemas. But it is also a masterful rewriting of other texts. Marsé's text is a rewriting not only of his own childhood or his own novels (Sherzer) but also of the classical detective story that began with Edgar Allan Poe, and its offshoot, the hardboiled detective story, which was brought to the cinema in *film noir*. Attention to these intertexts will be crucial to understanding how they serve the boys in the effort of psychological survival. But in his construction of space, climate, and time in the story, Marsé is also rewriting Leopoldo Alas's *La Regenta;* both texts use the high-low opposition, the dislocation of time, and the dissolution of the earth-water opposition in order to create a moral framework for their plots, though to very different effect.

In the Spanish postwar period, the use of the imagination, fuelled by popular culture, was nothing less than a crucial survival tool, as has been attested by many leading Spanish intellectuals (Martín Gaite, *El cuarto* 179; *Canciones para después de una guerra;* Vázquez Montalbán xx). If Marsé's boys play at being detectives, it is because play is a multifaceted process that contributes in multiple ways to their survival. William Sherzer points out that the play of the fictional boys in "Historia de detectives" is based on the real play of Marsé and his friends on the streets of Barcelona in his childhood (85–6). In this chapter, I draw on the writings of child psychoanalyst Selma Fraiberg and psychologist Marjorie Taylor, as well as drama therapists Robert Landy and Sue Jennings, to examine what effects the role-play of these fictional adolescents would have on their ability to stay alive. By exploring what is *psychologically* real in the boys' intimate engagement with the detective genre and other movie roles, I will show how playing the role of the detective enables the boys to resolve, at least in part, several dilemmas, both emotional and practical, that threaten their survival in the unremittingly harsh reality of postwar Spain. Thus, where Sherzer and Fernández have rightly emphasized the importance of the boys' telling of stories to one another in "Historia de detectives," I will focus more on the importance of their *activity*, as they imitate Humphrey Bogart and follow people across the city.[2]

A plot summary is in order for those unfamiliar with Marsé's story, which takes place about a decade after the end of the Civil War. Four boys, sons of the losers of the war, play at being detectives, inspired especially by *film noir*. Their "headquarters" is a ruined Lincoln Continental mired in a field of mud in the poorest quarter of the city. The oldest boy, Juanito Marés, is the head detective who gives the orders. He remains in the car as the younger boys – Roca, David, and Jaime – tail people across the city, attempting to deduce what their situation is. One of these boys, Roca, narrates the story. Over the course of the story, Roca will follow Sra. Yordi, an attractive woman new to their neighbourhood and the mother of a small child, often in tears, who, gossip tells, has been abandoned by her husband. As she walks through the city, Roca will eavesdrop on her unwilling conversation with a Francoist baker, and then on her encounter with a man in a bar, with whom she soon afterwards leaves in a taxi. Meanwhile, David is following an actor, dressed in pajamas and a robe and slippers, made up for the theatre. Curiously, the actor appears to be following Roca. While Roca and Sra. Yordi are in the bar, the actor remains outside, looking in the window and crying like a baby. Unaware of his surroundings, he drops a wallet that David picks up; it contains an old photograph of a happy couple, and five *duros*, a significant amount of money at the time. Having told their stories back at the Lincoln, the boys listen as Marés weaves a story about the two adults. The actor, he says, was actually following Sra. Yordi, and is her husband, who has abandoned her not for lack of love but because he is hiding from the police. Where the younger boys believe Sra. Yordi is going to the bar to meet her lover, Marés believes that the man in the bar is actually a member of the Falange, with whom Sra. Yordi has asked to meet in order to get a favour for her husband the actor, perhaps by providing a guarantee of loyalty to the regime that might get him out of trouble. Sex is the price she will have to pay for this favour. The boys are sceptical that the actor is actually related to Sra. Yordi. The next day, the younger boys learn that the actor has hanged himself, and rush to the scene to see the macabre spectacle; Marés observes them mockingly, sure that the suicide corroborates his deductions. The story closes a few days later when Marés obliges the boys to return the wallet to Sra. Yordi, who examines the photo and the money, murmurs "Gracias," and walks away, neither affirming nor denying that these objects belong to her. The story ends without any certainty as to whether Marés has correctly "solved" the case.

Carmela Hernández García sees the principal function of the game the boys play as an escape into a "dorada ficción," in which they will stay until the suicide forces them back into reality (52). The escape, she argues, is a necessity: "Hay que ignorar el ambiente inmundo del barrio para poder sobrevivir" [They must ignore the filthy atmosphere of the neighbourhood in order to survive] (53). William Sherzer reads the story metafictionally, showing how the oldest boy, who gives the orders and makes the deductions, is called Juanito Marés and is a thinly disguised version of the author. Reading Marés's relationship to the story's narrator, Roca, as a representation of the relationship between the author and the first-person narrator, Sherzer sees the story as an autobiographical look backward, a dialogue with Marsé's previous works, and a representation of Marsé's own youth among a group of poor boys on the streets of Barcelona. He notes that, both in "Historia de detectives" and in Marsé's earlier novel *Si te dicen que caí*, "young boys invent fantastic adventures in order to escape from [their] poverty-stricken world" (86).

Álvaro Fernández has a very different view of the relationship between the film-inspired stories the boys tell and the surrounding reality, and his observations lay crucial foundations for my own study. These stories, inspired by real people around the boys, but saturated with fictional elements derived from popular culture, are called *aventis* by Marsé, and they first appear in the novel *Si te dicen que caí*. They are essentially oral stories, made up on the spur of the moment, and Fernández points out that the role of the listeners is that of an active public, who may insist that the story be changed by casting doubt on any of its elements. These *aventis* have several functions, according to Fernández. First, in a world where everything is falling apart, they make it possible to tell a story: "Contar, en las novelas de Marsé, implica poner en juego un marco cultural degradado (cine 'malo,' novelas 'baratas') ... y aplicarlo sobre una realidad más degradada aún – la miserable (material y culturalmente) posguerra civil – para estetizarla y poder llevar adelante la narración" [Telling a story, in Marsé's novels, involves taking a degraded cultural framework ("bad" films, "cheap" novels) ... and applying it to an even more degraded reality – the culturally and materially wretched post–Civil War period – in order to aestheticize it and be able to keep the narration going] (66).

Secondly, these stories, formed of a mixture of pop culture and surrounding reality, provide a possible role for poor boys on the losing side who have been condemned to poverty and idleness by the Regime:

"Las aventis constituyen la única posibilidad de vislumbrar un protagonismo, de tener una identidad *otra* que los redima de la condena con que el régimen perseguirá a sus enemigos" [*Aventis* constitute the only possibility of glimpsing a way to play an important role, to have a different identity that could redeem them from the sentence with which the regime persecuted its enemies] (Fernández 68–9). Furthermore, the boys' *aventis* incorporate rumours and gossip that circulate in the neighbourhood, rumours about denunciations and arrests, rumours about the dictatorship that can't be published or spoken on the street, and allow them to circulate, mixed with fictional elements from the movies; the effect is to permit the articulation of speech by those for whom it is prohibited and marginalized. Finally, the *aventis* work to transform the value system imposed by the dictatorship: "los géneros menores se vuelven trascendentes; los marginados, héroes; los héroes, traidores" [minor genres become important; the marginalized become heroes; the heroes, traitors] (70).

Fernández makes it clear that these stories are much more than an escape, if indeed they are an escape at all. They do aestheticize the surrounding reality, but only to better critique it. The stories are such inseparable mixtures of American movies and Spanish postwar reality that the surrounding reality is never really absent. The result, says Fernández, is that the *aventis*, even though they are saturated with fiction, appear to the reader to be more "real" than the absurd reality the boys are living in, and function to replace that reality with one that restores relevance and meaning to the lives of those excluded under Franco (73).

It's worth recalling a few key points about life in postwar Spain to understand the context in which the boys imitate detectives. The harsh years between 1939 and 1952 were known as "los años del hambre" and "el tiempo de silencio" [the "years of hunger" and the "time of silence"]. These were the years when Franco hunted down and executed his political enemies, both officially, through kangaroo courts, and unofficially, where Falangist militiamen would "take someone for a ride," leaving them in the countryside with a bullet between their eyes. Everyone was being investigated to determine his or her political loyalties. Hundreds of thousands of people were jailed, and those who were lucky enough to survive faced daily humiliations on the streets. Cataluña, which had supported the Republic in order to maintain its regional autonomy, was singled out for extra punishments; speaking Catalan was forbidden on the streets, and Barcelona, which had been bombed for months during the Civil War, was left in ruins for well over a decade. Meanwhile, people struggled to survive on tiny rations and were forced to buy food at exorbitant prices on the black market in order to stay alive. While much of Spain lived in hunger and terror, the regime trumpeted triumphal rhetoric about the "New Spain" it was creating.

The psychological threats to survival were as serious as the physical threats of execution, imprisonment, starvation, or epidemics. The regime consistently treated the defeated as subhuman, denying their personhood. Whether in prison or walking the streets, they were subjected to systematic "re-education" programs intended to break their spirit and recreate them as Francoists. They were forced to hide their past and camouflage themselves by making the Fascist salute, appearing regularly at Mass, and attending all the institutions at which they would be indoctrinated in Francoist values. They had to hide and silence their past and their real feelings. Furthermore, since they were defined as the "anti-Spain," they were denied any role in the new society that Franco was building. The danger was that the defeated, faced with constant humiliation and silencing, would internalize the Francoists' vilifying view of them, and cease to exist psychologically. As I have argued in detail elsewhere, in this context, playing roles from popular culture became for many Spaniards a way to stay alive psychologically. By choosing a role from popular culture that was at odds with the roles imposed on them by the regime, they could express some of their real feelings and dissident views, under the cover of just imitating a Hollywood movie star or a Spanish *copla* singer. Thus intense engagement with the fictional world of the movies became a way to affirm the clandestine self and survive psychologically.[3] The invitation to play roles through the movies was pervasive; as Steven Marsh has noted, in 1947, Spain had more movie theatres per capita than any other country except the United States (114–15). People also frequented the cinemas because they were heated, an attractive benefit at times of chronic cuts in electricity. Spaniards would sit through a double feature with a variety show in the middle every Saturday afternoon. Role-play, then, was far from just the activity of young boys in Marsé's circles, but a generalized practice.[4]

In this context of generalized threats of physical and psychological annihilation, the young boys in Marsé's story face enormous obstacles to their survival and development. They live in the poorest neighbourhood of Barcelona. Their fathers are jailed or suffering from alcoholism.

Their mothers never appear in the story, but we may infer that they work all day and then stand in line with their ration cards to get food. There is no school for the boys, and therefore no better future. They have no guides in growing up. Moreover, as we will see, they are defined by the winners of the war as delinquents, criminals, "Reds," and *charnegos* (the derogatory term used by Catalans to describe the many Andalusians who had migrated to Barcelona in search of work). They are hungry, stealing food from stalls as they follow Sra. Yordi and the man in pajamas down the streets.

The boys lack adequate male role models. At the level of "reality" represented in "Historia de detectives," men are either Francoist oppressors, like the baker or the man at the bar, or defeated Republicans who have fallen into despair and indigence. The story is populated by vagabonds, who sleep at night hugging their wine bottles in the same wrecked car that by day serves the boys as detective headquarters. Roca observes several of these indigents as he follows Sra. Yordi, describing "el vagabundo que empuja renqueante un cochecito de niño cargado de botellas y trapos viejos, y que tropieza en el bordillo y a punto está de caerse, pobre diablo" [the vagabond who limps along, pushing a stroller full of bottles and old rags, who stumbles on the curb and almost falls, poor devil] (13). Another vagabond pulls a wicker basket with a small boy clothed in rags sitting on empty champagne bottles (20). Later, David sees a young man wrapped in a ragged military blanket who collapses on the street, unable to respond when others try to wake him up, even though his eyes are open. But the most heart-rending description comes when Roca gives us an example of Juanito Marés's uncanny ability to detect "el dolor del alma de las personas" [people's deep emotional pain]: "Un día que vimos al señor Elías llorando en la taberna, solo, sentado en un rincón y escuchando en la radio una marcha militar, Marés dijo que el hombre lloraba porque la radio le estaba recordando una hija suya que hacía de puta en Zaragoza, detrás de un cuartel de Infantería" [One day when we saw Mr Elías crying in the tavern, seated alone in a corner and listening to a military march on the radio, Marés said that the man was crying because the radio was reminding him of his daughter, who was a prostitute in Zaragoza, behind an infantry barracks] (29). The boys will later confirm the truth of this story. So the boys are faced with the dilemma that their only possible models of adult behaviour are either the corrupt Francoists who oppress them or the defeated Republicans who have given in to despair. Neither option is a possibility if they are to survive psychologically.

The location of the boys' headquarters is in itself a threat to their psychological survival. The Lincoln is mired in a field known as el Campo de la Calva, so called because the Moors in Franco's army "jugaron aquí un partido de fútbol con la cabeza cortada y rapada de una puta, y dicen que de tanto patearla y hacerla rodar, la cabeza se quedó lisa y pulida como una bola de billar, sin nariz ni ojos ni orejas, y que la mandíbula se soltó y que al final del partido la enterraron con la boca abierta" [played a soccer game here with the head of a prostitute, shaved and cut off, and they say that from being kicked and rolled so much, the head became smooth and polished like a billiard ball, without a nose or eyes or ears, and that the jaw got loose, and that at the end of the game they buried it with its mouth open] (10). The fact that the boys later excavate the field and find only the skull of a dog does nothing to take away the impact of this terrifying story. While the story may be only legend, its terrorizing effects on the boys are real. From the beginning, then, the very concept of "reality" is presented as permeated with legend.

The wrecked Lincoln is stuck in the field, surrounded by "un montón de cosas muertas" [piles of dead things], old mattresses, broken armchairs, parts of old stoves. The Lincoln serves as a symbol of paralysis in years that those who experienced them called "los años de piedra, los años de plomo" [the years of stone, the years of lead].[5] Time brought no change; the rations of 1948 were no better than those of 1942; the bombed-out buildings from the war remained in ruins. Hope for a better future was threatened by this paralysis.

The boys' predicament in a hostile world is brought home through the ways space, weather, and time are constructed in the story, and here we find Marsé borrowing from, and rewriting, none other than Leopoldo Alas's *La Regenta*. The echoes begin with the vertical structure of the city. In Alas we begin with two scruffy boys atop the cathedral tower, looking down at the city below; they are described as "pilluelos" [little rascals] by the narrator, as they spit on passersby below (1:96). In Marsé, four equally ragged adolescent boys live in a neighbourhood perched high on a hill overlooking the rest of the city. Alas describes Vetusta with two adjectives separated by an "y"; it is first described tongue in cheek, as "la muy noble y leal ciudad" [the very noble and loyal city] (1:93), but we soon see it differently from atop the cathedral tower, which watches over "la ciudad pequeña y negruzca que dormía a sus pies" [the small and blackish city that slept at its feet] (1:94). Marsé uses this formula repeatedly:

> la ciudad misteriosa y corrompida (18)
>
> [the mysterious and corrupt city]
>
> la ciudad aterida y promiscua que se extendía a nuestros pies bajo un manto de neblina (32)
>
> [the numb and promiscuous city spread out at our feet under a mantle of fog]
>
> la ciudad lejana y andrajosa, dormida bajo un cielo desplomado (36)
>
> [the faraway and ragged city, asleep under a fallen sky]

Here the reader of *La Regenta* cannot help but recall the opening pages of the novel, where "la heroica ciudad dormía la siesta" [the heroic city was taking its nap] (1:93). The high-low opposition in both cases points up the corruption of the city seen down below.

The rain in *La Regenta* is likened to a whip that punishes the inhabitants of Vetusta: "Las nubes pardas, opacas ... se desgarraban y deshechas en agua caían sobre Vetusta ... en diagonales vertiginosas, como latigazos furibundos, como castigo bíblico" [the dark, opaque clouds ... were torn open, and, dissolving into water they fell on Vetusta ... in vertiginous diagonals, like the furious lashings of a whip, like a biblical punishment] (2:83). In Marsé's story, the boys conduct their investigation on a cold, rainy day, "lloviznando y con ráfagas de viento helado" [drizzling and with gusts of cold wind] (7). The elements are personified, as in the "viento racheado y cabrón," [squally, bastardly wind], a wind that will attack Sra. Yordi: "el viento la embistió por la espalda" [the wind attacked her from behind]. The combination of rain and wind becomes like a rodent: "la llovizna ahora peinada por el viento, afilada y gris como pelajos de rata" [the drizzle now combed by the wind, sharp and grey like a rat's fur] (15). And as in Alas, the elements are furious; Roca observes "una gigantesca nube de plomo en forma de puño alzándose iracundo contra el cielo" [a giant, leaden cloud shaped like a fist, raised in wrath against the sky] (29). People, too, are furious; Roca sees "un ciego furioso" [a furious blind man] striking the curb with his cane, waiting for someone to help him cross the street, and "escupiendo a las nubes" [spitting at the clouds] (20).

But the most important borrowing from *La Regenta* lies in that novel's dissolution of the opposition between earth and water to form the omnipresent mud of Vetusta. Harriet Turner has shown that the dissolution of contraries in the text allows the Vetustans to "smudge consciousness," leading ultimately to the dissolution of moral choice as the opposition between right and wrong is undermined ("From the Verbal to the Visual" 68). In "Historia de detectives," this dissolution is insistently described; the Lincoln is "varado en el mar de fango negro" [stuck in the sea of black mud] (13); the entire city is described "como una charca enfangada, una agua muerta" [like a muddy puddle, like stagnant water] (7). This continues even when the sun emerges from the clouds: "y la tarde se encendía como una luz roja arcillosa, como si fuera a llover barro" [and the afternoon lit up like a red claylike light, as if it were going to rain mud] (22). However, as shown below, the symbolic effect of the dissolution of contraries in Marsé is very different from that in *La Regenta.*

Finally, even time is dislocated, as this hostile climate is present in "un mes de abril que parecía noviembre" [an April that seemed like November] (8). Fernández has pointed out how Marsé's texts often allude to the war and postwar without naming them (71). I would argue that the dislocation of time and the dissolution of the earth-water opposition are indirect references to the fact that "reality" itself is distorted under Franco: time has been paralysed, repression and corruption have turned everything into mud, and the hostile attack of the climate on the characters represents the vengeful nature of the regime.[6]

But the greatest threat posed by the climate is that it compromises the boys' ability to *see*, to develop a perspective from outside the regime's obfuscating rhetoric of strict Catholic morality and its reality of corruption.[7] As Fernández puts it, in order to be able to tell stories about the postwar period, there has to be a gaze that generates them. As critics have noted, the first two, splendid paragraphs of the story indicate the difficulty in a contrast between bright, sunny days and grey days. On the bright days, the boys gaze far out to sea, imagining they can see the mermaids tattooed on the chests of the sailors and the rings in their ears. This "zoom" gaze comes from the movies (Fernández). But on grey days, "la mirada *se enreda* en el zarzal de neblinas y humos rasantes que atufan el laberinto de Horta y La Salud, y no consigue ir más allá. La ciudad se aplasta remota y gris, como una charca enfangada, una agua muerta" [the gaze *gets tangled up* in the brambles of the mist and steam at ground level that cloud up the labyrinth of Horta and La Salud, and it can't get beyond it. The city is squashed down, remote and grey, like a muddy puddle, like stagnant water] (7; my emphasis). The danger is that, between the rain, the fog, and the mud, the boys will be unable to gain a perspective on the Francoist city that will help them understand it and function within it, unlike their fathers, who have given in to despair. In the absence of other guides, the main resources at their disposal to interpret their world are the movies, which inject plot and forward motion into a reality of paralysis.

The action of the story begins when Marés quotes directly from a gritty police drama called *The Naked City* (1948), in which the older, Irish detective, played by Barry Fitzgerald, observes that a woman has "lovely long legs," and then orders his younger sidekick to tail her by saying, "Keep looking at 'em." Marés has to give the order several times, because Roca is afraid to start tailing Sra. Yordi. *The Naked City* is an ideal tool for boys trying to overcome their fear in a large city. The older detective has seen it all, knows how to "read" the suspects, and is unflappable in moments of danger, so that the younger detective has a reassuring father-figure to guide him. The teeming city (New York City in the film) is represented as intelligible if the detectives only stay methodical, put in enough legwork, and keep their cool.

The main influence on the boys' actions is the hard-boiled detective genre, which began in the novels of Dashiell Hammett and Raymond Chandler and was brought to the screen in movies like *The Maltese Falcon* (1941) and *The Big Sleep* (1946), with Humphrey Bogart playing the detective. This genre informs the way Roca describes the city, aestheticizing its danger, ugliness, and corruption. The world in these novels is much less morally pure than in *The Naked City*. People's motivations are hidden and complex. The detective can never be sure if the *femme fatale* is trustworthy, which is a problem, since he is often in love with her. The police and the DA's office have often been bought; and even the private detective himself is not always unequivocally on the side of law and order. Chandler presents the city as mysterious rather than intelligible. Despite the fact that the genre does not offer reassurance about the safety of the city, it does reassure in another way: by making danger and corruption familiar, by converting them into the stock ingredients of a film genre. It also provides a language in which to describe the city, and thus, symbolically, to control it.

Mutiny on the Bounty (Frank Lloyd, 1935) is the filter through which the boys see the Francoist baker who stops Sra. Yordi on the street and questions her. The baker informs Sra. Yordi that the boy tailing her and his friends are delinquents; that the Stetson hat Roca is wearing belonged to his father, who is in jail for being a Red and a separatist; and that their imitation of detectives will lead them into real crime as adults. The boys call him *Charles Lagartón*, after Charles Laughton, the actor who plays the tyrannical Captain Bligh in the film. A wonderfully appropriate film for the boys' purposes, it portrays the overthrow of the strong, unjust tyrant by a collectivity of previously oppressed men. To link the baker to Captain Bligh is to suggest that the boys will ultimately defeat him. He may be powerful and scary now, but the outcome is predetermined by the movie, and justice will prevail. Other popular texts that influence the boys are Fu Manchu films, which lead them to imagine Sra. Yordi as a sexualized oriental woman, and the Spanish series of Western novels called *El Coyote*.

How might playing the detective role affect the boys emotionally? Child psychology helps us understand how role-play could help the boys overcome their biggest obstacle: fear. Selma Fraiberg's classic book, *The Magic Years* (1959), tells us that toddlers who are afraid of wild animals or imaginary monsters cannot rely on their parents to be there every time they are afraid. They deal with these fears best by using their own imaginations. If a child is afraid of tigers, for example, he can invent an imaginary companion who is a tiger and follows his orders. Or he can become a tiger himself, and out-roar and out-threaten all the enemy tigers. The result is that "the child who has overcome his tigers in his play has learned to master his fear" (20). The boys in "Historia de detectives" are not toddlers, but they are facing a terrifying situation with no resources to help ease the fear. Imitating the tough, fearless Humphrey Bogart detective allows the boys to develop the courage they need to function in the city. Like the small child impersonating the tiger, the boys play the brave adult who is not afraid of the city until they are no longer so afraid, and are much closer to *being* that brave adult. Another aspect of the hard-boiled detective role also helps them develop bravery. They are following a woman in distress, who is crying and vulnerable. This allows them to try on the role of the rescuer, get in touch with feelings of strength, and imagine rescuing someone else in the way they themselves might unconsciously like to be rescued. So playing the role of the brave detective achieves the crucial psychological goal of managing their fears without becoming avoidant and unwilling to explore the city (Fraiberg 18). The crucial function of the detective role in overcoming fear is apparent in the fact that Marés has to order Roca several times to tail Sra. Yordi, because Roca is paralysed in the Campo de la Calva beside the wrecked Lincoln, "como si la boca abierta de la furcia calva, debajo de la tierra, se hubiese cerrado como un cepo en mis tobillos" [as if the open mouth of the bald whore, under the earth, had closed like a clamp on my ankles] (10). Later, back at the car, as Marés begins to tell the boys of his deductions, Roca thinks again about the bald woman and gets scared all over again:

> Pensé en el destino incierto de la señora de ojos de china bajo la lluvia, y pensé en el destino cumplido y atroz de la furcia calva cuya cabeza cercenada y calva yacía enterrada debajo de nosotros ...Y pensando confusamente en todo eso sentí un vértigo y me quedé de pronto como sordo o como atontado de las bombas. Me asusté e interrumpí a Marés ... (30)

> [I thought of the uncertain fate of the woman with oriental eyes, walking in the rain, and I thought of the horrible fate of the bald whore whose bald, cut-off head lay buried right under us ... And thinking with confusion about all this, I felt dizzy and I suddenly became like a deaf person, or someone stunned by bombs. I got scared, and interrupted Marés ...]

By the end of the story, despite their fear upon seeing the actor's body hanging in the air, the boys no longer need the detective role; this investigation, we are told, is their last.

Children will use the continuous impersonation of a single character, or the invention of an imaginary companion, to deal with new and unforeseen situations. The model for the impersonation or the companion will be selected to meet the particular psychological needs of the child (Taylor 63). This is what Marsé's boys do in choosing the detective role. Detection is precisely the art of gathering information, and the boys need information about their world to stay alive. In the process of investigating the adults around them, the boys learn how the system works. They know how the black market functions from following the baker and watching him traffic in bags of flour at the train station. They learn some of the reasons why women on the losing side might become prostitutes. They learn what kinds of favours the winners can dole out to the losers, such as a certificate of good conduct, necessary to hold a job in Franco's Spain. And they know the city in detail, including the places where food is easy to steal.

But playing the detective role fosters something more than survival skills, namely, healthy emotional development. Drama therapists such as Robert Landy see the human personality itself as a collection of roles; personality develops by taking on roles observed in the outside world. A healthy personality requires a wide variety of roles, and the ability to be flexible in playing them, improvising, and taking on new roles as needed. Sue Jennings argues that in the process of acting out roles in play, children develop the capacity to put themselves in the place of another person, to empathize, which then grounds their entire relationship with other human beings in everyday reality (61). Both Jennings and Landy see the movement between the alternative reality of play and everyday reality as crucial to healing and growth. Playing the role of a fictional character allows us to take emotional risks: creating a distance between ourselves and the characters we play bypasses our defences against our own pain. It therefore allows deep exploration of the feelings of the character, or of other characters, that a person would shy away from undertaking without the protection of the role (Andersen-Warren and Grainger 87).

I contend that the detective role, and other movie roles such as the cowboy, permit Marsé's boys to develop emotionally in several ways. First, children need adult models in order to mature emotionally, but, as we have seen, the boys are caught between Francoist oppressors and defeated Republican victims and cannot afford to identify with either. In contrast, Hollywood movies come from outside the Francoist reality, and they offer models of brave, strong men who are not Fascist, and who are fighting a corrupt system. Here we see illustrated Marjorie Taylor's assertion that the character impersonated will be chosen to meet the very specific psychological needs of the child. I argue that, contrary to conventional wisdom that sees popular culture as an escape, these films actually put the boys in touch with the problems of their own world and their own lives. Both detective *film noir* and cowboy movies feature a hero who represents justice and tough courage, pitted against a corrupt system in which the local authorities are implicated: the LA police of the Bogart films, the sheriff or a posse in cowboy movies. The movies name the boys' real problem of living in a world of violence, injustice, and corruption, and carve out a role for the courageous dissenter, a role which the movies portray as ultimately victorious.

Secondly, what Juanito Marés wants the younger boys to learn by playing detectives is much more emotional than factual. And here it is crucial to note that the author, Marsé, is not only rewriting the hard-boiled detective stories of Chandler and Hammett that are brought to the screen in *film noir* but also, less explicitly, turning on its head the conventions of their predecessors, the classic detective stories invented by Edgar Allan Poe and continued by Arthur Conan Doyle, Agatha Christie, and others. The classic detective story is much more optimistic and less cynical than the hard-boiled genre; the police are ineffectual but benign, there is only one murderer, and he or she ends up behind bars. The detective in these stories is primarily cerebral, excelling, as

Poe indicated in his first story, in the faculty of analysis. The classic detective story always begins with an elaborate illustration of the detective's uncanny ability to deduce the truth where no one else can see it, and this establishes the detective's authority in the mind of the reader.

Juanito Marés is constructed in dialogue with Poe's detective, Auguste Dupin, an aristocrat *venido a menos* [fallen on hard times] who has just enough money not to have to work. He lives isolated in his house, distanced from others, and he undertakes detective work primarily for the fun of exercising his analytical ability (he tells the narrator-sidekick, "an inquiry will afford us amusement," "Murders" 420). Juanito Marés has no money and lacks the protection of a house; we see him only in the wrecked car. But he is created out of echoes of Dupin, as both characters explicate their cases with their faces hidden behind clouds of smoke (from a pipe in Dupin's case, and cheap anisette cigarettes for Marés).[8] Marés, too, is presented as having extraordinary powers of deduction. But what he deduces are *feelings*, which in the classic detective story are kept at bay in order not to distress the reader: "Desde muy chico había dado muestras de esa extraña y terrible facultad: diríase que adivinaba el dolor del alma de las personas, que percibía su pena y su infortunio con sólo mirarlas a la cara o verlas pasar por la calle yendo al trabajo, por un detalle de nada" [From the time he was very little, he had shown signs of having that strange and terrible power: you could say that he guessed the pain in people's souls, that he perceived their sorrow and their misfortune just by looking them in the face or seeing them pass by on the street on their way to work, from a tiny detail] (28–9).

The proof of Marés's extraordinary powers is that he can deduce the tragic reasons why Sr. Elías is crying alone at the bar listening to a military band on the radio. With respect to Sra. Yordi, Marés's goal is to move the boys beyond their adolescent sexual obsession with her body. Initially, the younger boys project their desire onto her, and they imagine that the man she met at the bar, and with whom she leaves in a taxi, is her lover, with whom she is delighted to be having sex, even as the boys are talking about her. But the boys also have another reason for not initially identifying with Sra. Yordi; they cannot afford to do so emotionally. They are meeting in the Campo de la Calva, so they know what can happen to a victimized woman; we have already seen that when Roca thinks about Sra. Yordi in connection with the bald woman, he becomes paralysed with fear. The boys are victims themselves, too vulnerable to be able to afford to identify with a vulnerable woman on the losing side.

However, role-play helps them build courage, and Marés helps them build their powers of observation, precisely in order to be able to imagine how she is feeling, and to realize that her motives for meeting with this man are more complex:

> ... no es su querido ni su amante. ¿Desde cuándo una mujer enamorada acude tan triste, tan desganada de todo y llorando a una cita con su amante? Os digo que es otra cosa. ¿No habéis visto sus medias zurcidas, su gabardina tan corta y con el cinturón tan apretado bajo los pechos, y esos zapatos de mujer fatal que no le van a una señora tan fina ...? ¿No os parece que quiere gustar como sea a alguien, gustar mucho y de prisa y con vicio, y después vestirse de otra manera? Hay que verla como yo la estoy viendo, chicos, hacedme el puñetero favor de imaginarla de otra manera, si de verdad queréis destacar en este oficio de detectives. (31–2)

> [... he's not her lover. Since when does a woman in love go on a date with her lover so sad, so unwillingly, and crying? I'm telling you something else is going on. Didn't you see her darned stockings, her raincoat that is too short for her and with the belt tightened below her breasts, and those *femme fatale* shoes that don't belong on such a refined woman? Don't you think she wants to turn someone on, to have sex quickly and with depravity, and then dress differently? You have to see her the way I'm seeing her, kids, do me the damned favour of imagining her another way, if you really want to do well in this detective profession.]

Given that what the boys learn to detect in their investigations is emotional pain, they become more connected to the men and women who have lost the Spanish Civil War. As a result, they feel more connected to their surrounding world, which is crucial, for in Franco's New Spain, they feel isolated and relegated to the margins. Roca reflects on this isolation: "me puse a pensar no sé por qué en la ciudad aterida y promiscua que se extendía a nuestros pies bajo un manto de neblina, en las largas colas del sábado frente a los cines con calefacción, en los tranvías repletos bajando por las Ramblas ... Y nosotros aquí arriba rumiando musarañas" [I don't know why I started thinking about the numb and promiscuous city that was spread out at our feet under a mantle of fog, about the long lines on Saturdays in front of the movie theatres with heating, about the streetcars full to bursting, coming down the Ramblas ... And us up here letting our minds wander] (33). By the time the boys obey Marés's last order and hand the actor's wallet to Sra.

Yordi at the end of the story, they are much less fearful and more able to look after themselves (their pockets are full of freshly cooked garbanzos which they have just stolen). This will be their last case, for they no longer need to play the role, having developed the qualities it had to offer them.

Playing the role of the hard-boiled detective from the movies, then, offers the boys many practical and emotional skills they will need to survive. It gives them a role, whereas the system relegated them to sitting on a street corner with no school. It requires them to be curious, creative, observant, and engaged with the world around them. They learn to improvise when they are discovered tailing their suspects. They learn to be articulate about what they have observed. They gain a sense of mastery and empowerment, daring to challenge Marés's authority by the end of the story. And they develop their capacity for empathy with the adults around them.

One final consideration indicates why the boys' mastery of the detective role is so critical to their survival. Under Franco, everyone had to be a detective. The winners of the war were ordered to spy on the losers and to report any nonconformist conduct. This is what the baker is doing when he tries to find out why Sra. Yordi is so far from their neighbourhood. The losers had to gather information they desperately needed not only to survive, such as how to obtain food on the black market, but also to protect themselves against detective work by the winners.

Despite all of the positive effects of role-play on Roca, David, and Jaime, "Historia de detectives" does not posit that acting a part under any conditions will automatically help a character to cope with his or her situation in everyday reality. The story presents three categories of male characters on the losing side: those who live exclusively in the real world, those who are always playing a role, and those who alternate between everyday reality and the world of role-play. Those in the first category, who live constantly in the real world, have fallen into despair. The second category is that of the actor dressed in pajamas and slippers. If role-play is so helpful for coping with reality, why does the actor commit suicide? I believe there are two reasons. First, we have seen that children choose a role that helps them meet particular psychological needs and cope with specific problems. But Marés deduces that the actor is a third-rate performer who plays small roles in the amateur theatres of the neighbourhood; he does not choose his roles, but is stuck in the fixed role of the ageing ladies' man. Secondly, if Marés is correct, the actor is Sra. Yordi's husband, who lives across the city because he is hiding from the police. He wears his makeup and costume on the street for protection. For this reason, he cannot stop playing the role and re-enter everyday reality at all. He is trapped in his costume. When he sees his wife in the bar with another man and cannot intervene in the real situation that most concerns him, he commits suicide in costume, forever stuck in his role.

But the most ambiguous case in the story is that of Juanito Marés, the eldest boy who acts as detective boss. Marés has more skills to function in everyday reality than the younger boys, precisely because he is so comfortable moving from the world of the theatre or movies to everyday reality. His mother, we learn, is a fortune teller who surrounds herself with actors and variety artists down on their luck. From them, Marés has learnt how to guess at hidden motivations, how to develop and stick to a role, how to be a ventriloquist (he often speaks in a voice not his own) and an acrobat. He is well placed to coach the younger boys in role-play. Yet Marés is both more isolated and more angry than the younger boys. He uses the detective role as a shell that protects him from being vulnerable. The younger boys often leave him sitting alone in the Lincoln for hours at a time, smoking, with his feet wrapped around his neck, looking like a scorpion. His habit of speaking in a voice not his own distances him from the younger boys, as does the cloud of cigarette smoke which envelops him.

Marés is also distanced from the younger boys by anger. He shouts and screams at them, gives them orders, and is repeatedly described as "furious." At the scene of the suicide, he stands alone, looking mockingly at the younger boys rather than bonding with them. I believe that Marés's anger and his need for a protective shell come from a burden he carries which the younger boys do not share. The younger boys have each other to share their experiences with, and they have Marés as a mentor and father-figure. They are getting a kind of guidance in growing up from him. Marés, however, has no peers with whom to share his predicament, and gets no fathering. In Marsé's later novel, *El amante bilingüe*, we learn that Marés's father is an alcoholic magician who has almost completely abandoned the family. On one of his rare appearances at home, Juanito reproaches him for not spending time with his mother, never mentioning his own need for a father. He follows up by lending his father a *duro* (five *pesetas*) (*El amante* 43–5). Not only does he not receive fathering, he acts as a parent to his father, giving him money he really needs himself. Small wonder that he becomes embittered.

The role of the detective boss helps Marés to cope with his situation, exercising his creativity and giving him a sense of mastery, competence, and power. It connects him to the other boys, if only in a limited fashion. Marés's anger and isolation are not caused by the role-play through the movies, then, but by his ongoing isolation and lack of protection or love from his father. When he engages in fathering, it is laced with anger at not having received it himself.

Álvaro Fernández has noted how Marsé's stories invert and critique the official morality of the Franco regime, often in ways that are implicit rather than spelt out (67). In "Historia de detectives," Marsé effects this critique by inverting the formula of the classic detective story that begins with a murder, then introduces the detective and his powers, and moves through an investigation of suspects, the detective's revelation of the solution to the mystery, and the arrest of the criminal by the police (Cawelti 82). In "Historia de detectives," all of these elements are turned upside down; the boys investigate people before there is a crime. The story ends with a death, but it is a suicide, which makes "criminal" and "victim" the same person. Indeed, the real criminals in the story are the Francoists, whom the detectives have no power to bring to justice. Ironically, both the detectives and the "suspects" they follow are the victims. What is being deduced is primarily emotional pain rather than the intellectualized facts of the classic detective story. At the end, there is no resolution; we will never know if Juanito Marés is correct that the actor is really Sra. Yordi's husband. All of these inversions, which contrast with the classic formula familiar to the reader, serve to demonstrate that under dictatorship, those in power are the killers, and they cannot be brought to justice.

This story, written in 1987, bears significant similarities to the project of nineteenth-century realism, in its structure, aims, and theme. In 1870, when Galdós writes his "Observaciones sobre la novela contemporánea en España" [Observations on the Contemporary Spanish Novel] as a programmatic statement about the kind of novel Spain needs, it is no accident that he immediately turns to Cervantes as he decries foreign models and calls for a return to the novel of observation (106, 108). Nor is it an accident that he begins the *Novelas españolas contemporáneas* [Contemporary Spanish Novels] with *La desheredada* [The Disinherited Lady] (1881), a novel explicitly modelled on the *Quijote*. Galdós is writing after a long period of censorship and upheaval, once the Revolution of 1868 finally brought greater freedom of expression. He turns to Cervantes to construct a social critique of Spanish society and of recent historical events that have been lived by much of his original readership. He wants to use that memory to diagnose social ills, and through the stories of his characters, to effect a cure; thus he dedicates *La desheredada* to schoolteachers, whom he calls the true doctors for Spain's social ills. This novel is, among other things, a devastating critique of political corruption and economic parasitism in a society which has rendered honesty and hard work meaningless; this theme is picked up in "Historia de detectives" in the new context of the Franco regime. Marsé writes in 1987, once Spain's transition to democracy is complete, but his story is set in the harshest years of the Franco dictatorship, the 1940s and early 1950s. It's important to note that writers who wrote fiction during the postwar period itself were severely limited by a draconian censorship which forbade all reference to politics (wartime censorship standards were not relaxed until 1966). The *tremendismo* of the 1940s, exemplified in Cela's *La familia de Pascual Duarte*, presented marginalized characters who enact extreme violence, without apparent remorse or ethical framework. In the 1950s, dissident writers wrote novels of *realismo social* which had collective protagonists belonging to the poorer and more marginalized sectors of society. The writers could not directly denounce the situation of these characters, so they limited themselves to reproducing their dialogue, trying to create an implicit critique by simply presenting what *is*. The limits of such an endeavour led the novelists of the 1960s and 1970s to adopt more experimental forms of writing, and often to denounce the dictatorship in novels published outside Spain. It fell to the novelists of the 1970s and 1980s, then, to reconstitute both the memory of the postwar period as it was actually lived, a memory which had been covered over and falsified by Francoist official histories, and also to construct a critique of Francoist society that could not be done during the dictatorship. It is no accident that Marsé turns to Cervantes to achieve both ends, for the contrast between illusion/fiction/popular culture and "reality" allows for a deep critique of both levels. The aims and the Cervantine structure, then, are quite similar.

The theme of poor boys excluded from mainstream society also echoes and rewrites nineteenth-century realism. Marsé's focus on poor boys without schools who have been excluded from the dominant society and marked out as predestined to become delinquents should recall Mariano Rufete, el Majito, and their friends in *La desheredada*, whom we also see playing a game of imitation, in this case of General Juan Prim, whose deeds have become urban legend. Unfortunately, their war games lead to real violence, and don't provide them with a better future. We see these boys, however, through the descriptions of a bourgeois narrator who insists that they are genetically predestined to crime (93), even as he critiques the hypocrisy of the administration officials who wring their hands and talk about building schools while actually constructing a new bullring. Jo Labanyi has shown that the realist novel is obsessed with women and the working classes, those who have been excluded by the liberal social contract because they are not property owners (*Gender and Modernization* 53). The poor and the "deviant" in particular become the targets of social reform to control their behaviour, and realism, according to Labanyi, both critiques the excessive surveillance and punitive strategies brought to bear on the deviant and constitutes its own surveillance exercise, trying to document and hence to control those sectors of society which threaten bourgeois order (65, 78ff). In his portrayal of Mariano Rufete, Galdós's narrator alternates between sympathy for his hard labour and his lack of opportunities and the presentation of evidence that he is predestined to crime. (The contradiction is emblematic of the simultaneous guilt and prejudice of the bourgeoisie towards the poor.) Significantly, Mariano is almost completely inarticulate, unable to narrate his own experience.

Marsé's story also focuses on young boys defined as juvenile delinquents (the baker spells out their supposed criminal future to Sra. Yordi), also without schooling and living in extreme poverty. But Marsé shows us the world of Francoist corruption not through the eyes of a bourgeois narrator, as in *La desheredada*, but through the eyes of the young boys themselves, who not only actively imitate the movies but then narrate their own adventures. It is they who develop the powers of observation that allow them to diagnose and condemn the moral ills of their society. Those in power are now subject to portrayal by the excluded. And popular culture, the "low" which is so often condemned in realist fiction, here becomes redemptive, as American movie conventions allow for the creation of a new ethical framework to immunize the boys against Francoist corruption. As a result, Roca goes on to become the narrator of the story we read, rather than a delinquent, just like the author, Juan Marsé, who was once one of these boys.

The boys' imitation of hard-boiled detectives, then, can be considered a kind of "repair work" that helps them compensate for their poverty and their oppression, and allows them to create a new ethical foundation for their actions. And at another level, Marsé's creation of this story does repair work on a society falsified and corrupted by dictatorship, helping to reconstitute the memory of the defeated and, through critique, to propose new ethical foundations for a society in which all are included.

What is most *real* in "Historia de detectives," in sum, is the psychological activity described by Américo Castro as "incitación" [incitement] in which "the flame latent in the pages of certain books ... ignites bonfires in certain souls ready to become inflamed" (99). Just as Don Quixote was incited by the popular fictions of his day to take to the road and become a knight errant, so Marsé's boys are incited by detective and other fictions to create themselves by *doing* (Castro 110). They do so by playing roles from popular culture that exceed the limited roles imposed by the dominant society around them. It is this flame coming from popular culture, brought into everyday reality through the activity of role-play, that brings new life, plot, and purpose into a world characterized by death ("cosas muertas"), dissolution, and obfuscation.

And here it is the contrast with the use of popular culture in *La Regenta* that is instructive. In *La Regenta,* the narrator constructs everyday reality as the dissolution of contraries, particularly the fusion of water and earth to form mud, and the dissolution of the high-low opposition. Popular culture, emblematized in the serial novel, is represented as being a part of the "low" from the beginning. In *La Regenta,* the narrator uses these images of dissolution as a figure for the "moral dissolution" of the whole society. He purports to stand above the fallen world of his characters, but as Harriet Turner has done so much to show, he is actually implicated in the same forbidden desires, vindictiveness, and betrayal as they are.

Marsé, by contrast, eliminates the omniscient narrator and allows Roca, his first-person narrator, to use popular culture to create a world *in between* reality and fiction, a world where, in Cervantine fashion, the reader can never pinpoint exactly where one ends and the other begins. Marsé defends the production of such mixtures as a way to survive under the Francoist repression, and to maintain a dissident way of looking.[9] Thus, where *La Regenta* uses images of dissolution to denounce the moral corruption of the whole society, in "Historia de detectives," the fusion of earth and water points up the corruption of the winners, and the devastation that the repression has created among the defeated. It is not a moral judgment on the victims. At the end of *La Regenta,* Celedonio's toadlike kiss is emblematic of his own moral turpitude and that of the surrounding society. In "Historia de detectives," although Marsé presents us with boys who steal every day in order to eat, he also shows us how their imitation of the American Hollywood detective enables them to constitute a new moral centre that counters the corruption of the Francoists. This is emphasized when they return the wallet containing five *duros* to Sra. Yordi, despite being in desperate need of the money themselves. The boys' cynical, dissident gaze, fuelled by detective fiction, becomes a critique of the crimes around them. Amid the cold rain and wind that represent the hostility of the regime towards the vanquished, the boys, high on their hill, are like the afternoon light that eventually emerges, a light "[que] planea como un pájaro de oro sobre el mar de fango" [that glides like a golden bird over the sea of mud] (15).

NOTES

1 See Turner's remarkable chapter on "Metaphors of Mind" in *Benito Pérez Galdós:* Fortunata and Jacinta (ch. 3, 93–108).

2 I refer throughout to the edition of this story published in *Teniente Bravo* in 1987, by Seix Barral. Lumen later put out another edition of *Teniente Bravo* in which Marsé made revisions to the story. I found that the revisions detracted from the subtlety of the story, and have chosen to work with the original version. All translations in the essay are mine.

3 See Sieburth, *Survival Songs*, 32–8.

4 In the oral history of cinema-going directed by Jo Labanyi, interviewees recalled how children invented "guessing games based on acting out sequences from the movies." Fifty years later, the adults interviewed by Labanyi and her colleagues still retained "an extraordinarily detailed recall of the films they watched – often slipping into an animated reenactment" ("Mediation" 106).

5 Historian Juan José Carreras Ares recalled these terms in conversation with me on 1 June 2005.

6 On the paralysis of time during the dictatorship, see Martín Gaite, *El cuarto de atrás* 133.

7 In his documentary film *Canciones para después de una guerra*, Basilio Martín Patino has an elderly male voice-over sum up the problem: "Las cosas no eran como eran" [Things were not as they were]. And Martín Gaite refers to "aquella esquizofrenia entre lo que se decía que pasaba y lo que pasaba de verdad" [a kind of schizophrenia between what they told us was happening and what was really happening] (*Usos* 25).

8 See Poe, "The Purloined Letter" 497, 502.

9 In an as yet unpublished paper, Zachary Erwin has studied the importance of the "como si" [as if] construction in Marsé's creation of this "in-between" world. Álvaro Fernández describes how popular culture permits a critique of the dictatorship, by creating the possibility of *seeing* in a different way, from the margins: "En los relatos contaminados, en la visión del mundo desde la platea pringosa del cine de barrio en medio de la miseria, se alza una estrategia de representación que recupera la posibilidad de atisbar una verdad, una crítica social ... Precisamente, Marsé salva la verdad porque nunca la dice y la transforma en una trama que el lector puede encontrar entre los pliegues del relato, sin que éste se la imponga mediante la explicitación" [In contaminated stories, in a vision of the world from the sticky seats of a neighbourhood cinema in the midst of extreme poverty, rises a strategy of representation that recovers the possibility of glimpsing a truth, a social critique ... Marsé saves the truth precisely because he never articulates it, and he transforms it into a plot that the reader can find in the folds of the story, without it being imposed on him by being made explicit] (66–7).

WORKS CITED

Alas, Leopoldo. *La Regenta*. 2 vols. Ed. Gonzalo Sobejano. Madrid: Castalia, 1989. Print.

Andersen-Warren, Madeleine, and Roger Grainger. *Practical Approaches to Dramatherapy: The Shield of Perseus*. Preface by Anna Seymour. London: Jessica Kingsley, 2000. Print.

The Big Sleep. Dir. Howard Hawks. 1946. Warner Home Video, 2000. DVD.

Canciones para después de una guerra. Dir. Basilio Martin Patino. 1971. Diario El País, 2003. DVD.

Castro, Américo. "An Introduction to the *Quijote*." In *An Idea of History: Selected Essays of Américo Castro*, ed. and trans. Stephen Gilman and Edmund L. King. Columbus: Ohio State UP, 1977. 77–139.

Cawelti, John G. "The Formula of the Classical Detective Story." In *Adventure, Mystery and Romance*. Chicago: U of Chicago P, 1976. 80–105. Print.

Chandler, Raymond. *The Big Sleep*. 1st ed. New York: A.A. Knopf, 1939. Print.

– *Farewell, My Lovely*. New York and London: A.A. Knopf, 1940. Print.

Erwin, Zachary. "Las (ir)realidades del *como si* en 'Historia de detectives' de Juan Marsé." Unpublished paper.

Fernández, Álvaro. "Un canto en la tiniebla. Miradas, voces y memoria en la poética de Juan Marsé." *Iberoamericana* 3.11 (2003): 65–87. Print.

Fraiberg, Selma. *The Magic Years: Understanding and Handling the Problems of Early Childhood*. New York: Scribner, 1959. Print.

Hammett, Dashiell. *The Maltese Falcon*. New York: A.A. Knopf, 1930. Print.

Hernández García, Carmela. "El Juego En 'Historia de Detectives' de Juan Marsé." *Hispanófila* 34.2 (1991): 49–60. Print.

Jennings, Sue. *Introduction to Dramatherapy: Theatre and Healing. Ariadne's Ball of Thread*. Philadelphia: Jessica Kingsley, 1998. Print.

Labanyi, Jo. *Gender and Modernization in the Spanish Realist Novel*. New York: Oxford UP, 2000.

– "The Mediation of Everyday Life: An Oral History of Cinema-Going in 1940s and 1950s Spain: An Introduction to a Dossier." *Studies in Hispanic Cinemas* 2.2 (2005): 105–8. Print. http://doi.org/10.1386/shci.2.2.105_3.

Landy, Robert. *Persona and Performance: The Meaning of Role in Drama, Therapy, and Everyday Life*. New York and London: Guilford P, 1993. Print.

The Maltese Falcon. Dir. John Huston. 1941. Warner Home Video, 2000. DVD.

Marsé, Juan. *El amante bilingüe*. Barcelona: Planeta, 1990. Print.

– "Historia de Detectives." In *Teniente Bravo*. Barcelona: Seix Barral, 1987. 5–39.

Marsh, Steven. "The Haptic in Hindsight: Neighbourhood Cinema-Going in Post-War Spain." *Studies in Hispanic Cinemas* 2.2 (2005): 109–16. Print. https://doi.org/10.1386/shci.2.2.109_3.

Martín Gaite, Carmen. *El cuarto de atrás*. Barcelona: Ediciones Destino, 1981. Print.

– *Usos amorosos de la posguerra española*. Barcelona: Editorial Anagrama, 1987. Print.

Mutiny on the Bounty. Dir. Frank Lloyd. 1935. Warner Home Video, 2004. DVD.

The Naked City. Dir. Jules Dassin. 1948. Image Entertainment, 1998. DVD.

Pérez Galdós, Benito. *La desheredada*. Madrid: Alianza, 2001.

– "Observaciones sobre la novela contemporánea en España." In *Benito Pérez Galdós: Ensayos de crítica literaria*, ed. Laureano Bonet. Barcelona: Península, 1990. 105–20.

Poe, Edgar Allan. "The Murders in the Rue Morgue." In *The Prose Tales of E.A. Poe: First Series*. New York: A.C. Armstrong and Son, 1889. 404–41. Print.

– "The Purloined Letter." In *The Prose Tales of E.A. Poe: First Series*. New York: A.C. Armstrong and Son, 1889. 494–513. Print.

Sherzer, William M. "Textual Autobiography in 'Historia de Detectives' and 'El Fantasma Del Cine Roxy.'" In *Rewriting the Good Fight*, ed. Frieda S. Brown, Malcolm Allan Compitello, and Victor M. Howard. East Lansing: Michigan State UP, 1989. 81–94. Print.

Sieburth, Stephanie. *Inventing High and Low*. Durham, NC, and London: Duke UP, 1994. Print.

– *Survival Songs: Conchita Piquer's "Coplas" and Franco's Regime of Terror.* Toronto, Buffalo, and London: U of Toronto P, 2014. Print.
Taylor, Marjorie. *Imaginary Companions and the Children Who Create Them.* New York: Oxford UP, 1999. Print.
Turner, Harriet. *Benito Pérez Galdós: Fortunata and Jacinta.* Cambridge: Cambridge UP, 1992. Print.
– "From the Verbal to the Visual in *La Regenta.*" In *"Malevolent Insemination" and Other Essays on Clarín*, ed. Noël Maureen Valis. Michigan Romance Studies, vol. 10. Ann Arbor: University of Michigan, 1990. 67–86. Print.
Vázquez Montalbán, Manuel. *Cancionero general del franquismo, 1939–1975.* Barcelona: Crítica, 2000. Print.

Contributors

Maryellen Bieder was a professor emerita of Spanish at Indiana University, Bloomington. She wrote extensively on late nineteenth-century and early twentieth-century authors Emilia Pardo Bazán and Concepción Gimeno de Flaquer, as well as Carmen de Burgos. Most recently she researched networks of women writers, including Pardo Bazán's literary friendships with Gabriela Cunninghame Graham and Blanca de los Ríos de Lampérez. In addition to her book, *Narrative Perspective in the Post-Civil War Novels of Francisco Ayala* (1979), she published widely on contemporary Spanish- and Catalan-language writers: Juan Goytisolo, Mercè Rodoreda, Manuel Vázquez Montalbán, Carme Riera, and Marina Mayoral. She also worked on Spanish visual culture.

Peter A. Bly is currently a professor emeritus at Queen's University, Kingston, Ontario, Canada. He was editor of *Anales Galdosianos* (1990–2002), while simultaneously serving as secretary-treasurer of the International Association of Galdós Scholars, later serving as president from 2009 to 2012. The majority of his nine books and over 150 articles and book reviews deal with the work of Benito Pérez Galdós. Other authors studied include Leopoldo Alas, Juan Valera, Emilia Pardo Bazán, José María de Pereda, Armando Palacio Valdés, Eduardo López Bago, Eça de Queiroz, Émile Zola, Federico García Lorca, and Ramón Sender, as well as the authors of *Poema de Mio Cid* and *El Libro de Alexandre.*

Mary L. Coffey is an associate professor of Spanish and Senior Associate Dean at Pomona College. She has published numerous book chapters and articles on nineteenth- and twentieth-century Spanish literature and culture, with a focus on *costumbrismo*, realism, and naturalism, in journals such as *Revista Hispánica Moderna*, *Bulletin of Hispanic Studies*, *Anales Galdosianos*, and the *Arizona Journal of Cultural Studies*. Her book, *Ghosts of Colonies Past and Present: Spanish Imperialism in the Early Works of Benito Pérez Galdós* is under contract with Liverpool University Press, with expected publication in early 2020. She served as president of the Asociación Internacional de Galdosistas from 2011 to 2014.

David T. Gies is Commonwealth Professor of Spanish Emeritus at the University of Virginia and former chair of his department. He has published seventeen books, including *Theatre and Politics in Nineteenth-Century Spain* (Cambridge, 1988), *The Theatre in Nineteenth-Century Spain* (Cambridge, 1994), *The Cambridge Companion to Modern Spanish Culture* (1999), *The Cambridge History of Spanish Literature* (2004), *Eros y amistad* (2016), and *The Eighteenth Centuries* (coedited, 2017). He has authored 135 scholarly articles, and he edits *DIECIOCHO*, a journal dedicated to the study of the Spanish Enlightenment. He has received the University of Virginia Outstanding Teaching Award, the Thomas Jefferson Award, and, in 2007, the Encomienda de Número de la Orden de Isabel la Católica from His Majesty Juan Carlos, King of Spain. He serves as Honorary President of the Asociación Internacional de Hispanistas and of the National Honor Society, Sigma Delta Pi, and is a Corresponding Member of the Spanish Royal Academy.

Rebecca Haidt is a professor of Spanish at the Ohio State University. She has written numerous articles and chapters on eighteenth- and nineteenth-century literary and cultural topics, and authored three books: *Embodying Enlightenment* (1998), *Seduction and Sacrilege* (2002), and *Women, Work and Clothing in Eighteenth-Century Spain* (2011). Her current projects include essays on convict transportation in eighteenth-century theatre and a book on *costumbrismo*.

Catherine Jaffe is a professor of Spanish at Texas State University. Her research focuses on women during the Enlightenment in Spain, translation, and modern Spanish literature. She coedited *Eve's Enlightenment: Women's Experience in Spain and Spanish America, 1726–1839* (2009) and coauthored *Maria Lorenza de los Ríos, marquesa de Fuerte-Hijar: vida y obra de una escritora del Siglo de las Luces* (2019). She is co-editing *The Routledge Companion to the Hispanic Enlightenment*.

Roberta Johnson is a professor emerita at the University of Kansas and an adjunct professor in the Department of Spanish and Portuguese at UCLA. Her books include *Carmen Laforet* (Twayne, 1981); *El ser y la palabra en Gabriel Miró* (Fundamentos, 1985); *Crossfire: Philosophy and the Novel in Spain 1900–1934* (U of Kentucky P, 1993); *Las bibliotecas de Azorín* (Caja de Ahorros del Mediterráneo, 1996); and *Gender and Nation in the Spanish Modernist Novel* (Vanderbilt UP, 2003). She coedited *Antología del pensamiento feminista español 1726–2011* (Cátedra, 2013) with Maite Zubiaurre and *A New History of Iberian Feminisms* (U Toronto P, 2018) with Silvia Bermúdez. Her most recent book is *Major Concepts in Spanish Feminist Theory* (SUNY Press, 2019). She has published more than one hundred articles on twentieth- and twenty-first-century Spanish literature and thought, and has served or continues to serve on a large number of national and international committees and editorial boards. Roberta Johnson has been the recipient of numerous awards and honours, including the Order of Isabel la Católica from His Majesty Juan Carlos, King of Spain.

Susan M. McKenna is an associate professor of Spanish at the University of Delaware, where she teaches courses in Spanish language, literature, and culture. She is the author of *Crafting the Female Subject: Narrative Innovation in the Short Fiction of Emilia Pardo Bazán* (Catholic U of America P, 2009) as well as articles on Pardo Bazán, Juan Valera, Galdós, Sor Juana Inés de la Cruz, and Cervantes, published in *Hispanic Review, Hispanófila, Letras peninsulares,* and *Revista Hispánica Moderna.* Her current research focuses on the American playwright and author Barrie Stavis and his relationship to the Spanish Civil War. The study explores the dynamics of transatlantic cultural transfer in Stavis's modernism, especially in regard to his search for idioms and dramatic forms that could re-engage the stage with political reform and social justice.

Cristina Patiño Eirín has been a professor of Spanish literature at the Universidad de Santiago de Compostela in Spain since 1998. A specialist in the works of Emilia Pardo Bazán, she is author of *"El encaje roto" Antología de cuentos de violencia contra las mujeres* (Zaragoza, Contraseña Editorial, 2018) and *Poética de la novela en la obra crítica de Emilia Pardo Bazán* (Santiago de Compostela, Universidad, 1998) and co-author of the critical edition of Pardo Bazán's *Pascual López. Autobiografía de un estudiante de medicina* (Santiago de Compostela, Ara Solis/Consorcio de Santiago, 1996). She has published numerous articles on Pardo Bazán's work and nineteenth-century Spanish literature and has participated in the organization of symposia. She served as an organizer of an international conference on the work of Pardo Bazán and as editor of the conference proceedings. She is an active member of a research group focused on the promotion and publication of critical editions and analyses of Pardo Bazán's work. Patiño Eirín is a member of GREGAL (Grupo de Estudios Galdosianos).

Randolph D. Pope is a professor emeritus at the University of Virginia, where he was Commonwealth Professor of Spanish and Comparative Literature. He has served as chair of the Department of Spanish, Italian, and Portuguese and director of the Comparative Literature Program. He also served as the director of Graduate Studies in Spanish. Born in Chile, he studied Spanish literature and classics at the Universidad Católica de Valparaíso. He received an MA and PhD in Spanish from Columbia University in New York. His field of specialization is the Peninsular novel and autobiography, but he has also written extensively on other topics, such as Latin American literature, cultural studies, literature and architecture, literature and the arts, and literature and philosophy. He has published three books and over one hundred scholarly essays. He has twice directed an NEH Summer Seminar for College Teachers on Spanish autobiography in the European context. Randolph Pope's specialties include the novel, especially nineteenth- to twenty-first-century Spanish novels, autobiography, and comparative literature.

Enrique Rubio Cremades is Catedrático de Literatura Española at the Universidad de Alicante in Spain. He has been a visiting professor at various international institutions, including the University of Texas at Austin, Florida International University in Miami, Universität Bielefeld (Germany), Universitá degli Studi de Milano (Italy), Université de Nantes and the Université de Toulouse (France), and the Universidad de Santiago de Chile. He is currently the president of the Asociación Internacional de Estudios sobre el Romanticismo Español e Hispanoamericano as well as president of the Sociedad de Literatura Española del Siglo XIX. He has served as cultural ambassador to the United States in 1990 and 1991. He has published several monographs on nineteenth-century Spanish literature (on the realist-naturalist novel, on journalism, and on *costumbrista* literature as well as on authors Clarín, Valera, and Mesonero Romanos) as well as more than one hundred articles in journals, anthologies, and conference proceedings, specializing in writers from the eighteenth, nineteenth, and twentieth centuries. Other publications include critical editions of the works of novelists and *costumbrista* writers from the nineteenth century (Larra, Mesonero Romanos, Valera, Fernán Caballero, López Soler, and Gil y Carrasco). He has been the director of the Biblioteca Virtual Miguel de Cervantes and in that capacity has edited its digital holdings of the complete works of Galdós, Valera, Fernán Caballero, Mesonero Romanos, Alarcón, Alberto Lista, and Luis Coloma. He currently directs the websites "Novela histórica" and "Liberales Españoles."

Stephanie Sieburth is a professor of Spanish in the Department of Romance Studies at Duke University, where she teaches nineteenth- and twentieth-century Spanish literature and culture. She is the author of *Reading La Regenta* (Purdue Monographs in Romance Languages and Literatures, 1990); *Inventing High and Low* (Duke UP, 1994); and *Survival Songs: Conchita Piquer's "Coplas" and Franco's Regime of Terror* (U of Toronto P, 2014). *Survival Songs* was published in translation by Cátedra in 2016, under the title *Coplas para sobrevivir: Conchita Piquer, los vencidos y la represión franquista.*

Joyce Tolliver (University of Illinois at Urbana-Champaign) is a specialist in modern Spanish literature and culture, with a particular focus on discourse and gender. Her books include *Cigar Smoke and Violet Water: Gendered Discourse in the Stories of Emilia Pardo Bazán* (Bucknell, 1998); *"El encaje roto" y otros cuentos/"Torn Lace" and Other Stories*, published in the MLA Texts and Translations Series; and *Disciplines on the Line: Feminist Research on Spanish, Latin American, and U.S. Spanish Women* (Juan de la Cuesta, 2004). Her more recent research focuses on Spain and the Philippines at the end of the Spanish empire.

Margot Versteeg is a professor of Spanish at the University of Kansas. A native of the Netherlands, Versteeg has published numerous articles on nineteenth- and early twentieth-century literature and culture and is the author of *De fusiladores y morcilleros: el discurso cómico del género chico 1870–1910* (Rodopi, 2000) and *Jornaleros de la pluma: Hacia la (re)definición del papel del escritor periodista en la revista Madrid Cómico* (Iberoamericana/Vervuert, 2011). Her recently finished book project, *Propuestas para (re)construir una nación: el teatro de Emilia Pardo Bazán* (Purdue UP, 2019), focuses on the theatrical production of Emilia Pardo

Bazán. Versteeg coedited, with Susan Walter (University of Denver), a volume on Pardo Bazán in the MLA's Approaches to Teaching World Literatures series.

Linda M. Willem is the Betty Blades Lofton Professor of Spanish at Butler University. She received her PhD from UCLA. Her area of specialization is nineteenth-century Spanish literature, with a primary focus on the novels of Benito Pérez Galdós. She currently is the president of the Asociación Internacional de Galdosistas, Inc., having previously served two terms as its secretary-treasurer. She is a four-time recipient of National Endowment for the Humanities awards and currently is on the editorial board of *Anales Galdosianos*. Her secondary research area is Spanish film and television. She has published books with the University of North Carolina and the University of Mississippi presses, has edited editions of works by Galdós and Pardo Bazán, and currently has a contract with Palgrave Macmillan for a book on twenty-first-century adaptations of nineteenth-century Spanish novels. Her thirty-five articles and book chapters have appeared in such venues as *Hispania, MLN, Letras Peninsulares, Hispanic Journal, Romance Notes, Bulletin of Spanish Studies,* and *Literature/Film Quarterly,* as well as in volumes published by Bucknell University Press and the Modern Language Association. She has also presented papers and invited lectures at over forty national and international conferences.

Index

Toronto Iberic

1 Anthony J. Cascardi, *Cervantes, Literature, and the Discourse of Politics*
2 Jessica A. Boon, *The Mystical Science of the Soul: Medieval Cognition in Bernardino de Laredo's Recollection Method*
3 Susan Byrne, *Law and History in Cervantes' Don Quixote*
4 Mary E. Barnard and Frederick A. de Armas (eds), *Objects of Culture in the Literature of Imperial Spain*
5 Nil Santiáñez, *Topographies of Fascism: Habitus, Space, and Writing in Twentieth-Century Spain*
6 Nelson Orringer, *Lorca in Tune with Falla: Literary and Musical Interludes*
7 Ana M. Gómez-Bravo, *Textual Agency: Writing Culture and Social Networks in Fifteenth-Century Spain*
8 Javier Irigoyen-García, *The Spanish Arcadia: Sheep Herding, Pastoral Discourse, and Ethnicity in Early Modern Spain*
9 Stephanie Sieburth, *Survival Songs: Conchita Piquer's* Coplas *and Franco's Regime of Terror*
10 Christine Arkinstall, *Spanish Female Writers and the Freethinking Press, 1879–1926*

11 Margaret Boyle, *Unruly Women: Performance, Penitence, and Punishment in Early Modern Spain*
12 Evelina Gužauskytė, *Christopher Columbus's Naming in the* diarios *of the Four Voyages (1492–1504): A Discourse of Negotiation*
13 Mary E. Barnard, *Garcilaso de la Vega and the Material Culture of Renaissance Europe*
14 William Viestenz, *By the Grace of God: Francoist Spain and the Sacred Roots of Political Imagination*
15 Michael Scham, Lector Ludens: *The Representation of Games and Play in Cervantes*
16 Stephen Rupp, *Heroic Forms: Cervantes and the Literature of War*
17 Enrique Fernandez, *Anxieties of Interiority and Dissection in Early Modern Spain*
18 Susan Byrne, *Ficino in Spain*
19 Patricia M. Keller, *Ghostly Landscapes: Film, Photography, and the Aesthetics of Haunting in Contemporary Spanish Culture*
20 Carolyn A. Nadeau, *Food Matters: Alonso Quijano's Diet and the Discourse of Food in Early Modern Spain*
21 Cristian Berco, *From Body to Community: Venereal Disease and Society in Baroque Spain*
22 Elizabeth R. Wright, *The Epic of Juan Latino: Dilemmas of Race and Religion in Renaissance Spain*
23 Ryan D. Giles, *Inscribed Power: Amulets and Magic in Early Spanish Literature*
24 Jorge Pérez, *Confessional Cinema: Religion, Film, and Modernity in Spain's Development Years (1960–1975)*
25 Joan Ramon Resina, *Josep Pla: Seeing the World in the Form of Articles*
26 Javier Irigoyen-García, *"Moors Dressed as Moors": Clothing, Social Distinction, and Ethnicity in Early Modern Iberia*
27 Jean Dangler, *Edging toward Iberia*
28 Ryan D. Giles and Steven Wagschal (eds), *Beyond Sight: Engaging the Senses in Iberian Literatures and Cultures, 1200–1750*
29 Silvia Bermúdez, *Rocking the Boat: Migration and Race in Contemporary Spanish Music*
30 Hilaire Kallendorf, *Ambiguous Antidotes: Virtue as Vaccine for Vice in Early Modern Spain*
31 Leslie Harkema, *Spanish Modernism and the Poetics of Youth: From Miguel de Unamuno to* La Joven Literatura
32 Benjamin Fraser, *Cognitive Disability Aesthetics: Visual Culture, Disability Representations, and the (In)Visibility of Cognitive Difference*

33 Robert Patrick Newcomb, *Iberianism and Crisis: Spain and Portugal at the Turn of the Twentieth Century*
34 Sara J. Brenneis, *Spaniards in Mauthausen: Representations of a Nazi Concentration Camp, 1940–2015*
35 Silvia Bermúdez and Roberta Johnson (eds), *A New History of Iberian Feminisms*
36 Steven Wagschal, *Minding Animals in the Old and New Worlds: A Cognitive Historical Analysis*
37 Heather Bamford, *Cultures of the Fragment: Uses of the Iberian Manuscript, 1100–1600*
38 Enrique Garcia Santo-Tomás (ed), *Science on Stage in Early Modern Spain*
39 Marina Brownlee (ed), Cervantes' *Persiles* and the Travails of Romance
40 Sarah Thomas, *Inhabiting the In-Between: Childhood and Cinema in Spain's Long Transition*
41 David A. Wacks, *Medieval Iberian Crusade Fiction and the Mediterranean World*
42 Rosilie Hernández, *Immaculate Conceptions: The Power of the Religious Imagination in Early Modern Spain*
43 Mary L. Coffey and Margot Versteeg (eds), *Imagined Truths: Realism in Modern Spanish Literature and Culture*

www.ingramcontent.com/pod-product-compliance
Lightning Source LLC
LaVergne TN
LVHW090146080826
844660LV00013B/694/J

9781487505172